FEDERAL AGE DISCRIMINATION IN EMPLOYMENT LAW

Slowing Down The Gold Watch

By

CHARLES D. EDELMAN
Member New York and North Carolina Bars

And

ILENE C. SIEGLER, PH. D.
Assistant Professor of Medical Psychology
Department of Psychiatry
Duke University Medical Center
and
Senior Fellow, Center for the Study of Aging and Human Development
Duke University

THE MICHIE COMPANY
Law Publishers
CHARLOTTESVILLE, VIRGINIA

TO OUR PARENTS

PREFACE

This book originated as a paper we wrote for presentation at the Tenth International Congress of Gerontology held in Jerusalem, Israel in June, 1975.

The importance of the subject matter and the fact that the Federal Age Discrimination in Employment Act of 1967 provided a relatively recent, discrete area for investigation which could be reviewed in its entirety led us to expand our paper into its present form.

The ADEA represents an initial attempt by the Federal government to deal with a segment of a unique form of discrimination which some have termed "ageism." Ageism or discrimination against the older members of society is unique in many respects. It is the one type of discrimination that everyone can expect to face. It is also the only type of discrimination which can be expected to be practiced against those who had previously practiced it themselves. Indeed, the term ageism itself could at one time and in certain societies have been used to define a practice not of discrimination against older persons but rather of discrimination in their favor.

Compared to those subjected to other forms of discrimination, older persons have been relatively quiet in seeking redress. That, of course, is understandable for many reasons, including the fact that until recently the older members of society have not seen themselves as a group with common interests but rather as members of many groups with disparate interests constituted on bases other than age. In addition, the inevitability of getting old and the general disengagement from active participation in society of the elderly helps to explain the absence, until recently, of any organized opposition in the United States to age discrimination.

While, as the foregoing indicates, age discrimination has special characteristics and qualities, age discrimination in general, and age discrimination in employment specifically, share with all other types of discrimination those characteristics which at the same time make it both appropriate and inappropriate for resolution by

v

Federal statutory means. The national scope of the problem and the particular suitability of bright line statistical tests for determining the presence of blatant age discrimination militate in favor of a Federal, legal approach. On the other hand, the subtle presence of age discrimination in isolated cases may be so difficult to uncover and prove that no law can be expected to root it out. Of course, the generally unreasoned prejudices concerning, and the misconceptions which support, age discrimination can only truly be eliminated by education rather than laws however strong or actively enforced.

We do not believe that those employers and others who engage in age discrimination in connection with employment are necessarily acting irrationally or solely by reason of prejudice. To the contrary, unlike other forms of discrimination in employment, age discrimination is at times the result of economically rational decision making. Thus, for example, an employer faced with a choice of two prospective employees of equal ability might decide to choose a twenty-five year old over a fifty year old applicant on the theory that the younger person has forty years of his working life ahead of him while the older employee has only fifteen years at most before the common age of retirement. Assuming that the younger employee once hired does not leave until his retirement, the employer obtains almost three times the service for the one employment decision by choosing the younger as opposed to the older applicant. Thus, however minimal the training required of the new employee may be, the employer ultimately saves at least one, and possibly more, training periods by hiring the younger applicant. Whatever the expense involved in training the new employee, those expenses are likely to be amortized over a longer period in the case of the younger person. As the cost of training increases, of course, the significance of the disparity in the applicants' ages increases.

The Federal Age Discrimination in Employment Act of 1967 represents a policy judgment, concurred in by most of the states, that whatever economic advantages may accrue to employers by permitting them to discriminate on the basis of age are completely overshadowed by the damaging economic and psychological effects on a significant segment of the population by allowing such discrimination.

PREFACE

An examination of the legal efforts of the Federal government to deal with age discrimination in employment in the form of a legal treatise provides an opportunity to review the history of constitutional and non-Federal attempts to challenge age discrimination in employment and of the Federal statute itself and to study in depth the Federal courts' response to actions brought under the ADEA. Such an approach is more likely to uncover additional steps which must be taken to reduce, if not eliminate, employment discrimination based on age; problems with the means chosen which do not appear from the face of the statute; and alternative possibilities for reaching the objectives set by the Congress in enacting the Federal Age Discrimination in Employment Act.

This book is also intended to provide practicing attorneys with a complete statement of the law as it has developed in the nine years since the passage of the Federal statute. Whether an attorney deals exclusively with the legal problems of older persons or handles cases of age discrimination in employment as part of a general practice, the ever increasing number of cases brought under the Federal Age Discrimination in Employment Act is evidence of the importance of this area of the law.

We wish to thank Hal Parsons-Lewis, Esq., of the New York Bar, for reviewing the first draft of this book and providing us with many helpful comments and suggestions. We, of course, take full responsibility for the final product.

Charles D. Edelman
Ilene C. Siegler

Chapel Hill, North Carolina
January, 1977

vii

CONTENTS

Page

PREFACE v

CHAPTER 1 — INTRODUCTION 1

CHAPTER 2 — THE OLDER WORKER 3

CHAPTER 3 — BACKGROUND INFORMATION IN GERONTOLOGY 11
  A. Demographic Profile of the Aging Now and in the
     Future 11
  B. Physical and Attitudinal Aspects of Aging 13
     1. Physical Aspects 13
     2. Attitudinal Aspects 15
  C. The Older Worker 17
     1. Industrial Gerontology: Studies in the Workplace 18
     2. Training and Testing the Older Worker 22
     3. Functional Age 27
     4. Basic Research in the Laboratory 31
  D. Social Gerontology and Policy 32
     Research in Social Gerontology 33

CHAPTER 4 — THE LEGAL ATTACK ON AGE DISCRIMINATION
             IN EMPLOYMENT 37
  A. Constitutional and Equitable Challenges to Age
     Discrimination in Employment 37
     1. The "Right" to Obtain and Keep Employment ... 37
     2. Age Discrimination in Employment 40

CHAPTER 5 — STATE STATUTES DEALING WITH AGE
             DISCRIMINATION IN EMPLOYMENT 59
  A. Fair Employment Practices Law 60
     1. Enforcement 61
  B. Human Rights Law 65
  C. Age Discrimination in Employment Laws 65
  D. Conclusion 67

CHAPTER 6 — THE FEDERAL RESPONSE TO AGE DISCRIMINA-
             TION IN EMPLOYMENT PRIOR TO 1967 69

Page

CHAPTER 7 — THE FEDERAL AGE DISCRIMINATION IN
EMPLOYMENT ACT 73
A. Purposes 76
B. Education and Research 77
C. Definitions 79
D. Age Limits 83
E. Prohibited Employer Practices 85
F. Prohibited Employment Agency Practices 88
G. Prohibited Labor Organization Practices .... !90
G-1. Waiver of Rights Under the ADEA 90
H. General Prohibitions 91
I. Prohibited Advertising Practices 91
J. Lawful Practices 97
    1. Bona Fide Occupational Qualifications 99
    2. Differentiations Based on Reasonable Factors
       Other Than Age 108
    3. Bona Fide Seniority Systems 117
    4. Bona Fide Employee Benefit Plans 117
    5. Bona Fide Employee Pension and Retirement Plans 125
    6. Bona Fide Apprenticeship Programs 129
    7. Job Applications 131
    8. Discharge or Other Discipline for Good Cause .. 133
K. Enforcement of the ADEA 134
    1. Posting of Notices 135
    2. Investigations by Secretary of Labor 136
    3. Procedure for Initiation of Legal Action 137
       a. Preliminary Procedures for Individuals 137
          i. Federal-State Relationship 138
          ii. Notice to Secretary of Labor 146
          iii. Notice to Alleged Discriminator 159
       b. Preliminary Procedures for Individuals and the
          Secretary of Labor 159
       Conciliation, Conference and Persuasion 159
L. Statute of Limitations 163
M. Defense Based on Administrative Action 166
N. Civil Actions Under the ADEA by Individuals 167
O. Civil Actions Under the ADEA by Secretary of Labor 170
P. Injunctive Proceedings 171

CONTENTS

Page

Q. Class Actions and Consent to Suit 171
R. Availability of Jury Trial 179
S. Burden of Proof 182
T. Methods of Proof 192
U. Remedies for Violation of the ADEA 195
   1. Reinstatement and Compelled Employment 196
   2. Damages 197
     a. Wrongful Discharge 197
     b. Refusal to Hire 201
     c. Refusal to Refer 201
     d. Other Violations 205
   3. Liquidated Damages 205
   4. Permanent Injunctive Relief 208
   5. Attorney's Fees and Costs 211
   6. Interest on Damages 213
V. Age Discrimination in Federal Government
   Employment 214
W. Recordkeeping 216
   1. Employers 217
   2. Employment Agencies 219
   3. Labor Organizations 220
   4. Inspection of Records 221
   5. Recordkeeping Exceptions 222
X. Exemptions from the ADEA 222
Y. Study of Involuntary Retirement 224
Z. Criminal Penalties 225
AA. Annual Report to Congress 225
BB. Appropriations 226

CHAPTER 8 — THE ADEA IN RETROSPECT 227
CHAPTER 9 — THE FUTURE AND THE ADEA 239
  A. Involuntary Retirement 239
  B. Maximum Age Limit 240

CHAPTER 10 — CONCLUSION 243
APPENDICES 245

	Page
Appendix A	245
1. Federal Age Discrimination in Employment Act of 1967	245
2. Related Statutes	259
Appendix B	267
Regulations of the United States Secretary of Labor Promulgated Pursuant to Sections 7 (a), 8, and 9 of the Federal Age Discrimination in Employment Act of 1967	267
Appendix C	290
Notice Prepared by the United States Secretary of Labor Pursuant to Section 8 of the Federal Age Discrimination in Employment Act of 1967	291
Appendix D	293
Summary of Provisions Under State Laws Pertaining to Discrimination in Employment Because of Age as of February 1, 1976	293
TABLE OF CASES	329
INDEX	343

Chapter 1

INTRODUCTION

> The happy reality that comes after job severance because of age has to do with independence. No longer is one bound by boss, hierarchy, tradition, the careful ascent of promotional ladders, nor apprehensions regarding duties, obligations, pay and pensions.
>
> One is free to say yea or nay, to work half or twice as hard, or intermittently or not at all — free to moonlight or to quit if disenchanted.
>
> To be in this capacity provides an unusual degree of liberty. Decisions are personal and based on aptitudes and inclinations. No longer are there fetters and one is no longer obligated or required to undertake a task. Little stands in the way of being true to oneself, to one's own philosophy and ideals.[1]

The infrequently heard view of termination of employment based on age expressed by Dr. Perera should serve as a reminder that not all older persons want or need the financial or psychological rewards of continued regular employment. Such persons have no personal interest in nor are they the focus of attempts to deal with age discrimination in employment. They should, however, be kept in mind because any solution to the problem of age discrimination in employment which prevents or discourages the withdrawal of such persons from the regular labor force at an appropriate time must be assiduously avoided if the solution to one problem is not to create another one both for persons like Dr. Perera and for those others who would enter into or advance within the labor force upon the retirees' withdrawal.

The efforts of the last half century in the United States to meet the problem of age discrimination in employment have revolved primarily around those who are capable of continuing to work and who must look to regular employment even in old age for the basic necessities of life. As Maggie the Cat noted in Tennessee Williams' *Cat On A Hot Tin Roof,*

> You can be young without money but you can't be old without it. You've got to be old with money because to be old without it is just too awful, you've got to be one or the other, young or with money, you can't be old without it.[2]

---

1. Perera, *Finding Golden Threads Among the Silver,* N.Y. Times, March 6, 1974, at 37, col. 4. Dr. Perera was, prior to his retirement, a professor of medicine and associate dean of the Columbia University College of Physicians and Surgeons.

2. P. 38 (New Directions ed. 1955).

1

Age Discrimination in Employment

This book describes the efforts in the United States to deal with age discrimination in employment by legal means. It is a treatise on Federal age discrimination in employment law and provides a case study of an attempt to use a legal approach to deal with a facet of the larger problem of age discrimination in American society.

Chapter 2

THE OLDER WORKER

To understand the magnitude of the problem of age discrimination in employment in the United States, it is necessary to first focus on the older worker's place in the labor force of the United States.

The total noninstitutional population over 15 years of age of the United States in June, 1974 was 150,710,000.[1] The total civilian labor force over 15 years of age was 92,546,000 of which 87,167,000 persons were employed and 5,380,000 were unemployed.[2] At the same time there were 55,952,000 people who were not in the labor force.[3] The following tables show the employment status of the noninstitutional, civilian population of the United States over 15 years of age by numbers and percentages, respectively:

Table A[4]

(In thousands)

Age	Total Civilian Labor Force	Employed Civilian Labor Force	Unemployed Civilian Labor Force	Not In Labor Force
16 and over	92,547	87,167	5,379	55,952
16 to 19	10,416	8,363	2,053	5,640
20 to 24	13,483	12,233	1,250	4,182
25 to 29	11,507	10,973	534	4,174
30 to 34	9,328	9,037	291	3,843
35 to 39	8,241	7,997	244	2,901
40 to 44	8,343	8,100	244	2,870
45 to 49	8,688	8,469	219	3,051
50 to 54	8,466	8,283	183	3,375

---

1. U.S. Department of Labor, Bureau of Labor Statistics, 21 (1) Employment and Earnings 19 (July 1974) (hereinafter *Employment and Earnings*). All statistics in this chapter are as of June, 1974 unless otherwise indicated.

2. *Id.*

3. *Id.*

4. *Id.* at 21-22.

Table A—Continued
(In thousands)

Age	Total Civilian Labor Force	Employed Civilian Labor Force	Unemployed Civilian Labor Force	No. In Labor Force
55 to 59	6,671	6,508	163	3,517
60 to 64	4,469	4,353	118	4,618
65 to 69	1,756	1,692	64	5,896
70 and over	1,179	1,160	19	11,887

Table B[5]

Age	Percentage of Total Civilian Labor Force	Percentage of Employed Civilian Labor Force	Percentage of Unemployed Civilian Labor Force
16 to 19	11.3	9.6	38.2
20 to 24	14.6	14.0	23.2
25 to 29	12.4	12.6	9.9
30 to 34	10.1	10.4	5.4
35 to 39	8.9	9.2	4.5
40 to 44	9.0	9.3	4.5
45 to 49	9.4	9.7	4.1
50 to 54	9.1	9.5	3.4
55 to 59	7.2	7.5	3.0
60 to 64	4.8	5.0	2.2
65 to 69	1.9	1.9	1.2
70 and over	1.3	1.3	.4

As appears from the foregoing tables, the various age groups provided a proportion of the total employed civilian labor force nearly identical to the portion of the total labor force which they represented. The same relationship, however, did not carry over to the unemployed portion of the civilian labor force where the younger age groups constituted a disproportionate part of the total

---

5. *Id.*

4

unemployed civilian labor force. Thus, persons 45 and over constituted 33.7 percent of the civilian labor force but only 14.3 percent of the unemployed while those under 30 represented 38.3 percent of the civilian labor force and 71.3 percent of the unemployed.

A similar relationship exists between age and rate of unemployment as the following table shows:

Table C [6]

Age	Percentage In Civilian Labor Force Employed	Percentage In Civilian Labor Force Unemployed
16 and over	94.2	5.8
16 to 19	80.3	19.7
20 to 24	90.7	9.3
25 to 29	95.4	4.6
30 to 34	96.9	3.1
35 to 39	97.0	3.0
40 to 44	97.1	2.9
45 to 49	97.5	2.5
50 to 54	97.8	2.2
55 to 59	97.6	2.4
60 to 64	97.4	2.6
65 to 69	96.4	3.6
70 and over	98.4	1.6
Average	95.1	4.9

The preceding table indicates that the rate of unemployment is greater among those between 16 and 29 and that unemployment among those 40 and over is significantly below the average. However, the rate of unemployment which declines with increasing

6. *Id.*

5

age for persons from 16 to 54 years of age climbs again for those between 55 and 69.[7]

The unemployment rates must, however, be considered together with the lengths of the duration of unemployment of the age groups before their significance can be appreciated. The following tables set forth the length of unemployment by age group:

Table D[8]
(In thousands)

Age	Number of Unemployed	Unemployed Less Than 5 Weeks	Unemployed 5 to 14 Weeks	Unemployed 15 to 26 Weeks	Unemployed 27 Weeks and Over
16 and over	5,380	3,226	1,231	543	379
16 to 19	2,053	1,528	366	106	53
20 to 24	1,250	745	310	121	73
25 to 34	825	418	233	117	57
35 to 44	488	240	122	68	57
45 to 54	401	156	100	77	69
55 to 64	280	110	72	45	54
65 and over	83	30	28	10	16

---

7. As is indicated in Table A, pp. 3, 4, *supra*, the 70 and over group includes only 19,000 persons.

8. *Employment and Earnings, supra,* at 31.

Table E[9]

Age	Average (Mean) Duration of Unemployment in Weeks	Less Than 5 Weeks Unemployment as a Percentage of Unemployed	15 Weeks and over Unemployment as a Percentage of Unemployed
16 and over	8.7	60.0	17.1
16 to 19	5.3	74.4	7.7
20 to 24	7.9	59.6	15.6
25 to 34	9.7	50.7	21.1
35 to 44	12.4	49.3	25.6
45 to 54	15.0	38.8	36.4
55 to 64	16.0	39.2	35.2
65 and over	15.0	35.5	31.2

As the tables indicate, persons over 44 had an average duration of unemployment almost twice the national average and their length of unemployment was as likely to be 15 or more weeks as less than 5 weeks while younger workers were twice as likely to be unemployed for less than 5 weeks than 15 weeks or more. These statistics are consistent with the findings of a United States Department of Labor report prepared for the 1971 White House Conference on Aging which concluded that

> The difficulties older workers encounter in the labor market are expressed in the length of their periods of unemployment rather than in the incidence of unemployment. Unemployment rates tend to be relatively low for older workers.[10]

The reasons which have been identified for the longer duration of unemployment of older persons include: lack of occupational

---

9. *Id.*

10. U.S. Department of Labor, Bureau of Labor Statistics, Bulletin 1721-*The Employment Problems of Older Workers* 6 (1971) (hereinafter *Employment Problems*).

mobility,[11] lack of geographic mobility,[12] and, most importantly, discrimination because of their age.[13]

No attempt has been made herein to define "the older worker" who is subjected to age discrimination in employment. The United States Department of Labor has stated that

> Although age 65 is considered the beginning of old age for many purposes, the older worker generally is defined as those workers aged 45 or older. The rational in this case for a dividing line of 45 years is that cross-sectional data show at this age the onset of an increase in withdrawals of men from the labor force, an increase in the prevalence of part-time and part-year workers, a decline in annual and weekly earnings, and a lengthening of the duration of unemployment — all factors that increase in subsequently older age groups.[14]

The foregoing definition adopts a chronological view of "the older worker." A similar approach has been adopted by the Congress and various state legislatures in enacting statutes dealing with age discrimination in employment which are limited

---

11. *Id.* at 10.

12. *Id.* at 10-12.

13. See pp. 16-17, 69-73. *See generally* Kovarsky and Kovarsky, *Economic, Medical and Legal Aspects of the Age Discrimination Laws in Employment,* 27 Vand. L. Rev. 839, 844-65 (1974) (where the authors list and discuss ten common "justifications" given by employers for age discrimination in the employment setting and conclude that the excuses given by employers are generally not supported by the facts); and Rosen and Jerdee, *Too Old or Not Too Old,* 55(6) Harv. Bus. Rev. 97 (Nov.-Dec 1977), reporting on the results of a survey of Harvard Business Review subscribers from which the authors concluded that

> Managers perceive older employees to be relatively inflexible and resistant to change. Accordingly, managers make much less effort to give an older person feedback about needed changes in performance.

> Few managers provide organizational support for the career development and retraining of older employees.

> Promotion opportunities for older people are somewhat restricted, particularly when the new positions demand creativity, mental alertness, or capacity to deal with crisis situations. [*Id.* at 98.]

The authors attribute the differential treatment of younger and older workers to unconscious age stereotypes rather than conscious discrimination.

14. *Employment Problems, supra,* at 2 n. 1.

in their coverage to persons in specified age groups. That is not, however, the only possible approach to the definitional problem. One alternative is a functional approach applied on an individual basis. A conflict has developed between these two approaches and those espousing them which has been reflected by the courts.[15]

The remainder of this book is devoted to a review of the scientific literature concerning older workers and to a description and evaluation of the legal attempt to deal with age discrimination in employment in the United States.

---

15. *See* pp. 42-44, 51-58, 100-07, *infra.*

Chapter 3

BACKGROUND INFORMATION IN GERONTOLOGY

This chapter presents an overview of the results of gerontological studies. Gerontology is the scientific study of aging and combines work from a variety of disciplines that seek to understand the processes of aging. Gerontology is a relatively new field. The Gerontological Society, the major umbrella professional organization, was founded in 1949 while the National Institute of Aging, (NIA), the newest of the research institutes within the National Institutes of Health, was created in 1974.[1] Among the priorities of NIA are: the need to develop functional criteria other than age to be used in employment decisions, to seek ways to provide financial security for individuals beyond the typical retirement age, and to study the distribution of work and leisure over the lifespan.[2] Another recent sign of interest in the problems of aging was the successful effort to retain the Special Committee on Aging of the United States Senate in February of 1977, suggesting that those concerned with problems of aging now have an effective lobbying organization to represent the concerns of the 23 million older citizens in the United States.[3]

A. DEMOGRAPHIC PROFILE OF THE AGING NOW AND IN THE FUTURE

The number of older people in the population is increasing in both absolute numbers and as a percentage of the total population. In 1776, the population of the United States was approximately 2.5 million, life expectancy at birth was 38-39 years and the number of individuals aged 65 and older was 50,000 or about 2 percent of the total. By 1900 there were 3 million older people or about 4 percent of the total population and in mid-1975 there were 22.4 million older people or about 10 percent of the total.[4] Current life expectancy, calculated for individuals born in 1974 is 68.9 years for

---

1. Butler, *Early Directions for the NIA,* 16 Gerontologist 293 (1976).
2. National Institute of Aging, *Our Future Selves* (1976).
3. N.Y. Times, Feb. 2, 1977, at B4, col. 2 (city ed.).
4. H. Brotman, *Every Tenth American,* in *Senate Special Committee on Aging, 1976 Developments in Aging* xv.

men and 72.4 years for women.[5] Life expectancy is an index of the proportion of a cohort that can expect to live to old age and, with increasing age, the life expectancy increases such that individuals who are currently 65 years old can expect to live 12.8 more years if male and 16.3 years if female.[6] This gain in life expectancy has been accomplished by advances in medical care, primarily at the younger ages by reductions in infant mortality. It has been estimated that the average life expectancy would naturally peak somewhere around 90 years of age. In order to extend the lifespan, major alterations in the biological mechanisms presumed to control the processes of aging would have to be discovered.[7]

The elderly are also one of the fastest growing segments of the population. Between 1960 and 1970 the population under 65 grew by 13 percent while the population now 65 grew by 21 percent.[8] Within the older population, the oldest group, those 75 and older grew by 52 percent compared to those 65 to 74 who increased by 26 percent over the past 15 years.[9] Estimates for the future suggest that there will be no dramatic increases in lifespan. A regular progression of medical knowledge and health care should, however, lead to a slow reduction in mortality. Thus, under the assumption of zero population growth, by the year 2000, there will be 31.6 million older persons or about 11.5 percent of the population.[10]

It is important to recognize that the elderly are not a homogeneous group. Not only are the age groups within the older population increasing at different rates, but differences in health are also apparent. For example, of the 960,300 older people in

---

5. Brotman, *Life Expectancy,* 17 Gerontologist 12 (1977).

6. E. Shanas and G.L. Maddox, *Aging, Health and Health Resources,* in *Handbook of Aging and the Social Sciences* 596, 601 (R. Binstock & E. Shanas eds. 1976).

7. L. Hayflick, *Brain Function and Biological Age* (March, 1974) (unpublished paper presented at 19th annual Veterans Administration Symposium).

8. H. Brotman, *Every Tenth American, supra,* at xvi.

9. *Id.*

10. B.L. Neugarten and R.J. Havighurst, *Aging and the Future,* in *Social Policy, Social Ethics and the Aging Society* 1, 4 (B.L. Neugarten & R.J. Havighurst eds. 1976).

nursing homes in 1973-1974, 17 percent were age 65 to 74, 40 percent were 75 to 84, and 43 percent were 85 and older.[11]

Also, most older people are women. The sex ratio of men to women between the ages of 65 and 74 is 100 to 130 and after age 74 the ratio is 100 to 171.[12] This differential life expectancy between the sexes also leads to higher degrees of widowhood for older women.

Dr. Bernice L. Neugarten has suggested that for policy reasons one helpful way to think about older people is to make a distinction between the young-old and the old-old. The young-old are those age 55 to 74 and the old-old those 75 and over.

The young-old is a particularly interesting group. This group, which increasingly has the option to retire early, is also one that is relatively well educated and in fairly good health. Also it is this group that has probably been the most subject to age discrimination. Current projections suggest that this group will continue to maintain excellent standards of functioning.[13]

B. PHYSICAL AND ATTITUDINAL ASPECTS OF AGING

1. *Physical Aspects.* Dr. Alex Comfort has made a useful distinction between physical aging and sociogenic aging.[14] Physical aging refers to the processes of change observed in humans and animals over time. In this context, aging is defined as a natural process, that is, one that is independent of disease. The American Medical Association's Committee on Aging has concluded that there is no disease entity that is the result purely of the passage of time.[15] Descriptions of aging processes by biologically-oriented researchers suggest that a very prominent characteristic of aging systems is a reduction in the reserve capacity of the system to

11. H. Brotman, *Every Tenth American, supra,* at xvi.

12. *Id.* at viii.

13. *See* Neugarten, *The Future and the Young Old,* 15(2) Gerontologist, 1, 5-7 (1975). *See also* V.L. Bengston and N.E. Cutler, *Generations and Intergenerational Relationships,* in *Handbook of Aging and the Social Sciences* 130, 152 (R. Binstock & E. Shanas eds. 1976).

14. Comfort, *Age Prejudice in America,* 7 Soc. Policy 1, 3-4 (1976).

15. F.C. Swartz, *Characteristic Health Problems of Older Americans,* in *The Neglected Older Americans* 1, 7 (J.C. Cull & R.E. Hardy eds. 1973).

return itself to a resting level after a stress of some sort.[16] This may be a reflection of the sum total of stresses which have acted upon the body over the lifetime.

A current focus of research is an attempt to specify what is causal in aging. The endocrine and immune systems are thought to be important in understanding control mechanisms related to aging.[17] The evidence suggesting the importance of genetic factors has long been recognized; but the precise mechanisms involved are not well understood.[18] Scientific work on the biological aspects of aging is accelerating in most of the biomedical areas. Most of this work is aimed at uncovering the mechanisms involved, employing both human and animal models.[19] Also the speciality of geriatric medicine has begun to receive recognition from the medical profession.[20]

A major question in understanding physical aging involves distinguishing aging from disease. As individuals age, there tends to be an accumulation of various disease processes. When an individual dies at a young age there tends to be one specific cause of death, when an individual dies in old age there can be as many as thirteen to fifteen causes of death.[21] Much of the available information, especially that obtained from longitudinal studies of

---

16. P.S. Timiras, *Developmental Physiology and Aging* 408-12 (1972), *See also* Zorzoli, *Biological Aspects of the Aging Process*, 49 Pub. Health News 135, 138-39 (1968).

17. Bylinsky, *Science Is on the Trail of the Fountain of Youth,* Fortune, July, 1976 at 134-40.

18. Jarvik, *Thoughts on the Psychobiology of Aging,* 30 Am. Psych. 576, 577 (1975). *See also* L.F. Jarvik & D. Cohen, *A Biobehavioral Approach to Intellectual Changes with Aging,* in *The Psychology of Adult Development and Aging* 220-280 (C. Eisdorfer & M.P. Lawton eds. 1973).

19. *See Handbook of the Biology of Aging* (C.E. Finch & L. Hayflick eds. 1977). *See also Neurobiology of Aging* (R.D. Terry & S. Gershon eds. 1976); and *Aging and the Brain* (C.M. Gaitz ed. 1972).

20. J.C. Brockelhurst & T. Hanley, *Geriatric Medicine for Students* (1976). *See also Textbook of Geriatric Medicine* (J.C. Brockelhurst ed. 1973) and *Clinical Geriatrics* (I. Rossman ed. 1971).

21. Comfort, *Age Prejudice in America, supra,* at 3.

aging, indicates that many of the declines we associate with old age are more correctly attributable to changes in health.[22]

Various systems in the body also age at different rates.[23] This can be assessed by looking at the age-related nature of various causes of death. Deaths from coronary heart disease are highest in males during their 40's,[24] deaths from cancer peak in the 40's to 60's, deaths due to failures in the cardiovascular system occur in the 70's and 80's.[25] However, many of these changes start much earlier in the lifespan. For example, arteriosclerosis starts in childhood,[26] changes in the visual and auditory systems start in the 20's and 30's [27] and peak muscular strength starts declining in the 30's; however the rate of change through the middle years is relatively slow and major changes are not noticed until the organism is no longer able to compensate for declining capacity. That time varies widely for individuals and is also dependent on the particular demands on the person.

2. Attitudinal Aspects. Sociogenic aging is defined as the prejudices, misconceptions, and stereotypes about aging and the elderly imposed by modern society on older people. It is Dr. Comfort's view that 75 percent of the problems with aging fall into this category, and such problems are, in the abstract, easier to solve because they primarily involve a change in societal attitude.

---

22. The NIMH longitudinal study worked with 47 men, of whom all were very healthy. Upon examination, a sub-group called "supra healthy" was identified. The report on the initial evaluation can be found in *Human Aging I* (J.E. Birren, R.N. Butler, S.W. Greenhouse, L. Sokoloff & M.R. Yarrow eds. 1971). The report on the eleven year follow-up is in *Human Aging II* (S. Granick & D. Patterson eds. 1974). *See also* L.W. Thompson and G. R. Marsh, *Psychophysiological Studies of Aging.* in *The Psychology of Adult Development and Aging* 112, 129-30 (C. Eisdorfer & M.P. Lawton eds. 1973).

23. *See* K. Goldman, *Decline in Organ Function with Age,* in *Clinical Geriatrics* 19-48 (I. Rossman ed. 1971). *See also* D.B. Bromley, *The Psychology of Human Ageing* 78-121 (1974).

24. P.S. Timiras, *Developmental Physiology and Aging, supra,* at 498.

25. *Id.* at 471.

26. *Id.* at 477.

27. *Id.* at 415. *See also* Corso, *Sensory Processes and Age Effects in Normal Adults,* 26 J. Gerontology 90 (1971); and R.A. McFarland, *The Sensory and Perceptual Processes in Aging,* in *Theory and Method of Research in Aging* 9 (K.W. Schaie ed. 1968).

He sums this up with the question: "One wonders how Archie Bunker would feel about immigrants if he knew that on his 65th birthday he would turn into a Puerto Rican."[28]

Dr. Robert N. Butler has coined the term "ageism" to describe the deep and profound prejudice which many harbor towards the old.[29] Common reasons that employers give for not hiring older workers have to do with presumed mental and physical infirmities, presumed problems in motivation of older workers, increased costs for older workers in salary and benefits, increased turnover and lack of comfort by younger employees in working as supervisors for older people.[30] However, it appears whenever there is a great demand for manpower in the economy the arguments used to buttress age discrimination seem to disappear.[31] The data reviewed later in this chapter suggest that most of the problems with older workers can be solved and that the cost/benefit ratio with regard to older workers can be seen to balance on the benefit side of the equation.

One recent study systematically examined the extent and pervasiveness of age stereotypes in a group of undergraduates and relators who were attending a special institute at a school of business. The respondents were told that they were about to meet a person who was either 30 or 60 years old. Respondents then rated the hypothetical persons on a variety of scales which assessed performance capacity, potential for development, stability, and interpersonal skills. The younger man was seen as higher on dimensions of performance capacity (e.g., more productive, efficient, motivated, and capable of working under pressure); the

---

28. Comfort, *Age Prejudice in America, supra,* at 4. Comfort may not be correct here. By attributing 75 percent of the problems of aging to society's view, he may err on the optimistic side.

29. R.N. Butler, *Why Survive?: Being Old in America,* 11-12 (1975). *See also* S. de Beauvoir, *Coming of Age* (1973).

30. Kovarsky and Kovarsky, *Economic, Medical and Legal Aspects of Age Discrimination Laws in Employment,* 27 Vand. L. Rev. 839, 845 (1975).

31. *Id.* at 846. *See also* J.M. Kreps, *Employment, Income and Retirement Problems of the Aged* 3 (1963); L. Harris & Associates, *The Myth and Reality of Aging in America* (1975); and Stagner, *An Industrial Psychologist Looks at Industrial Gerontology,* 2 Int'l. J. Aging Hum. Dev. 29, 30 (1971).

older man was seen as more accident prone. The younger man was characterized as ambitious, eager, future-oriented, adaptable, receptive to new ideas, while the older man was seen as more rigid and dogmatic. Stability was seen as favoring the older man. In the interpersonal skills dimension, the various characteristics were distributed independent of the age of the target stimulus.

Older respondents saw a smaller difference between the hypothetical target persons on the performance capacity scale but still favored the younger man, suggesting further confirmation for Butler's ageism notion, causing even the person discriminated against to adopt the dominant culture's negative view of himself.[32]

A second study assessed the validity of the stereotype of increased psychiatric symptomatology in middle-aged workers. Seven hundred and forty-five workers and their spouses in five New Jersey plants, the majority of whom were assembly line workers, were studied. Self-reported psychiatric symptoms were evaluated. Respondents over forty had significantly fewer symptoms than the younger workers. There were no differences between those respondents between 40 and 60. Indeed, job satisfaction increased with age; such that 77 percent of the workers under age 30, 90 percent of the workers between 30 and 60, and 97 percent of the workers over 60 reported a high degree of satisfaction with their jobs. The authors suggest that their findings provide evidence that coping capacity in the workplace is increased in those over 40 years of age.[33]

C. THE OLDER WORKER

In evaluating research on older workers, it is important to keep in mind one important methodological point. The results of the studies are based on persons of specified ages at a specific

32. Rosen and Jerdee, *The Nature of Job Related Age Stereotypes,* 61 J. Appl. Psych. 180, 181-82 (1976). *See also* Rosen and Jerdee, *Too Old or Not Too Old,* 55(6) Harv. Bus. Rev. 97 (Nov.—Dec. 1977), reporting on the results of a similar study of age stereotypes conducted by means of a survey of Harvard Business Review subscribers. The authors concluded that "[r]esponses to the survey suggest that, because of managerial actions based on age stereotypes, older employees are potential victims of unjust treatment." *Id.* at 98.

33. Siassi, Crocetti and Spiro, *Emotional Health, Life and Job Satisfaction in Aging Workers,* 2 Indus. Gerontology 289 (1975).

historical point in time. Projections for the future suggest that the elderly will be better educated and have received better health care, and will, thus, maintain their competence longer than current generations of middle-aged and older persons.[34] Additionally, current research in the behavioral and social sciences where the cohort or birth year of the individual has been taken into account suggests that, in many circumstances, this variable can explain more about the behavior of the individual than age can.[35]

1. *Industrial Gerontology: Studies in the Workplace.* Industrial gerontology is defined as the study of the employment and retirement problems of middle-aged and older workers.[36]

Efficiency of work varies not only by age but also by the type of work. Studies of output per man-hour were made in a variety of industries: 5,000 workers in twenty-two manufacturing plants in footwear and furniture industries, 6,000 clerical workers in five federal agencies and twenty-one private companies, and 6,000 mail sorters in United States Post Offices, between 1956 and 1961. The performance of workers at ages 35 to 44 was set equal to one hundred and the performance of workers from under 25 to those 65 and over was compared to the standard middle-aged group. Just considering the groups above 44: 45 to 54, 55 to 64, and 65 and over, the ratings for men in the footwear industry were: 97.7, 92.5 and 81.1, respectively; in furniture: 96.1, 94.5 and 93.6; for office workers: 100.1, 98.6 and 101.2; and for mail sorters: 100.1, 98.5 and 93.3.[37] Thus, while there was some fall off particularly in the footwear industry after 65 years of age, the trends were gradual,

---

34. Sarason, Sarason and Crowden, *Aging and the Nature of Work,* 30 Am. Psych. 584, 586 (1975). *See also* K.W. Schaie and K. Gribben, *Adult Development and Aging,* in 26 Ann. Rev. Psych. 65, 70 (M.R. Rosenzweig and L.W. Porter eds. 1975).

35. Schaie, *Translations in Gerontology — From Lab to Life — Intellectual Functioning,* 29 Am. Psych. 802, 806 (1974).

36. N. Sprague, *Industrial Gerontology,* in *Toward an Industrial Gerontology,* v (H.L. Sheppard ed. 1970). *See also* Meier and Kerr, *Capabilities of Middle Aged and Older Workers,* 3 Indus. Gerontology 147 (1976). Annotated bibliographies in the area are: Hanson, *Age and Physical Capacity to Work,* Indus. Gerontology 20 (Winter 1972); and Kelleher and Quirk, *Age, Functional Capacity and Work,* Indus. Gerontology 80 (Fall 1973).

37. Adapted from Table 18.5, in M.W. Riley and A. Foner, *Aging and Society* 426 (1968).

and for office workers, did not indicate any loss of efficiency with increased age.

Older workers are also thought to be more accident prone. A study of sixty-two men aged 23 to 63 in a Birds Eye plant found that age was not related to accident proneness.[38]

Older people are also thought to be more rigid. Dr. Shelia M. Chown investigated the role of rigidity as measured by nineteen different tests of rigidity in three different work situations and two laboratory experiments. In four of the investigations there was a large age spread. In each of the situtations some adaptation or change was required of the individuals and performance criteria were established in each situation. Age was inversely related to performance on all of the measures except one, but the measures of rigidity were more highly related than age in all of the situations. This research suggests that direct measures of rigidity, rather than age, are more accurate predictors of successful adaptation on the job.[39]

In his chapter on the 'right to work', Dr. Butler addressed the question of productivity and creativity in older people and called attention to well-known historical figures from Sophocles to Shaw who made major contributions in their old age.[40] A recent article in the New York Times Magazine focused on current contributors.[41] Detractors always point out that the superior individuals who achieve are different from the average man-in-the-street; but these people miss the point. If we observe excellence, creativity, and productivity in late life, then indeed the individuals who so achieve might be special, but their existence is proof of the fact that age, by itself, is no barrier to continued achievement.[42]

---

38. Kunce, *Vocational Interests and Accident Proneness*, 51 J. Appl. Psych. 223 (1967).

39. Chown, *The Effect of Flexibility-Rigidity and Age in Adaptability in Job Performance*, Indus. Gerontology 105 (Spring 1972).

40. R.N. Butler, *Why Survive?: Being Old in America, supra*, at 76.

41. H.D. Shapiro, *Do Not Go Gently . . .*, N.Y. Times Magazine, February 6, 1977, at 37.

42. Two classic studies present the relationships between age and achievement across a variety of fields: H.C. Lehman, *Age and Achievement* (1953) and Dennis, *Creative Productivity Between the Ages of 20 and 80 Years*, 21 J. Gerontology 1 (1966).

One of the most comprehensive systems of matching the worker to the job, useful in dealing with problems of employment for older workers, is a system developed by Dr. Leon F. Koyl.[43] Dr. Koyl's system focuses on a joint assessment of the fitness of the individual and the requirements of the job. Both the individual and the job are rated on a seven category scale called the GULHEMP. GULHEMP is an acronym for the functional components of the required competence of the workers for the job: *G*eneral physique, *U*pper extremities, *L*ower extremities, *H*earing, *E*yesight, *M*entality and *P*ersonality. Each function is rated from superior competence with no restrictions or limitations to total incompetence and a profile is developed. Each job in a particular industrial setting is also evaluated on the same set of criteria stressing the minimum skills required for adequate performance of the job. In order to decide if the individual is fit for the job, the individual's profile must be at, or above, the requirements for the job in all seven areas of competence.[44]

The GULHEMP system is not limited to the assessment of older workers, but can deal with a wide range of individuals including the middle-aged and older worker and does provide a system of determining the functional performance of an individual independent of age, sex, or race. Profiles of various individuals can be made at regular intervals or upon hiring, and again when questions of promotion, retirement, or changes in health status of an individual suggest that an additional evaluation would be useful. For example, it can be used to show whether the current lowered profile of an individual who may have lost competence when compared to him or herself at an earlier age is still above what is required for adequate performance of a specific job.[45]

The manual describing the GULHEMP system is an extremely useful practical volume, and a fine illustration of a system that both allows for individual differences in functional ability and is able to do so in an age-fair way. The manual deals very effectively with a variety of common diseases and discusses their probable

43. L.F. Koyl, *Employing the Older Worker: Matching the Employee to the Job* (1974).
44. *Id.* at 21-22, 37, 40-44.
45. *Id.* at 38.

impact on performance. Disabilities are evaluated in terms of remaining ability. The system has been in use at de Havilland Aircraft Ltd. in Toronto, Canada, for over a decade.[46] As a result of the success of the program there, the Institute of Industrial Gerontology, under the sponsorship of the National Council on the Aging and the Manpower Administration of the U.S. Department of Labor, funded a demonstration project in Portland, Maine which was called the Industrial Health Counseling Service (IHCS).

The IHCS project started in 1971. During the first three years of the project, 2,400 job applicants were evaluated and 51 percent of them were placed in jobs. Approximately 1,800 jobs with more than one hundred firms in the Portland area were evaluated.[47]

Data were collected on program participants over a seven month period, including 534 people who were followed after employment.[48] The unemployment rate for the participants was reduced from 94 percent to 30 percent. By age, 71 percent of those under 25, 73 percent of those 25 to 44, 63 percent of those 55 to 64, and 48 percent of those over 65 years of age were placed in jobs.[49]

The GULHEMP system was evaluated by comparing two age groups (under 54, and 55 and over). As would be expected, the two groups differed in educational attainment. Nine percent of the younger group had an eighth grade education or less compared to 23 percent of the older group. Level of education was related to employment only for the younger group. More of the older group were referred by the state employment service and more of the younger workers who got jobs got better jobs than their previous ones, while the older workers who got jobs had new jobs at the same level as their old jobs.[50] The GULHEMP ratings were directly related to age, but in general, the ratings were more important

---

46. *Id.* at 5.
47. Batten, *Application of a Unique Industrial Health System,* Indus. Gerontology 38 (Fall 1973).
48. Quirk and Skinner, *IHCS: Physical Capacity, Age and Employment,* Indus. Gerontology 49, 50 (Fall 1973).
49. *Id.* at 51.
50. *Id.* at 53-55.

than age in job placement. During the same time period involved in the study, only 13 percent of workers over 45 were placed by the Maine Employment Service, while even the lowest placement group in the IHCS project, those over 65, had a placement rate of 48 percent. As a result of the project, those who did not find jobs were disqualified based on their lack of functional ability rather than their age.

Data from three employers were analyzed to evaluate the cost/benefit ratio of the program to industry. IHCS employees used sick leave .36 percent of the time, while comparable employees (hired at the same time, in similar jobs, but not hired through the project) used sick leave 4.29 percent of the time.[51] Estimated cost for the IHCS project was $100 per person ($25 for the medical evaluation and $75 for the evaluation of the job). Thus, the success of the program, over time, in avoiding costly selection errors, and reducing the amount of lost time due to sick leave, was seen as providing a net benefit to the industries using the system.[52]

The IHCS project shows that the technology exists to evaluate workers' capacities in an age-fair way. The GULHEMP system is one such model.

2. *Training and Testing the Older Worker.* Older people can learn new work skills and the efficiency of that learning can be improved by the use of special techniques. The studies reviewed in this section focus on special retraining of older persons in work situations and on issues in testing of older people for employment.

Some of the major work in this area has been done by the Industrial Training Research Unit (ITRU) in Cambridge, England, and is summarized in a volume by Drs. Eunice Belbin and R. Meredith Belbin.[53] The ITRU develops training programs for industrial workers, and consults with respect to and evaluates programs in industrial settings. The volume contains a set of case examples and illustrations of the principles found useful in training and retraining mature adult workers.

51. Levine, *Benefits and Costs to Industry,* Indus. Gerontology 63, 65 (Fall 1973).

52. *Id.* at 70. *See also* Indus. Gerontology 71 (Fall 1973), for comments by company representatives involved in the program.

53. E. Belbin and R.M. Belbin, *Problems in Adult Retraining* (1972). For an annotated bibliography in this area *see* Clifford, *Learning Ability and Age,* Indus. Gerontology 50 (Winter 1972).

in job placement. During the same time period involved
dy, only 13 percent of workers over 45 were placed by
e Employment Service, while even the lowest placement
the IHCS project, those over 65, had a placement rate of
t. As a result of the project, those who did not find jobs
qualified based on their lack of functional ability
n their age.

rom three employers were analyzed to evaluate the
fit ratio of the program to industry. IHCS employees
leave .36 percent of the time, while comparable employees
he same time, in similar jobs, but not hired through the
sed sick leave 4.29 percent of the time.[51] Estimated cost
HCS project was $100 per person ($25 for the medical
and $75 for the evaluation of the job). Thus, the success
gram, over time, in avoiding costly selection errors, and
he amount of lost time due to sick leave, was seen as
a net benefit to the industries using the system.[52]

S project shows that the technology exists to evaluate
apacities in an age-fair way. The GULHEMP system is
model.

ing and Testing the Older Worker. Older people can
work skills and the efficiency of that learning can be
y the use of special techniques. The studies reviewed
ion focus on special retraining of older persons in work
and on issues in testing of older people for employment.
the major work in this area has been done by the
Training Research Unit (ITRU) in Cambridge, England,
marized in a volume by Drs. Eunice Belbin and R.
Belbin.[53] The ITRU develops training programs for
workers, and consults with respect to and eval-
rams in industrial settings. The volume contains
case examples and illustrations of the principles
l in training and retraining mature adult workers.

Benefits and Costs to Industry, Indus. Gerontology 63, 65 (Fall 1973).
0. *See also* Indus. Gerontology 71 (Fall 1973), for comments by
esentatives involved in the program.
in and R.M. Belbin, *Problems in Adult Retraining* (1972). For an
liography in this area *see* Clifford, *Learning Ability and Age,* Indus.
0 (Winter 1972).

and for office workers, did not indicate any loss of efficiency with
increased age.

Older workers are also thought to be more accident prone. A
study of sixty-two men aged 23 to 63 in a Birds Eye plant found
that age was not related to accident proneness.[38]

Older people are also thought to be more rigid. Dr. Shelia M.
Chown investigated the role of rigidity as measured by nineteen
different tests of rigidity in three different work situations and two
laboratory experiments. In four of the investigations there was a
large age spread. In each of the situations some adaptation or
change was required of the individuals and performance criteria
were established in each situation. Age was inversely related to
performance on all of the measures except one, but the measures
of rigidity were more highly related than age in all of the
situations. This research suggests that direct measures of rigidity,
rather than age, are more accurate predictors of successful
adaptation on the job.[39]

In his chapter on the 'right to work', Dr. Butler addressed the
question of productivity and creativity in older people and called
attention to well-known historical figures from Sophocles to Shaw
who made major contributions in their old age.[40] A recent article
in the New York Times Magazine focused on current
contributors.[41] Detractors always point out that the superior
individuals who achieve are different from the average
man-in-the-street; but these people miss the point. If we observe
excellence, creativity, and productivity in late life, then indeed the
individuals who so achieve might be special, but their existence is
proof of the fact that age, by itself, is no barrier to continued
achievement.[42]

38. Kunce, *Vocational Interests and Accident Proneness,* 51 J. Appl. Psych. 223
(1967).

39. Chown, *The Effect of Flexibility-Rigidity and Age in Adaptability in Job
Performance,* Indus. Gerontology 105 (Spring 1972).

40. R.N. Butler, *Why Survive?: Being Old in America, supra,* at 76.

41. H.D. Shapiro, *Do Not Go Gently . . . ,* N.Y. Times Magazine, February 6, 1977,
at 37.

42. Two classic studies present the relationships between age and achievement
across a variety of fields: H.C. Lehman, *Age and Achievement* (1953) and Dennis,
Creative Productivity Between the Ages of 20 and 80 Years, 21 J. Gerontology 1
(1966).

One of the most comprehensive systems of matching the worker to the job, useful in dealing with problems of employment for older workers, is a system developed by Dr. Leon F. Koyl.[43] Dr. Koyl's system focuses on a joint assessment of the fitness of the individual and the requirements of the job. Both the individual and the job are rated on a seven category scale called the GULHEMP. GULHEMP is an acronym for the functional components of the required competence of the workers for the job: *G*eneral physique, *U*pper extremities, *L*ower extremities, *H*earing, *E*yesight, *M*entality and *P*ersonality. Each function is rated from superior competence with no restrictions or limitations to total incompetence and a profile is developed. Each job in a particular industrial setting is also evaluated on the same set of criteria stressing the minimum skills required for adequate performance of the job. In order to decide if the individual is fit for the job, the individual's profile must be at, or above, the requirements for the job in all seven areas of competence.[44]

The GULHEMP system is not limited to the assessment of older workers, but can deal with a wide range of individuals including the middle-aged and older worker and does provide a system of determining the functional performance of an individual independent of age, sex, or race. Profiles of various individuals can be made at regular intervals or upon hiring, and again when questions of promotion, retirement, or changes in health status of an individual suggest that an additional evaluation would be useful. For example, it can be used to show whether the current lowered profile of an individual who may have lost competence when compared to him or herself at an earlier age is still above what is required for adequate performance of a specific job.[45]

The manual describing the GULHEMP system is an extremely useful practical volume, and a fine illustration of a system that both allows for individual differences in functional ability and is able to do so in an age-fair way. The manual deals very effectively with a variety of common diseases and discusses their probable

---

43. L.F. Koyl, *Employing the Older Worker: Matching the Employee to the Job* (1974).

44. *Id.* at 21-22, 37, 40-44.

45. *Id.* at 38.

---

impact on performance. Disabiliti
remaining ability. The system ha
Aircraft Ltd. in Toronto, Cana
a result of the success of the
of Industrial Gerontology, unde
tional Council on the Aging and
of the U.S. Department of Labor,
in Portland, Maine which was
Counseling Service (IHCS).

The IHCS project started in 19
of the project, 2,400 job applicant
of them were placed in jobs. Appl
than one hundred firms in the Po

Data were collected on program
period, including 534 people
employment.[48] The unemploymer
reduced from 94 percent to 30 per
under 25, 73 percent of those 25
64, and 48 percent of those over
jobs.[49]

The GULHEMP system was
groups (under 54, and 55 and ov
groups differed in educational
younger group had an eighth gr
23 percent of the older group.
employment only for the young
were referred by the state emp
younger workers who got jobs
ones, while the older workers
same level as their old jobs.[50] Th
related to age, but in general,

---

46. *Id.* at 5.

47. Batten, *Application of a U*
Gerontology 38 (Fall 1973).

48. Quirk and Skinner, *IHCS: Phys*
Gerontology 49, 50 (Fall 1973).

49. *Id.* at 51.

50. *Id.* at 53-55.

---

than age
in the st
the Main
group in
48 percer
were dis
rather th

Data f
cost/bene
used sick
(hired at
project) u
for the II
evaluation
of the pro
reducing
providing

The IH
workers'
one such
2. *Train*
learn new
improved
in this sec
situations
Some of
Industrial
and is sur
Meredith
industrial
uates pro
a set of
found usef

---

51. Levine
52. *Id.* at
company rep
53. E. Bell
annotated bil
Gerontology

The ITRU programs begin with a recognition of the fact that the adult faced with the task of retraining often approaches the program with a high degree of anxiety due, in part, to a poor educational background or to the length of time that has passed since being in a training environment. The authors suggest methods of group training that help build confidence and types of learning experiences that allow the adult to be an active problem solver.

During learning, it is important that errors be corrected before they become incorporated into the older person's performance. Because the older learner does appear to be a more cautious learner, the progress may tend to be slower, but the eventual amount of learning may be the same or better than that of younger trainees. The authors suggest that practical training on smaller, conceptually relevant, parts of the task to be learned should be taught first, then the parts should be put together and, once learned, practiced up to speed. The studies indicate that this is a particularly good way to teach some of the psychomotor skills involved in skilled industrial performance. The book is an excellent source of ideas about methods of adult retraining which sets out principles that could be adapted for a variety of situations.

Home study and programmed instructions were found to be particularly appropriate for older learners as they allow individuals to progress at their own rates. For example, in a study of programmed learning, it was found that the younger trainees learned more in ten one-half hour sessions while the older trainees did better with five one-hour sessions. Thus, while it took the same amount of time to train the two groups, the distribution of the time was important in maximizing benefits for the different age groups.[54] Another study of programmed learning in the laboratory, investigated the amount of time required for two groups (20 versus 73 years old) to study programmed text about anatomy and physiology. Both groups were relatively well educated (students and retired faculty) and on a pre-test of the information scored at the same level (13.8 and 13.9 answers correct). The material was

---

54. Neale, Toye and Belbin, *Adult Training: The Use of Programmed Instruction,* 42 Occupational Psych. 21 (1968).

presented in a one hundred frame linear program. The tests were conducted immediately after the completion of the learning program by both groups. Both had improved their scores significantly, and had learned about the same amount of information (23.80 for the young group, 27.43 for the older group). The main difference was in the time taken by each group. The younger group took 45 minutes on the average with a standard deviation of 10.26 minutes while the older group took 102.53 minutes on the average with a standard deviation of 44.85 minutes.[55] Thus, given sufficient time, the old mastered the material as well as the young.

The work of the ITRU has been particularly useful in coping with automation, where a firm is interested in finding a way to retrain its workforce many of whose members are middle-aged and older people. One interesting case study is the change over from a cargo warehouse operated "by hand" to an automated system. One third of the workforce to be retrained was over forty and the principles developed by the ITRU were used in the retraining program. The program was highly successful and the success of those participating in the program was not related to age.[56]

Testing of older workers for employment requires "age fair" testing instruments.[57] Discrimination in testing occurs when the test performance is not related to ability to do the job. This is a problem of test validity. The problem is not limited to assessments which involve older workers, but rather is a characteristic of all measuring instruments used to assess individual characteristics. Standards for psychological tests used in such cases must meet the criteria provided by the American Psychological Association defining various types of validity which in essence require that the

---

55. Siemen, *Programmed Material as a Training Tool for Older Persons*, 3 Indus. Gerontology 183 (1976).

56. E. Belbin and R.M. Belbin, *Problems in Adult Retraining, supra*, at 153-59. *See also* Mullan and Gorman, *Facilitation of Adaptation to Change: A Case Study in Retraining Middle Aged and Older Workers at Aer Lingus*, Indus. Gerontology 20 (Fall 1972).

57. *See* Jenkins, *Age Discrimination in Employment Testing*, Indus. Gerontology 42 (Winter 1972). For a discussion of similar issues related to sex discrimination, *see* L. Kanowitz, *Sex Roles in Law and Society* (1973).

24

test must measure what it is designed to measure.[58] The types of functional evaluation represented by the GULHEMP and by the on-the-job evaluations suggested by Drs. Belbin and Belbin avoid a lot of problems, but are not always practical. Many employment services and firms rely on paper and pencil tests because they are cheaper, quicker, and, if valid, can provide important information for use in making hiring decisions.

One large scale study of paper and pencil tests with adults was conducted by the Adult Development Study. In this testing program, a series of multiple choice exams on general vocabulary and specific content areas (e.g., health, finances) were developed for adults aged 20 to 80 years of age.[59] Each vocabulary test was analyzed separately for age groups by decade as well as for educational level of the groups. Analyses were also done on the particular items that made up the test. The results indicated that performance was maintained through the 40's and, for some of the tests and items, maximum performance was obtained by the group consisting of persons in their 60's.[60] The age patterns for the high and low education grouping showed similar age patterns, with the lower educational group scoring lower at each age than their better educated peers. This research indicates that it is possible to build a test so that you can predict which age group will do well on a particular set of items. Thus, an older individual can be evaluated against expected performance for his or her age group as well as against a standard set for all age groups.

A test that has received some scrutiny and is in use by the United States Employment Service is the General Aptitude Test Battery (GATB). Dr. Robert C. Droege investigated the validity of the GATB across the adult age range.[61] Most research on the development of aptitude batteries has been done with younger people. The validity for older persons of such tests needs to be

---

58. American Psychological Association Standards for Educational and Psychological Tests (no date, available from APA).

59. R.H. Monge and E.F. Gardner, *A Program of Research in Adult Differences in Cognitive Performance and Learning* (1973).

60. *Id.* at 29.

61. Droege, *Effects of Aptitude Score Adjustments by Age Curves on Prediction of Job Performance*, 51 J. Appl. Psych. 181 (1967).

determined separately. Work with the GATB indicated that all scales except Verbal Aptitude declined with age. Age curves were constructed over the range of 17 to 72 allowing for the calculation of age norms.[62] The United States Employment Service has a continuing program of test validation for specific occupations. Information from studies of eleven occupational groups was used in Droege's study. All eleven studies were conducted longitudinally. That is, individuals were evaluated with the GATB prior to starting the job, but the GATB was not used in selection or placement. Each individual's performance on the job was later rated by his supervisor or based on a work sample or by instructors for those in training programs. Each of the eleven occupational groups studied had a broad age range (16 to 23 on the young end and 37 to 60 on the old end). The measure of validity was the correlation between the score the individual received on the GATB, raw score or score adjusted for age, and the rating on the job. The differences for the validity coefficients corrected for age compared to those with the raw scores were small, the largest being .09, with the median difference equal to .00.[63] Thus, it appears that the GATB is an appropriate test across the adult age range (through the 60's).

The GATB is composed of nine aptitudes measured by twelve different tests. The aptitudes measured are Intelligence, Verbal Aptitude, Numerical Aptitude, Spatial Aptitude, Form Perception, Clerical Perception, Motor Coordination, Finger Dexterity, and Manual Dexterity. GATB scores have been shown to be related to both age and social class (SES).[64] For example, on numerical ability, aptitude declined with age in all class groups, however the scores of the oldest high SES men were better than those of the youngest low SES men; whereas for manual dexterity, there were large age differences and no differences between classes.

---

62. *Id.* at 182-183. *See also* Droege, Crambert and Henkin, *Relationship Between GATB Aptitude Scores and Age for Adults,* 42 Personnel Guidance J. 502 (1963).

63. *Id.* at 183 and Tables 4, 5 at 185.

64. Fozard and Nuttall, *General Aptitude Test Battery Scores for Men Differing in Age and Socioeconomic Status,* 55 J. Appl. Psych. 372-79 (1971); and Fozard and Carr, *Age Differences and the Psychological Estimates of Abilities and Skills,* Indus. Gerontology 75 (Spring 1972).

Therefore, in using the results of the GATB for counseling purposes, it is important to evaluate the test results by what would be expected on the basis of age and social class. There is, however, a counterargument to specific age/class norms. That is that a specific job may require a certain set of minimum qualifications and while the test performance may vary due to those characteristics, given the test is valid, the same minimum standards of performance should be applied to all persons.[65] The functional types of assessment appear to suffer from fewer problems but are certainly more time consuming and costly.

3. *Functional Age.* Functional age is a theoretical construct that has been important in the development of understanding of the meaning of age differences in performance. The construct is intuitively appealing and captures such common sense notions as "you are as young as you feel" and "you are as old as your arteries." Additionally, it focuses on the fact that the various systems within the body age at different rates, thus allowing an individual to have more than one functional age, as well as the fact that there are large individual differences among people of the same chronological age. Among a group of the same age, it is possible to try to rank order the group from the functionally youngest to the functionally oldest. The construct has been important in terms of theory and as a stimulus for research. While the empirical research guided by the search for an appropriate measure of functional age has been a major contributor to understanding age differences in functioning and the development of normative data across the lifespan, it has failed in its *own* goal of replacing chronological age with a more valid indicator of functioning.[66]

The construct of functional age became important during World War II, when it became necessary to employ large numbers of older workers in war industries, and techniques were needed to identify which older workers would be suitable. In 1943, Dr. Ross A. McFarland studied the problem and concluded that, if properly

---

65. Fozard and Carr, *supra,* at 83.

66. Costa and McCrae, *Functional Age: A Conceptual and Empirical Critique* (Paper presented at NIA Conference on Epidemology of Aging, March, 1977).

placed, the older workers could not only do the job but had higher job stability and fewer accidents and lost less time from work than the younger workers.[67]

Dr. McFarland concluded that the wrong question had been asked about work and age. Instead of focusing on declines in performance seen with increased age, he suggested that question should be when in the aging process is the physiological and psychological deterioration no longer compensated for by past experience, including adaptations which have been made to offset declining capacities.[68]

Three major studies have been organized around the construct of functional age.[69] Drs. Alastair Heron and Shelia Chown studied three hundred men and two hundred and forty women representative of the British population grouped by decades from the 20's to the 70's distributed by occupation and social class.[70] Johan M. Dirken and his co-workers studied three hundred and sixteen industrial workers between the ages of 30 and 70 who were drawn from a cross-section of Dutch industry.[71] In the United States a group of investigators at the Normative Aging Study studied 2,000 men screened for health in the Boston area.[72]

In all three studies, a wide variety of physiological and psychological constructs were studied. In the Heron and Chown study, the twenty-six measures were carefully investigated and age differences were calculated separately for the sexes. Special attention was paid to investigate differences due to different social class groupings. Once these normative patterns were identified,

---

67. McFarland, *The Need for Functional Age Measurements in Industrial Gerontology*, Indus. Gerontology 1 (Fall 1973).

68. *Id.* at 11.

69. *See also* Furukawa, Inoue, Kajiya, Inada, Tokasugi, Fukui and Abe, *Assessment of Biological Age by Multiple Regression Analysis*, 30 J. Gerontology 422 (1975); and Webster and Logie, *A Relationship Between Functional Age and Health Status in Female Subjects*, 31 J. Gerontology 546 (1976).

70. A. Heron and S. Chown, *Age and Function* (1967).

71. *Functional Age of Industrial Workers* (J.M. Dirken ed. 1972).

72. *Normative Aging Study*, 3 Int'l J. Aging Hum. Dev't. 143 (1972). *See also* Costa and McCrae, *Functional Age: A Conceptual and Empirical Critique, supra*, for longitudinal data after 5 and 10 years.

the average performance for each decade was determined. It was then possible to compare the scores of an individual of a given age with the average scores for each age group. They investigated functional age by building a profile for the individual, for example, for a 65 year old man, if his functional age was equal to his chronological age, then all of his functional age scores should equal 65.

The range of functional ages can be illustrated by comparing two of the case studies, A1 and C2. Both were men aged 65 from the middle class. A1 scored in the upper ranges on measures of intelligence, C2 in the middle to lower ranges. A1 had younger functional ages on ten of the measures, older functional ages on four of the measures and was his own age for two of the measures. C2 had younger functional ages on six of the measures, older ages on eight of the measures, and his own age for two of the measures.[73]

While changes associated with increasing age were reported, the variation among individuals increased with the age of the people studied. Thus, not only are generalizations about the aged unsound, but chronological age is a very poor guide to the state of the individual's functioning. Additionally, aging is not a unitary process, performance in one kind of task did not necessarily predict performance on another.[74]

The other two studies followed a different approach. Both the Dutch group and the Boston group measured a large number of variables across a broad age range and attempted to use the measures to develop a set of regression equations based on a smaller number of variables that predicted the individual's functional age. The criterion of this measure of functional age was its correlation with chronological age. The Dutch group developed an equation that included performance measures of the efficiency of the cardiovascular system and the respiratory system, reaction time, hearing and cognitive performance. With this equation they categorized the sample by their functional ages. Only 26 of their 316 men had functional ages equal to their chronological ages, 198 men had ages within five years; 97 had functional ages between

73. A. Heron and S. Chown, *Age and Function, supra*, at 123-33.
74. *Id.* at 137-44.

five to ten years different, 15 people were greater than ten years off from their measured age. Overall, 235 were younger than their actual age and 145 were older. The evaluation for functional age developed by the Dutch group takes about one and a half hours to administer and, thus, might have practical application.[75]

The Boston study developed six functional ages: laboratory age, auditory age, anthropometric age, ability age, personality age, and social age.[76] In summarizing the work of the group of investigators, the six functional ages were factor analyzed.[77] The six functional ages were represented by thirty-one variables that were derived from the much larger battery. In addition, the chronological age of each person and two measures of socioeconomic status, occupation and education, were added. The factor analysis resulted in four factors named functional age, socioeconomic status, strength, and size. The correlation between chronological age and those factors were .82, -.31, .22, and -.03, respectively. Three of the functional ages were represented on the functional age factor: anthropometric, ability, and auditory age.

The Boston study is unique in that it is the only longitudinal study of functional age. The longitudinal follow-up data after five and ten years were used to investigate the validity of the functional age construct. Drs. Paul Costa and Robert McCrae reasoned that the functionally older men should age more rapidly and thus show greater changes over the ten year period than the functionally younger men and that predictions based on functional age should be more efficient than predictions based on chronological age for a variety of performance measures. Their results indicated that none of the tests for functional age produced results supporting the utility of the construct, and thus suggest that functional age as an indicator to replace chronological age is a flawed concept.[78] The functional age research did not meet its stated goal but has been useful nonetheless in pointing out that the relationships are

75. *See* note 71, *supra.*

76. *Normative Aging Study, supra,* at 145.

77. Nuttall, *How Many Functional Ages Are There?,* in *Symposium on Personality, Age and Social Indices* 13 (1973).

78. Costa and McCrae, *Functional Age: A Conceptual and Empirical Critique, supra,* at 19-31.

complex, no one single indicator of function, be it chronological or some derived index, will serve. Instead, specific assessments of the competencies required for the performance of a particular set of tasks, while time consuming, are the best way to measure the competence of an individual at any age.

4. *Basic Research in the Laboratory.* Most psychological research done in the United States on the intellectual and cognitive abilities of older persons has been done in the laboratory and not in applied work settings. Both types of research are critical in our understanding of the functioning of the older person. There are many excellent review chapters and books available for the reader who wishes more depth in this important area.[79] A brief summary of the implications of that body of work will be discussed here.

In many respects the older person and his cognitive and learning performance can be described as practical. Dr. A.T. Welford points out that difficulties in learning can be overcome, and that part of the problem may be motivational. The "cost" of learning for the older person may be greater (require more time, increased concentration). Therefore, the benefit to be derived from the learning must really pay off and be seen by the older person to be of use.[80] Many of the tasks presented to people in the laboratory seem to have no direct application for the older persons themselves, and, thus, performance may suffer. An equally important problem can be seen when the older person makes the decision that it is worth performing up to maximum capacity generating, as a result, an undue amount of anxiety that may also act to impair performance.[81]

---

79. Excellent reviews of the literature in the area of cognitive performance can be found in the following volumes: *Handbook of the Psychology of Aging* (J.E. Birren & K.W. Schaie eds. 1977); J.L. Fozard and J.C. Thomas, *Psychology of Aging: Basic Findings and Some Psychiatric Applications*, in *Modern Perspectives on the Psychiatry of Old Age* 108 (J.G. Howells ed. 1975); J. Botwinick, *Aging and Behavior* (1973); *The Psychology of Adult Development and Aging* (C. Eisdorfer & M.P. Lawton eds. 1973); R.D. Savage, P.G. Britton, N. Bolton, and E.H. Hall, *Intellectual Functioning in the Aged* (1973); *Human Aging and Behavior* (G.A. Talland ed. 1968); J. Botwinick, *Cognitive Processes in Maturity and Old Age* (1967); *Behavior Aging and the Nervous System* (A.T. Welford & J.E. Birren eds. 1965).

80. Welford, *Motivation, Learning and Age*, 7 Int'l J. Aging Hum. Dev. 189 (1976).

81. C. Eisdorfer, *Arousal and Performance: Experiments in Verbal Learning and a Tentative Theory*, in *Human Aging and Behavior* 189 (G.A. Talland ed. 1968).

A second characteristic of older persons is that given a particular challenge or stress the older person will need to exert more energy to meet it and will take longer to get back to the resting level and be ready to repeat the event all over again.[82] This phenomenon is most often seen in the laboratory in conjunction with the slowing of behavior. Speed may not always be required for adequate job-related performance but it is a critical variable, theoretically, in our understanding of the changes that come with age in the brain and the central nervous system.[83]

A third major point the research is just beginning to focus on is the ecological constraints on behavior, particularly with reference to human performance engineering where changes in the system may be used to improve efficiency at any age but would be particularly useful for older persons.[84]

A fourth major point is that the role of age in explaining behavior must be carefully applied. Often, poor health, rather than age, is what causes poor performance.[85] An additional point to be remembered is that many people with marginal skills survive into old age.[86]

D. SOCIAL GERONTOLOGY AND POLICY

Many of the decisions which effect older people can be seen to have little relationship to the individual's psychological characteristics, but rather are based on the fact that older people are treated as a group for purposes of social policy. Social gerontology focuses on how the social system interacts with aging.

---

82. J.L. Fozard and J.C. Thomas, *Psychology of Aging: Basic Findings and Some Psychiatric Applications, supra,* at 115.

83. Birren, *Translation in Gerontology — From Lab to Life,* 29 Am. Psych. 808 (1974).

84. J.L. Fozard and J.C. Thomas, *Psychology of Aging: Basic Findings and Some Psychiatric Applications, supra,* at 116. *See also* J.L. Fozard and J.C. Thomas, *Why Engineering Psychologists Ought to Get Interested in Aging* (Paper presented at American Psychological Association Convention, August 1973).

85. *See* note 22, *supra.*

86. L.E. Gottesman, C.E. Quarterman and G.M. Cohn, *Psychosocial Treatment of the Aged,* in *The Psychology of Adult Development and Aging* 378, 387 (C. Eisdorfer & M.P. Lawton eds. 1973).

Research in this area comes from a variety of social science disciplines including sociology, economics, political science, and policy sciences.

Research in Social Gerontology. As with laboratory work in psychology, there has been a tremendous amount of work done in this area. There are many excellent books and review chapters available.[87] Some of the major findings and issues are reviewed below.

Retirement has been a major focus of this literature. Many of the authors point out that retirement is a relatively recent phenomenon that has come with the development of industrial societies. As the proportion of the population that lives until retirement age, and beyond, has increased, so has the importance of retirement. Retirement functions for society as a way of providing a proscribed exit from the workforce, generally at a fixed time, that allows those in the system to move up and those outside of the system a way in. Definitions of retirement are not simple. Individuals may retire at a certain age or after completion of a certain number of years, and this can either be by the choice of the employee or under a mandatory system. Also a small but significant number of older persons change jobs around retirement age, often going from full-time to part-time work. Thus, it is not uncommon for an individual to have "retired" a number of times. Individuals who leave the workforce during the young adult years due to health reasons are considered disabled, but older workers who leave the workforce due to health are often considered retired. Most workers in the United States upon retirement are covered by

---

87. For excellent reviews in the area of Social Gerontology *see*: *Handbook of Aging and the Social Sciences* (R. Binstock & E. Shanas eds. 1976); J.M. Kreps and R.L. Clark, *Sex, Age and Work* (1975); R.E. Barfield and J.N. Morgan, *Early Retirement: The Decision and Experience* (1974); R.E. Barfield, *The Automobile Worker and Retirement: A Second Look* (1974); J. Schultz, G. Carrin, H. Krupp, M. Peschke, E. Sclar, and J. Van Steenberge, *Providing Adequate Retirement Income* (1974); R.C. Atchley, *The Social Forces in Later Life,* 153-76 (1972); *Retirement* (F.M. Carp ed. 1972); Jaffe, *The Retirement Dilemma,* Indus. Gerontology 1 (Summer 1972); M.W. Riley, M. Johnson and A. Foner, *Aging and Society* 160-97 (1972); E. Claque, B. Palli and L. Kramer, *The Aging Worker and the Union* (1971); G.F. Streib and C.J. Schneider, *Retirement in American Society: Impact and Process* (1971); *Adjustment to Retirement* (R.J. Havighurst, J.M.A. Munnichs, B.L. Neugarten & H. Thomae eds. 1969).

some sort of income replacement plan. For example, in 1970, 91 percent of men and 45 percent of women 65 and over were covered by the social security system; for those aged 40 to 49, 99 percent of the men and 67 percent of the women are covered.[88] In addition, approximately 52 percent of men and 23 percent of women have private pension coverage. Many government workers, at all levels, are not covered by the social security system; but instead have a pension system.[89] However, on the average, the amount of income replaced by social security and pensions is low. In 1972 the median benefit from private pensions was $2,080 for men and $970 for women per year.[90] Social security benefits, while increasing dramatically in recent years, provided in 1975 an average monthly benefit of a minimum of $101.40 for a worker retiring at age 65, $193 for an aged widow, a maximum of $341.70 for a worker retiring at age 65, and $512.60 for a couple both aged 65.[91] Benefits are reduced if the individual chooses to retire at age 62.

The social security system is currently the source of much controversy. One issue is the retirement test. The retirement test limits the amount a person may earn and still receive benefits. The argument for this is that social security is a retirement program that was designed to replace earnings lost by cessation of work. Thus, the fact that 'unearned income' (from rents, annuities, investments or other pensions) does not reduce benefits produces no conflict. The contributory nature of the social security system suggests to people that social security is an annuity and a form of deferred income and, therefore, should be treated like other pensions.[92] Current regulations provide a system which allows a limited amount of earnings before benefits are reduced, with the

---

88. Social Security Administration, *Reaching Retirement Age: Findings from a Survey of Newly Entitled Beneficiaries* 75-93 (1976).

89. *Id.* at 4.

90. J.H. Schultz, *Income Distribution and the Aging,* in *Handbook of Aging and the Social Sciences* 561, 580 (R. Binstock & E. Shanas eds. 1976).

91. Senate Special Committee on Aging, *1976 Developments in Aging, supra,* at 62.

92. Quirk, *The Retirement Test: The Debate Continues,* 2 Indus. Gerontology 76 (1975). *See also* Institute of Gerontology, Univ. of Michigan, *Social Security: The First 35 Years* (1970).

limitation no longer applicable after seventy-two years of age, and appear, as a result, to be compatible with neither argument.

Mandatory retirement is the second issue of current importance. Estimates of the number of individuals subject to mandatory retirement are hard to come by. Some authors count those forced to retire because of declining health as mandatory retirees, others do not. Additionally, the difficulty in keeping up with changes in union practices and in private pensions schemes, both of which tend to provide benefits on the basis of some mandatory date of retirement and include incentives for retiring before the maximum date, also complicate the issue.

Dr. James H. Schultz has reworked data from the Social Security Administration's Survey of Newly Entitled Beneficiaries and has come up with the following estimates: of a retirement cohort, 54 percent are subject to mandatory retirement rules; of the 54 percent, 30 percent choose to retire early while 24 percent retire at the maximum age; of the 24 percent, 10 percent do so willingly and 14 percent unwillingly; of the 14 percent unwilling, 4 percent are unable to work due to health limitations and 10 percent are able to work; of the 10 percent able to work, about 3 percent are able to find another job and 7 percent are unable to find another job. Thus, his estimate suggests a relatively small percentage of the cohort of retirees, each year, wish to continue working.[93]

Mandatory retirement schemes appear to be popular because they provide a high degree of administrative convenience. Many individual companies do not have mandatory retirement systems, but the definitive set of studies comparing these particular industries with the rest of the variations in the system have yet to be done. The consensus appears to be that mandatory retirement, while it may not be equitable or morally correct, appears to be uniformly fair and, with the growth of pensions and increased social security benefits, provides a reasonable compromise within the marketplace. A paradox is the expressed desire for work by older people included in the arguments against

---

93. Schultz, *The Economics of Mandatory Retirement*, 1 Indus. Gerontology 1 (1974).

mandatory retirement [94] while an increasing number of individuals opt for retirement at age 62 under the social security system and under early retirement schemes associated with pension systems.

Studies of early retirement have shown that many prefer this option given proper inducements.[95] Thus, it is at least a reasonable supposition that if the age discrimination in employment laws were amended to provide protection against age discrimination in employment regardless of age, it would provide for a small proportion of older individuals' desperately needed protection, but probably would not cause massive disruptions in the workplace. Indeed, the demographic projections suggest that we cannot afford the trend towards early retirement for only if the retirement age moves closer to 70 will we be able to provide a reasonable standard of living for all of the population, young and old.[96]

---

94. *See* P. Woodring. *Why 65?*, Sat. Rev., August 7, 1976, at 18; J.A. McCracken, *The Company Tells Me I'm Old*. Sat. Rev., August 7, 1976, at 21; J.M. Johnson, *Is 65 Old?*, 7 Soc. Policy 9 (1976); R.N. Butler, *Why Survive?: Being Old in America, supra*, at 64-102; L.D. Cain, *Mandatory Retirement: The Murgia Decision and its Likely Consequences*, 3 Indus. Gerontology 233 (1976).

95. *See* R.E. Barfield and J.N. Morgan, *Early Retirement: The Decision and Experience, supra;* and Social Security Administration, *Reaching Retirement Age: Findings from a Survey of Newly Entitled Beneficiaries, supra.*

96. R.L. Clark, *The Influence of Low Fertility Rates and Retirement Policy on Dependency Costs* (Unpublished manuscript, 1977); R.L. Clark and J.J. Spengler, *Changing Demography and Dependency Costs* (Unpublished manuscript, 1977); and J.M. Kreps, J.J. Spengler, R.L. Clark and R.S. Herren, *Economic Implications for Older Americans of a Stationary Population* (1976).

Chapter 4

THE LEGAL ATTACK ON AGE DISCRIMINATION IN EMPLOYMENT

The legal challenge to age discrimination in employment has, of necessity, involved a two-pronged attack. The first prong is statutes, rules, and regulations prohibiting age discrimination in employment. The second is lawsuits based on constitutional and equitable principles where there either are no statutes covering age discrimination in employment or where the statutes which do exist do not cover a particular situation or individual. For example, many of the statutes, rules, and regulations prohibiting age discrimination in employment have a limited applicability generally related to the age of the persons covered and whether the employer involved is a public or private entity. Accordingly, the existence of statutory protection has not reduced the importance of litigation based on constitutional and equitable principles challenging age discrimination in employment.

A. CONSTITUTIONAL AND EQUITABLE CHALLENGES TO AGE DISCRIMINATION IN EMPLOYMENT

1. *The "Right" To Obtain and Keep Employment.* The importance of an individual's having the opportunity to obtain and keep employment has long been recognized by individual judges and by courts in the United States. There has not, however, been developed any well-defined body of generally applicable law governing what might be termed "a constitutional right to employment."

In considering the question of whether there is a "right" to obtain and keep employment, judges have looked to the Declaration of Independence and the Fourteenth Amendment of the United States Constitution. The latter provides, in part, that

> No State shall make or enforce any law which shall abridge the privileges or immunities of citizens of the United States; nor shall any State deprive any person of life, liberty, or property, without due process of law; nor deny to any person within its jurisdiction the equal protection of the laws.[1]

---

1. Amendment XIV, § 1.

One of the first judges to identify a right to employment was Justice Bradley of the United States Supreme Court in his concurring opinion in *Butchers' Union Co. v. Crescent City Co.*[2] where he stated that

> The right to follow any of the common occupations of life is an inalienable right. It was formulated as such under the phrase "pursuit of happiness" in the Declaration of Independence, which commenced with the fundamental proposition that "all men are created equal, that they are endowed by their Creator with certain inalienable rights; that among these are life, liberty and the pursuit of happiness." This right is a large ingredient in the civil liberty of the citizen.[3]

* * *

> I hold that the liberty of pursuit — the right to follow any of the ordinary callings of life — is one of the privileges of a citizen of the United States.[4]

The Supreme Court in *Allgeyer v. Louisiana*[5] subsequently quoted Justice Bradley's remarks with approval stating that "they well describe the rights which are covered by the word 'liberty' as contained in the Fourteenth Amendment."[6]

In *Truax v. Raich*,[7] the Supreme Court found an Arizona law restricting the employment of non-citizens to be unconstitutional holding, *inter alia,* that

> It requires no argument to show that the right to work for a living in the common occupations of the community is of the very essence of the personal freedom and opportunity that it was the purpose of the [Fourteenth] Amendment to secure.[8]

---

2. 111 U.S. 746, 760 (1884).
3. *Id.* at 762.
4. *Id.* at 764.
5. 165 U.S. 578, 589-90 (1897).
6. *Id.* at 590.
7. 239 U.S. 33 (1915).
8. *Id.* at 41. That statement was recently cited with approval in Hampton v. Mow Sun Wong, 426 U.S. 88, 102-103 and n. 23 (1976).

The importance of the general right to obtain and keep employment has, perhaps, been most eloquently expressed by Justice Douglas of the Supreme Court in his dissenting opinion in *Barsky v. Board of Regents.*[9] Justice Douglas there stated that

> The right to work, I had assumed, was the most precious liberty that man possesses. Man has indeed as much right to work as he has to live, to be free, to own property. The American ideal was stated by Emerson in his essay on Politics, "A man has a right to be employed, to be trusted, to be loved, to be revered." It does many men little good to stay alive and free and propertied, if they cannot work. To work means to eat. It also means to live. For many it would be better to work in jail, than to sit idle on the curb. The great values of freedom are in the opportunities afforded man to press to new horizons, to pit his strength against the forces of nature, to match skills with his fellow man.[10]

The courts and judges cited above and others [11] have found in the Fourteenth Amendment at least a right to obtain and keep employment free from discrimination, arbitrary interference or prohibitions, and unreasonable and unnecessary restrictions. However, the protection afforded by the Fourteenth Amendment is limited to "state action"; that is, acts of the fifty states and lesser instrumentalities of government. Thus, it provides no protection from discrimination in private employment situations where there is no state involvement.[12]

Although the Fourteenth Amendment does not apply to the Federal portion of the dual system of government established in the United States Constitution, under certain circumstances similar protection against discriminatory action by the Federal government has been found in the guarantee contained in the Fifth Amendment to the United States Constitution which provides, in

---

9. 347 U.S. 442, 472 (1954).

10. *Id.* at 472.

11. *See, e.g.,* New State Ice Co. v. Liebmann, 285 U.S. 262, 278 (1932); Corey v. City of Dallas, 352 F. Supp. 977, 980 (N.D. Tex. 1972) ("The right to earn a livelihood by following one's legitimate occupation is a right implicit in the Fourteenth Amendment."), *rev'd on other grounds,* 492 F. 2d 496 (5th Cir. 1974).

12. *See* Hines v. Cenla Community Action Comm., Inc., 474 F. 2d 1052, 1058 (5th Cir. 1973); Vaughn v. Chrysler Corp., 382 F. Supp. 143, 144 (E.D. Mich. 1974).

part, that "No person shall ... be deprived of life, liberty, or property, without due process of law; ...." [13] Again, however, the protection applies only to Federal employment or employment having Federal involvement. [14]

2. *Age Discrimination in Employment.* In the absence of statutes prohibiting age discrimination in employment or in instances where such statutes are inapplicable, persons claiming to have been subjected to age discrimination in employment have sought protection in the courts relying upon the Fifth and Fourteenth Amendments, where applicable, and the courts' inherent equitable powers. The persons bringing such suits have, generally, been state and federal employees who were originally excluded from many statutes prohibiting age discrimination in employment; airline flight personnel; and railroad employees.

Railroads and railway unions have commonly entered into collective bargaining agreements providing for forfeiture of all seniority rights by operating employees and their retirement from service at a specified age, typically seventy. The employees covered by such agreements have challenged the agreements arguing, *inter alia,* that such agreements discriminate against them and favor fellow employees under the specified age and, in taking away their seniority rights, divest them of property without due process of law in violation of the Fourteenth Amendment and similar provisions of state constitutions. The courts have consistently rejected all such arguments holding that the unions were the lawful bargaining representatives of the employees and that compulsory retirement was a valid subject of such bargaining; that seniority rights arise only by reason of provisions of collective bargaining agreements and can, therefore, be taken away without constitutional infirmity by provisions of, or amendments to, collective bargaining agreements; and that compulsory retirement provisions are not discriminatory by favoring younger employees over older workers since each employee would be affected equally,

---

13. *See* Shapiro v. Thompson, 394 U.S. 618, 641-42 (1969), and the cases cited therein.

14. *See* Hines v. Cenla Community Action Comm., Inc., *supra*.

although at different times, when they reach the specified retirement age.[15]

A case closely related to the railway union cases is *Retail Clerks Union, Local 770 v. Retail Clerks International Association*.[16] The plaintiffs alleged that the defendant union's adoption of a bylaw providing for mandatory retirement at age 65 of officers and employees of the union and its chartered locals discriminated against them on the basis of age in violation of the Fifth and Fourteenth Amendments to the United States Constitution. The Court held that plaintiffs had failed to state a claim upon which relief could be granted and dismissed the action finding that there was neither the requisite allegation of state or Federal action in the origination or perpetration of the challenged bylaw nor the use of the power of the state to enforce or encourage private discrimination so as to constitute the kind of necessary state action.

The Court, further, noted that the union's stated purpose for adopting the bylaw was to establish uniform retirement requirements while allowing a transition period to avoid organizational dislocation and individual hardship, and that there was no proof that the bylaw was enacted with the specific intent of depriving the plaintiffs of their livelihood or that the bylaw would not be uniformly and non-discriminatorily applied to all those to whom it was applicable. Reviewing the cases, the Court found that

> Age classifications of persons of advanced years have not been held to be constitutionally or statutorily infirm.[17]

---

15. *See, e.g.,* Goodin v. Clinchfield R.R., 125 F. Supp. 441 (E.D. Tenn. 1954), *aff'd per curiam,* 229 F. 2d 578 (6th Cir.), *cert. denied,* 351 U.S. 953 (1956); Ricks v. Norfolk and Western Ry, 185 F. Supp. 119 (E.D. Va. 1960); Jones v. Martin, 1 CCH Employ. Prac. Dec. ¶9649 (S.D. Fla., April 16, 1956) n.o.r.; McMullans v. Kansas, Oklahoma and Gulf Ry., 129 F. Supp. 157 (E.D. Okla. 1955), *aff'd,* 229 F. 2d 50, 55 (10th Cir.) ("There is nothing illegal or immoral about a contract for compulsory retirement. It is a principle now commonly accepted in industry and other lines of endeavor, including employees of the United States. 5 U.S.C. § 715."), *cert. denied,* 351 U.S. 918 (1956); Flowers v. Brotherhood of Locomotive Firemen and Enginemen, 212 Ga. 142, 91 S.E.2d 41 (Sup. Ct. 1956); Lamon v. Georgia Southern & Florida Ry., 212 Ga. 63, 908 S.E.2d 658 (Sup. Ct. 1955).

16. 359 F. Supp. 1285 (C.D. Cal. 1973).

17. *Id.* at 1287.

The Court held that
> Not all discrimination between classes of persons is violative of the law. The test is whether distinctions which are drawn are rationally related to the purpose for drawing of the distinctions.[18]

and that the mandatory retirement bylaw of the union was a rational and permissible means of achieving a rational and permissible objective.

The airline pilot cases are of particular interest because they involve challenges to a Federal regulation and provide examples of a court-created defense to claims of age discrimination in employment similar to the "bona fide occupational qualification" defense found in many statutes dealing with age discrimination in employment. The regulation in question prohibits airlines from using the services of any person as a pilot if he has reached his sixtieth birthday and prohibits any person from serving as an airline pilot if he has reached his sixtieth birthday.[19] In *Chew v. Quesada*,[20] the plaintiff pilot argued that the United States Congress did not have the power, even in the interest of safety, to make age the conclusive criterion for compulsory retirement and it followed that the Congress had not delegated and could not delegate such power to the defendant Administrator of the Federal Aviation Agency who prescribed the challenged regulation. The Court rejected plaintiff's claim and held that the regulation was promulgated in a valid exercise of a validly delegated Congressional power and was reasonably related to the achievement of the Administrator's purpose and duty of promoting safety in air commerce. In the course of its opinion, the Court noted that the Administrator had proposed the regulation

> after extensive investigation and study, which led the defendant to believe that the existing absence of any maximum age limit for pilots should be remedied in light of medical information regarding the increased probability of sudden incapacitating maladies in any group reaching 60....[21]

---

18. *Id.*

19. The current version of the regulation is found at 14 C.F.R. § 121.383 (c) (1974).

20. 182 F. Supp. 231 (D.D.C. 1960).

21. *Id.* at 232.

In subsequent attacks on the regulation, the courts have reached an identical result. Thus, in *Air Line Pilots Association, International v. Quesada,*[22] the Court rejected the plaintiffs' claim that the regulation violated due process because it modified the pilots' rights without affording each pilot affected a hearing holding that

> All private property and privileges are held subject to limitations that may reasonably be imposed upon them in the public interest. Only when the limitations are too stringent in relation to the public interest to be served are they invalid. The limitations here are entirely reasonable.[23]

The Court also turned aside plaintiffs' assertion that the age sixty limitation was arbitrary and discriminatory and without relation to any requirements of safety holding that the Administrator of the Federal Aviation Agency had a reasonable basis for his exercise of judgment in promulgating the regulation [24] and that

> It is not the business of courts to substitute their untutored judgment for the expert knowledge of those who are given authority to implement the general directives of Congress.[25]

In *O'Donnell v. Shaffer,*[26] the Court upheld the F.A.A.'s rejection of a petition by the airline pilots association for reconsideration of the age sixty rule. The Court quoted the following from the decision of the Acting Administrator,

---

22. 276 F. 2d 892 (2d Cir. 1960); *summary judgment granted for defendant,* 6 CCH Aviation Cas. 18, 085 (S.D.N.Y., June 14, 1960) n.o.r., *aff'd per curiam.,* 286 F.2d 319 (2d Cir.), *cert. denied,* 366 U.S. 962, *rehearing denied,* 368 U.S. 870 (1961).

23. 276 F.2d at 896.

24. The Court referred to the Administrator's findings that the number of commercial pilots over sixty years of age had been few but was increasing rapidly; that older pilots because of their seniority often flew the newest, largest, and fastest planes; that available medical studies showed that sudden incapacitation due to heart attacks became more frequent as men approach age sixty and medical knowledge was such that it was impossible to predict with accuracy those individuals most likely to suffer attacks; that a number of foreign airlines had mandatory retirement ages of sixty or less; and that numerous aviation safety experts had advocated a maximum age of sixty or younger. *Id.* at 898.

25. *Id.*

26. 491 F.2d 59 (D.C. Cir. 1974).

Before the chronological basis for termination of service can be replaced by a system based on physiological and psychological factors, those factors must be capable of identification and application within the framework of the FAA medical examination. . . .In this regard, an increase in the number of medical examinations administered to a given pilot, as suggested by some of the testimony at the hearing, would not be an effective deterrent to incapacitation inasmuch as the indices of such incapacitation are not now sufficiently developed.[27]

The theme of increased risk of sudden incapacity due to disease among older persons is often raised in cases of alleged age discrimination in employment and particularly in the transportation industry. Of course, it is not simply the age of the employees but the determinations of legislatures, courts, and administrative agencies that there is at present an inability to predict the sudden onslaught of debilitating disease which has led to the choice of chronological limits in particular occupations. The fact that persons such as airline pilots, railroad engineers, and bus drivers [28] are responsible for the lives of others and their sudden unpredictable incapacitation could be disastrous to those in their charge, has led the courts to uphold a chronological age limitation or qualification for persons seeking employment in those positions in the absence of reliable individualized predictors.

When a state or Federal employee or potential employee alleges age discrimination in connection with employment, he or she has recourse to the Fourteenth or Fifth Amendments, respectively. One of the leading cases in this area is *Weiss v. Walsh.*[29] In that case, the plaintiff, a seventy year old philosopher and educator, alleged that he had been given a firm offer of an Albert Schweitzer

---

27. *Id.* at 61.

28. *See* pp. 100-107, *infra.*

29. 324 F. Supp. 75 (S.D.N.Y. 1971), *aff'd without opinion,* 4 CCH Employ. Prac. Dec. ¶7572 (2d Cir., October 29, 1971) n.o.r.; *motion to dismiss denied,* 4 CCH Employ. Prac. Dec. ¶7650 (S.D.N.Y., January 11, 1972) n.o.r.; *judgment for defendants,* 5 Fair Employ. Prac. Cas. 1099 (S.D.N.Y., March 7, 1972) n.o.r., *aff'd without opinion,* 461 F.2d 846 (2d Cir. 1972), *cert. denied,* 409 U.S. 1129, *rehearing denied,* 410 U.S. 970 (1973).

Professorship by Fordham University and had then been denied the appointment because of his age. The Albert Schweitzer Professorships are awarded and funded by the State of New York. The Court held that, on the facts, there was no discrimination against plaintiff and judgment was ordered entered for the defendants. In denying plaintiff's motion for a preliminary injunction preventing the awarding to another candidate during the pendency of the action of the Schweitzer Chair to which plaintiff laid claim, the Court noted, *inter alia,* that

> the absence of specific reference to age in the Fourteenth Amendment does not alone insulate age classification from constitutional scrutiny....***. But being a classification that cuts fully across racial, religious, and economic lines, and one that generally bears some relation to mental and physical capacity, age is less likely to be an invidious distinction.[30]

The Court held that
> Notwithstanding great advances in gerontology, the era when advanced age ceases to bear some reasonable statistical relationship to diminished capacity or longevity is still future. It cannot be said, therefore, that age ceilings upon eligibility for employment are inherently suspect, although their application will inevitably fall unjustly in the individual case. If the precision of the law is impugnable by the stricture of general applicability, vindication of the exceptional individual may have to attend the wise discretion of the administrator. On its face, therefore, the denial of a teaching position to a man approaching seventy years of age is not constitutionally infirm.[31]

The Court did note, however, that if
> the age ceiling on eligibility for the state-endowed chairs has not been consistently applied, the Equal Protection Clause [of the Fourteenth Amendment] might have been violated.[32]

A similar approach has been taken by courts faced with challenges to laws and regulations providing for the mandatory

---

30. 324 F. Supp. at 77.
31. *Id.*
32. 324 F. Supp. at 78.

retirement of Federal and state employees. Thus, for example, it has been held that there is no constitutional infirmity in: a county civil service policy and regulations imposing mandatory retirement at age 65;[33] a state statute requiring the retirement of city fire department members at age 60 unless they can continue to pass mental and physical qualification tests, in which case they can continue until their sixty-fifth birthday;[34] a state law permitting boards of school directors to terminate the service of any professional employee who has attained the age of 62 except one who is a member of the state old age and survivors system who may be terminated at age 65 or the age at which such employee becomes eligible to receive full benefits under the Federal Social Security Act;[35] a state law requiring the mandatory retirement of state policemen at age 60;[36] a state law providing that contractual continued service of teachers must cease at the end of the school term following their sixty-fifth birthday and that any subsequent employment must be on an annual basis;[37] and a state law requiring primary and secondary school teachers who are members of the state employees retirement system to retire at age 65 unless

---

33. Armstrong v. Howell, 371 F. Supp. 48 (D. Neb. 1974).

34. Gardner v. Nation, 522 P.2d 1281 (Wyo. Sup. Ct. 1974).

35. Frantz v. Baldwin — Whithall School Dist., 8 Pa. Commw. Ct. 639, 304 A.2d 531 (1973).

36. McIlvaine v. Pennsylvania State Police, 6 Pa. Commw. Ct. 505, 296 A.2d 630, 633 (1972) ("The fact that a particular police officer is physically fit and able to perform his duties or that minds may differ upon the particular mandatory retirement age selected by the legislature is not proof of want of bona fides as to the qualification otherwise applied uniformly and nondiscriminatorily to the selected class."), aff'd, 454 Pa. 129, 309 A.2d 801 (Sup. Ct. 1973), appeal dismissed, 415 U.S. 986 (1974).

37. Kennedy v. Community Unit School Dist. No. 7, Champaign County, Ill., 23 Ill. App. 3d 382, 319 N.E.2d 243, 246 (App. Ct., 1974),

> It is a matter of general and common knowledge that many persons expect to and do retire from employment at the age of 65 years. Such age marks the eligibility for benefits both under the Social Security Act of the United States and many public and private pension plans. It is thus apparent that the classification is not "inherently suspect and subject to close judicial scrutiny." [Citation omitted.] If no fundamental right is concerned a statutory classification which is reasonable and bears a rational relationship to a proper State objective, there is no denial of constitutional equal protection. [Citation omitted.]

their application to be retained is annually approved by their school board.[38]

County policemen, who had elected under a state law to contribute to a retirement fund and authorized deductions to be made from their salaries in order to become eligible to retire at one-half of their final average salary after serving 20 years, were denied relief on their constitutional claims of age discrimination when they were involuntarily retired at age 59 because the statute creating the retirement system required those electing to participate therein to agree to retire at the end of the month in which they attained the age of 59.[39]

Claims of age discrimination in connection with employment were also unsuccessful in *Kingston v. McLaughlin,*[40] where sitting judges of the Massachusetts state courts alleged that an amendment to the Massachusetts' constitution requiring the retirement of state judges when they reach the age of 70 violated their constitutional rights.

In *Cookson v. Lewiston School District No. 1,*[41] a 56 year old teacher challenged the decision of the board of trustees of the defendant school district not to renew her contract and to, thereby, deny her tenure alleging, *inter alia,* age discrimination violating her right to equal protection of the laws under the Fourteenth Amendment. Plaintiff had been advised by the superintendent of

---

38. Lewis v. Tucson School Dist. No. 1, 23 Ariz. App. 154, 531 P.2d 199 (Ct. App.), *cert. denied,* 423 U.S. 864 (1975).

39. Bouffier v. Frank, 12 Fair Employ. Prac. Cas. 955 (E.D.N.Y., February 19, 1975) n.o.r.

40. 359 F. Supp. 25 (D. Mass. 1972), *aff'd without opinion,* 411 U.S. 923 (1973). *See also* Rubino v. Ghezzi, 512 F.2d 431 (2d Cir.) *(per curiam), cert. denied,* 423 U.S. 891 (1975); and Aronstam v. Cashman, 132 Vt. 538, 325 A.2d 361 (Sup. Ct. 1974), upholding mandatory retirement ages for judges. *Cf.* Anderson, *Age Discrimination: Mandatory Retirement From the Bench,* 20 Loyola L. Rev. 153 (1974), in which a sitting judge argues that

> discrimination because of age is as invidious to the equal protection and due process guarantees of the Constitution of the United States as prejudicial treatment based on race, religion, sex or national origin.

41. 351 F. Supp. 983 (D. Mont. 1972).

schools that the reasons for the board's action were her prior illness during the school year, she was 56 years old and only average teaching could be expected from her, and during her three years of teaching she had had one unsuccessful year of teaching English. The Court, in ordering the action dismissed, expressed a particularly conservative and unsympathetic view toward age discrimination in employment:

> The equal protection clause does forbid the consideration of some differences such as color or religious belief or political opinion, but it has not yet been held by any controlling court that the 14th amendment forbids school boards to consider age as an employment factor, and I would not break trail in that direction. It may be that a school faculty should be composed of young people all recently educated, filled with enthusiasm, and relatively close in age to their pupils. It may be that a faculty should be balanced — that the enthusiasm of the young teachers should be tempered by the experience and maturity of the older ones. It may be that a faculty should be composed of old or middle-aged people, though I doubt it. I have no capacity to determine even in the abstract what the ideal faculty should be in terms of the age of its members, and certainly I have no capacity to determine the ages of the teachers that should be hired for a particular faculty at a particular time. I am sure, however, that age is a factor that ought to be considered by those close to the problem in the employment of teachers and that in the interests of education it ill behooves a federal district judge using the Constitution as his excuse to force school boards to ignore what may be a very important factor in the selection of a staff. It is my opinion that plaintiff has no 14th amendment rights based upon the school board's consideration of her age.[42]

While the reluctance of the Court in *Cookson* to advance beyond the frontiers established by other courts is understandable in a legal system which relies on precedent such as the United States common law system, there is little to justify the Court's failure to consider the specific individual before it and its focusing only on the general question of faculty age distribution where there was,

---

42. *Id.* at 986-87.

apparently, no claim that a decision for the plaintiff would result in a major revision of the age characteristics of school faculties since it is unusual for a teacher to be in her tenure year at age 56.

The foregoing cases paint a very pessimistic picture for those who choose to, or must, rely on a constitutional or equitable challenge to age discrimination in employment.[43]

An indication that a change is unlikely in the immediate future in the courts' generally unsympathetic response to challenges to mandatory retirement policies under the Fifth Amendment or the Fourteenth Amendment is provided by *Weisbrod v. Lynn*.[44] In that case, the Court of Appeals reversed the District Court's decision, which denied plaintiff's motion for the convening of a three-judge court to consider the constitutionality of a Federal law providing for mandatory retirement of Federal civil service employees at age 70[45] and dismissed the complaint, holding that the plaintiff's

> challenge in this instance presents a constitutional issue of sufficient substance as to warrant consideration by a three-judge court.[46]

---

43. *See* Serwer, *Mandatory Retirement at Age 65 — A Survey Of The Law,* 1 Indus. Gerontology (n. s.) 11, 22 (1974), where the author notes that

almost entirely unsuccessful have been those employees who have claimed their employer's retirement policy violates the equal protection clause of the Fourteenth Amendment.

See generally Comment, *The Constitutional Challenge to Mandatory Retirement Statutes,* 49 St. John's L. Rev. 748 (1975); Comment, *Mandatory Retirement: The Law, the Courts, and the Broader Social Context,* 11 Willamette L. J. 398 (1975); Note, *Constitutional Attacks on Mandatory Retirement: A Reconsideration,* 23 U.C.L.A. L. Rev. 549 (1976); Note, *Age Discrimination in Employment,* 50 N.Y.U. L. Rev. 924, 927-45 (1975); Note, *Too Old to Work: The Constitutionality of Mandatory Retirement Plans,* 44 So. Cal. L. Rev. 150 (1971).

44. 494 F. 2d 1101 (D.C. Cir. 1974) *(per curiam), on remand,* 383 F. Supp. 933 (D.D.C. 1974) (three-judge court), *aff'd without opinion,* 420 U.S. 940 (1975), *motion for leave to file petition for rehearing denied,* 423 U.S. 886 (1975).

45. 5 U.S.C. § 8335 (1970).

46. 494 F.2d at 1102. A three-judge court is convened to give initial consideration to actions seeking an injunction restraining the enforcement, operation, or execution of a state or Federal statute on the ground that it is unconstitutional. There is a right of direct appeal to the United States Supreme Court from a three-judge court's decision. 28 U.S.C. §§ 1253, 2281, 2282, 2284 (1970).

On remand, however, the three-judge court dismissed the action on the ground that the United States Supreme Court had recently dismissed the appeal in *McIlvaine v. Pennsylvania* [47] "for want of a substantial federal question." [48] The United States Supreme Court affirmed that determination without opinion.[49] An identical result on the same ground was reached in an action challenging the New York State constitutional and statutory provisions requiring the mandatory retirement at age 70 of New York City Civil Court judges.[50]

In *Cannon v. Guste*,[51] a Louisiana statute which required state civil service employees to retire at age 65 if they were eligible to retire under either the Federal Social Security law or any state public employment retirement system unless their appointing authority certified that it was to the agency's advantage to retain them for one year was upheld in the face of a multiple ground constitutional attack. The three-judge District Court, in rejecting plaintiff's arguments, held that

> This court is satisfied that there is a rational basis for maintaining the mandatory retirement requirement at age sixty-five in that it is fairly and substantially related to the state's valid economic objective of maintaining an efficient, vigorous and healthy civil service, and of establishing a feasible system for promotions of younger employees.***. The contention that age is a suspect

---

47. 415 U.S. 986 (1974). Discussed at p. 46, n. 36, *supra.*

48. 383 F. Supp. 933 (D.D.C. 1975). That ground for decision disregards the fact that the *McIlvaine* case involved a challenge to a state retirement statute while *Weisbrod* involved a Federal employee, a Federal statute, and the right to assert a claim under the Fifth Amendment to the United States Constitution not present in the former case.

49. 420 U.S. 940 (1975).

50. Rubino v. Ghezzi, 512 F.2d 431 (2d Cir.) *(per curiam), cert. denied,* 423 U.S. 891 (1975). To the same effect is Gault v. Garrison, 523 F.2d 205 (7th Cir. 1975) *(per curiam),* withholding decision on a challenge to Illinois statutory provisions requiring, in effect, mandatory retirement of public school teachers at age 65 until determination by the United States Supreme Court of the appeal from the District Court's decision in Murgia v. Commonwealth of Mass. Bd. of Retirement, 376 F. Supp. 753 (D. Mass. 1974), discussed pp. 51-58, *infra.*

51. 10 CCH Employ. Prac. Dec. ¶10,460, 11 Fair Employ. Prac. Cas. 675 (E.D. La., May 5, 1975) *(per curiam)* (three-judge court) n.o.r., *aff'd without opinion,* 423 U.S. 918 (1975).

classification demanding proof of a compelling state interest is infirm and unsupported jurisprudentially. [Citation omitted.]***.

Plaintiff has not established that she possessed a constitutionally protectible property interest in her employment prior to dismissal: a mere unilateral, subjective expectation that her request for continued employment of one year would receive the requisite final approval . . . is insufficient.*** 52

The most damaging blow to the constitutional challenge to age discrimination in employment was delivered in *Murgia v. Commonwealth of Massachusetts Board of Retirement.*[53] Plaintiff brought the action to challenge a Massachusetts statute requiring that the state board of retirement retire members of the uniformed branch of the Massachusetts State Police when they reach age 50 or complete 20 years of service, whichever occurs later. Plaintiff, the executive officer and lieutenant colonel of the uniformed branch, alleged that the statute discriminated against him in violation of the equal protection clause of the Fourteenth Amendment to the United States Constitution since he would shortly be retired at 50 with over 24 years of service. The plaintiff moved for a preliminary injunction restraining his forced retirement pending a final determination of the case and for the convening of a three-judge court.

The single judge, applying the traditional analysis, found: that age had not been held to be a suspect classification such as religion or race requiring special scrutiny by the courts; that

[e]arly retirement even of high-ranking officers gives younger men a chance for promotion and ensures that commanders possess the physical vigor to accompany

52. 10 CCH Employ. Prac. Dec. ¶10,460, at 5984-85, 11 Fair Employ. Prac. Cas. at 676. The same result was reached in Talbot v. Pike, 533 F.2d 331 (6th Cir. 1976) (upholding a rule requiring retirement at age 70 of employees of the Cleveland Metropolitan Park District pursuant to statutory authorization contained in the law establishing Ohio's Public Employee Retirement System).

53. 345 F. Supp. 1140 (D. Mass. 1972), *rev'd and remanded,* 9 CCH Employ. Prac. Dec. ¶10,007 (1st Cir., September 10, 1973) (order) n.o.r., *on remand,* 376 F. Supp. 753 (D. Mass. 1974) (holding statute unconstitutional) (three-judge court), *reversed,* 427 U.S. 307 (1976) *(per curiam);* 386 F. Supp. 179 (D. Mass. 1974) (relief) (three-judge court), *aff'd without opinion,* 421 U.S. 972 (1975).

their men in the field. These are surely legitimate purposes. Mandatory retirement at the age of 50 is at least a rational, if not the only, means of achieving them.[54]

and that it would be only exceptional cases where persons would retire under the statute at over 50 years of age. Accordingly, the Court held that the complaint did not raise a substantial constitutional question and denied the request for a preliminary injunction and the convening of a three-judge court.

However, a three-judge court subsequently convened pursuant to an order of the Court of Appeals rejected the traditional approach. That Court held that it was not necessary to determine whether age was a suspect classification or the right to employment was a fundamental interest since the lesser standard of a showing by the plaintiff that the statute lacked a rational basis had been met and the plaintiff had at least a recognizable interest in retaining his employment which the state could not deny arbitrarily and irrationally. The Court found that the mandatory retirement of uniformed state policemen at 50 years of age bore no fair and substantial relation to the object of the legislation and declared the statute to be unconstitutional and void.

The Court disposed of the traditional arguments raised by the defendant state as follows:

Its argument that early retirement enhances the morale of the younger members, in a sense assumes the point. Of course, if there are only younger members, they are happier than the older members who are being eliminated. This does not add up on balance, but merely advances the time of ultimate happiness. The same can be said with respect to the alleged desirability of rapid promotion; the attractiveness of quick promotion must be weighted against the unattractiveness of early retirement. Furthermore, to the extent that the purpose of early retirement is said to be to empty higher ranking positions after they have been occupied by one person for a reasonable time, the cut-off at 50 years is of questionable consequence since it is unrelated to the period of time the retiree has occupied his last position.

---

54. 345 F. Supp. at 1142-43.

The alleged desirability of facilitating rapid promotion by early retirement, rather than a justification, will be seen on analysis to be age discrimination per se.[55]

The Court identified the only question requiring serious consideration to be whether mandatory retirement at age 50 was rationally related to maintaining a vigorous, healthy person. The Court noted that plaintiff's experts conceded that "there is a general relationship between advancing age and decreasing physical ability to respond to the demands of the job." [56] At the same time, the state did not dispute plaintiff's experts' testimony that

the relation between chronological age and functional age varies greatly from one individual to the next.[57]

To the state's argument that in matters of this sort it is administratively reasonable to select an arbitrary cut-off and that irrationality is not established by the fact that certain individuals are disadvantaged thereby, the Court accepted the necessity of choosing arbitrary standards in certain areas and that in such a case

[t]o satisfy the minimal standards of rationality the line must be drawn within a range where fairness, or some appreciable state interest, exists, even if no specific point within that range is preferable to any other.[58]

However, in the case before it the Court held that no arbitrary standard was called for since

Individual testing is not impracticable but, rather, is already the order of the day. There is no suggestion that it is more burdensome to examine an officer at age 50 than it was at age 49.[59]

The Court noted, further, there was no scientific justification presented by the state in support of the reasonableness of the age

---

55. 376 F. Supp. at 754-55.
56. 376 F. Supp. at 755.
57. *Id.*
58. *Id.*
59. *Id.*

chosen such as a showing of a greater risk at the higher age that the prognosis based upon testing would be less reliable.[60] The Court then concluded that

> Recognizing the public interest in protecting individuals' right to work, and against discrimination on account of age ... we are compelled to strike down the present age distinction where plaintiff has established the absence of any factual basis therefor.[61]

The three-judge court ordered the plaintiff reinstated to the position and the rank he held at the time of his retirement and required the defendants to pay the regular court costs, but denied the plaintiff back pay and attorneys' fees.[62]

On appeal to the United States Supreme Court, however, the decision of the three-judge court was reversed in a *per curiam* opinion which upheld the constitutionality of the Massachusetts statute.[63] The Supreme Court, noting the cursory consideration it had given to prior cases involving constitutional challenges to age discrimination in employment,[64] held that challenges to mandatory retirement statutes based upon the Equal Protection Clause of the Fourteenth Amendment to the United States Constitution were to be determined under the "rationality" standard, which involves a determination of whether the age classification chosen by the state for mandatory retirement is rationally related to furthering a

---

60. The Court noted that in Airline Pilots Assoc., Int'l v. Quesada, *supra*, p. 43, the court pointed to a study documenting the F.A.A.'s assertion that by age 60, in spite of medical testing, a critical area had been reached for airline pilots.

61. 376 F. Supp. at 756. The Court did feel it necessary to note that Massachusetts was the only state compulsorily retiring police officers before age 55 and that it was not faced with deciding whether it would reach the same result if a more customary retirement age had been specified in the statute. However,

> we would anticipate the question of mandatory retirement at age 70 not to be the same as at age 50, but perhaps we say this because of the increasing difficulties that a plaintiff might have to show that at that greater age the state had not made out a factually rational argument. [376 F. Supp. at 756 n. 9.]

62. 386 F. Supp. 179 (D. Mass. 1974) (relief) (three-judge court), *aff'd without opinion,* 421 U.S. 972 (1975).

63. 427 U.S. 307 (1976) *(per curiam).*

64. 427 U.S. at 308-309 n. 1.

legitimate state interest. The Supreme Court rejected the use of the strict scrutiny standard noting that that standard was applicable only to those classifications which impermissibly interfere with the exercise of a fundamental right or operate to the peculiar disadvantage of a suspect class.[65]

The Supreme Court held that a right of governmental employment was not *per se* fundamental and that the class of uniformed police officers over 50 years of age did not constitute a suspect class for purposes of equal protection analysis. In the view of the Supreme Court,

> a suspect class is one "saddled with such disabilities or subjected to such a history of purposeful unequal treatment, or relegated to such a position of political powerlessness as to command extraordinary protection from the majoritarian political process." While the treatment of the aged in this Nation has not been wholly free of discrimination, such persons, unlike, say, those who have been discriminated against on the basis of race or national origin, have not experienced a "history of purposeful unequal treatment" or been subjected to unique disabilities on the basis of stereotyped characteristics not truly indictive of their abilities. ***. [The Massachusetts statute] cannot be said to discriminate only against the elderly. Rather, it draws the line at a certain age in middle life. But even old age does not define a "discrete and insular" group, [citation omitted], in need of "extraordinary protection from the majoritarian political process." Instead, it marks a stage that each of us will reach if we live out our normal span. Even if the statute could be said to impose a penalty upon a class defined as the aged, it would not impose a penalty

---

65. 427 U.S. at 312-13. The Supreme Court gave the following examples of "fundamental rights": right of a uniquely private nature — Roe v. Wade, 410 U.S. 113 (1973) (abortion); right to vote — Bullock v. Carter, 405 U.S. 134 (1972); right of interstate travel — Shapiro v. Thompson, 394 U.S. 618 (1969); rights guaranteed by the First Amendment — Williams v. Rhodes, 393 U.S. 23 (1968); right to procreate — Skinner v. Oklahoma ex rel. Williamson, 316 U.S. 535 (1942). 427 U.S. at 312 n. 3.
The following examples of "suspect" classes were given: alienage — Graham v. Richardson, 403 U.S. 365 (1971); race — McLaughlin v. Florida, 379 U.S. 184 (1964); ancestry — Oyama v. California, 332 U.S. 633 (1948). 427 U.S. at 312 n. 4.

upon a class defined as the aged, it would not impose a distinction sufficiently akin to those classifications that we have found suspect to call for strict judicial scrutiny.[66]

Resorting to the "rational basis" standard, the Supreme Court found that the Massachusetts legislature sought, through the mandatory retirement statute, to protect the public by assuring physical preparedness of its uniformed police and that, "[s]ince physical ability generally declines with age,"[67] mandatory retirement at age 50 seemed to remove from police service those whose fitness for uniformed work had presumptively declined with age. A result held to be rationally related to the state's objective, particularly since there was "no indication that [the statute] has the effect of excluding from service so few officers who are in fact unqualified as to render age 50 a criterion wholly unrelated to the objective of the statute."[68]

In holding that the Massachusetts statutory retirement system did not deny the plaintiff equal protection of the laws, the Supreme Court noted that it was not ignoring the substantial economic and psychological effects upon an individual of premature and compulsory retirement, denigrating the ability of elderly citizens to continue to contribute to society, or deciding that the Massachusetts statute was wise or that a better system could not be devised, but was only holding that Massachusetts' choice not to determine fitness after age 50 by individual testing did not mean that the objective of assuring physical fitness is not rationally furthered by a maximum age limitation even though it may not be the best means to accomplish that purpose. Quoting from *Dandridge v. Williams*,[69] the Supreme Court stated that

> where rationality is the test, a State "does not violate the Equal Protection Clause merely because the classification made by its laws are imperfect."[70]

---

66. 427 U.S. at 313-14.
67. 427 U.S. at 315.
68. 427 U.S. at 315-16.
69. 397 U.S. 471, 485 (1970).
70. 427 U.S. at 316.

Of the eight Justices that decided the *Murgia* case only Justice Marshall dissented from the Supreme Court's decision.[71] He found the Massachusetts statute so "overinclusive" that, regardless of which standard was used, it resulted in a deprivation of the plaintiff's Fourteenth Amendment rights. Justice Marshall noted also that, in his view, the Court's decision did not imply that all mandatory retirement laws are constitutionally valid and

> [t]hat the Court concludes it is rational to legislate on the assumption that physical strength and well-being decrease significantly with age does not imply that it will reach the same conclusion with respect to legislation based on assumptions about mental or manual ability. Accordingly, a mandatory retirement law for all government employees would stand in a posture different from the law before us today.[72]

The Supreme Court's decision in *Murgia,* and particularly the reasoning by which it determines that age is not a suspect class requiring strict judicial scrutiny under the Fourteenth Amendment's Equal Protection Clause, is open to substantial criticism. The Court's reference to a lack of history of unequal treatment of older workers is contrary to the findings of Congress in enacting the Federal Age Discrimination In Employment Act of 1967,[73] the findings of the Secretary of Labor,[74] and others.[75] In addition, the absence of any "history" is more logically explainable by the relatively recent growth in the numbers of older persons in the population and the percentage of older persons who either have to or want to continue working. The increase in the numbers of mandatory retirement laws and of the people affected by them suggests that we are now living through the "history" which the

71. 427 U.S. at 317-27.

72. 427 U.S. at 327 n. 8.

73. 29 U. S. C. § 621 (a) (1970).

74. Report of the Secretary of Labor to the Congress Under Section 715 of the Civil Rights Act of 1964, *The Older American Work* r — *Age Discrimination in Employment* (June 1965), discussed pp. 69-71, *infra.*

75. *See, e.g.,* M. Barron, *The Aging American* (1961), *See also* President Lyndon B. Johnson's Special Message to the Congress Proposing Programs for Older Americans, Public Papers of the Presidents of the United States — Lyndon B. Johnson — 1967 — Book I 32 (G. P. O. 1968).

Court could not find. The "majoritarian political process" to which the Supreme Court referred is also present in the younger workers anxious for the jobs and positions held by older workers who support mandatory retirement and the society as a whole with its youth orientation. Against that tide older workers have, indeed, been politically powerless.

The most significant response to age discrimination in employment to date has been Federal, state and local statutes which prohibit, in varying degrees, such discrimination. There follows a discussion of such statutes.

Chapter 5

STATE STATUTES DEALING WITH AGE
DISCRIMINATION IN EMPLOYMENT

There are presently in force in 39 of the 50 states, Puerto Rico, the Virgin Islands, the District of Columbia, and Guam statutes which prohibit age discrimination in employment to a greater or lesser extent.[1] These statutes fall into three general categories: fair employment practices (FEP) laws prohibiting discrimination in employment on grounds such as race, religion, national origin, sex, and age; statutes dealing only with age discrimination in employment; and human rights laws prohibiting discrimination in, for example, employment, public accommodations, and housing on grounds such as those previously enumerated.[2] The first such statute was enacted in Colorado in 1903.[3]

The following discussion provides a brief review of the three types of state statutes. The importance of such laws was increased by the inclusion in the Federal statute dealing with age discrimination in employment of a provision giving limited primacy to state procedures for dealing with claims of age discrimination in employment in those states having statutes meeting specified minimum standards; thereby giving recognition to the Federal nature of the United States constitutional scheme and encouraging the enactment of state laws dealing with age discrimination in employment.[4]

---

1. _See_ Employment Standards Administration, U.S. Dep't of Labor, _A Report Covering Activities Under the Act During 1975,_ at 21, 32-58 (1976). A summary of the state, commonwealth, and territorial laws covering age discrimination in employment is set forth in Appendix D. to this book.

2. For an extended discussion of state statutes dealing with age discrimination in employment and a proposal for a uniform law covering the area, see Note, _Age Discrimination in Employment: The Problem of the Older Worker,_ 41 N.Y.U.L. Rev. 383 (1966) (hereinafter _Problem of the Older Worker)._

3. _Problem of the Older Worker_ at 388 n. 42.

4. _See_ pp. 138-146, _infra._

A. FAIR EMPLOYMENT PRACTICES LAWS

FEP statutes generally cover three types of potential discriminators in connection with employment — employers, employment agencies, and labor unions.[5]

"Employer" is generally defined to include any private person or entity employing more than a specified number of persons within the state and the state or any political subdivision thereof.[6] An exception is occasionally made for religious, fraternal, charitable, or sectarian organizations permitting them to hire persons of a single sex or religion.[7]

FEP statutes typically declare it to be an "unfair employment practice" for

(a) an employer to refuse to hire or employ or to discharge an individual or to discriminate against an individual in compensation or in the terms, conditions, or privileges of employment upon the specified grounds;[8]

(b) an employment agency to fail or refuse to classify properly or to refer for employment or to otherwise discriminate against an individual upon the specified grounds;[9]

(c) a labor organization to exclude or expel from membership or to otherwise discriminate against an individual or to do any act which would deprive, limit, or otherwise act so as to adversely affect an individual's status as an employee or an applicant for employment upon the specified grounds;[10] and

(d) an employer, an employment agency, or a labor organization to advertise employment opportunities in such a manner as to

---

5. *See, e.g.,* Conn. Gen. Stat. Ann. § 31-126 (Cum. Supp. 1976); Del. Code Ann., tit. 19, § 711 (1975); Mich. Stat. Ann. § 17.458(3a) (1975 rev. vol.).

6. *See, e.g.,* Conn. Gen. Stat. Ann. § 31-122(f) (Cum. Supp. 1976) ("three or more persons"); Del. Code Ann., tit. 19, § 710 (1975) ("4 or more persons"); Mich. Stat. Ann. § 17.458(2)(a) (1975 rev. vol.) ("8 or more persons").

7. *See, e.g.,* Del. Code Ann., tit. 19, § 710 (1975).

8. *See, e.g.,* Conn. Gen. Stat. Ann. § 31-126(a) (Cum. Supp. 1976); Del. Code Ann., tit. 19, § 711(a) (1975); Mich. Stat. Ann. § 17, 458(3a) (a) (1975 rev. vol.).

9. *See, e.g.,* Conn. Gen. Stat. Ann. § 31-126(b) (Cum. Supp. 1976); Del. Code Ann., tit. 19, § 711(b) (1975); Mich. Stat. Ann. § 17.458(3a) (b) (1975 rev. vol.).

10. *See, e.g.,* Conn. Gen. Stat. Ann. § 31-126(c) (Cum. Supp. 1976); Del. Code Ann., tit. 19, § 711(c) (1975); Mich. Stat. Ann. § 17.458(3a) (c) (1975 rev. vol.).

restrict such employment so as to discriminate against an individual upon the specified grounds.[11]

In each FEP statute there are specific limitations on the scope of the prohibition, if any, against age discrimination in employment which, for example, may limit the protection afforded by the statute to persons falling within specified age limits,[12] and exclude from the statute's coverage a "bona fide occupational qualification";[13] an employee unable to satisfactorily perform his duties;[14] a bona fide retirement policy or system or welfare or benefit plan of an employer where such policy, system, or plan is not a subterfuge to evade the purposes of the statute;[15] and an apprenticeship program.[16]

1. *Enforcement.* Enforcement of FEP statutes is generally delegated to either a department of the executive branch of state government[17] or, more commonly, an administrative agency specifically created for the task.[18]

Any person claiming to be aggrieved by a violation of an FEP statute must file a complaint in writing with the designated state agency stating the name of the party allegedly violating the FEP

---

11. *See, e.g.,* Conn. Gen. Stat. Ann. § 31-126(f) (Cum. Supp. 1976); Mich. Stat. Ann. § 17.458(3a) (d) (1) (1975 rev. vol.).

12. *See, e.g.,* Cal. Labor Code § 1420.1(a) (West Cum. Supp. 1976) ("between the ages of 40 and 64"); Del. Code Ann., tit. 19, § 710 (1975) ("between the ages of 40 and 65"); Mich. Stat. Ann. § 17.458(3a) (a) (1975 rev. vol.) ("between the ages of 18 and 60"). A provision such as that found in Michigan's FEP law containing a lower age limit below, for example, 40 has the unfortunate possible side-effect of dividing limited resources and personnel between younger and older workers and, thereby, reducing the efforts made on behalf of older workers by state enforcement officials.

13. *See, e.g.,* Conn. Gen. Stat. Ann. § 31-126(a), (b), (c), (f) (Cum. Supp. 1976); Del. Code Ann., tit. 19, § 711 (e) (1) (1975); Mich. Stat. Ann. § 17.458(3a) (d) (1975 rev. vol.).

14. *See, e.g.,* Mich. Stat. Ann. § 17.458(3a) (e) (1975 rev. vol.).

15. *See, e.g.,* Conn. Gen. Stat. Ann. § 31-126 (Cum. Supp. 1976); Del. Code Ann., tit. 19, § 711(h) (1975); Mich Stat. Ann. § 17.458(3a) (e) (1975 rev. vol.).

16. *See, e.g.,* Conn. Gen. Stat. Ann. § 31-126 (Cum. Supp. 1976); Mich. Stat. Ann. § 17.458(3a) (a) (1975 rev. vol.). *Contra,* Del. Code Ann., tit. 19, § 711(d) (1975).

17. *See, e.g.,* Del. Code Ann., tit. 19, § 712(a) (1975) (state department of labor).

18. *See, e.g.,* Conn. Gen. Stat. Ann. §§ 31-122(h), 31-123, 31-127 (Cum. Supp. 1976) ("commission on human rights and opportunities"); Mich. Stat. Ann. §§ 3.548(5), 3.548(6) (1969 rev. vol.) ("civil rights commission").

statute (employer, employment agency, labor union, etc.) and setting forth the particulars of the alleged violation.[19] The complainant is required to file his complaint within a specified time after the alleged act of discrimination.[20]

Upon the filing of a complaint, the designated state agency is required to commence an investigation of the complainant's allegation.[21] If, after the completion of the investigation, the designated state agency finds that there is reasonable cause to believe that the alleged violation of the FEP statute has occurred, the agency is required to attempt to eliminate the unfair employment practice complained of by conference, conciliation and persuasion with the alleged violator.[22] This provision is consistent with the general philosophy of attempting to eliminate unfair employment practices by informal means rather than formal adjudication with an accompanying saving in time and limited resources. Accordingly, there is often a provision prohibiting disclosure of allegations of unfair employment practices until after informal procedures have been exhausted without success.[23]

If the informal procedures of conference, conciliation, and persuasion do not result in the elimination of the alleged discriminatory practice, a formal written complaint is issued by the designated state agency specifying the charges together with a notice setting a hearing on the complainant's allegations and requiring the alleged discriminator — the respondent — to appear

---

19. *See, e.g.,* Conn. Gen. Stat. Ann. § 31-127 (Cum. Supp. 1976); Del. Code Ann., tit. 19, § 712(b) (1975); Mich. Stat. Ann. § 17.458(7) (b) (1975 rev. vol.).

20. *See, e.g.,* Conn. Gen. Stat. Ann. § 31-127 (Cum. Supp. 1976) ("within one hundred and eighty days after the alleged act of discrimination"); Del. Code Ann., tit. 19, § 712(d) (1975) ("within 90 days after the alleged unlawful employment practice or 120 days after discovery thereof, whichever is the later"); Mich. Stat. Ann. § 17.458(7) (b) (1975 rev. vol.) ("within 90 days after the alleged act of discrimination").

21. *See, e.g.,* Conn. Gen. Stat. Ann. § 31-127 (Cum. Supp. 1976); Del. Code Ann., tit. 19, § 712(b) (1975); Mich. Stat. Ann. § 17.458(7) (c) (1975 rev. vol.).

22. *See, e.g.,* Conn. Gen. Stat. Ann. § 31-127 (Cum. Supp. 1976); Del. Code Ann., tit. 19, § 712(c) (1975); Mich. Stat. Ann. § 17.458(7) (a), (c) (1975 rev. vol.).

23. *See, e.g.,* Conn. Gen. Stat. Ann. § 31-127 (Cum. Supp. 1976); Del. Code Ann., tit. 19, § 712(b), (c) (1975); Mich. Stat. Ann. § 17.458(7) (c) (1975 rev. vol.).

at the hearing and answer the complaint. All parties usually have a right to be represented by counsel at the hearing.[24]

At the hearing, the parties, the complainant — often represented by counsel for the designated state agency — and the respondent, present testimony under oath and other evidence with a verbatim transcript kept of the proceedings before one or more hearing officers.[25]

After the conclusion of the hearing, the hearing officer or officers are required to render a written opinion either deciding that the complainant and his counsel have proven the charges of an unfair employment practice in accordance with the designated standard of proof or ordering the complaint dismissed.[26]

If the respondent is found to have engaged in an unfair employment practice in violation of the FEP statute, the designated state agency is empowered to issue an order requiring it to cease and desist from the unlawful employment practice and, under most statutes, to take such affirmative or other action as is consistent with the purposes of the FEP statute including, but not limited to, hiring, reinstatement, or upgrading of employees with or without back pay, or admission or restoration to union membership, as may be appropriate.[27]

Persons aiding or abetting or attempting to aid and abet violations of an FEP statute are often covered by provisions which

---

24. *See, e.g.,* Conn. Gen. Stat. Ann. § 31-127 (Cum. Supp. 1976); Del. Code Ann., tit. 19, § 712(e) (1975); Mich. Stat. Ann. § 17.458(7)(d) (1975 rev. vol.).

25. *See, e.g.,* Conn. Gen. Stat. Ann. § 31-127 (Cum. Supp. 1976); Del. Code Ann., tit. 19, § 712(f) (1975); Mich. Stat. Ann. § 17.458(7) (g) (1975 rev. vol.).

26. *See, e.g.,* Conn. Gen. Stat. Ann. § 31-127 (Cum. Supp. 1976) ("upon all evidence"); Del. Code Ann., tit. 19, § 712(g) (1975); Mich. Stat. Ann. § 17.458(7)(h), (i) (1975 rev. vol.) ("the preponderance of the evidence on the record considered as a whole").

27. *Id. See, e.g.,* Williams v. Entenmann's Bakery, 2 CCH Employ. Prac. Guide ¶5114 (Conn. Comm'n on Human Rights and Opportunities, October 30, 1972) (ordering, *inter alia,* the hiring of persons found to have been denied employment on the basis of age without justification and payment of back pay equal to the difference between the amount they earned since the filing of their complaint and the amount they would have earned had they been hired by respondent).

make their acts violations as well, regardless of whether they would otherwise be subject to the statute.[28]

Either party to an unfair employment practice proceeding may appeal to the courts, subject to the completion of appellate procedures within the agency where available, from a decision of the designated state agency. Upon such an appeal, the standard of judicial review is severely limited as is generally the case with judicial review of administrative determinations.[29]

As part of the effort to inform the public as to the existence of rights and procedures for enforcing them under the FEP statutes, those statutes often require persons subject to their provisions to post a specified notice or poster describing individual's rights and the method of asserting them.[30]

---

28. *See, e.g.,* Conn. Gen. Stat. Ann. § 31-126(e) (Cum. Supp. 1976). *See also* Del. Code Ann., tit. 19, § 711(c) (3) (1975) (unfair employment practice for labor organization to cause or attempt to cause an employer to discriminate against an individual). In Pittsburgh Press Co. v. Pittsburgh Comm'n on Human Relations, 413 U.S. 376 (1973), the United States Supreme Court upheld an injunction prohibiting a newspaper from aiding in sex discrimination by publishing job advertisements under "male" and "female" columns as directed by advertisers.

29. *See, e.g.,* Conn. Gen. Stat. Ann. § 31-128 (1972) ("The findings of the hearing tribunal as to the facts, if supported by substantial and competent evidence, shall be conclusive."); Del. Code Ann., tit. 19, § 712(h) (1975) ("The Court may reverse or modify the order if substantial rights of the petitioner have been prejudiced because the findings of fact of the department are clearly erroneous in view of the reliable probative and substantial evidence on the whole record."); Mich. Const. art. VI, § 28 (providing for review by a court on an appeal from an order, decision, or ruling of an administrative officer or agency and requiring affirmance thereof if supported by "competent, material and substantial evidence on the whole record."). *See, e.g.,* Board of Educ. of West Haven v. Commission on Civil Rights of the State of Conn., 153 Conn. 652, 220 A.2d 278 (Sup. Ct. 1966); University of Conn. v. Conn. Comm'n on Human Rights and Opportunities, 4 CCH Employ. Prac. Dec. ¶7758, 4 Fair Employ. Prac. Cas. 1242 (Conn. Super. Ct., December 23, 1971) n.o.r., *affirming sub. nom* Baskin v. University of Conn., 2 CCH Employ. Prac. Guide ¶5054 (Conn. Comm'n on Human Rights and Opportunities, June 14, 1971); Remick v. Burge, 39 Mich. App. 444, 197 N.W.2d 868 (Ct. of App. 1972).

30. *See, e.g.,* Del. Stat. Ann., tit. 19, § 716 (1975); Mich. Stat. Ann. § 17.458(9) (1975 rev. vol.).

B. HUMAN RIGHTS LAWS

Some states have included what are, in effect, fair employment practices provisions in their human rights laws which deal with discrimination, for example, in housing and public accommodations as well as employment. Those statutes which include "age" among the covered types of discrimination in employment are virtually identical with the FEP statutes discussed above.[31]

C. AGE DISCRIMINATION IN EMPLOYMENT LAWS

While the FEP laws and the human rights statutes containing provisions dealing with age discrimination in employment are basically similar in their coverage, exemptions, and enforcement procedures, the statutes dealing solely with age discrimination in employment differ widely.

Some age discrimination in employment laws are similar to the FEP laws and the human rights statutes.[32] Others provide very limited or no enforcement procedures thereby severely restricting their effectiveness.[33]

---

31. The following human rights laws are examples of such statutes: N.J. Stat. Ann. §§ 10:5-12[a], [b], [c], [d], [e], 10:5-13, 10:5-14, 10:5-14.1, 10:5-15 to 10:5-19, 10:5-21, 10:5-24 (1976); New York, N.Y., Admin. Code §§ B1-7.0[1], [1-a], [3-a], [6]-[9], B1-8.0 to B1-12.0 (1970 & Cum. Supp. 1973); N. Y. Exec. Law §§ 290-292 [1]-[7], [17]-[19], 293-296[1], [1-a], 297, 297-a, 298-300 (McKinney 1972 & Cum. Supp. 1976-1977); Pa. Stat. Ann., tit. 43, §§ 951-953, 954(a)-(h), 955(a)-(g), (j), 956, 957, 959-962, 963 (1964 & Cum. Supp. 1976-1977); W. Va. Code Ann. §§ 5-11-1, 5-11-2, 5-11-3(a) to (i), (q), 5-11-4, 5-11-8, 5-11-9(a)-(e), 5-11-10 to 5-11-17 (1971 & Cum. Supp. 1976).

32. See, e.g., Ind. Code Ann. §§ 22-9-2-1 to 22-9-2-11 (Burns 1974) (limited to persons between 40 and 65 years of age).

33. The Illinois statute, while similar in substance to the FEP statutes and human rights laws with the exception of its application to all discrimination in employment because of age without limits, provides no enforcement procedures other than a criminal penalty providing that any person willfully failing, neglecting, or refusing to comply with its terms is guilty of a petty offense and subject to a fine of not less than $50 nor more than $100 for each offense. Ill. Ann. Stat., ch. 48, §§ 881-887 (Smith-Hurd Cum. Supp. 1976-1977).

The Massachusetts statute while declaring it to be against public policy to dismiss from employment or refuse to employ any person between 45 and 64 years of age because of the person's age, provides only that upon a determination by the designated state agency that an employer has not observed the provisions of the statute it may cause the employer's name and the fact of its non-observance to be

A third category of age discrimination in employment laws apply only to public employees.[34]

Perhaps the strangest legislative action concerning age discrimination in employment was a resolution of the Montana legislature declaring it to be against the public policy of the state and an unfair employment practice for an employer or his agent, except in the case of a bona fide occupational qualification or need, because an individual is between 40 and 65 years of age to arbitrarily refuse to hire or employ him, or to bar or discharge him from employment, or to discriminate against him in compensation or in the terms, conditions or privileges of employment, or to fail or refuse to classify him properly or refer him for employment, or to advertise employment opportunities in a manner so as to restrict employment so as to discriminate against such person.[35] The resolution was not enacted into law and, thus, was without force or effect.[36]

---

published in newspapers within the state and in such other manner as is deemed appropriate — Mass. Ann. Laws, ch. 149, §§ 24A-24J (Law. Co-op 1976). In Johnson v. United States Steel Corp., 348 Mass. 168, 202 N.E.2d 816 (Sup. Jud. Ct. 1964), the Court dismissed plaintiff's suit for damages which alleged discharge without cause based on age holding that nowhere in the statute is a civil remedy provided for a violation of its provisions and finding no basis for implying one.

Ohio law simply provides that no employer shall refuse an applicant an opportunity for an interview for employment or discharge an employee between 40 and 64 who is physically able to perform the duties and otherwise meeting the established requirements of the industry and laws pertaining to the relationship between employer and employee. Ohio Rev. Code Ann. § 4101.17 (Anderson 1973). There is no provision concerning enforcement or prosecution of violators.

Obviously statutes such as the foregoing provide no real protection for employees or persons seeking employment who are subjected to age discrimination. They provide neither for affirmative action to correct violations of the statutes nor for compensation of persons discriminated against through the payment of damages.

34. *See, e.g.,* Fla. Stat. Ann. § 112.043 (1975 rev.); Tex. Rev. Civ. Stat. Ann., art. 6252-14 (1970).

35. House Joint Resolution No. 12, 37th Mont. Legislative Assembly, 1961 Sess. Laws of State of Mont. 840 (1961).

36. *See* Cookson v. Lewistown School Dist. No. 1, 351 F. Supp. 983, 985 n. 1, 987 (D. Mont. 1972).

D. CONCLUSION

In the more than seventy years since enactment of the first state law dealing with age discrimination in employment, only three-quarters of the states have enacted statutes providing older workers with legal protection against age discrimination in employment. The statutes which have been enacted vary greatly in the protection given, the breadth of coverage, and the means, if any, provided individuals for obtaining redress for actions in violation of the statutes.

The patchwork quilt which has resulted from individual state and local action has proved, at best, only moderately successful in dealing with the problem of age discrimination in employment. It finally became apparent, in an era of increasing Federal concern with discrimination in all its forms and substantial growth in the average age of the population of the United States, that Federal action was necessary if truly effective means were to be provided for dealing with the increasingly serious problem of age discrimination in employment. The next section of this book describes the Federal response and reviews the reception afforded the Federal action in the courts.

Chapter 6

THE FEDERAL RESPONSE TO AGE DISCRIMINATION IN EMPLOYMENT PRIOR TO 1967

Before 1967, the United States government had done little to deal with age discrimination in employment. One exception was a statute prohibiting the use of appropriated funds to pay a Federal employee who established a maximum age requirement for entrance into the Federal civil service.[1]

In 1963, the United States Congress was considering legislation which became Title VII of the Civil Rights Act of 1964.[2] Title VII deals with discrimination in employment based on "race, color, religion, sex, or national origin."[3] It was suggested that age discrimination be included in the statute but the proposal was rejected in an effort to assure passage without delay of a statute covering the other types of discrimination, particularly racial discrimination.[4] There was, however, included as Section 715 of Title VII a provision requiring the Secretary of Labor to make a report by June 30, 1965 to the United States Congress on age discrimination in employment including therein "such recommendations for legislation to prevent arbitrary discrimination in employment because of age as he determines advisable."[5]

---

1. 5 U.S.C. § 3307 (Supp. V 1975). Excluded from the statute's coverage are air traffic controllers, the United States Park Police, law enforcement officers, and firefighters. This statute is based on a provision of the Independent Offices Appropriation Act, 1957, ch. 452, § 302, 70 Stat. 355.

2. 42 U.S.C. §§ 2000e to 2000e-15 (1970 & Supp. V 1975), *as amended,* 42 U.S.C. §§ 2000e-16, 2000e-17 (Supp. V 1975).

3. 42 U.S.C. § 2000e-2 (1970 & Supp. V 1975). *See generally Developments in the Law-Employment Discrimination and Title VII of the Civil Rights Act of 1964,* 84 Harv. L. Rev. 1109 (1971).

4. Hearings on H.R. 405 before the General Subcommittee on Labor of the House Committee on Education and Labor, 88th Cong., 1st Sess. 22, 38-39, 69, 92, 109, 430, 478-79 (1963).

5. 42 U.S.C. § 2000e-14 (1970 & Supp. V 1975).

The Secretary of Labor's Report [6] stated that:

> The firmest conclusion from this year long study is that the most serious barriers to the employment of older workers are erected on just enough basis of fact to make it futile as public policy, and even contrary to the public interest, to conceive of all age restrictions as "arbitrary" and to concentrate on the prohibition of practices which include this element. [7]

The Report recommended four programs:

> First: Action to eliminate arbitrary age discrimination in employment.
> Second: Action to adjust institutional arrangements which work to the disadvantage of the older workers.
> Third: Action to increase the availability of work for older workers.
> Fourth: Action to enlarge educational concepts and institutions to meet the needs and opportunities of older age.[8]

With respect to the first proposal, the Report found that, despite studies and educational efforts by Federal and state governments and nonprofit, employer, and labor organizations and state laws dealing with age discrimination in employment,

> There is persistent and widespread use of age limits in hiring that in a great many cases can be attributed only to arbitrary discrimination against older workers on the basis of age and regardless of ability.[9]

The Report stated in this connection that nothing short of statutory means could meet the problem and that state statutes, though increasing in number, were in some cases not implemented at all and, with few exceptions, state resources had been inadequate to insure effective compliance.[10] Accordingly, the Report concluded that

---

6. Report of the Secretary of Labor to the Congress Under Section 715 of the Civil Rights Act of 1964, *The Older American Worker — Age Discrimination in Employment* (June 1965), conclusions and recommendations reprinted in CCH [July, 1965-July, 1968 Transfer Binder] Labor L. Rep. Employ. Prac. ¶8001.

7. *Id.* at 21.
8. *Id.*
9. *Id.*
10. *Id.* at 21-22.

> The elimination of arbitrary age limits on employment will proceed much more rapidly if the Federal Government declares clearly and unequivocally, and implements so far as is practicable, a national policy with respect to hiring on the basis of ability rather than age.[11]

A first, limited, formal Federal step toward dealing with age discrimination in employment had previously been taken by President Lyndon B. Johnson in 1964. In an Executive Order, President Johnson declared it the policy of the Executive branch of the Federal government that (1) contractors and subcontractors engaged in the performance of Federal contracts not discriminate against persons because of their age in connection with the employment, advancement, or discharge of employees, or in connection with the terms, conditions, or privileges of their employment except upon the basis of a bona fide occupational qualification, retirement plan, or statutory requirement and (2) that contractors and subcontractors, or persons acting on their behalf, not specify in solicitations or advertisements for employees to work on Federal government contracts a maximum age limit for such employment unless it is based on a bona fide occupational requirement, retirement plan or statutory requirement.[12]

Executive Order No. 11141 did not contain any means for enforcing its provisions. The regulations implementing the policy set forth in that Executive Order provide only for bringing that policy to the attention of business concerns and requesting compliance therewith.[13]

---

11. *Id.* at 22.
12. Exec. Order No. 11141, 3 C.F.R. at 112 (1974).
13. 41 C.F.R. §§ 1-12.1000 to 1-12.1003 (1975).

71

Chapter 7

THE FEDERAL AGE DISCRIMINATION
IN EMPLOYMENT ACT

With the experience gained under the various state statutes dealing with age discrimination in employment and Executive Order No. 11141 and the information contained in the Secretary of Labor's 1965 Report, the Federal government finally acted to deal with the problem on a broad front.

On January 23, 1967, President Lyndon B. Johnson, in a Special Message to the Congress Proposing Programs for Older Americans, recommended that Congress enact a law prohibiting arbitrary and unjust discrimination in employment because of a person's age, covering workers aged 45 to 65. In support of his recommendation, President Johnson stated, in part, that

> Hundreds of thousands not yet old, not yet voluntarily retired, find themselves jobless because of arbitrary age discrimination. * * *.
>
> Today, more than three-quarters of a billion dollars in unemployment insurance is paid each year to workers who are 45 or over. * * *. In 1965, the Secretary of Labor reported to the Congress and the President that approximately half of all private job openings were barred to applicants over 55; a quarter were closed to applicants over 45.
>
> In economic terms, this is a serious — and senseless — loss to a nation on the move. But the greater loss is the cruel sacrifice in happiness and well-being which joblessness imposes on these citizens and their families.[1]

On December 16, 1967, President Johnson signed into law the first Federal statute dealing on a broad scale with age discrimination in employment.[2] The ADEA became effective on

---

1. Public Papers of the Presidents of the United States — Lyndon B. Johnson — 1967 — Book I 32, 37 (G. P. O. 1968).

2. *See* Statement by the President After Signing the Age Discrimination in Employment Act of 1967, Public Papers of the Presidents of the United States — Lyndon B. Johnson — 1967 — Book II 1154-55 (G. P. O. 1968).

June 12, 1968. Discrimination in employment based on age occurring before that date is not covered by the ADEA.[2a]

The Federal Age Discrimination in Employment Act of 1967 [3] (ADEA) was enacted in the light of considerable experience with state laws dealing with age discrimination in employment. Not surprisingly, the United States Congress borrowed heavily from the state statutes in drafting the ADEA.[4]

The following discussion of the ADEA incorporates a description of the provisions of the statute, the decisions of courts interpreting and applying the ADEA, the regulations of the Wage and Hour Division of the United States Department of Labor,[5] and opinions

---

2a. See Hayes v. Southern Pac. Co., 12 CCH Employ. Prac. Dec. ¶11, 196, at 5504, 13 Fair Employ. Prac. Cas. 753, 756 (C.D. Cal., August 18, 1976) n.o.r.; Monroe v. Penn-Dixie Cement Corp., 335 F. Supp. 231 (N.D. Ga. 1971); Opinion Letter of Deputy Wage-Hour Administrator, 8 Lab. Rel. Rep. 401:5201 (June 7, 1968); Opinion Letter of Wage-Hour Administrator, 8 Lab. Rel. Rep. 401:5208 (August 2, 1968); Opinion Letter of Wage-Hour Administrator, 8 Lab. Rel. Rep. 401:5211 (August 12, 1968). But see Donnelly v. Exxon Research & Eng'r Co., 11 CCH Employ. Prac. Dec. ¶10,860, 12 Fair Employ. Prac. Cas. 417 (D.N.J., October 30, 1974) n.o.r., aff'd without opinion, 521 F.2d 1398 (3rd Cir. 1975), where the District Court held that the ADEA applied to the involuntary retirement of an employee who was first notified of the retirement before the effective date of the statute but was not actually retired until after the effective date of the ADEA.

3. 29 U.S.C. §§ 621-634 (1970), as amended, 29 U.S.C. §§ 630(a), (b), (c), (f), 633a, 634 (Supp. V 1975).The Federal Age Discrimination in Employment Act of 1967 is reprinted in full in Appendix A. to this book.

4. H.R. Rep. No. 805, 90th Cong., 1st Sess., reprinted in [1967] U. S. Code Cong. and Admin. News 2213, 2215 (1968) ("H.R. Rep. No. 805"). This report of the Education and Labor Committee of the House of Representatives described and recommended passage of the bill which became the ADEA to the full House of Representatives. Such "legislative history" is looked to by the courts and those responsible for administering the ADEA for assistance in interpreting it.

5. 29 C.F.R. Parts 850, 860 (1974). Part 850 sets forth, inter alia, regulations implementing the provision of the ADEA which gives the Secretary of Labor the power to require the keeping of records necessary or appropriate for the administration of the statute, 29 U.S.C. § 626(a) (1970), and to "establish such reasonable exemptions to and from any or all provisions of the ADEA as he may find necessary and proper in the public interest," 29 U.S.C. § 628 (1970). Part 860 implements the statutory authorization to the Secretary of Labor to "issue such rules and regulations as he may consider necessary or appropriate for carrying out" the ADEA, 29 U.S.C. § 628 (1970). The regulations of the Secretary of Labor issued

issued by the Wage-Hour Administrator of the Wage and Hour Division of the United States Department of Labor in response to specific inquiries from persons subject to or entitled to protection under the ADEA.[6]

---

pursuant to the foregoing statutory authority are reprinted in full in Appendix B. to this book.

The foregoing regulations interpreting the ADEA adopted by the agency responsible for enforcing the statute hold a special significance before the courts. In Griggs v. Duke Power Co., 401 U.S. 424, 433-34 (1971), the United States Supreme Court, in considering regulations of the Equal Employment Opportunity Commission under Title VII of the Civil Rights Act of 1964, held that

> The administrative interpretation of the Act by the enforcing agency is entitled to great deference.

To the same effect see Hodgson v. Tamiami Trail Tours, Inc., 531 F. 2d 224, 230 (5th Cir. 1976); Brennan v. Root, 8 CCH Employ. Prac. Dec. ¶9531, at 5335 (E.D.N.C., May 21, 1974) n.o.r.; Hodgson v. American Hardware Mut. Ins. Co., 329 F. Supp. 225, 228-29 (D. Minn. 1971); Brennan v. Hughes Personnel, Inc., 8 CCH Employ. Prac. Dec. ¶9571, at 5475 (W.D. Ky., May 22, 1974) n.o.r., amended, 8 CCH Employ. Prac. Dec. ¶9679 (W.D. Ky., June 25, 1974) n.o.r. In the latter case, the Court stated that while a regulation adopted by the Secretary of Labor under the ADEA

> is not controlling, it does constitute the administrative agency's interpretation of the statute to which the Court may properly resort for guidance.

The courts do not, however, always follow the administrative agency's interpretations. Thus, for example, the same interpretation of the ADEA which was approved by the Court in Brennan v. Hughes Personnel, Inc., supra, and in Hodgson v. Career Counsellors Int'l, Inc., 5 CCH Employ. Prac. Dec. ¶7983, at 6627, 5 Fair Employ. Prac. Cas. 129, 130 (N.D. Ill., September 28, 1972) n.o.r., was rejected by the Court in Brennan v. Paragon Employment Agency, Inc., 356 F. Supp. 286 (S.D. N.Y. 1973), aff'd without opinion, 489 F.2d 752 (2d Cir. 1974).

6. See Opinion Letter of Deputy Wage-Hour Administrator, 8 Lab. Rel. Rep. 401:5201 (June 4, 1968). Opinion letters interpreting a statute, like regulations of the administrative agency responsible for enforcing the statute, are "entitled to be given great weight by the court in deciding the proper interpretation of the" ADEA, Hart v. United Steelworkers of America, 350 F. Supp. 294, 296 (W.D. Pa. 1972), appeal dismissed and remanded for vacation of judgment as moot, 482 F.2d 282 (3rd Cir. 1973) (per curiam).

A. PURPOSES

In Section 2 of the ADEA, the United States Congress stated that the purpose of the ADEA was

> to promote employment of older persons based on their ability rather than age; to prohibit arbitrary age discrimination in employment; to help employers and workers find ways of meeting problems arising from the impact of age on employment.[7]

Congress acted in light of findings that, in the face of rising productivity and affluence, older workers found themselves disadvantaged in their efforts to retain employment and especially to regain employment when displaced from jobs; that the setting of arbitrary age limits, regardless of potential for job performance, had become a common practice and that certain otherwise desirable practices may work to the disadvantage of older persons; that the incidence of unemployment, especially long-term unemployment with resultant deterioration of skill, morale, and employer acceptability, was, relative to the younger ages, high among older workers and that their numbers were great and growing and their employment problems grave; and that the existence in industries affecting commerce of arbitrary age discrimination in employment burdened commerce and the free flow of goods.[8]

The purposes of the ADEA were succinctly stated by the Court in *Brennan v. Paragon Employment Agency, Inc.,*[9]

> The Act was intended to alleviate the serious economic and psychological suffering of people between the ages of 40 and 65 caused by widespread job discrimination against them. * * *. The Congress hoped that it would substitute individual ability for generalization founded on ignorance and irrational prejudice as the relevant standard for hiring, promoting and retaining older people.

---

7. 29 U.S.C. § 621(b) (1970). The House of Representatives' Report stated that

the bill outlines a national policy against discrimination in employment on account of age, provides a vehicle for enforcement of the policy, and establishes broad guidelines for its implementation. H.R. Rep. No. 805, 7, [1967] U.S. Code Cong. and Admin. News at 2220.

8. 29 U.S.C. § 621(a) (1970).

9. 356 F. Supp. 286, 288 (S.D.N.Y. 1973), *aff'd without opinion*, 489 F.2d 752 (2d Cir. 1974).

The multiple effects of age discrimination in employment were noted by the Court in *Rogers v. Exxon Research and Engineering Company* [10] in the following language

> It is difficult enough for anyone to encounter and to surmount the psychological and physiological problems of the aging process. Simultaneously to find oneself arbitrarily discharged because the clock has struck a certain hour adds substantially, ..., to these already formidable stresses. The cumulative effect of an arbitrary and illegal termination of a useful and productive older employee is a cruel blow to the dignity and self-respect of one who has devoted his life to productive work, and can take a dramatic toll.

B. EDUCATION AND RESEARCH

The ADEA takes an interestingly multi-faced approach to age discrimination in employment. Not only does it declare certain types of age discrimination in employment impermissible and provide a means for dealing with prohibited acts but also the ADEA encourages efforts to eliminate the problem before it arises by means of education and publicity to dispel the unfounded myths which lead to age discrimination. As a United States Senate Committee working paper notes,

> ADEA was enacted not only to enforce the law, but to provide the facts that would help change attitudes. [11]

Section 3 of the ADEA directs the United States Secretary of Labor to undertake studies and provide information to labor unions, management, and the general public concerning the needs and abilities of older workers and their potentials for continued employment and contribution to the economy. To achieve the purposes of the ADEA, the Secretary of Labor is directed in the same section of the statute to carry on a continuing program of education and information including the undertaking and promotion of research, the publication and dissemination of information, the fostering of expansion of opportunities and

---

10. 404 F. Supp. 324, 329 (D.N.J. 1975).

11. U. S. Senate, Special Committee on Aging, *Improving the Age Discrimination Law — A Working Paper*, 93d Cong. 1st Sess., at (iii) (September 1973) (hereinafter *Improving the Age Discrimination Law).*

potentials of older persons through the public employment service system and cooperation with public and private agencies, and the sponsoring and assisting of state and community informational and educational programs.[12]

The House of Representatives' Report states that

> These functions can do much to correct age discriminatory employment practices and are therefore vital to the overall effectiveness of the bill. They are means of affecting salutory changes in attitude which will induce compliance with the simple justice the proposal espouses, thereby making enforcement measures unnecessary. This viewpoint was corroborated by many of the witnesses, including representatives of the State agencies and labor and management.[13]

---

12. 29 U.S.C. § 622(a) (1970).

Summaries of the educational and information activities of the Secretary of Labor are contained in the annual reports of the Secretary of Labor to the United States Congress required by the ADEA, 29 U.S.C. § 632 (1970). *See* Employment Standards Administration, U.S. Dep't of Labor, *A Report Covering Activities Under the Act During 1976,* at 17 (1977); Employment Standards Administration, U.S. Dep't of Labor, *A Report Covering Activities Under the Act During 1975,* at 16 (1976); Employment Standards Administration, U.S. Dep't of Labor, *A Report Covering Activities Under the Act During 1974,* at 20 (1975); Employment Standards Administration, U.S. Dep't of Labor, *A Report Covering Activities Under the Act During 1973* at 6 (1974); Employment Standards Administration, U.S. Dep't of Labor, *A Report Covering Activities Under the Act During 1972* at 5 (1973); Employment Standards Administration, U.S. Dep't of Labor, *A Report Covering Activities Under the Act During 1971* at 5-6 (1972); Workplace Standards Administration, U.S. Dep't of Labor, *A Report Covering Activities in Connection with the Act During 1970* at 6-7 (1971); Wage and Labor Standards Administration, U.S. Dep't of Labor, *A Report Covering Activities in Connection with the Act During 1969,* pt. IV at 3 (1970).

An example of the educational and cooperative efforts engaged in by the Department of Labor under the ADEA is provided by a speech given by Wage-Hour Administrator Robert D. Moran before the National Council of Senior Citizens on June 5, 1969, which is excerpted in CCH [Transfer Binder — New Developments, June, 1969 — December, 1969] Lab. L. Rep. ¶8031.

13. H.R. Rep. No. 805, 3, [1967] U.S. Code Cong. and Admin. News at 2216.

C. DEFINITIONS

Person, as used in the ADEA, includes, *inter alia*, individuals, partnerships, and corporations.[14]

Employer means a person engaged in an industry affecting commerce[15] who has twenty or more employees for each working day in each of twenty or more calendar weeks in the current or preceding calendar year, any agent of such a person, a state or political subdivision of a state, and any interstate agency but not the United States or a corporation wholly-owned by the United States Government.[16] In *Woodford v. Kinney Shoe Corporation*,[17]

14. 29 U.S.C. § 630(a) (Supp. V 1975).

15. The reference to "commerce" provides a predicate for Federal action. The terms "commerce" and "industry affecting commerce" are defined to meet constitutional restrictions by limiting the term "commerce" to trade, traffic, commerce, transportation, transmission, or communication: among the states of the United States, between a state and a place outside it, within the District of Columbia or a possession of the United States, or between points in one state but through a point outside it, 29 U.S.C. § 630(g), (h) (1970). The "commerce clause" of the United States Constitution gives the United States Congress the power "[t]o regulate Commerce . . . among the several states. . . ." U.S. Const., art. I, § 8. The phrase "industry affecting commerce" reaches the fullest breadth of that clause — Opinion Letter of Deputy Wage-Hour Administrator, 8 Lab. Rel. Rep. 401:5221 (December 9, 1968).

An employer is in an industry affecting commerce where it uses or sells goods which are produced outside the state in which it is located or serves persons who come from outside the state — Opinion Letter of Wage-Hour Administrator, 8 Lab. Rel. Rep. 401:5209 (August 7, 1968). *See also* Opinion Letter of Wage-Hour Administrator, 8 Lab. Rel. Rep. 401:5210 (August 1, 1968).

Protection under the ADEA extends to all employees of a covered employer and not merely to those engaged in interstate activities. Opinion Letter of Deputy Wage-Hour Administrator, 8 Lab. Rel. Rep. 401:5221 (December 9, 1968).

16. 29 U.S.C. § 630(b) (Supp. V 1975); 29 C.F.R. § 860.31 (1974). A city is a political subdivision of a state, Opinion Letter of Acting Wage-Hour Administrator (WH-341), 2 CCH Employ. Prac. Guide ¶5355 (June 23, 1975); as is a town, Opinion Letter of Acting Wage-Hour Administrator (WH-360), 2 CCH Employ. Prac. Guide ¶5366 (August 19, 1975); a private, non-profit corporation meeting the other requirements of the ADEA would be an "employer" covered by the statute, Opinion Letter of Wage-Hour Administrator, 8 Lab. Rel. Rep. 401:5215 (September 9, 1968); a covered employer is governed by the ADEA's terms as to any of his acts which occur in the United States even though their principal effect may be outside the

17. 369 F. Supp. 911, 916 (N.D. Ga. 1973).

it was held that, while the mere fact that one corporation was the wholly-owned subsidiary of another would not make the former the latter's agent or instrumentality,

---

United States as, for example, where employees are hired in the United States for overseas work, Opinion Letter of Wage-Hour Administrator, 8 Lab. Rel. Rep. 401:5217 (September 24, 1968); an employee of the American subsidiary of a foreign company with total foreign and domestic employment of more than the statutory number of employees is entitled to the protection of the ADEA where its terms and provisions otherwise apply, Opinion Letter of Wage-Hour Administrator (WH-105), 8 Lab. Rel. Rep. 401:5233 (December 29, 1970).

The reduction from the original requirement of at least 25 employees and the inclusion of states and their political subdivisions, which became effective May 1, 1974, was effected by the Fair Labor Standards Amendments of 1974, Pub. Law No. 93-259, § 28(a)(1), (2), 88 Stat. 74. The implementation of portions of the Fair Labor Standards Amendments of 1974, including those making the ADEA applicable to states and political subdivisions thereof, was stayed pending determination of an action challenging their constitutionality. National League of Cities v. Brennan, 406 F. Supp. 826 (D.D.C. 1974) (three-judge court), *stay granted,* 419 U.S. 1321 (1974) (before Burger, C.J.), *stay continued,* 419 U.S. 1100 (1975). On June 24, 1976, in National League of Cities v. Usery, 426 U.S. 833 (1975), the Supreme Court held that the Fair Labor Standards Amendments of 1974 interfered with traditional aspects of state sovereignty and exceeded the powers granted to Congress under the Commerce Clause of the United States Constitution. The Supreme Court reversed the District Court's decision denying the plaintiff cities and states declaratory and injunctive relief against the application of the amendments to them and remanded the case for further proceedings.

The Supreme Court's opinion in the *National League of Cities* case discusses only those portions of the Fair Labor Standards Amendments of 1974 which bring states and political subdivisions thereof within the coverage of the Fair Labor Standards Act of 1938. No reference is made to the amendments to the ADEA. However, since the constitutional authority for enactment of the Fair Labor Standards Act of 1938 and the ADEA is the Commerce Clause of the United States Constitution, *see* 29 U.S.C. § 621(a)(4) (1970), there is a serious question as to whether the 1974 amendments to the ADEA survived the Supreme Court's decision. A final resolution of that question will have to await the District Court's decision on remand.

One District Court has held that the *National League of Cities* decision did not invalidate the extension of the coverage of the ADEA to states, political subdivisions of states, and agencies and instrumentalities of states. In a well reasoned opinion, the Court in Usery v. Board of Educ. of Salt Lake City, 12 CCH Employ. Prac. Dec. ¶11,184, 13 Fair Employ. Prac. Cas. 717 (D. Utah, September 1, 1976) n.o.r., held that, unlike the minimum wage and maximum hours laws, the degree of Federal intrusion in integral state functions involved in the extension of the applicability of the ADEA to the states was minimal since it imposed only a limited negative obligation on the states not to arbitrarily use age as an employment

A parent corporation can be held liable under the Age Discrimination Act for the discriminatory employment practices of its subsidiary corporation if the parent corporation so controls the subsidiary that the subsidiary is merely the agent or instrumentality of the parent.... Put differently, an employee of the parent company's agent-subsidiary is an employee of the parent company for the purposes of the Age Discrimination Act.[18]

Employment agency is defined as any person regularly undertaking with or without compensation to procure employees for an employer, including an agent of such a person but excluding

---

criterion. The District Court, further, held that Congress had the power to regulate discriminatory state employment practices under the Commerce Clause

> where the national interest in employment significantly outweighs the state's interest in discriminatory employment policies and practices. [12 CCH Employ. Prac. Dec. ¶11,184, at 5445, 13 Fair Employ. Prac. Cas. at 719.]

The Court also found that the Congress had the power to extend the coverage of the ADEA to the states under Section 5 of the Fourteenth Amendment to the United States Constitution as a prohibition on state action denying equal protection of the laws. This alternative ground for decision was based on the District Court's finding that there was no clear expression by Congress in the ADEA as to whether the Commerce Clause or the Fourteenth Amendment provided the constitutional foundation for the statute. However, as is noted above, Section 2(a)(4) of the ADEA seems to suggest that Congress relied on its power under the Commerce Clause in enacting the ADEA. The District Court's discussion of the Fourteenth Amendment as a ground for its decision is understandable in light of the Supreme Court's opinion in *National League of Cities v. Usery, supra,* which found a lack of Congressional power to act under the Commerce Clause but specifically reserved decision on whether power to affect the integral operations of state governments existed under Section 5 of the Fourteenth Amendment, 426 U.S. at 852 n. 17.

18. *See also* Brennan v. Ace Hardware Corp., 362 F. Supp. 1156, 1157-58 (D. Neb. 1973) (an office of a corporation is not a separate employer under the ADEA, the employer is the corporation as one entity), *aff'd,* 495 F.2d 368 (8th Cir. 1974); Hodgson v. Poole Truck Line, Inc., 4 CCH Employ. Prac. Dec. ¶7668, 4 Fair Employ. Prac. Cas. 265 (S.D. Ala., January 13, 1972) (enjoining defendants from future violations of the ADEA based on a violation at one of its various places of business) n.o.r.; Opinion Letter of Wage-Hour Administrator, 8 Lab. Rel. Rep. 401:5204 (July 12, 1968) (the ADEA applies to all operations, departments, stations, and other organizational units of an employer who is otherwise subject to the statute).

an agency of the United States.[19] An employment agency which regularly procures employees for at least one employer covered by the ADEA falls within the coverage of the ADEA with respect to all of its activities for both covered and non-covered employers.[20] It should be noted that, while the term "employer" is limited to persons "affecting commerce" and having a minimum number of employees, there is no such limitation on employment agencies which are covered if they regularly provide services for any covered employer. As one court has noted,

> While the legislative history is silent as to the reasons for the distinction, it may fairly be explained as a recognition by the Congress of the desperate responsibilities and needs of the two categories.[21]

Employee, as used in the ADEA, includes an individual employed by an included employer but excludes elected officials of states and their political subdivisions, any persons chosen by such officials to be on their personal staff, any appointees on the policy-making level or immediate advisors with respect to the exercise of the constitutional or legal powers of their offices other than employees subject to the civil service laws of a state government, governmental agency, or political subdivision.[22] Despite the

---

19. 29 U.S.C. § 630(c) (Supp. V 1975); 29 C.F.R. § 860.35(a) (1974). The Fair Labor Standards Amendments of 1974, Pub. Law No. 93-259, § 28(a)(3), 88 Stat. 74, eliminated, *inter alia,* an exclusion of agencies of states or their political subdivisions.

A medical school which assists its graduates to secure employment is not an employment agency under the ADEA. The school's principal function is the education and training of its students. Cannon v. University of Chicago, 406 F. Supp. 1257 (N.D. Ill. 1976) (holding that defendants alleged refusal to admit plaintiff to medical school on the basis of her age did not state a claim upon which relief could be granted under the ADEA where plaintiff alleged that the defendant's discriminatory refusal to admit her based, *inter alia,* upon her age would lead directly to a failure to refer her for employment).

20. 29 C.F.R. § 860.35(b) (1974); Brennan v. Root, 8 CCH Employ. Prac. Dec. ¶9531, at 5335 (E.D.N.C., May 21, 1974) n.o.r.

21. Brennan v. Paragon Employment Agency, Inc., 356 F. Supp. 286, 288 (S.D.N.Y. 1973), *aff'd without opinion,* 489 F.2d 752 (2d Cir. 1974).

22. 29 U.S.C. § 630(f) (Supp. V 1975). The special exclusions and inclusions were added by the Fair Labor Standards Amendments of 1974, Pub. Law No. 93-259, § 28(a)(4), 88 Stat. 74, to deal with the simultaneous addition of states and their political subdivisions as covered employers.

specific terms of the definition, the Secretary of Labor's regulations recognize that to be consistent with the other provisions of the ADEA the term "employee" must be read to "apply to any person who has a right to bring an action under the Act, including an applicant for employment." [23]

Labor organization means a labor organization engaged in an industry affecting commerce [24] and any agent of such an organization including any organization of any kind, any agency, or employee representation committee, group, association, or plan so engaged in which employees participate and which exists for the purpose, in whole or part, of dealing with employers concerning grievances, labor disputes, wages, rates of pay, hours, or other terms or conditions of employment, and any conference, general committee, joint or system board, or joint council so engaged which is subordinate to a national or international labor organization. [25]

D. AGE LIMITS

The protection from age discrimination in employment provided by the ADEA is limited by Section 12 of the statute to individuals who are at least 40 years of age but less than 65 years of age. [26]

---

23. 29 C.F.R. § 860.30 (1974); Hart v. United Steelworkers of America, 350 F. Supp. 294, 297 (W.D. Pa. 1972), *appeal dismissed and remanded for vacation of judgment as moot,* 482 F.2d 282 (3rd Cir. 1973) (*per curiam*). The ADEA applies to all employees supervisory as well as non-supervisory and would, thus, apply as well to applicants for supervisory positions, Opinion Letter of Wage-Hour Administrator (WH-136), 2 CCH Employ. Prac. Guide ¶5027, 8 Lab. Rel. Rep. 401:5234 (May 28, 1971). The ADEA is applicable to officers as well as employees. Opinion Letter of Wage-Hour Administrator, 8 Lab. Rel. Rep. 401:5211 (August 12, 1968).

24. "Labor organization engaged in an industry affecting commerce" is defined in Section 11(e) of the ADEA, 29 U.S.C. § 630(e) (1970).

25. 29 U.S.C. § 630(d) (1970). A local union composed entirely of public employees of the United States government or a corporation wholly-owned by the United States government would not be subject to the ADEA because the members' employer would not be covered by the statute since "labor organization" is defined with reference to "employees" which, in turn, refers to "employers" from which the United States and its wholly-owned corporations are excluded. Opinion Letter of Assistant Secretary of Labor, 8 Lab. Rel. Rep. 401:5224 (December 26, 1968).

26. 29 U.S.C. § 631 (Supp. V 1975).

The choice of an upper limit of 65 was presumably based primarily on the fact that social security retirement benefits become available to eligible male workers at that age.[27] The choice of that age for social security purposes has been said to have resulted from political decisions and default rather than a determination based on scientific data.[28]

The lower limit did receive Congressional consideration. The House of Representatives' Report noted that

> The committee altered the lower age limit from 45 in the original bill to 40, in that testimony indicated this to be the age at which age discrimination in employment became evident. It is also the lower age limit found in most State statutes bearing on this subject. The committee declined to further lower the age limitation. . . . [I]t was felt a further lowering of the age limit proscribed by the bill would lessen the primary objective; that is, the promotion of employment opportunities for older workers.[29]

The statutory protection applies only to persons within the specified age limits. Following attainment of age 65, an individual is no longer covered by the ADEA or entitled to the protection it

---

27. *See* Agatstein, *The Age Discrimination in Employment Act of 1967: A Critique,* 19 N.Y.L. Forum 309, 321-22 (1973); Comment, *Age Discrimination and the Over-Sixty-Five Worker,* 3 Cum.-Sam. L. Rev. 333, 334-35 (1972). The legislative history of the ADEA contains no discussion of the upper age limit. However, the United States Department of Labor stated, in response to a question asked by Senator Jacob Javits while the ADEA was pending before the Congress, that the upper age limit of 65 was chosen because

> While substantial numbers of employees perform productive work for many years past age 65, for the majority of workers this is the usual retirement age and an age at which pensions become payable under the Old Age Survivors and Disability Insurance Program of the Social Security Act, as well as many private pension plans. [BNA Daily Labor Report No. 103 — 5/26/67, at F-2.]

28. Cain, *The Growing Importance of Legal Age in Determining the Status of the Elderly,* The Gerontologist 167, 169-70 (April 1974).

29. H.R. Rep. No. 805, 6, [1967] U.S. Code Cong. and Admin. News at 2219.

affords to those below 65.[30] Similarly, those below age 40 have no rights under the ADEA.[31]

The ADEA covers not only discrimination based on age against those in the specified age bracket and in favor of younger persons but also discrimination based on age between persons within the bracket.[32]

It has been held that a person complaining of a violation of the statute has the burden of proving that he was within the protected age bracket at the time of the discriminatory act.[33]

E. PROHIBITED EMPLOYER PRACTICES

Section 4(a) of the ADEA declares it to be unlawful for a covered employer to fail or refuse to hire or to discharge any individual within the protected age bracket or to otherwise discriminate

---

30. Hart v. United Steelworkers of America, 482 F.2d 282, 283 (3rd Cir. 1973) *(per curiam), dismissing appeal and remanding for vacation of judgment as moot,* 350 F. Supp. 294, 297 (W.D. Pa. 1972); Billingsley v. Service Tech. Corp., 6 CCH Employ. Prac. Dec. ¶8874, at 5720, 6 Fair Employ. Prac. Cas. 404, 410 (S.D. Tex., April 5 and 24, 1973) n.o.r. While the ADEA does not authorize discrimination in favor of the 40 to 65 age group, its terms and provisions do not apply to individuals less than 40 or over 65 years of age. Opinion Letter of Wage-Hour Administrator, 8 Lab. Rel. Rep. 401:5209 (August 7, 1968).

31. Klapp v. Civil Service Comm., 11 CCH Employ. Prac. Dec. ¶10,878 (C.D. Cal., October 29, 1975) n.o.r.; Bishop v. Jelleff Associates, Inc., 398 F. Supp. 579, 586 n. 3 (D.D.C. 1974). Opinion Letter of Assistant Wage-Hour Administrator (WH-44), 8 Lab. Rel. Rep. 401:5231 (June 4, 1970); American Airlines v. State Comm'n for Human Rights, 29 App. Div. 2d 178, 286 N.Y.S. 2d 493 (1st Dept. 1968) (decided under New York Law).

32. 29 C.F.R. § 860.91 (1974). The ADEA does not, however, restrain age discrimination against those below 40 or over 65 or between such persons. *Id.* Opinion Letter of Wage-Hour Administrator, 8 Lab. Rel. Rep. 401:5209 (August 7, 1968).

33. Kincaid v. United Steelworkers of America, 5 CCH Employ. Prac. Dec. ¶8462, 5 Fair Employ. Prac. Cas. 235 (N.D. Ind., July 25, 1972) n.o.r. There is also an unfortunate and erroneous suggestion in that decision that a defendant who engages in conduct prohibited under the ADEA with respect to an individual based on its determination that the individual is not within the protected age bracket does not violate the statute where its determination is not arbitrary but is, instead, supported by substantial evidence before it and made fairly and in good faith. There is no such defense to a violation of the statute and the Court's reliance on the fact that one purpose of the ADEA is "to prohibit arbitrary age discrimination in employment," 29 U.S.C. § 621(b) (1970), is clearly misplaced.

against any such individual with respect to his compensation, terms, conditions, or privileges of employment because of such individual's age; to limit, segregate, or classify employees in any way which would deprive any individual within the protected age bracket of employment opportunities, or otherwise adversely affect his status as an employee, because of such individual's age; or to reduce the wage rate of any employee in order to comply with the ADEA.[34]

The term "compensation" includes all types and methods of remuneration paid to or on behalf of or received by an employee for his employment.[35]

The phrase "terms, conditions, or privileges of employment" includes, but is not limited to, job security, advancement, status, and benefits.[36]

The prohibition against a reduction in wage rate of any employee by an employer seeking to bring itself into compliance with the ADEA would, for example, prevent an employer discriminating in wage rate against an employee in the protected age bracket from complying with the ADEA by reducing the wage rate of the favored employees who are not within the protected age bracket. The employer would, instead, have to raise the wage rate of the disfavored, protected employee.[37] Nor could the employer bring

---

34. 29 U.S.C. § 623(a) (1970).

35. 29 C.F.R. § 860.50(b) (1974).

36. 29 C.F.R. § 860.50(c) (1974). Examples include fringe benefits, promotion, demotion or other disciplinary action, hours of work (including overtime), leave policy (including sick leave, vacation, holidays), career development programs, seniority or merit systems (governing such conditions as transfer, assignment, job retention, layoff and recall). *Id.* Also included are regular rotation of assignments and equalization of overtime hours, Opinion Letter of Wage-Hour Administrator, 8 Lab. Rel. Rep. 401:5204 (July 12, 1968). Thus, the Acting Wage-Hour Administrator has advised that a proposed provision in a college faculty tenure, retention, and retirement policy which would deny sabbatical leaves to persons in cases where the leaves would become effective after the persons had reached 60 years of age would violate the ADEA since age was the disqualifying factor in denial of the benefit. Opinion Letter of Acting Wage-Hour Administrator (WH-248) (November 30, 1973) n.o.r.

37. 29 C.F.R. § 860.75 (1974).

itself into compliance with the ADEA by transferring either the favored employee or the disfavored protected employee to another position

> since the transfer itself would appear discriminatory under the particular facts and circumstances.[38]

The prohibition against age discrimination with respect to "terms" or "conditions" of employment is not, however, absolute. Thus, for example, the Wage-Hour Administrator has opined that, in the case of bus drivers required to take periodic physical examinations to assure that they meet certain minimum physical standards, requiring older drivers to take more frequent examinations is not unreasonable, provided that the employer's health standards are uniformly applied to persons of all ages.[39] He has also stated that it would not violate the ADEA for fringe benefits, such as vacations or sick leave, to be based on length of service where age plays no part in the establishment of such benefits.[40]

In an advisory opinion under the provisions of the Fair Labor Standards Amendments of 1974 making the ADEA applicable to the states and their political subdivisions,[41] the Acting Administrator of the Wage-Hour Division stated that a Florida statute, which provided that no person over 45 years of age could thereafter become a member of the classified service of a specified city unless normal recruitment measures fail to produce the required qualified applicants in which case the age limitation could be waived by the city's civil service board provided that the over-45

---

38. *Id.* Similarly, an employer cannot negotiate an agreement with an older worker within the protected age bracket to employ him with no participation in the employer's pension plan. Opinion Letter of Wage-Hour Administrator, 8 Lab. Rel. Rep. 401:5220 (November 13, 1968).

39. Opinion Letter of Wage-Hour Administrator (WH-137), 2 CCH Employ. Prac. Guide ¶5028 (June 24, 1971). The letter does note that

> where examinations required for older employees are at such frequent intervals as to be unreasonable considering the purpose of and need for physical examinations in relation to the particular occupation, we believe the practice would be discriminatory within the meaning of the Act.

40. Opinion Letter of Wage-Hour Administrator, 8 Lab. Rel. Rep. 401:5216 (September 10, 1968).
41. Pub. Law No. 93-259, § 28(a)(2), 88 Stat. 74.

applicants waived any and all rights to participate in any pension system maintained for employees of the city except social security benefits, would violate the ADEA by restricting entrance into the classified service of the city to individuals 45 years of age and under.[42] The Acting Administrator further stated that, since the prohibitions of Section 4(a) of the ADEA are directed toward employers, the city and not the state legislative body would be liable for any violations.

Under the same amendment, the Acting Wage-Hour Administrator advised that an agreement between a town and its police benevolent association which allowed the police commission to retire a police employee solely because of age, at age 52, would violate the ADEA since it is unlawful thereunder to discharge or force into retirement when eligible any individual within the protected age bracket because of their age.[43] The Acting Administrator, further, noted that the labor agreement would not provide a defense or bring the employer within any of the exceptions to the ADEA. Nor could employees over 52 years of age legally be required to periodically request continuation of their employment pursuant to a provision of the same labor agreement when employees generally are not required to do so.

Similarly, a state law requiring that, in the event that reductions in fire department personnel are made necessary for reasons of economy, the men oldest in age and service be placed on pension was held to be violative of the ADEA.[44]

F. PROHIBITED EMPLOYMENT AGENCY PRACTICES

Section 4(b) of the ADEA makes it unlawful for an employment agency to fail or refuse: to refer for employment, or otherwise to discriminate against, any individual within the protected age bracket because of such individual's age, or to classify or refer for

---

42. Opinion Letter of Acting Wage-Hour Administrator (WH-341), 2 CCH Employ. Prac. Guide ¶5355 (June 23, 1975).

43. Opinion Letter of Acting Wage-Hour Administrator (WH-360), 2 CCH Employ. Prac. Guide ¶5366 (August 19, 1975).

44. Opinion Letter of Acting Wage-Hour Administrator (WH-302), 2 CCH Employ. Prac. Guide ¶5334 (April 24, 1975).

employment any such individual on the basis of such individual's age.[45]

A covered employment agency is subject to the prohibitions of the ADEA with respect to all of its actions on behalf of all employers covered or not and would, therefore, violate the statute if it discriminated in connection with a referral to an employer not covered by the ADEA if it regularly procured employees for one covered employer.[46]

Since the determination of whether an employment agency is covered by the ADEA is based not on its size but on its clients and a covered employment agency is prohibited from "otherwise" discriminating against an individual in the protected age bracket, a covered employment agency would appear to be prohibited from discriminating in the hiring of its own employees even if it would not be covered under the ADEA's definition of "employer." [47]

An employment agency violates the ADEA even if it engages in an act prohibited by the ADEA at the request of an employer client. Such an employment agency would also be subject to the prohibitions of the ADEA as an agent of the employer since the statute defines employer to include "any agent" of a covered employer.[48]

---

45. 29 U.S.C. § 623(b) (1970). Thus, a non-profit temporary help service working exclusively with people over 55 was denied an administrative exemption from the prohibitions of the ADEA since it preferred one group of older workers over another group equally entitled to the protection of the statute, Opinion Letter of Wage-Hour Administrator (WH-113), 8 Lab. Rel. Rep. 401:5232 (January 19, 1971).

46. 29 C.F.R. § 860.36(b) (1974).

47. 29 C.F.R. § 860.36(c) (1974). This interpretation of the ADEA was specifically rejected without analysis of the ADEA's prohibitions covering employment agencies in the generally retrogressive decision in Brennan v. Paragon Employment Agency, Inc., 356 F. Supp. 286 (S.D.N.Y. 1973), aff'd without opinion, 489 F.2d 752 (2d Cir. 1974), discussed pp. 92-94, infra.

48. 29 U.S.C. § 630(b) (Supp. V 1975). See Brennan v. Hughes Personnel, Inc., 8 CCH Employ. Prac. Dec. ¶9571 (W.D. Ky., May 22, 1974) n.o.r., amended, 8 CCH Employ. Prac. Dec. ¶9679 (W.D. Ky., June 15, 1974) n.o.r., where the defendant employment agency was held to have violated the ADEA when it refused to refer job applicants to its employer client because the latter had indicated a preference for persons not more than 35 years of age. This interpretation of the ADEA was specifically rejected without analysis of the ADEA's prohibitions covering employment agencies in Brennan v. Paragon Employment Agency, Inc., 356 F. Supp. 286 (S.D.N.Y. 1973), aff'd without opinion, 489 F.2d 752 (2d Cir. 1974).

G. PROHIBITED LABOR ORGANIZATION PRACTICES

It is unlawful for a labor organization, under Section 4(c) of the ADEA, to exclude or to expel from its membership, or otherwise to discriminate against, any individual within the protected age bracket because of his age; to limit, segregate, or classify its membership, or to classify or fail or refuse to refer for employment any such individual, in any way which would deprive or tend to deprive any such individual of employment opportunities, or would limit such employment opportunities or otherwise adversely affect his status as an employee or as an applicant for employment, because of such individual's age; or to cause or attempt to cause an employer to discriminate against such an individual in violation of the ADEA's prohibitions against age discrimination.[49]

G-1. WAIVER OF RIGHTS UNDER THE ADEA.

An individual within the protected age bracket may voluntarily waive his right to seek relief under the statute for a prior violation of the ADEA as, for example, part of a settlement of a claim under the statute.

However, an individual's rights under a retirement program can not be conditioned upon his not instituting litigation against his employer including litigation under the ADEA.[50]

---

49. 29 U.S.C. § 623(c) (1970). Thus, a labor organization covered by the ADEA would violate the statute with a policy which provides for an arbitrary age limit of 55 for membership, Opinion Letter of Acting Wage-Hour Administrator, 8 Lab. Rel. Rep. 401:5224 (January 23, 1969); a clause in a union contract negotiated by a covered labor organization which provides for an arbitrary age limit for employment in maintenance crew positions would constitute a violation of the ADEA by the labor organization in the absence of an applicable statutory exception, Opinion Letter of Wage-Hour Administrator, 8 Lab. Rel. Rep. 401:5213 (August 19, 1968); a contract between a union and independent contractors providing that the latter will not engage steamfitters for certain types of work who could not prove that they were over 50 was denied an exemption under the ADEA since it would discriminate based on age against individuals in the protected age bracket even though it was meant to guarantee some work to older steamfitters, Opinion Letter of Wage-Hour Administrator (WH-30), 8 Lab. Rel. Rep. 401:5230 (May 1, 1970); a collective bargaining agreement providing for a ratio of men 55 years of age or older to younger men of 1 to 5 meant to guarantee some work to able plumbers over 55 does not accord with the statute and the purpose would not serve as a defense to a charge of discrimination under the ADEA, Opinion Letter of Wage-Hour Administrator (WH-36), 8 Lab. Rel. Rep. 401:5230 (May 25, 1970).

50. Opinion Letter of Wage-Hour Administrator, 8 Lab. Rel. Rep. 401:5217 (September 26, 1968).

In *Ott v. Midland-Ross Corporation,*[51] plaintiff alleged that he had waived a properly asserted right to proceed against his former employer under the ADEA in a transaction which was induced by his employer's fraud. The Court of Appeals held that if plaintiff proved his allegations then the transaction was voidable by him and, if the transaction were set aside, then plaintiff could assert his original claim under the ADEA.

H. GENERAL PROHIBITIONS

Section 4(d) of the ADEA, generally, makes it unlawful for an employer to discriminate against any of its employees or applicants for employment; for an employment agency to discriminate against any individual; or for a labor organization to discriminate against any member thereof or applicant for membership because such individual, member, or applicant for membership has opposed any practice made an unlawful act under the ADEA, or because such individual, member, or applicant for membership has made a charge, testified, assisted, or participated in any manner in an investigation, proceeding, or litigation under the ADEA.[52]

The importance of this protection for those, regardless of age, who assert rights under the ADEA, challenge practices prohibited thereunder, or participate in enforcement proceedings under the ADEA cannot be overstated since one of the primary means by which discriminatory practices are uncovered is the complaints of employees and applicants for employment.

I. PROHIBITED ADVERTISING PRACTICES

Section 4(e) of the ADEA declares it unlawful for a covered employer, labor organization, or employment agency to print or publish, or cause to be printed or published, any notice or advertisement relating to employment by such an employer, or

---

51. 523 F.2d 1367 (6th Cir. 1975).
52. 29 U.S.C. § 623(d) (1970). The Wage-Hour Administrator has opined that a clause in a retirement program to the effect that litigation by an employee will result in forfeiture of his rights under the program would be unlawful insofar as it may be applied to those who seek redress under the ADEA, Opinion Letter of Wage-Hour Administrator, 8 Lab. Rel. Rep. 401:5217 (September 26, 1968). *See* 29 C.F.R. § 860.120(c) (1974).

membership in or any classification or referral for employment by such a labor organization, or any classification or referral for employment by such an employment agency, indicating any preference, limitation, specification, or discrimination based on age.[53]

The Secretary of Labor has issued regulations providing that the placing of help wanted notices or advertisements containing terms and phrases such as "age 25 to 35," "young," "boy," "girl," "college student," "recent college graduate," or others of a similar nature discriminates against the employment of older persons and will be considered violations of the ADEA.[54] The courts have, with one notable exception, upheld this regulation.[55]

However, in *Brennan v. Paragon Employment Agency, Inc.,*[56] where an employment agency placed advertisements in a newspaper seeking "college students," "girls," "boys," and "June graduates" as its own employees, the Court specifically refused to follow the Secretary of Labor's regulations holding that

---

53. 29 U.S.C. § ¡23(e) (1970). The Wage-Hour Administrator has opined that this provision also covers notices of personnel available for employment that are sent out by employment agencies to prospective employers. Opinion Letter of Wage-Hour Administrator (WH-139), 2 CCH Employ. Prac. Guide ¶5029 (June 29, 1971).

54. 29 C.F.R. § 860.92(b) (1974). *Cf.* Opinion Letter of Wage-Hour Administrator (WH-106), 8 Lab. Rel. Rep. 401:5231 (January 6, 1971) (help wanted advertisement for "Girl Friday" not violative of the ADEA since it does not generally indicate an age preference).

55. *See* Brennan v. Approved Personnel Services, Inc., 529 F.2d 760 (4th Cir. 1975), *reversing,* 8 CCH Employ. Prac. Dec. ¶9810, 11 Fair Employ. Prac. Cas. 683 (M.D.N.C., September 20, 1974) n.o.r.; Brennan v. Hughes Personnel, Inc., 8 CCH Employ. Prac. Dec. ¶9571 (W.D. Ky., May 22, 1974) ("recent graduates") n.o.r., *amended,* 8 CCH Employ. Prac. Dec. ¶9679 (W.D. Ky., June 25, 1974) (" 'recent college graduates,' 'young,' 'boy,' 'girl,' or others of a similar nature") n.o.r.; Hodgson v. Western Textile Co., 7 CCH Employ. Prac. Dec. ¶9383 (N.D. Ill., April 26, 1974) ("young girl") n.o.r.; Brennan v. C/M Mobile, Inc., 8 CCH Employ. Prac. Dec. ¶9532, 8 Fair Employ. Prac. Cas. 551 (S.D. Ala., March 6, 1974) ("new grad," "college student," "prefer coll. student") n.o.r.; Hodgson v. Career Counsellors Int'l, Inc., 5 CCH Employ. Prac. Dec. ¶7983, 5 Fair Employ. Prac. Cas. 129 (N.D. Ill., September 28, 1972) ("girl") n.o.r.

56. 356 F. Supp. 286 (S.D.N.Y. 1973), *aff'd without opinion,* 489 F.2d 752 (2d Cir. 1974).

The purpose of the Act was to prevent persons aged 40 to 65 from having their careers cut off by unreasonable prejudice. It was not intended to prevent their children and grandchildren from ever getting started. There is nothing in the Act that authorizes the Secretary of Labor to prohibit employers from encouraging young persons whether or not in college to turn from idleness to useful endeavor. I find such encouragement to be in the public interest and therefore based on "reasonable factors other than age".[57]

A review of the applicable provisions of the ADEA and its legislative history suggests that the Court in *Brennan v. Paragon Employment Agency, Inc.* erred both with respect to its statement of the purposes of the ADEA and its interpretation of the provisions of the statute dealing with prohibited advertising practices.[58] First, the purpose of the ADEA is not simply to "prevent persons aged 40 to 65 from having their careers cut off by unreasonable prejudice" but rather

to promote employment of older persons based on their ability rather than age; [and] to prohibit arbitrary age discrimination in employment; ....[59]

Consistent with those purposes, the ADEA prohibits, *inter alia,* an

advertisement relating to employment ... indicating any preference, limitation, specification, or discrimination, based on age.[60]

The use of "college student," "girls," "boys," and "June graduates" clearly indicates a preference, limitation, specification,

---

57. 356 F. Supp. at 288-89. *See also* Levien, *The Age Discrimination in Employment Act: Statutory Requirements and Recent Developments,* 13 Duq. L. Rev. 227, 241 n. 92 (1974) (stating without analysis that the regulation "seems both extreme and inflexible").

58. *Accord,* Gilfix, *First Hired-First Fired: Age Discrimination in Employment,* 50 Cal. State Bar J. 462, 511 (1975); Note, *Proving Discrimination Under the Age Discrimination in Employment Act,* 17 Ariz. L. Rev. 495, 507 (1975).

59. 29 U.S.C. § 621(b) (1970). *See also* H.R. Rep. No. 805, 4, 8, [1967] U.S. Code Cong. and Admin. News at 2217, 2220 ("[T]he primary purpose of the bill — hiring of older workers ....").

60. 29 U.S.C. § 623(e) (1970). *See also* H.R. Rep. No. 805, 9, [1967] U.S. Code Cong. and Admin. News at 2221.

and discrimination based on age and discourages employment of older persons based on their age rather than their ability.

Second, the Secretary of Labor's interpretation does not, as stated by the Court, prevent children and grandchildren from ever getting started. It simply requires them to compete on equal terms with older persons based on ability, not the arbitrary criteria of age. When faced with the same issues the Court in *Brennan v. Hughes Personnel, Inc.*[61] specifically rejected the determination in the *Paragon Employment Agency, Inc.* case and held that the Secretary of Labor's regulation

> is in fulfillment of and in accordance with the statutory language used by Congress. . ..[62]

In *Hodgson v. Approved Personnel Service, Inc.,*[63] the Court of Appeals upheld the Secretary of Labor's interpretation of Section 4(e) and reversed the determinations of a District Court [64] which were contrary to the regulations of the Secretary of Labor. However, the Court of Appeals rejected the Department of Labor's suggestion that, with respect to advertisements which contained certain "trigger words," the use of those words should be deemed *per se* violations of the ADEA. While recognizing that the Department's suggestion had the dual virtues of simplicity and facilitation of enforcement, the Court of Appeals held that "the discriminatory effect of an advertisement is determined not by 'trigger words' but rather by its context." [65]

The Court of Appeals affirmed the District Court's holding that the defendant's advertisements relating to specific positions containing the following phrases violated the ADEA: "Prefer recent college grad," "recent high school grad," "some sales experience or recent college grad," "1-2 years out of college," "any recent degree," "recent grads," "college grads," "Recent Math

---

61. 8 CCH Employ. Prac. Dec. ¶9571 (W.D. Ky., May 22, 1974) n.o.r., *amended,* 8 CCH Employ. Prac. Dec. ¶9679 (W.D. Ky., June 25, 1974) n.o.r.

62. 8 CCH Employ. Prac. Dec. ¶9571, at 5475.

63. 529 F.2d 760 (4th Cir. 1975).

64. Brennan v. Approved Personnel Services, Inc., 8 CCH Employ. Prac. Dec. ¶9810, 11 Fair Employ. Prac. Cas. 683 (M.D.N.C., September 20, 1974) n.o.r.

65. 529 F.2d at 765.

Grad," "Recent college grad ideal," "Prefer recent technical school grad," "sharp recent grad," "High School grads 1972" and "College Grads 1972."

In addition, the Court of Appeals held that the defendant's advertisements containing the following phrases also violated the ADEA reversing the determinations of the District Court: "those unable to continue in college" and "do not plan to return to school," [66] "girl" and "career girls." [67]

The Court of Appeals affirmed the District Court's holding that the following did not violate the ADEA: "Returning Vets" and "Returning Servicemen" and "Returning Veterans," [68] "first job" and "excellent first job." These two holdings would appear to ignore the realities of how the phrases would be understood by persons within the protected age bracket reading the advertisements. Such persons might logically consider themselves excluded from applying for such positions.

The phrases "Junior Secretary," "Jr. Accountant," and "Junior Programmer," were upheld on the grounds that neither the statute nor the regulations promulgated thereunder mentioned the term, "junior" and the Court of Appeals' belief that

> the adjective "junior" when applied to an employee's job description designates the scope of his duties and responsibilities within the employer's organization, and does not carry connotations of youth prohibited by the Act.[69]

"All-American type" and "athletically inclined" were held "merely to state qualifications relating to personal appearances

---

66. "The obvious suggestion is that school- or college-age applicants will be given preference. The Act forbids this sort of advertisement." 529 F.2d at 767 n. 14.

67. "We think the term 'girl' as used and understood in the vernacular does carry connotations of youth, and advertisements soliciting 'girls' or 'career girls' for specific positions implicitly suggest that older applicants need not apply." 529 F.2d at 767 n. 14.

68. "[W]ere time-related to the end of the Vietnam war. We share the district court's feeling that the purpose of the Act was not then obstructed by such advertisements. We also note that not all returning veterans are young." 529 F.2d at 767 n. 14.

69. 529 F.2d at 765.

and physical characteristics which can exist in persons of any age." [70]

Lastly, the Court of Appeals held that

> an employment agency advertisement directed to "recent graduates" as part of a broad, general limitation to a specific class of prospective customers coming into the job market at a particular time of year to use the services it offers does not violate the Act. But when these same words are used in reference to a specific employment opportunity, we think there is an implication that persons older than the normal "recent graduate" need not apply. Thus, such ads violate the Act. Acceptable advertisements of this type may emphasize the services and performance record of the agency itself, but must avoid representations of anticipated salaries as well as descriptions, general or specific, of job opportunities available to members of the class. [71]

The Court of Appeals' analysis overlooks the fact that an employment agency which uses general advertisements directed to young people thereby discourages older persons from availing themselves of that agency's services and, thus, the opportunity to obtain the jobs available through that agency. Such advertisements have the same effect as one which offers to help "persons under 40" to obtain employment. Such an advertisement would seem to clearly indicate a "preference, limitation, specification, or discrimination, based on age" which is prohibited by the ADEA. [72] An employment agency could as easily advertise generally for persons looking for employment by including in the advertisement language making it clear that both young and older applicants are wanted. Such advertisements would both serve to provide the type of information needed by persons not familiar with the procedure for finding employment and not violate the spirit and the letter of the ADEA.

The Secretary of Labor's regulations also provide: that specifications such as "age 40 to 50," "age over 50," or "age over

---

70. 529 F.2d at 767 n. 14.
71. 529 F.2d at 766.
72. 29 U.S.C. § 623(e) (1970).

65" are also considered prohibited as are "retired persons," or "supplement your pension" where they are intended and applied so as to discriminate against others within the protected group; [73] that help wanted notices or advertisements can include a term or phrase such as "college graduate" or other educational requirement or specify a minimum age less than 40; [74] and that, while use of the phrase "state age" in a help wanted notice or advertisement is not in itself a violation of the ADEA, because such a request may tend to deter older applicants or otherwise indicate age discrimination employment notices or advertisements including such a request or any similar term will be closely scrutinized to make sure the request is for a permissible purpose and not ones proscribed by the ADEA.[75]

J. LAWFUL PRACTICES

The ADEA recognizes that not all refusals to hire or terminations of older persons represent instances of age discrimination in employment. Accordingly, it provides in Section 4(f) that it is not unlawful for a covered employer, employment

---

73. 29 C.F.R. § 860.92(b) (1974). Such specifications would not be prohibited if they are shown to be based on reasonable factors other than age — Opinion Letter of Acting Wage-Hour Administrator, 8 Lab. Rel. Rep. 401:5221 (January 7, 1969). Advertisements which discriminate in favor of the 40 to 65 year old group at worst discriminate against those outside the protected age bracket and are not prohibited by the ADEA. *Id.*

74. 29 C.F.R. § 860.92(c) (1974).

75. 29 C.F.R. § 860.92(d) (1974). *See also* Opinion Letter of Deputy Wage-Hour Administrator, 8 Lab. Rel. Rep. 401:5201 (June 4, 1968). The same position has been taken with respect to requests for a job applicant's age made by covered employers in pre-employment inquiries, [Opinion Letter of Wage-Hour Administrator, 8 Lab. Rel. Rep. 401:5202 (July 5, 1968)]; employment applications, [Opinion Letter of Wage-Hour Administrator, 8 Lab. Rel. Rep. 401:5207 (July 31, 1968)]; and resumes used by personnel agencies, [Opinion Letter of Wage-Hour Administrator, 8 Lab. Rel. Rep. 401:5206 (July 29, 1968)]. The Wage-Hour Division has, further, opined that, while such inquiries are not prohibited by the ADEA if made for a permissible purpose and not for purposes prohibited by the statute, the applicant must be informed that the request is not made for an improper purpose as by means of a reference in an application form to the ADEA and the fact that it prohibits age discrimination with respect to persons between 40 and 64 years of age. Opinion Letter of Wage-Hour Administrator, 8 Lab. Rel. Rep. 401:5202 (July 5, 1968).

Of course, nothing in the ADEA prohibits an individual advertising for employment from specifying his age, 29 C.F.R. § 860.92(e) (1974).

agency, or labor organization [1] to take any action otherwise prohibited under the ADEA where age is "a bona fide occupational qualification" reasonably necessary to the normal operation of the particular business, or where a differentiation is based on reasonable factors other than age; [2] to observe the terms of a bona fide seniority system or any bona fide employee benefit plan such as a retirement, pension, or insurance plan which is not a subterfuge to evade the purposes of the ADEA, except that no such employee benefit plan excuses the failure to hire any individual within the protected age bracket; or [3] to discharge or otherwise discipline such an individual for good cause.[76] In addition, the Secretary of Labor has, by regulation, provided an exemption from the provisions of the ADEA for bona fide apprenticeship programs [77] and rules governing job applications.[78]

The House of Representatives' Report notes that an additional exception was considered and rejected:

> The committee declined to incorporate a specific exception for management training programs since it was believed so broad an exemption in the law might open a very wide door of possible abuse. Almost any training, or opportunity for acquiring experience on a job, might be construed as leading to future advancement to management positions. The committee recognizes, however, that bona fide age requirements do exist for some positions designed to give employees knowledge and experience which can reasonably be expected to aid in developing capabilities required for future advancement to executive, administrative, or professional positions, and expects the Secretary [of Labor] to appropriately recognize such requirements.[79]

---

76. 29 U.S.C. § 623(f) (1970).

77. 29 C.F.R. § 860.106 (1974).

78. 29 C.F.R. § 860.95 (1974).

79. H.R. Rep. No. 805, 4, [1967] U.S. Code Cong. and Admin. News at 2217. *Cf.* Ill. Ann. Stat., ch. 48, § 884(2) (Smith-Hurd Cum. Supp. 1976):

> In the employment of a person in a capacity in which the knowledge and experience to be gained might reasonably be expected to aid in developing capabilities required for future advancement to supervisory, managerial, professional or executive positions, an age distinction may be exercised as one of the reasonable demands of the position to which the person is employed.

1. *Bona Fide Occupational Qualifications.* Section 4(f)(1) of the ADEA recognizes an exemption from the prohibitions of the statute for bona fide occupational qualifications (BFOQ).[80] The Labor and Education Committee of the House of Representatives, using the example of truck drivers, stated that,

It is, of course, not the purpose of this legislation to require the employment, regardless of age, of one not otherwise qualified in such instances.[81]

The Secretary of Labor has, by regulation, provided that whether an occupational qualification will be deemed to be "bona fide" and reasonably necessary to the normal operations of a particular business will be determined on the basis of all pertinent facts surrounding each particular situation, but that it is anticipated that the exception will have limited scope and application and that as such it must be construed narrowly.[82] The burden of proving that this exception applies is the responsibility of the employer, employment agency, or labor organization relying upon it.[83]

Examples of bona fide occupational qualifications include: Federal statutory and regulatory compulsory age limitations for hiring or retirement which make no reference to the individual's actual physical condition at the terminal age when such conditions are clearly imposed for the safety and convenience of the public, such as commercial airline pilots,[84] and special, individual

---

80. 29 U.S.C. § 623(f)(1) (1970).

81. H.R. Rep. No. 805, 7, [1967] U.S. Code Cong. and Admin. News at 2220.

82. 29 C.F.R. § 860.102(b) (1974).

83. *Id.* Thus, the Wage-Hour Administrator has opined that where it cannot be established that age is actually a bona fide occupational qualification reasonably necessary to the operation of a particular business, neither an employment agency's lack of knowledge that age is not a bona fide occupational qualification in the particular case nor its reliance on an employer's representation that it is such an occupational qualification can relieve the agency from the statutory consequences of an act prohibited by the ADEA. Opinion Letter of Wage-Hour Administrator, 8 Lab. Rel. Rep. 401:5207 (July 31, 1968).

84. 29 C.F.R. § 860.102(d) (1974). *See also* Opinion Letter of Wage-Hour Administrator, 8 Lab. Rel. Rep. 401:5203 (July 5, 1968); Opinion Letter of Wage-Hour Administrator, 8 Lab. Rel. Rep. 401:5204 (July 11, 1968). The Federal regulation concerning airline pilots is discussed at pp. 42-44, *supra.*

occupational circumstances, for example, actors required for youthful or elderly roles and persons used to advertise or promote the sale of products designed for and directed to appeal exclusively to either youthful or elderly consumers.[85]

The leading cases under the ADEA involving the defense of bona fide occupational qualifications are *Hodgson v. Greyhound Lines, Inc.*[86] and *Hodgson v. Tamiami Trail Tours, Inc.*[87] Both cases involved challenges under the ADEA to an industry-wide practice among inter-state bus companies of not hiring new drivers aged 40 or above. The defendant bus companies each asserted the defense of bona fide occupational qualification alleging that as a result of their seniority systems new bus drivers had the most arduous and irregular assignments and that hiring a new driver at 40 or above did not provide enough time to train him properly with the result that their being required to hire driver-ap-

---

85. 29 C.F.R. § 860.102(e) (1974). However, the Acting Wage-Hour Administrator has opined that the ADEA would prohibit specifying an age description in advertising for applicants to work in special teen and college shops since it is based on the assumption that every individual above a chosen age limit is unable to perform the duties of sales personnel satisfactorily in such shops. While some individuals may be so disqualified, those who are able to perform the job despite their age are arbitrarily discriminated against. Opinion Letter of Acting Wage-Hour Administrator, 8 Lab. Rel. Rep. 401:5222 (January 8, 1969).

An unusual example is provided by a proceeding brought under a state age discrimination law. In Smith v. New Viceroy Restaurant, 2 CCH Employ. Prac. Guide ¶8034 (Wash. State Board Against Discrimination, November 18, 1965), the complainants challenged the requirement of an employer that cocktail waitresses be "sexy" as age discrimination against older women. In rejecting the complaint, the Board noted that

> Some older women are "sexy" .... and some younger women are not. Thus a condition of employment that cocktail waitresses be "sexy" is not strictly an age condition, although it is a condition that older women, as a class, may find more difficult to meet. [2 CCH Employ. Prac. Guide ¶8034, at 6056.]

and held that the state discrimination law "was designed to prevent and eliminate discrimination against older women in jobs they are able to fill, rather than to require that every job be described so that older persons may fill it." 2 CCH Employ. Prac. Guide ¶8034, at 6057.

86. 499 F.2d 859 (7th Cir. 1974), *cert. den. sub. nom.* Brennan v. Greyhound Lines, 419 U.S. 1122 (1975), *reversing* 354 F. Supp. 230 (N.D. Ill. 1973).

87. 4 CCH Employ. Prac. Dec. ¶7795, 4 Fair Employ. Prac. Cas. 728 (S.D. Fla., March 31, 1972) n.o.r., *aff'd*, 531 F.2d 224 (5th Cir. 1976).

plicants age 40 or more would seriously affect the safety of passengers.

In the *Tamiami Trail Tours, Inc.* case, the District Court upheld that defendant's claimed exemption. The Court noted that

> Congress has ... mandated ... the common sense proposition that a bona fide occupational qualification is appropriate and must be made available when reasonably necessary to the normal operation of a particular business. ***. By so doing, Congress has sought to temper the ideals embodied in the Act with the practical knowledge that differentiation based on age is reasonably necessary to the normal operation of some particular business or to specific positions within some businesses. The touchstone for the BFOQ exemption provided under the Act is a finding that age is a reasonable requirement, necessitated by normal business operations and having a manifest relationship to the employment in question.[88]

The Court held that

> Where the defendant can demonstrate that its assertion of a bona fide occupational qualification ... is predicated upon an objective factual basis which gives it, as an employer, reasonable cause to believe that age differentiation in hiring bus drivers is necessary and proper for purposes of efficient business operations and the furtherance of the public interest, then the pre-requisites of the exemption have been satisfied and such exemption must be allowed.[89]

Reviewing decisions in cases alleging sex discrimination under Title VII of the Civil Rights Act of 1964, the Court held that the defendant would meet its burden of proof if it showed that "the essence of its business would be undermined by hiring drivers over forty years of age..." [90] and that

> defendant need not deal with each applicant over forty years of age on an individual basis by considering his particular functional ability to perform safely the duties of a driver notwithstanding his age, if it is not practical to do so.[91]

---

88. 4 CCH Employ. Prac. Dec. ¶7795, at 6049, 4 Fair Employ. Prac. Cas. at 730.
89. 4 CCH Employ. Prac. Dec. ¶7795, at 6049, 4 Fair Employ. Prac. Cas. at 731.
90. 4 CCH Employ. Prac. Dec. ¶7795, at 6050, 4 Fair Employ. Prac. Cas. at 731.
91. 4 CCH Employ. Prac. Dec. ¶7795, at 6050, 4 Fair Employ. Prac. Cas. at 732.

The Court found that the functional age, as distinguished from the chronological age, of a driver-applicant could not be determined with sufficient reliability to meet the special safety obligations of motor carriers of passengers; that, as persons grow older, the natural process of aging produces a decline in sensory perception, motor reflexes and reaction time, stamina, etc. and that older drivers with seniority can compensate by choosing regular, easier routes such as daytime runs while new, older drivers could not; and that

> Defendant's only concern is the possible one-time occurrence where a driver fails to function properly or collapses altogether due to an age-related physiological or psychological malfunction or breakdown. The risks involved in defendant's business are too great, and a single life is too valuable to deny the existence of defendant's bona fide occupational qualification defense as demonstrated by the evidence.[92]

On the other hand, the District Court in the *Greyhound Lines* case rejected the claimed bona fide occupational qualification defense. The Court found, *inter alia,* that Federal regulations required periodic physical examinations of drivers; that physical examinations were no more valid a test of driving ability of a 25 year old than of a 45 year old; that it could not state with definitive certainty

> that such physical examinations as are given would be capable or incapable of discovering the physical and sensory changes common to all men nor that those changes are necessarily caused only by the aging process nor that such changes in and of themselves make an interstate bus operator less safe in the normal operation of defendant's business.[93]

and that, while older drivers with seniority had more regular runs than new drivers, they both were subject to the same regulations as to the number of hours they were permitted to drive and the

---

92. 4 CCH Employ. Prac. Dec. ¶7795, at 6052, 4 Fair Employ. Prac. Cas. at 733.
93. 354 F. Supp. at 235.

number of hours between runs. The District Court held that the defendant had

> not met the burden of demonstrating that its policy of age limitation is reasonably necessary to the normal and safe operation of its business nor that age is a bona fide occupational qualification within the meaning of the Act.[94]

In reaching its decision, the District Court disagreed on two crucial points with the conclusions reached by the District Court in the *Tamiami Trail Tours, Inc.* case although no reference was made to that previously decided case. First, the District Court held that

> If ever there were an opportunity for "individual consideration" surely this is one for through its screening process defendant has ample opportunity to exclude those individuals it finds unsuitable for interstate bus driving.[95]

Second, the District Court held that

> Safety is the foremost concern involved herein not only for defendant but for plaintiff and this Court as well, but I cannot accept the contention that persons over 40 cannot become safe bus drivers. *I believe strongly that functional capacity and not chronological age ought be the most important factor as to whether or not an individual can do a job safely.* This determination must be made repeatedly throughout the employee's employment experience. The human variances involved are myriad; there is no way to generalize as to the physical capability and physiological makeup of an individual. Nor is there a way to project how an individual will be affected by the aging process.[96] (Emphasis added.)

On appeal, the Court of Appeals reversed the District Court's determination in the *Greyhound Lines* case and upheld the defendant's bona fide occupational qualification defense. The Court of Appeals held that the District Court had applied the wrong

---

94. 354 F. Supp. at 239.
95. *Id.*
96. *Id.*

standard of proof and that, as a public transportation carrier entrusted with the lives and well-being of passengers which must continually strive to employ the most highly qualified persons available,

> Greyhound must demonstrate that it has a rational basis in fact to believe that elimination of its maximum hiring age will increase the likelihood of risk of harm to its passengers. Greyhound need only demonstrate, however, a minimal increase in risk of harm for it is enough to show that elimination of the hiring policy might jeopardize the life of one more person than might otherwise occur under the present hiring practice.[97]

The Court of Appeals found that it was not clear that functional age is readily or practicably determinable; it was questionable whether the defendant could practically scrutinize the continued fitness of drivers between 40 and 64 on a frequent and regular basis; and for long-term Greyhound drivers the effect of the aging process on driver safety records was offset by experience as Greyhound drivers, a factor not attainable by newly hired drivers over 40. The Court of Appeals concluded that

> Greyhound has amply demonstrated that its maximum hiring age policy is founded upon a good faith judgment concerning the safety needs of its passengers and others. It has established that its hiring policy is not the result of an arbitrary belief lacking in objective reason or rationale.[98]

---

97. 499 F.2d at 863.

98. 499 F.2d at 865. The decision of the Court of Appeals is criticized in XVI B.C. Indus. & Com. L. Rev. 688, 691 (1975) ("the Seventh Circuit's decision in Greyhound frustrates congressional intent, as expressed in the enactment of the ADEA, by permitting arbitrary and unreasonable age discrimination through an overly broad application of the BFOQ exception."); Gilfix, *First Hired-First Fired: Age Discrimination in Employment,* 50 Calif. State Bar J. 462, 466, 508 (1975); Note, *Age Discrimination in Employment,* 50 N.Y.U.L. Rev. 924, 946-49 (1975). (Noting that since Greyhound had no data on the safety record of newly hired drivers over the age of 35 because it had never hired applicants over that age and the Court of Appeals was unwilling to allow such data to be generated because it would require experimenting with the lives of passengers, the age discrimination of the past was, in effect, allowed to justify such discrimination in the present and the future).

The Fifth Circuit Court of Appeals affirmed the District Court's determination in the *Tamiami Trail Tours, Inc.* case that age was a bona fide occupational qualification.[99] As a result, an identical result was reached in both of the bus driver cases. The Fifth Circuit reviewed the decision of the Seventh Circuit in the *Greyhound Lines* case and, while agreeing with the result reached on the merits, held that the Seventh Circuit had not correctly interpreted the Fifth Circuit's previously enunciated tests for determining whether an employer relying on a BFOQ defense had carried its burden. Those tests were set forth in two Fifth Circuit decisions under Title VII of the Civil Rights Act of 1964.[100]

The first, or so-called *Weeks,* test places the burden on an employer relying on the bona fide occupational qualification defense of proving that it has reasonable cause to believe, that is, a factual basis for believing, that all or substantially all members of the protected class would be unable to perform safely and efficiently the duties of the job involved. However, even if the employer cannot carry that burden, it can still rely upon the defense if it demonstrates that it is impossible or highly impractical to deal with members of the protected class on an individualized basis, in which case the employer may apply a reasonable general rule. That burden may, for example, be met by an employer which establishes that some members of the otherwise protected class

> possess a trait precluding safe and efficient job performance that cannot be ascertained by means other than knowledge of the applicant's membership in the class.[101]

However, the employer's burden would not be met by an allegation that added expense would be incurred by individualized dispositions of employment applications.[102]

---

99. 531 F.2d 224 (5th Cir. 1976).

100. Diaz v. Pan Am. World Airways, Inc., 442 F.2d 385 (5th Cir.), *cert. denied,* 404 U.S. 950 (1971); Weeks v. Southern Bell Tel. and Tel. Co., 408 F.2d 228 (5th Cir. 1969).

101. Hodgson v. Tamiami Trail Tours, Inc., *supra,* 531 F.2d at 235.

102. 531 F.2d at 235 n. 26.

The second, or so-called *Diaz,* test construed the statutory requirement that the claimed bona fide occupational qualification be "reasonably necessary" to the operation of the employer's business to limit qualification for the defense to those cases in which the "essence" of the business operation would be undermined by not hiring persons outside the protected class exclusively.[103] The Fifth Circuit rejected the interpretation of the Seventh Circuit in the *Greyhound* case which saw the *Weeks* and *Diaz* tests as inconsistent and relied on the latter while rejecting the former. The Fifth Circuit held that

> the Diaz requirement of a correlation between the job description and the essence of the business operation is a condition precedent to the application of Weeks' BFOQ exception to the ban on hiring discrimination. As such, Diaz affirms and elaborates on the Weeks rationale. Diaz was not an exception to Weeks based on the third party safety factor. It represented an evaluation of Weeks to cover attempts by employers to discriminate on the basis of job descriptions not related to the essence of the employer's business.[104]

The Fifth Circuit in the *Tamiami* case stated that it was the *Diaz* element of the bona fide occupational qualification defense test which brings into play the third-party safety factor since the safe transportation of bus passengers from one point to another was asserted by the defendant-employer to be reasonably necessary to the essence of its business. Further,

> The greater the safety factor, measured by the likelihood of harm and the probable severity of that harm in case of an accident, the more stringent may be the job qualifications designed to insure safe driving.[105]

Looking to the specific facts before it, the Fifth Circuit noted that neither party had suggested that Tamiami's stringent job qualifications for the position of bus driver were either unrelated to the essence of its business or unreasonable in light of the safety

---

103. 531 F.2d at 235.
104. 531 F.2d at 235 n. 27.
105. 531 F.2d at 236.

risk and that Tamiami had, therefore, satisfied the *Diaz* prong of its bona fide occupational qualification test. Since Tamiami had not attempted to establish a factual basis for believing that substantially all job applicants over 40 years of age would be unable to drive buses safely, it was required under *Weeks* to demonstrate that passenger-endangering characteristics of the over-40 years old job applicants could not practically be ascertained by some hiring test other than automatic exclusion on the basis of age. The Court of Appeals reviewed the findings of the District Court and the evidence which supported those findings and held that the lower court's determination that there was no practical basis other than automatic exclusion on the basis of age for ascertaining the passenger-endangering characteristics was not clearly erroneous. Accordingly, the District Court's decision was affirmed.

The *Greyhound Lines* and *Tamiami Trail Tours, Inc.* cases are, obviously, unique in that the courts were faced with questions of public interest and safety not present in most cases brought under the ADEA. In this aspect, the bus company cases are closely related to the railroad and airline cases discussed previously.[106] At the same time, they demonstrate that there is no mechanistic process at work but rather courts with different attitudes and approaches which may lead to different results on nearly identical facts or identical results on different theories.

Outside of businesses involving hazardous work or public safety, the availability of the bona fide occupational qualification exception has been closely restricted. Thus, the Wage-Hour Administrator opined that a proposed plan of an employer with a need for qualified lawyers to permit certain of its technical employees under the age of 35 to pursue studies leading to a degree in law, preparatory to a career as a patent attorney, and to reimburse them for all expenses associated with the undertaking, would neither be eligible for the bona fide occupational qualification exception or in compliance with the ADEA.[107] The

---

106. See pp. 40-44, *supra*.

107. Opinion Letter of Wage-Hour Administrator, 8 Lab. Rel. Rep. 401:5228 (March 13, 1970).

Wage-Hour Administrator noted that the employer could require that employees wishing to participate in the tuition plan meet certain specified mental, physical, and educational standards but could not assume that merely because an individual employee has reached some particular age that he no longer possesses the necessary qualifications to participate in the program. The Wage-Hour Administrator, further, held that the cost of the program in relation to the amount of service as a patent attorney which could be expected from the trainees did not seem relevant to the matter of occupational qualification but rather was a calculation largely dependent upon the age of the trainee and assumptions concerning amounts of expected service.

2. *Differentiations Based on Reasonable Factors Other Than Age.* The exemption in Section 4(f)(1) for differentiations based on reasonable factors other than age in connection with employment [108] presents a threshold problem concerning the reason for its inclusion in the ADEA. Since the statute prohibits only specified types of discrimination based on age in connection with employment, the ADEA does not prohibit differentiations or discrimination based on factors other than age. That is true whether the factors used are reasonable, such as inability to perform a particular job, or unreasonable, such as the number of letters in a person's name or the month and day of their birth. Accordingly, there would not appear to have been any need for a specific exemption for differentiation based upon reasonable, or unreasonable, factors other than age since such differentiations were never prohibited by the ADEA in the first place. The only logical explanation is that the differentiations based on reasonable factors other than age exemption was included in order to make clear what was, in any case, implicit. Admittedly, this argument leaves unexplained the inclusion of the word "reasonable," but there is no apparent basis for justifying that.[109]

108. 29 U.S.C. § 623(f)(1) (1970).

109. It has been suggested that the inclusion of the reasonableness requirement might be read to give a court the power to determine whether the factors other than age upon which a defendant relies in defending an action brought under the ADEA are rational on purely economic grounds. If the court determines that those factors are irrational from a business standpoint, then the court could require the defendant to prove that its actions were not motivated by the plaintiff's age and could even

The scope of the exemption from the prohibitions of the ADEA for "differentiations based on reasonable factors other than age," like that for bona fide occupational qualifications, is not specified in the statute. The Secretary of Labor's regulations note that no precise and unequivocal determination can be made as to the scope of the exception and whether such differentiations exist must be decided on the basis of all the particular facts and circumstances surrounding each individual situation.[110] The regulations reiterate that it was not the purpose or intent of the Congress in enacting the ADEA to require the employment of anyone regardless of age who is disqualified from performing a particular job but rather to insure that age, within the limits prescribed by the ADEA, is not a determining factor in the making of any decision regarding hiring, dismissal, promotion or any other term, condition or privilege of employment of an individual.[111]

The Secretary of Labor's regulations and the House of Representatives' Report make it clear that the propriety of a particular differentiation must be determined on a case-by-case basis and not on the basis of any general or class concept, with unusual working conditions given weight according to their individual merit.[112]

---

conduct an inquiry into the defendant's employment practices to determine whether they indicated the presence of age discrimination. Note, *Proving Discrimination Under the Age Discrimination in Employment Act,* 17 Ariz. L. Rev. 495, 518-19 (1975). However, there is no support in the legislative history of the ADEA or in the cases decided under the statute, *id.* at 517, for such an interpretation. *See also* Kovarsky and Kovarsky, *Economic, Medical and Legal Aspects of the Age Discrimination Laws in Employment,* 27 Vand. L. Rev. 839, 880-83 (1974), where the authors suggest that the inclusion of the word "reasonable" might be meant to provide a guide for the Department of Labor and the courts in considering a claim that a particular action was based on factors other than age. Where the factors relied upon are "reasonable" the credibility of the alleged discriminator would be increased but where the factors are "unreasonable" then doubt would be cast upon the intentions of the alleged discriminator. Presumably, closer scrutiny would then be justified to determine whether age was, in fact, a motivating factor.

110. 29 C.F.R. § 860.103(b) (1974).
111. 29 C.F.R. § 860.103(c) (1974).
112. 29 C.F.R. § 860.103(d) (1974); H.R. Rep. No. 805, 7, [1967] U.S. Code Cong. and Admin. News at 2219-20.

As with the bona fide occupational qualification exception, the differentiation exception will be construed narrowly with the burden of proof in establishing the applicability of the exception resting upon the employer, employment agency, or labor union which seeks to invoke it.[113]

The Secretary's regulations do provide general guidelines indicating factors which are among those which may be recognized as supporting a differentiation based on reasonable factors other than age.[114] Those factors include physical fitness requirements based on pre-employment or periodic physical examinations relating to minimum standards for employment provided that the standards are reasonably necessary for the specific work to be performed and are uniformly and equally applied to all applicants for the particular job category, regardless of age. This would include job situations which necessitate stringent physical requirements due to inherent occupational factors such as the safety of the individual employees or of other persons in their charge, or those occupations which by their nature are particularly hazardous such as iron workers, bridge builders, sandhogs, underwater demolition men and similar job classifications which require rapid reflexes or a high degree of speed, coordination, dexterity, endurance, or strength. However, a claim for recognition of a differentiation will not be permitted on the basis of an employer's assumption that every employee over a certain age in a particular type of job usually becomes physically unable to perform the duties of the job.[115]

---

113. 29 C.F.R. § 860.103(e) (1974).

114. 29 C.F.R. § 860.103(f) (1974).

115. 29 C.F.R. § 860.103(f)(1)(iii) (1974) (the regulation notes that there is medical evidence to support the contention that that assumption is generally incorrect). *See also* Opinion Letter of Wage-Hour Administrator, 8 Lab. Rel. Rep. 401:5203 (July 11, 1968); Opinion Letter of Wage-Hour Administrator, 8 Lab. Rel. Rep. 401:5206 (August 1, 1968).

The regulations caution that even in situations where experience has shown that most elderly persons do not have certain qualifications which are essential to those who hold certain jobs, some may have them even though they have attained an advanced age, 29 C.F.R. § 860.103(g) (1974). *See* Opinion Letter of Wage-Hour Administrator, 8 Lab. Rel. Rep. 401:5205 (July 26, 1968) (help wanted advertisement specifying age limitation for oil field workers required to carry heavy steel

The regulations also recognize evaluation factors such as quantity or quality of production or educational level as an acceptable basis for differentiation when, in an individual case, such factors are shown to have a valid relationship to job requirements and where the criteria or personnel policies establishing such factors are applied uniformly to all employees, regardless of age.[116]

The general assertion that the average cost of employing older workers as a group is higher than the average cost of employing younger workers as a group has been declared not to be a recognizable differentiation under the ADEA unless one of the other statutory exceptions applies since the classification, or grouping, of employees solely on the basis of age, for the purpose of comparing costs or for any other purpose necessarily rests on the assumption which is contrary to the terms of the ADEA [117] that the age factor alone may be used to justify a differentiation.

---

equipment would violate the ADEA since it assumes that all older workers could not perform the job); Opinion Letter of Wage-Hour Administrator, 8 Lab. Rel. Rep. 401:5211 (August 12, 1968) (strenuous manual outdoor labor); Opinion Letter of Wage-Hour Administrator, 8 Lab. Rel. Rep. 401:5213 (August 27, 1968) (age not bona fide occupational qualification in connection with employment in a newspaper's classified advertising department); Opinion Letter of Wage-Hour Administrator, 8 Lab. Rel. Rep. 401:5214 (August 30, 1968) (construction work); Opinion Letter of Wage-Hour Administrator, 8 Lab. Rel. Rep. 401:5221 (November 15, 1968) (unloading of trucks and heavy stock work).

116. 29 C.F.R. § 860.103(f)(2) (1974). This would include pay which is based on piece-rate or incentive systems so long as the system is not applied to older workers as a group based on the assumption that they have a lower productivity. Opinion Letter of Wage-Hour Deputy Administrator, 8 Lab. Rel. Rep. 401:5205 (July 19, 1968). Similarly, the exception might apply to a company pension plan providing, *inter alia*, for involuntary retirement of employees ceasing to meet the company's evaluation factors having a valid relationship to job requirements if uniformly applied to all employees regardless of age. Opinion Letter of Wage-Hour Administrator (WH — 289), 2 CCH Employ. Prac. Guide ¶5295 (October 10, 1974). The latter view was adopted, without citing the Opinion Letter, by the District Court in Donnelly v. Exxon Research & Engineering Co., 11 CCH Employ. Prac. Dec. ¶10,860, 12 Fair Employ. Prac. Cas. 417 (D.N.J., October 30, 1974) n.o.r., *aff'd without opinion,* 521 F.2d 1398 (3rd Cir. 1975).

117. 29 C.F.R. § 860.103(h) (1974). *See* Donnelly v. Exxon Research & Eng'r Co., 11 CCH Employ. Prac. Dec. ¶10,860, at 7639, 12 Fair Employ. Prac. Cas. 417, 422 (D.N.J., October 30, 1974) n.o.r., *aff'd without opinion,* 521 F.2d 1398 (3rd Cir. 1975),

Also listed among the actions which would be discriminatory under the ADEA is a declaration by an employer that he will hire only persons receiving old age insurance benefits under the Federal Social Security system since it could result in discrimination against other individuals in the protected age bracket willing to work for the wages and under the conditions offered even though the wages and conditions are particularly attractive to Social Security recipients who are in some cases limited as to the amount of wages they can earn and still receive benefits and are, therefore, particularly interested in part-time work.[118]

An employer's condition as to the number or schedule of hours for a particular job may be a differentiation based on a reasonable factor other than age.[119]

The use of a validated employee test is not, of itself, a violation of the ADEA when the test is: specifically related to the requirements of the job, fair and reasonable, administered in good faith and without discrimination on the basis of age, and properly evaluated.[120]

---

upholding against a challenge based on this sub-section of the Secretary of Labor's regulations, a policy requiring the termination of any employee, regardless of his age, whose productivity measured in dollars was less than 75 per cent of his salary.

118. 29 C.F.R. § 860.104(a)(1) (1974) (specification of Social Security recipients cannot be used as a convenient reference to persons of sufficient age to be eligible for old age benefits nor may an employer give preference in hiring to an individual solely because he is receiving such benefits). *See* Opinion Letter of Wage-Hour Administrator, 8 Lab. Rel. Rep. 401:5209 (August 7, 1968). For age and earnings restrictions on eligibility to receive Social Security old age insurance benefits, *see* 42 U.S.C. §§ 402, 403, 415 (1970 & Supp. V 1975).

119. 29 C.F.R. § 860.104(a)(2) (1974). Thus, it would not violate the ADEA for an employer to fail to employ a job applicant in the protected age bracket who is unwilling to accept the number or schedule of hours required by the employer as a condition for a particular job because the job applicant is receiving Social Security benefits and is limited in the amount of wages he may earn without losing such benefits, *id. See also* Opinion Letter of Deputy Wage-Hour Administrator, 8 Lab. Rel. Rep. 401:5202 (June 10, 1968).

120. 29 C.F.R. § 860.104(b) (1974). The regulation notes, however, that due to a tremendous increase in the use of tests in schools younger persons may generally have had greater experience in test-taking than older persons and that younger job applicants may, therefore, have an advantage over older applicants where an employee test is used as the sole tool or the controlling factor in the job selection

Since the ADEA does not prohibit a covered employer, employment agency, or labor organization from refusing to hire an individual within the protected age bracket not because of his age but because he is a relative of a person already employed by the firm or organization, such a differentiation would be based on a reasonable factor other than age.[121]

The House of Representatives' Report suggested an additional differentiation with dangerous counter-productive implications when it stated, with reference to industries having a disproportionately high number of older workers in the work force resulting in some cases from a decline in total employment in an industry coupled with the exercise of seniority rights, that

> The committee does not intend that the legislation be administered in such a way as to worsen a situation as this, or to prevent an employer from achieving a reasonable age balance in his employment structure. It is expected that the Secretary [of Labor] will recognize these particular situations and treat them according to their individual merits on a case-by-case basis.[122]

Such an exception to the prohibitions of the ADEA could result in just such a differentiation based on age alone in hiring new employees in such industries as is specifically declared unlawful by the statute.

The purpose of the differentiation exception was explained by the District Court in *Hart v. United Steelworkers of America*.[123] The Court in that case denied plaintiffs' request for an injunction to prevent enforcement of a provision of the defendant union's constitution making persons who would attain 65 years of age before the end of the nominating period ineligible for nomination

---

process since older applicants, though they may have greater on-the-job experience, have been out of school longer. Accordingly, situations in which an employee test is used as the sole tool or the controlling factor in the employment selection process will be carefully scrutinized to ensure that the test is used for a permissible purpose and not ones prohibited by the ADEA. *Id.*

121. 29 C.F.R. § 860.104(c) (1974).

122. H.R. Rep. No. 805, 7, [1967] U.S. Code Cong. and Admin. News at 2219-20.

123. 350 F. Supp. 294 (W.D. Pa. 1972), *appeal dismissed and remanded for vacation of judgment as moot*, 482 F.2d 282 (3rd Cir. 1973) (*per curiam*).

to an office in the international union even if the individual was not yet 65 when nominated. The Court stated that

> While employees and job applicants are entitled to protection under the Act when they have been arbitrarily discriminated against because of age they are not entitled to relief where there has been merely a reasonable differentiation on some basis not intended as a subterfuge to avoid application of the Act. Kincaid v. United Steelworkers of America, No. 71H-229(2) (N.D. Ind.-Hammond Division, July 25, 1972).[124]

Litigation in which the differentiation exception is raised as a defense has often involved reductions in force caused either by adverse business conditions or changes in a business. In *Bishop v. Jelleff Associates, Inc.,*[125] the Court held that

> the statute is not violated in the case of terminations or other employer decisions which are premised upon a rational business decision made in good faith and not actuated by age bias. To conclude otherwise would make the federal courts a super board of directors reviewing bona fide management decisions, a procedure Congress clearly did not intend by passage of this Act.[126]

While giving deference to the business judgment of an employer, the Court held that a reduction in force which was not across the board, but rather, simply a reduction in the older employee force, violated the ADEA since reductions which were predominantly of older employees for no apparent, rational reason other than age were violative of the spirit of the ADEA.

On the other hand, reductions in force which included older workers have been upheld where the choice of specific employees was based on factors other than age which were uniformly applied. In *Stringfellow v. Monsanto Company,*[127] the defendant was required by economic factors to reduce substantially the nature, scope, and extent of a plant which necessitated the elimination of a large number of preexisting jobs and a substantial reduction in

---

124. 350 F. Supp. at 297.
125. 398 F. Supp. 579 (D.D.C. 1974).
126. 398 F. Supp. at 593.
127. 320 F. Supp. 1175 (W.D. Ark. 1970).

the number of its employees. All employees who were terminated were given an opportunity to receive an explanation as to the reasons for their termination and an opportunity for a review of the evaluation made of their job performance. The Court found that defendant had utilized a plan of evaluation for determining and selecting terminees on the basis of performance and ability to perform the jobs remaining at the plant. The Court held that

> The method of the company's impartial evaluation of the ability and job performance of each of the plaintiffs and other employees evaluated by Monsanto was based upon established factors and criteria ordinarily utilized for such purpose. The Court concludes that the differentiation resulting from the application of such factors and criteria in the plan of evaluation which Monsanto used was based on reasonable factors other than age and in the opinion of the Court constitutes a lawful practice envisioned under 29 U.S.C. § 623(f).[128]

In *Gill v. Union Carbide Corporation*,[129] the defendant decided which employees were to be terminated as part of a reduction in force by the use of guidelines for the use of divisional directors whose decisions were reviewed by boards established to scrutinize those who had been selected for possible termination. The guidelines provided that "ability" and "effectiveness" were to be evaluated first and were to be the controlling considerations. Other factors to be considered were each employee's value to the continuing programs, versatility, uniqueness — a specialty important to the division or plant, personal problems, and company service. The latter factor required personnel with less than three years' service to be considered first for termination unless the quality factors were exceptional, personnel of less than 40 years of age with relatively short service to be considered next with quality factors being important, and personnel with long service and over 40 years of age to be given most consideration for retention. The Court, noting the positive value given to age in the evaluation process, dismissed the action.[130]

---

128. 320 F. Supp. at 1180-81.
129. 368 F. Supp. 364 (E.D. Tenn. 1973).
130. The Court also rejected the plaintiff's claim that the evaluation system employed was inadequate because, unlike the procedure followed in Stringfellow

The differentiation exception has also been held available to employers discharging employees found to be the most expendable regardless of their age,[131] to employers discharging employees not fully qualified to perform their jobs while retaining those employees who were,[132] and to an employer encouraging young persons to work by advertising for employees who were "college students," "girls," "boys," and "June graduates." [133]

On the other hand, it has been suggested that the reasonable factors other than age exemption may be applicable as well to a unique situation where the qualification to perform the job is not denied. Decisions involving the hiring and the granting of tenure to persons within the protected age bracket in the university setting are made based upon evaluations of relative quality rather than the simple adequacy of particular individuals. The factors taken into account in making those decisions often involve primarily subjective determinations and predictions of future development and performance as opposed to objective reviews of past performance. The former are, of course, far more difficult for a defendant university to verbalize and for a court to evaluate.[134]

---

v. Monsanto Co., *supra,* the divisional director who evaluated him did not consult with plaintiff's immediate superior in determining his professional ability and productivity and plaintiff was not given an opportunity to consult with those in decision-making positions and to comment upon his evaluation. The Court held that such procedures were not the *sine quo non* for the defendant to show that reasonable factors other than age were used and that each case must rest upon its own facts and circumstances.

131. Price v. Maryland Cas. Co., 391 F. Supp. 613, 625 (S.D. Miss. 1975) ("Certainly the Act does not contemplate that private industry may not retrench in times of austerity.").

132. Hinote v. Dworshak Dam Constructors, 6 CCH Employ. Prac. Dec. ¶8892 (D. Idaho, July 13, 1973) n.o.r.

133. Brennan v. Paragon Employment Agency, Inc., 356 F. Supp. 386 (S.D.N.Y. 1973), *aff'd without opinion,* 489 F.2d 752 (2d Cir. 1974), discussed p. 92-94, *supra.*

134. Haslam, *Age Discrimination in Campus Employment,* 4 Human Rights 321, 336-37 (1975). The author argues not that university faculty decisions should be exempted from ADEA but that the differences between commercial and academic enterprises be recognized and that those responsible for enforcing the statute should be sensitive to those differences in the performance of their legal responsibilities.

3. *Bona Fide Seniority Systems.* A seniority system may be qualified by such factors as merit, capacity, or ability, but to qualify as "a bona fide seniority system" under Section 4(f)(2) of the ADEA [135] the system must be based on length of service as the primary criterion for the equitable allocation of available employment opportunities and prerogatives among workers.[136]

Since seniority systems not only distinguish between employees on the basis of their length of service but also afford greater rights to those who have the longer service, adoption of a purported seniority system which gives those with longer service less rights and results in discharge or less favored treatment of those within the protected age bracket of the ADEA may, depending on the circumstances, be a "subterfuge to evade the purposes" of the ADEA and, thus, not within the exception for such systems. Similarly, a seniority system which has the effect of perpetuating discrimination on the basis of age which may have existed prior to the effective date of the ADEA would not be covered by the exception.[137]

Unless the essential terms and conditions of an alleged seniority system have been communicated to the affected employees and can be shown to be applied uniformly to all of those affected regardless of age, it will be regarded as lacking the necessary bona fides to qualify for the exception.[138]

4. *Bona Fide Employee Benefit Plans.* The exception contained in Section 4(f)(2) of the ADEA makes it lawful for a covered employer, labor organization, or employment agency to observe the terms of a bona fide employee benefit plan which is not a

---

135. 29 U.S.C. § 623(f)(2) (1970).

136. 29 C.F.R. § 860.105(a) (1974). A bona fide seniority system may be operated on an occupational, departmental, plant, or company wide unit basis. *Id.* Such a system could include, for example, rotation of job assignments and the equalization or allocation of overtime hours. Opinion Letter of Wage-Hour Administrator, 8 Lab. Rel. Rep. 401:5204 (July 12, 1968).

137. 29 C.F.R. §860.105(b) (1974).

138. 29 C.F.R. § 860.105(c) (1974). The Secretary of Labor's regulations also provide that a seniority system which violates Title VII of the Civil Rights Act of 1964 will not be regarded as bona fide under the ADEA. 29 C.F.R. § 860.105(d) (1974).

subterfuge to evade the purposes of the ADEA so long as it does not result in the failure to hire any individual.[139] That provision deals with one of the major grounds upon which employers have attempted to justify their refusal to hire older workers. Employers have argued [1] that the cost differential between younger and older workers of certain employee benefit plans was so great that they could not afford to allow older workers to participate and, where the plan required all employees to participate, they have had to set maximum age restrictions on hiring, and [2] that hiring older workers who do not participate in employee benefit plans or do not accumulate sufficient service before normal retirement to qualify for a pension or to qualify for a sufficient pension to meet the employee's basic needs would result in bad public relations for the employer which might be accused of retiring an employee with no or an inadequate pension.[140]

The exception for bona fide employee benefit plans meets the first argument by permitting differentiation based on age while prohibiting refusals to hire older workers on the ground of such benefit plans.[141] Publicity as to the provisions and purposes of the ADEA together with the recently enacted Federal pension reform law [142] can, at least in part, deal with the second argument. The Court in *Hodgson v. American Hardware Mutual Insurance Company* [143] described the resulting statutory scheme as follows:

> [C]onceptually there is no difference between a mandatory retirement age of sixty-two and a refusal to

---

139. 29 U.S.C. § 623(f)(2) (1970).

140. Note, *Age Discrimination in Employment: The Problem of the Older Worker,* 41 N.Y.U.L. Rev. 382, 401-404 (1966).

141. The Wage-Hour Administrator has stated that

> the exception was enacted because of Congressional concern that the costs of retirement, pension or insurance plans would become prohibitive if employers could not continue to observe their terms and conditions as established in accordance with sound actuarial formulas. Thus, the purpose of section 4(f) (2) was to protect existing retirement, pension and insurance plans and to enable employers to hire older workers without jeopardizing the continued maintenance and operation of such plans.

Opinion Letter of Wage-Hour Administrator (No. 287), 2 CCH Employ. Prac. Guide ¶5282 (April 29, 1974).

142. Employee Retirement Income Security Act of 1974, Pub. L. No. 93-406, 88 Stat. 829 (1974).

143. 329 F. Supp. 225, 229 (D. Minn. 1971).

hire anyone who is sixty-two years old. This is particularly significant in light of the language in §4(f) [setting forth the lawful exceptions to the prohibitions of the ADEA]. Although it permits an employer to observe the terms of a bona fide retirement program, the last clause of §4(f)(2) — "except that no such employee benefit plan shall excuse the failure to hire any individual" — does not permit the employer to refuse to hire someone because of the terms of such a program. Thus an employer may discriminate according to age by refusing to permit an employee over the maximum entry age — fifty-five years for women in the instant case — to enroll in the Plan or by retiring a person who is a Plan member prior to age sixty-five. However, §4(f)(2) seems to clearly prohibit a refusal by defendant to hire a sixty-three year old woman based on the Plan's compulsory retirement age or a refusal to hire a fifty-six year old woman because she would be unable to participate in the Plan. The legislative history indicates that the latter situation is the one which Congress was most concerned about. A requirement that newly hired older workers be entitled to the same retirement benefit provisions as younger ones would make the cost of funding such retirement plans prohibitive and discourage employers from adopting them. However, it is germane that the language of §4(f)(2) clearly encompasses the former circumstances and that the employer interests which the Act overrides are substantially the same in both cases.

The House of Representatives' Report states that the exception applies both to employee benefit plans existing at the time of enactment of the ADEA and those established thereafter, including the establishment and the maintenance of such plans, and

> serves to emphasize the primary purpose of the bill — hiring of older workers — by permitting employment without necessarily including such workers in employee benefit plans.[144]

This statement and others made during the consideration of the ADEA by Congress led the Wage-Hour Administrator to conclude that it was the intent of Congress to subordinate the importance of adequate pension benefits for older workers in favor of the

---

144. H.R. Rep. No. 805, 4, [1967] U.S. Code Cong. and Admin. News at 2217.

employment of such workers, without necessarily making equal treatment under pension plans a condition of that employment, and to state that

> it is the general position of the Department of Labor that we are not at this time prepared to conclude that the exclusion of a newly-hired individual from a bona fide employee benefit plan is a violation of the statute, where the terms and provisions of the Age Discrimination in Employment Act otherwise apply. Similarly, we are not at this time prepared to conclude that an employer will violate the statute if an excluded employee is not provided with other compensatory benefits in lieu of those provided in the pension or retirement plan involved.[145]

The result, however tentatively adopted, reached by the Wage-Hour Administrator is not mandated by the ADEA and may be contrary to its provisions and its spirit. As has been noted above, the ADEA provides that no employee benefit plan shall excuse the failure to hire any individual. This prohibition can be read to mean that an employer cannot refuse to hire an individual within the protected age bracket simply because the employment would increase the cost to the employer of its employee benefit plan. In addition, an employer permitted to exclude older workers from its employee benefit plan even on an equal cost, as opposed to an equal benefit, basis might, by means of advising older job applicants they would be ineligible to participate in employee benefit plans, discourage them from accepting employment.[146] There is, thus, a danger that permitting employers to totally exclude older workers from employee benefit plans might result in employers using that authorization as a subterfuge to evade the purposes of the ADEA and to totally or largely exclude older workers from their work force. The difficulty of proving this form of discrimination where the older job applicant appears to have rejected the employer,

---

145. Opinion Letter of Wage-Hour Administrator, 8 Lab. Rel. Rep. 401:5227, at 401:5228 (February 9, 1970).

146. It is, however, relevant to note that some benefits which an older employee could expect to accumulate before retirement might be so small as to have little bearing on his decision to accept or reject a particular position.

rather than the more typical and obvious form of age discrimination in employment where the employer rejects the older job applicant, raises serious questions as to the wisdom of the Administrator's position.

The ADEA does not define either "bona fide" or "employee benefit plan" although it does specify examples such as retirement, pension, and insurance plans. The Wage-Hour Administrator has opined that

> In this connection, the term "bona fide" given its generally understood meaning, describes a plan established in good faith to provide certain fringe benefits for employees, and not as a device or subterfuge to avoid the purposes of the Act.[147]

He has further stated that not all employee benefit plans come within the provision, only those similar to the kind enumerated in the ADEA.[148] Thus, a profit-sharing plan as such would not fall within the terms of the statute unless it is the essential purpose of such a plan financed from profits to provide retirement benefits for employees in which case the exception may apply if the plan is "bona fide" under its particular facts and circumstances.[149]

---

147. Opinion Letter of Wage-Hour Administrator (WH-138), 2 CCH Employ. Prac. Guide ¶5030, at 3050, 8 Lab. Rel. Rep. 401:5235 (June 29, 1971). An employee benefit plan put into effect before consideration and enactment of the ADEA in 1967 could not, in the view of some courts, be a device or subterfuge to avoid the purposes of the statute. *See* Brennan v. Taft Broadcasting Co., 500 F.2d 212, 215 (5th Cir. 1974); DeLoraine v. MEBA (Marine Engineers' Beneficial Association) Pension Trust, 499 F.2d 49 (2d Cir. 1974), *cert. denied,* 419 U.S. 1009 (1974); Steiner v. National League of Professional Baseball Clubs, 377 F. Supp. 945, 948 (C.D. Cal. 1974).

148. As the Court of Appeals noted in Brennan v. Taft Broadcasting Co., *supra.*

> The key phrase is "employee benefit plan." The words, "retirement, pension, or insurance," are added in a clearly descriptive sense, not excluding other kinds of employee benefit plans if, conceivably, there could be any. [500 F.2d at 215.]

149. Opinion Letter of Acting Wage-Hour Administrator, 8 Lab. Rel. Rep. 401:5225 (February 18, 1969); 29 C.F.R. § 860.120(b) (1974).

The Wage-Hour Administrator has opined that a profit-sharing thrift plan would not qualify under the retirement plan exception where it provided for mandatory

The Wage-Hour Administrator has refused to give his approval to a retirement pension plan providing, *inter alia,* for involuntary retirement at the employer's discretion of employees ceasing to meet the employer's employment standards which combined attitude, production standards, punctuality, etc., noting that

> As a general rule we have reservations about the bona fides of a plan that does not by its provisions spell out its conditions and limitations and instead is governed by a undefined policy entirely within the discretion of the employer outside the plan. It has been our experience that the operation of a plan in practice is of equal significance as the explicit terms of the plan in determining an employer's compliance status.[150]

The foregoing certainly does not exhaust the inquiry into the meaning of the term "bona fide." For example, in *Donnelly v. Exxon Research & Engineering Co.*[151] the District Court rejected the defendant's argument that a retirement plan which pre-dated the enactment of the ADEA was, for that reason, immune from attack under the statute. The Court held that

> The antiquity of the plan, the fact that it was in existence before the passage of the statute is, in the view of this Court at least, without any legal significance. Once Congress spoke and legislated in this area plans, even of such long-standing antiquity as this one, must give way. And practices, no matter how long established, that would vary from the Congressional intent, must give way as well. Indeed, the very purpose of Congress entering the area was obviously to correct long-standing abuses

employee contributions, its costs were not geared to the age of participating employees, and contributions depended upon the amount of the company's profits, if any, and the payroll deductions authorized by participants amounting to not less than three per cent of their annual earnings. The Wage-Hour Administrator compared that plan with a true retirement plan where contributions depend upon amounts which are actually necessary to provide stipulated retirement benefits to participants. Opinion Letter of Wage-Hour Administrator (No. 287), 2 CCH Employ. Prac. Guide ¶5282 (April 29, 1974).

150. Opinion Letter of Wage-Hour Administrator (WH-289), 2 CCH Employ. Prac. Guide ¶5295, at 3540 (October 10, 1974).

151. 11 CCH Employ. Prac. Dec. ¶10,860, 12 Fair Employ. Prac. Cas. 417 (D.N.J., October 30, 1974) n.o.r., *aff'd without opinion,* 521 F.2d 1398 (3rd Cir. 1975).

in which employees were discriminated against, solely and entirely because they were older employees. And the mere fact that a corporation may have emblazoned that kind of indiscriminate inequality into a plan, is not to be permitted to defeat an Act of Congress which is passed thereafter to correct that very abuse.[152]

The Court's view does not seem to recognize that a retirement plan adopted long before the enactment of the ADEA could not have been adopted as a subterfuge to avoid the purposes of the statute. That was, apparently, the thrust of the defendant's argument. That position does, however, unduly restrict the meaning of the term "bona fide" since continuation of an old benefit plan after enactment of the ADEA could be a subterfuge to avoid the purposes of the statute.

It has been suggested that a court reviewing an employee benefit plan under the ADEA should consider not only whether the age restrictions in the plan were intended to evade the statutory purposes but also whether the age restrictions were unrelated to the economic viability of the plan itself. If either question is answered in the affirmative, one writer would have the court disallow the employer's reliance on the employee benefit plan exception.[153] If a "bona fide plan" is more than simply a plan which is not a subterfuge to avoid the purposes of the statute, then the foregoing proposal has merit.

There are, unfortunately, no guidelines indicating how far a court should go in determining whether a particular benefit plan was, in fact, established in a good faith effort to provide fringe benefits for employees or as a protective cover for prohibited discrimination against older workers. It would certainly be appropriate to require the courts to consider the background to the establishment of a particular benefit plan, including the reasons for its adoption, and the reasonableness of the terms of the plan, such as the size of the benefits involved and the discretion retained

---

152. 11 CCH Employ. Prac. Dec. ¶10,860, at 7636, 12 Fair Employ. Prac. Cas. at 419.

153. Note, *Age Discrimination in Employment,* 50 N.Y.U.L. Rev. 924, 949-51 (1975).

by the employer in implementing the plan with respect to specific individuals.[154]

A mandatory early retirement pension plan permitting termination of employees over 55 years of age with ten or more years of pension credited service with permanent partial disability resulting in excessive absenteeism, decreased production, and frequent application for and receipt of sickness and accident payments was upheld against challenges under the ADEA [155] and a state law prohibiting age discrimination in employment.[156]

The ADEA does not specify what is meant by "subterfuge to evade the purposes of this Act." One writer has suggested that

> The "subterfuge" clause logically applies to those age-based plans which arbitrarily discriminate against older workers, i.e., those that are not necessary to the fiscal viability of pension and retirement plans, evade the purposes of the Act and therefore do not come within the benefit-plan exception.[157]

Under the exception, an employer does not have to provide older workers within the protected age bracket with the same pension, retirement or insurance benefits which he provides for younger workers as long as any differential is in accordance with the terms of a bona fide benefit plan.[158] A retirement, pension or insurance plan will fall within the exception where the actual amount of payments made or costs incurred on behalf of an older worker are

---

154. *See* Kovarsky and Kovarsky, *Economic, Medical and Legal Aspects of the Age Discrimination Laws in Employment*, 27 Vand. L. Rev. 839, 907-908 (1974), urging that courts should consider in determining the bona fides of a pension plan under the ADEA whether the plan was adopted by an employer on its own or jointly with a union; the age provided for compulsory retirement; the circumstances, if any, under which retirement can be postponed; whether the plan provides for compulsory or voluntary retirement; and the amount of the benefits paid under the plan.

155. Thompson v. Chrysler Corp., 406 F. Supp. 1216 (E.D. Mich. 1976).

156. Thompson v. Chrysler Corp., 382 F. Supp. 1317 (E.D. Mich. 1974).

157. Note, *Age Discrimination in Employment,* 50 N.Y.U. L. Rev. 924, 949-50 n. 138 (1975).

158. 29 C.F.R. § 860.120(a) (1974); Opinion Letter of Wage-Hour Administrator, 8 Lab. Rel. Rep. 401:5227, at 401:5228 (February 9, 1970); Opinion Letter of Acting Wage-Hour Administrator, 8 Lab. Rel. Rep. 401:5224 (January 23, 1969).

equal to those made or incurred on behalf of a younger worker even though the older worker may, as a result, receive a lesser amount of pension or retirement benefits or insurance coverage.[159]

It is permissible for an employer to provide varying benefits to employees under a bona fide plan where the differentiation is based on length of service.[160]

5. *Bona Fide Employee Pension and Retirement Plans.* The exception in Section 4(f)(2) of the ADEA[161] to the general prohibitions of the ADEA for bona fide pension and retirement plans which are not subterfuges to evade the purposes of the statute were originally interpreted as permitting an employer to involuntarily retire employees at a fixed age, irrespective of the specific age chosen even though it was within the protected age bracket, provided that the retirement was pursuant to such a

---

159. 29 C.F.R. § 860.120(a) (1974); Opinion Letter of Wage-Hour Administrator, 8 Lab. Rel. Rep. 401:5218 (September 18, 1968); Opinion Letter of Wage-Hour Administrator, 8 Lab. Rel. Rep. 401:5220 (November 13, 1968). Thus, for example, an employer could legally make identical insurance premium payments for all his employees even though older workers would, thereby, receive less coverage than younger workers. *Id.*

The Acting Wage-Hour Administrator has opined, with respect to a state law which prohibited individuals over the age of 45 from becoming members of a specified city's classified service unless they waived any and all rights to participate in any pension system maintained for employees of the city, that

> we do not believe that the absolute exclusion from any pension benefits would be justified for all individuals over age 45; although there may be some subsequent age at which a total or partial exclusion would be justified on the basis of cost.

Opinion Letter of Acting Wage-Hour (WH-341), 2 CCH Employ. Prac. Guide 5355, at 3730 (June 23, 1975).

160. *Cf.* 29 C.F.R. § 860.120(a) (1974). ("when such benefits are determined by a formula invoking age *and* length of service requirements") (emphasis added), *with* Opinion Letter of Wage-Hour Administrator, 8 Lab. Rel. Rep. 401:5216 (September 10, 1968),

> fringe benefits such as vacations or sick leave based upon length of service would not be deemed a violation of the act. This would, of course, be true only where the factor of age had *no* part in the establishment of such benefits. (Emphasis added.)

161. 29 U.S.C. § 623(f)(2) (1970).

plan.[162] Such a plan might, alternatively, provide for retirement at a fixed date rather than on the exact date when an employee reached the age of mandatory retirement.[163]

However, the Secretary of Labor has more recently commenced actions against two railroads challenging their pension plans which impose mandatory retirement at ages younger than 65 on the ground that the plans violate the ADEA.[164] This position is inconsistent with the opinions of the Wage-Hour Administrator

---

162. Grossfield v. W. B. Saunders Co., 1 CCH Employ. Prac. Dec. ¶9941, 1 Fair Employ. Prac. Cas. 624 (S.D.N.Y., December 31, 1968) n.o.r.; 29 CFR § 860.110(a) (1974); Opinion Letter of Deputy Wage-Hour Administrator (WH-29), 8 Lab. Rel. Rep. 401:5229 (April 16, 1970); Opinion Letter of Acting Wage-Hour Administrator, 8 Lab. Rel. Rep. 401:5226 (April 29, 1969); Opinion Letter of Wage-Hour Administrator, 8 Lab. Rel. Rep. 401:5217 (September 13, 1968); Opinion Letter of Wage-Hour Administrator, 8 Lab. Rel. Rep. 401:5215 (September 6, 1968); Opinion Letter of Wage-Hour Administrator, 8 Lab. Rel. Rep. 401:5214 (September 6, 1968).

The United States Secretary of Labor has ruled that a proposal by the City of New York to require a specified number of its employees to retire with full benefits at 63 years of age as an economy measure, rather than the statutory mandatory retirement age of 65, would violate the ADEA, N.Y. Times, Dec. 19, 1974, at 1, col. 5.

But see Donnelly v. Exxon Research & Eng'r Co., 11 CCH Employ. Prac. Dec. ¶10,860, 12 Fair Employ. Prac. Cas. 417 (D.N.J., October 30, 1974) n.o.r., *aff'd without opinion*, 521 F.2d 1398 (3rd Cir. 1975), where the District Court, in considering the involuntary retirement of the plaintiff pursuant to a plan permitting involuntary retirement at age 55 and a policy requiring discharge of workers below 55 and retirement of workers aged 55 and above who failed to meet specified performance standards, held that

> A violation of law must be found, if it exists at all, in the manner and the means used by the defendant in involuntarily retiring the plaintiff. If there was, in the words of the regulation [29 C.F.R. § 860.103(1974)] a reasonable differentiation between the plaintiff and other employees, based on some factor other than age, then his termination is not a violation of statute [*sic*], albeit that it was done pursuant to a plan which permitted the defendant to pay him a pension rather than to terminate him without one. 11 CCH Employ. Prac. Dec. ¶10,860, at 7636, 12 Fair Employ. Prac. Cas. at 419.

163. *See, e.g.,* Grossfield v. W. B. Saunders Co., 1 CCH Employ. Prac. Dec. ¶9941, 1 Fair Employ. Prac. Cas. 624 (S.D.N.Y., December 31, 1968) (the December 31st nearest the employee's 65th birthday) n.o.r.; Opinion Letter of Deputy Wage-Hour Administrator, 8 Lab. Rel. Rep. 401:5219 (October 28, 1968).

164. N.Y. Times, June 20, 1974, at 23. Earlier challenges to the mandatory retirement provisions of railroad pension plans have been discussed at pp. 40-42, *supra*.

cited above which were issued shortly after the enactment of the ADEA and represents a revision of the Department of Labor's position. Indicative of this change is the following statement contained in the Department of Labor's annual report to Congress under the ADEA for 1974:

> An area of continuing concern is the whole question of mandatory retirement before age 65. Generally, the Department takes the position that such retirements are unlawful unless the mandatory retirement provision: (1) is contained in a bona fide pension or retirement plan, (2) is required by the terms of the plan and is not optional, and (3) is essential to the plan's economic survival or to some other legitimate purpose — i.e., is not in the plan for the sole urpose [sic] of moving out older workers, which purpose has now been made unlawful by the ADEA.[165]

It has properly been suggested by one commentator that the choice of a particular age for mandatory retirement pursuant to a pension or retirement plan below 65 years of age should be subject to challenge under the ADEA if the age chosen bears no reasonable relation to a particular job since the pension or retirement plan could then be said to not be bona fide but instead a subterfuge to evade the purposes of the statute.[166] There is, however, no support in the legislative history of the ADEA or, as yet, in the cases decided under the statute for that position.

A covered employer may not involuntarily retire an employee within the protected age bracket before age 65 if the employee is not a participant in a bona fide pension or retirement plan even though other employees of the same employer who are participants

---

165. Employment Standards Administration, U.S. Dept. of Labor, *A Report Covering Activities Under the Act During 1974* at 17 (1975).

166. Levien, *The Age Discrimination in Employment Act: Statutory Requirements and Recent Developments*, 13 Duq. L. Rev. 227, 242-43 (1974). *Cf.* Murgia v. Commonwealth of Mass. Bd. of Retirement, 376 F. Supp. 753 (D. Mass. 1974), *reversed*, 427 U.S. 307 (1976), discussed pp. 51-58, *supra. See also* Gilfix, *First Hired-First Fired: Age Discrimination in Employment*, 50 Cal. State Bar J. 462, 510 (1975), arguing that the Secretary of Labor's regulation permitting mandatory retirement before age 65 pursuant to a bona fide plan, 29 C.F.R. § 860.110 (1974), is "conceptually untenable" under the ADEA.

in such a plan can be involuntarily retired at an earlier age fixed in the plan.[167]

An employee who becomes eligible for retirement cannot on that ground be discharged or forced to retire unless the applicable pension or retirement plan requires the employee's mandatory retirement.[168]

An employer may permit an employee who is a participant in a bona fide pension or retirement plan to continue working after reaching the mandatory retirement age fixed in the plan without calling into question the bona fides of the plan or causing the plan to become ineligible for the exception provided for in the ADEA, even though other employee-participants in the plan are given a shorter waiver of the mandatory retirement provision of the plan or are required to retire at the age fixed in the plan.[169] Such a practice permits the older worker to continue working and, thus, is consistent with the purposes of the ADEA.

---

167. Hodgson v. American Hardware Mut. Ins. Co., 329 F. Supp. 225 (D. Minn. 1971); 29 C.F.R. § 860.110(b) (1974); Opinion Letter of Acting Wage-Hour Administrator, 8 Lab. Rel. Rep. 401:5226 (April 29, 1969); Opinion Letter of Wage-Hour Administrator, 8 Lab. Rel. Rep. 401:5215 (September 6, 1968).

168. Opinion Letter of Acting Wage-Hour Administrator (WH-360), 2 CCH Employ. Prac. Guide ¶5366 (August 19, 1975).

169. Steiner v. National League of Professional Baseball Clubs, 377 F. Supp. 945 (C.D.Cal. 1974); 29 C.F.R. § 860.110(a) (1974); Opinion Letter of Deputy Wage-Hour Administrator, 8 Lab. Rel. Rep. 401:5219 (October 28, 1968). In addition, an employer who allows an employee-participant in a bona fide pension or retirement plan to continue working beyond the mandatory retirement age may exclude the employee from receiving any additional pension benefit for work beyond the mandatory retirement date, Opinion Letter of Deputy Wage-Hour Administrator (WH-29), 8 Lab. Rel. Rep. 401:5229 (April 16, 1970). On the other hand, a covered employer was advised that it could not change its retirement plan to provide for the cessation of the accumulation of benefits under a retirement plan at an age within the protected age bracket which is lower than the age of mandatory retirement since such a provision would, in effect, reduce the total cost of employing workers older than the selected age and lower their wages by the amount previously contributed on their behalf and discriminate against them as opposed to younger workers. Opinion Letter of Wage-Hour Administrator, 8 Lab. Rel. Rep. 401:5216 (September 11, 1968).

Similarly, an employer can rehire former employees previously retired pursuant to a bona fide pension or retirement plan.[170] It has been held that an employer is under no obligation to rehire a former employee after he has been properly retired under a bona fide pension or retirement plan despite what appears to be a conflict between the provisions of the ADEA.[171]

The ADEA does not, of course, apply to plans requiring mandatory retirement at age 65 or older [172] or to employees working beyond that age.[173]

6. *Bona Fide Apprenticeship Programs.* The ADEA, unlike some state laws dealing with age discrimination in employment, contains

---

170. Opinion Letter of Wage-Hour Administrator, 8 Lab. Rel. Rep. 401:5217 (September 13, 1968) (The ADEA requires "that such an individual be considered in the same light as any other applicant."); Opinion Letter of Wage-Hour Administrator, 8 Lab. Rel. Rep. 401:5209 (August 7, 1968) ("provided that such employer does not discriminate on the basis of age against any other job applicant who is within the 40-65 age bracket").

171. Brennan v. Taft Broadcasting Co., 500 F.2d 212, 218 (5th Cir. 1974):

> The last clause in 29 U.S.C.A. § 623(f) (2) provides that "[no employee benefit plan] shall excuse the failure to hire any individual". Relying on the literal language of this section, the Secretary [of Labor] contends that the failure to hire "any individual" is illegal regardless of whether that individual has already been legally retired by the entity from whom he seeks the employment.
>
> The Secretary's construction would render meaningless the statutory language allowing employers "to observe the terms of bona fide employee benefit plans such as retirement ... plans".If retired employees must be rehired immediately, the right to insist on compliance with a plan is an illusion. Congress could not have possibly intended, or directed, such a contradictory result.

Cf. Opinion Letter of Wage-Hour Administrator, 8 Lab. Rel. Rep. 401:5204 (July 11, 1968), stating that there is no provision in the ADEA which would require an employer to provide other employment for individuals who are mandatorily retired under Federal regulatory requirements which provide for compulsory retirement without reference to an individual's actual physical condition at the terminal age when such conditions or qualifications are clearly imposed for the safety and convenience of the public.

172. Opinion Letter of Wage-Hour Administrator, 8 Lab. Rel. Rep. 401:5211 (August 12, 1968).

173. That is a matter for agreement between employer and employee. *Id.;* Opinion Letter of Wage-Hour Administrator, 8 Lab. Rel. Rep. 401:5212 (August 14, 1968).

no exception from its prohibitions for apprenticeship programs.[174] However, the Secretary of Labor has, by regulation, provided that the prohibitions contained in the ADEA will not be applied to bona fide apprenticeship programs meeting standards set by the Secretary [175] based on a determination that

> Age limitations for entry into bona fide apprenticeship programs were not intended to be affected by the Act. Entry into most apprenticeship programs has traditionally been limited to youths under specified ages. This is in recognition of the fact that apprenticeship is an extension of the educational process to prepare young men and women for skilled employment.[176]

While the Secretary of Labor presents no authority for his position, it is not unreasonable or clearly inconsistent with the legislative history of the ADEA.[177] The Wage-Hour Administrator

---

174. *See, e.g.,* Conn. Gen. Stat. Ann. § 31-126(4) (Cum. Supp. 1976); Del. Code Ann., tit. 19, § 711(e)(1) (1975); Cal. Labor Code § 1420.1(c) (West Cum. Supp. 1976); Mich. Stat. Ann. § 17.458(3a)(a) (1975) rev. vol.), *Contra,* Del. Code Ann., tit. 19, § 711(d) (1975); New York, N.Y., Admin. Code § B1-7.0[1-a](a) (1971); N.Y. Exec. Law § 296[1-a](a) (McKinney Cum. Supp. 1976); W. Va. Code § 5-11-9(d) (Cum. Supp. 1976). *See also* Judson v. Apprenticeship and Training Council, 9 Ore. App. 367, 495 P.2d 291 (Ct. of App. 1972); Brown and Williamson Tobacco Corp. and Int'l Assoc. of Machinists and Aerospace Workers, Local Number 681, Case No. 421-E (Ky. Commission on Human Rights, December 12, 1975) (holding that a labor management apprenticeship program meeting the Federal standards for exemption from the prohibitions of the ADEA, [*see* footnote 175, *infra,* and accompanying text] with a maximum age limit of 38 violated the state law against age discrimination in employment) n.o.r., *digested in* 2 CCH Employ. Prac. Guide ¶5362.

175. The standards for apprenticeship programs are set forth in 29 C.F.R. §§ 521.1, 521.3 (1974).

176. 29 C.F.R. § 860.106 (1974).

177. The Secretary of Labor would have the power to exclude apprenticeship programs from the prohibitions of the ADEA under Section 9 of the statute, 29 U.S.C. § 628 (1970), after conducting the proceeding required by that section. *See, however,* Release of U.S. Department of Labor dated February 5, 1969, CCH [Transfer Binder — New Developments, Aug. 1968 — April, 1969] Lab. L. Rep. ¶8075, announcing the Department of Labor's regulation exempting bona fide apprenticeship programs and stating that

> The Age Discrimination in Employment Act seemed to include apprenticeship,.... [*Id.* at 6128.]

One author, urging the courts to reject the regulation, notes that the exception for apprenticeship programs forecloses an important method by which persons within

has, further, advised an employer that, while its refusal to hire an inexperienced 62 year old applicant for a job requiring approximately three years of training when the individual applicant would have to retire at age 65 could result in a technical violation of the ADEA, the Wage-Hour Division would not be prepared to take enforcement action against the activity despite the fact that the training program did not meet the standards for a bona fide apprenticeship program.[178]

Where age is not a bona fide occupational qualification, the establishment in an agreement between a covered employer and a labor organization of a maximum age for entry into the employer's training program has been held to be in violation of the ADEA since the cost of the training program in relation to the amount of service which could be expected from the trainees "would not seem relevant to the matter of occupational qualification." [179]

7. *Job Applications.* The Secretary of Labor has provided by regulation special rules governing "job applications." The term is defined to include: all pre-employment inquiries about employment or applications for employment or promotion including, but not limited to, resumes or other summaries of the applicant's background as well as inquiries by employees concerning terms, conditions, or privileges of employment.[180]

The regulation states that a request on the part of an employer, employment agency, or labor organization subject to the provisions of the ADEA for information, such as "date of birth" or "state age," on an employment application form is not, in itself, a violation

the protected age bracket might obtain employment by means of a regulation promulgated under a statute meant to protect them. Gilfix, *First Hired-First Fired: Age Discrimination in Employment,* 50 Cal. State Bar J. 462, 510 (1975).

178. Opinion Letter of Wage-Hour Administrator (WH-119), 8 Lab. Rel. Rep. 401:5233 (January 20, 1971).

179. Opinion Letter of Acting Wage-Hour Administrator, 8 Lab. Rel. Rep. 401:5227 (May 1, 1969); Opinion Letter of Acting Wage-Hour Administrator, 8 Lab. Rel. Rep. 401:5226 (April 29, 1969).

180. 29 C.F.R. § 860.95(a) (1974).

of the ADEA. However, because such a request may tend to deter older applicants or otherwise indicate a discrimination based on age, employment applications which request such information by means of those or any similar phrases will be closely scrutinized to assure that the request is for a permissible purpose and not for purposes proscribed by the ADEA. The applicant is required to be advised that the purpose is not one proscribed by the statute as by means of a reference on the application form to the statutory prohibition in language to the effect that the ADEA prohibits discrimination on the basis of age with respect to individuals between 40 and 65 years of age.[181]

An employer can lawfully limit the active period of consideration given to a job application so long as he treats all applicants alike regardless of age. Thus, if an employer customarily retains employment applications in an active status for a period of 60 days, he will be in compliance with the ADEA if he retains those of individuals in the 40 to 65 age group for an equal period of consideration to that used in the case of younger persons. An employer can advise all applicants of such a practice by means of a legend on his application forms as long as this does not suggest any limitation based on age. The regulations further provide that if, however, it develops that such a legend is used as a device to avoid consideration of the applications of older persons or otherwise discriminate against them because of age, there would then appear to be a violation of the ADEA.[182]

The Acting Wage-Hour Administrator has opined that the mere failure of an employer to acknowledge responses to his advertisement of a job opening would not, without more, be sufficient to constitute prima facie evidence of age discrimination sufficient to support a complaint under the ADEA. Some evidence as to the application of an age limit or requirement contrary to the ADEA would be necessary to support such a complaint.[183]

---

181. 29 C.F.R. § 860.95(a) (1974).

182. 29 C.F.R. § 860.95(b) (1974). *See also* Opinion Letter of Acting Wage-Hour Administrator, 8 Lab. Rel. Rep. 401:5223 (January 27, 1969).

183. Opinion Letter of Acting Wage-Hour Administrator, 8 Lab. Rel. Rep. 401:5222 (January 7, 1969).

8. *Discharge or Other Discipline for Good Cause.* Section 4(f)(3) of the ADEA [184] permitting the discharge or disciplining of an individual for good cause simply puts persons in the protected age bracket in the same position as other persons and prevents them from taking unfair advantage of the protections afforded them by the ADEA.

In *Brennan v. Reynolds & Co.,*[185] the defendant-employer asserted that it had discharged the plaintiff for repeated tardiness and not, as claimed by plaintiff, because of her age. The Court, in upholding the defendant's "good cause" defense, noted that

> only where the "good cause" is unlawful may a court substitute its judgment for that of management as to what constitutes proper cause for discharge.[186]

and found that

> under Section 623(f)(3) once an employer has demonstrated that its employee's conduct is "good cause" for termination the statutory condition precedent has been satisfied and the employer's action is valid.[187]

The Court analyzed the "good cause" exception as follows:

> Section 621, [which sets forth the purposes of the ADEA,] is concerned about age discrimination. Its purpose is not to solve other problems about employment. In approving "discharge for good cause" as a defense to an action under 621, it is not my purpose to label as a "for good cause discharge" any kind of discharge other than one based "merely upon the age factor." Section 621 does not cast upon the Court the duty of determining that a discharge was, for reasons other than age, a justifiable discharge. It serves only to prevent discharge because of age alone. However, even when age is but one of a number of causes for discharge, the finding must be that the discharge was not "for good cause", within the meaning of 621. Otherwise Congressional intent expressed through the statute would be defeated. On the other hand, where the discharge is that of a person whose "age" by tradition and custom was excessive, where it actually was not the

---

184. 29 U.S.C. § 623(f)(3) (1970).
185. 367 F. Supp. 440 (N.D. Ill. 1973).
186. 367 F. Supp. at 443.
187. 367 F. Supp. at 444.

employer's consideration, discharge for other reasons would under the statute be a "good cause" for discharge.[188]

In *Bittar v. Air Canada*,[189] plaintiff's discharge for dereliction of duty was upheld under the good cause provision of the ADEA. The District Court also found that plaintiff had failed to establish that her termination was based upon age or any other cause prohibited by the ADEA.

A district court's conclusion that a discharge was for good cause was upheld on appeal as not clearly erroneous where the trial court held that there was no corroboration for plaintiff's claim that he was discharged because of his age, that it was reasonable to find that plaintiff's superior had concluded that plaintiff had failed to fulfill satisfactorily the business responsibility which had been assigned to him and that a change had to be made if the superior's responsibilities to their employer were to be fulfilled.[190]

K. ENFORCEMENT OF THE ADEA

The success of a broad remedial statute, such as the ADEA, in dealing with the problem which it was enacted to prevent is directly related to the manner in which, and the vigor with which, it is enforced and to the attitude of the courts before which enforcement of the statute is sought. Thus, if those charged with enforcing or interpreting a statute adopt a restrictive or antagonistic approach, the administrative and judicial actions brought under the statute and the decisions in such actions may

---

188. *Id.*

189. 10 Fair Employ. Prac. Cas. 1136 (S.D. Fla., September 25, 1974) n.o.r., *aff'd per curiam,* 512 F.2d 582 (5th Cir. 1975).

To the same effect *see* Leach v. Hilti, Inc., 414 F. Supp. 3 (E.D. Mo. 1975) (plaintiff's termination based on his poor sales performance not his age); Moses v. Falstaff Brewing Corp., 13 Fair Employ. Prac. Cas. 347 (E.D. Mo., June 15, 1976) (discharged due to termination of plaintiff's position and not to discriminatory action by defendant) n.o.r.

190. Surrisi v. Conwed Corp., 510 F.2d 1088 (8th Cir. 1975), *affirming* 10 Fair Employ. Prac. Cas. 706 (D. Minn., March 25, 1974) n.o.r. The Court of Appeals noted that the case did not present and the Court did not, therefore, express any opinion on the question of whether the defendant-employer had an obligation to offer the plaintiff continued employment in another available position commensurate with his ability.

result in an extra-legislative revision of the statute contrary to the intendment of the legislature which enacted it. Such a restrictive approach to a statute will not only result in decisions contrary to the legislative purpose in individual cases but will also discourage voluntary cooperation in eliminating the problem with which the legislation was meant to deal. On the other hand, such cooperation would be encouraged by a philosophical approach by the courts and administrators consistent with the objectives of the legislature in enacting the statute.[191]

The ADEA incorporates a dual faceted approach to enforcing its provisions consisting of formal and informal methods and official and private actions. Those procedures are described below.

The official administration and enforcement of the ADEA has been delegated by the Secretary of Labor to the Wage and Hour and Public Contracts Division of the United States Department of Labor which maintain regional, district, and field offices throughout the United States.[192]

1. *Posting of Notices.* Enforcement of the ADEA requires identification of possible violations. There are two general means by which possible violations can be uncovered — investigations by the Wage and Hour Division [193] and complaints by persons

---

191. *See* Moses v. Falstaff Brewing Corp., 525 F.2d 92, 93 (8th Cir. 1975) ("The Age Discrimination Act is remedial and humanitarian legislation. It is to be construed liberally to achieve its purpose of protecting older employees from discrimination."); Surrisi v. Conwed Corp., 510 F.2d 1088, 1090 (8th Cir. 1975), where the Court of Appeals stated that

We note that the Age Discrimination in Employment Act of 1967 is remedial in nature, * * *. It prohibits a particularly subtle form of discrimination, and the courts must be receptive to its purposes and accord it the intended scope.

Skoglund v. Singer Co., 403 F. Supp. 797, 801 (D.N.H. 1975),:

ADEA is remedial legislation with the broad purpose of ending age discrimination in the United States. 29 U.S.C. § 621. Remedial legislation should not be so narrowly read as to preclude achievement of its purpose; form should not be raised over substance.

192. Opinion Letter of Wage-Hour Administrator, 8 Lab. Rel. Rep. 401:5215 (September 9, 1968).

193. In a speech before the National Council of Senior Citizens on June 5, 1969, the Wage-Hour Administrator stated that "Generally, most of the investigations under the ADEA are conducted in conjunction with investigations under the FLSA [Fair Labor Standards Act] and other laws enforced by the Divisions." CCH

claiming that they have been discriminated against in violation of the ADEA.

Before individuals can assert claims of violations of the ADEA, persons covered by the ADEA must be made aware of the protections afforded them under the statute.[194] Accordingly, Section 8 of the ADEA requires every covered employer, employment agency, and labor organization to post and keep posted in conspicuous places upon its premises a notice prepared or approved by the Secretary of Labor setting forth the information he deems appropriate to effectuate the statute's purposes.[195]

2. *Investigations by Secretary of Labor.* The Secretary of Labor is given the power by Section 7(a) of the ADEA to make investigations necessary or appropriate for the administration of the statute by incorporation of certain provisions of the Fair Labor Standards Act of 1938 granting him the authority: (1) to require the attendance of witnesses and the production of books, papers, and documents; [196] (2) to utilize the bureaus and divisions of the United States Department of Labor to investigate and gather data from persons subject to the provisions of the ADEA and to enter and inspect such places and records, question such employees, and investigate such facts, conditions, practices, or matters as he may deem necessary or appropriate to determine whether any person has violated any provision of the statute, or which may aid in

---

[Transfer Binder — New Developments, June, 1969 — December, 1969] Lab. L. Rep. ¶8031, at 6055. He noted, however, that special investigations looking solely for age discrimination might be needed as well because larger firms rarely break the other laws administered by the Wage and Hour Division. *Id.* at 6056.

194. *See* Edwards v. Kaiser Aluminum & Chemical Sales, Inc., 515 F.2d 1195, 1197 (5th Cir. 1975).

195. 29 U.S.C. § 627 (1970). The Secretary of Labor's regulations require that "a notice must be posted in prominent and accessible places where it can readily be observed by employees, applicants for employment and union members." 29 C.F.R. § 850.10 (1974). The Secretary of Labor has designated a particular notice which must be posted pursuant to this section of the ADEA. The notice has been designated U.S. Department of Labor Employment Standards Administration Publication 1289. A reproduction of the current form of the Secretary of Labor's notice is contained in Appendix C. to this book.

196. 29 U.S.C. § 626(a) (1970) *incorporating* 29 U.S.C. § 209 (1970) (FLSA) *incorporating* 29 U.S.C. §§ 49, 50 (1970).

enforcing the provisions of the ADEA;[197] and (3) to utilize the services of state and local agencies and their employees with the consent and cooperation of state agencies charged with administering the state labor laws and to reimburse such state and local agencies and their employees for services rendered for such purposes.[198]

The ability of the Secretary of Labor to conduct investigations permits him not only to uncover violations of the ADEA and examine claims of violations made by individuals but also to obtain evidence which encourages informal settlements by violators and permits effective prosecution of actions where informal settlements cannot be negotiated.[199]

3. *Procedure for Initiation of Legal Action.* The ADEA provides for legal actions to redress violations of its provisions by both the Secretary of Labor and individuals alleging that they have been discriminated against.[200] However, prior to the filing of a legal action under the ADEA certain preliminary procedures must be complied with by the Secretary and by individuals.

a. PRELIMINARY PROCEDURES FOR INDIVIDUALS. Section 7(c) of the ADEA provides that any person aggrieved may bring a civil action in any court of competent jurisdiction for such legal or equitable relief as will effectuate the purposes of the statute. However, the right of a person to bring such an action terminates upon the commencement of an action by the Secretary of Labor

---

197. 29 U.S.C. § 626(a) (1970) *incorporating* 29 U.S.C. § 211(a) (1970) (FLSA).

198. 29 U.S.C. § 626(a) (1970) *incorporating* 29 U.S.C. § 211(b) (1970) (FLSA).

199. *See* Wallace, *Age Discrimination In Employment Under Federal Law,* 9 Ga. State Bar J. 114, 118 (1972). It has been suggested by one writer that individuals claiming to have been injured by a violation of the ADEA should be given access to the information obtained by the Secretary of Labor in the course of his investigations as a means of discouraging meritless private suits and encouraging settlement of justified private actions. Gilfix, *First Hired-First Fired: Age Discrimination in Employment,* 50 Cal. State Bar J. 462, 511-12 (1975). Such prelitigation "discovery" in a private setting would, however, be contrary to the normal American practice. In addition, the statutory grant of authority for such investigations by the Secretary of Labor does not provide for the release of information obtained in connection therewith to third parties. A prospective plaintiff can, in any event, quickly develop similar information by means of pre-trial discovery once he has commenced an action.

200. H.R. Rep. No. 805, 5-6, [1967] U.S. Code Cong. and Admin. News at 2118.

to enforce the rights of such "employee" under the ADEA.[201] The termination of the individual's right to maintain an action upon commencement of an action by the Secretary of Labor "covering the particular grievance for which vindication is sought" is meant to permit "the Secretary to discharge his responsibilities to achieve to the optimum the purposes of the act. . . ." [202]

i. Federal-State Relationship. — In recognition of the federal form of government in the United States, Section 14(a) of the ADEA provides that nothing therein shall affect the jurisdiction of any agency of any state performing like functions with regard to discriminatory employment practices on account of age except that upon commencement of an action under the ADEA such action supersedes any state action.[203]

In addition, Section 14(b) provides that where an alleged unlawful practice occurs in a state which has a law prohibiting discrimination in employment because of age and establishing or authorizing a state authority to grant or seek relief from such discriminatory practice, no suit may be brought under the ADEA "before the expiration of sixty days after proceedings have been commenced under the state law, unless such proceedings have been earlier terminated. . . ." [204]

---

201. 29 U.S.C. § 626(c) (1970). The word "employee" in Section 7(c) must be read to include applicants for employment and former employees if the purposes of the ADEA are to be effectuated. *See* Opinion Letter of Acting Wage-Hour Administrator, 8 Lab. Rel. Rep. 401:5222 (January 7, 1969); Opinion Letter of Wage-Hour Assistant Administrator (WH-136), 8 Lab. Rel. Rep. 401:5234 (May 28, 1971).

Although no court has decided the question, it would appear that once an individual brings an action under the ADEA the Secretary of Labor's power to commence an action and, thereby, terminate the individual's right to do so is ended. *But see* Bishop v. Jelleff Associates, Inc., 398 F. Supp. 579, 592 (D.D.C. 1974) ("[T]he Secretary [of Labor] is empowered to initiate proceedings to supersede pending litigation instituted under the Act. 29 U.S.C. § 626(c). ") *(dictum)*.

202. H.R. Rep. No. 805, 5, [1967] U.S. Code Cong. and Admin. News at 2218.

203. 29 U.S.C. § 633(a) (1970).

204. 29 U.S.C. § 633(b) (1970). The period is extended to 120 days during the first year after the effective date of such a state law. *Id.* Skoglund v. Singer Co., 403 F. Supp. 797, 801 (D.N.H. 1975) ("The purpose of Section 633(b) is to further state-federal relations. ***. Section 633(b) manifests Congressional intent to defer

If any requirement is imposed by a state authority for the commencement of state proceedings other than a requirement for the filing of a written and signed statement of the facts upon which the proceeding is based, the proceeding is deemed to have been commenced for the purposes of the ADEA provision at the time such a statement is sent by registered mail to the appropriate state authority.[204a]

These provisions are meant to preserve and encourage state legislation dealing with age discrimination in employment [205] since each such law increases the agencies, funds, and personnel engaged in fighting the problem. In the absence of such provisions, the ADEA might be held to preempt the area and would, in any case, stultify development of state procedures for dealing with age discrimination in employment. It should be noted that the short 60 day period generally allotted to proceedings in qualifying states is barely enough to permit attempts at informal settlements and is clearly not sufficient to permit conclusion of a state court action.

It is not, however, every state law relating to age discrimination in employment which is entitled to such special primacy. It is

> only where the State law prohibiting discrimination in employment because of age establishes or authorizes a state authority to grant or seek relief from such discriminatory practice.[206]

---

to the states' efforts to remedy age discrimination within their own boundaries. It allows the states a minimum of sixty days to attempt to redress a grievance prior to any federal judicial action in the case.").

204a. 29 U.S.C. § 633(b) (1970).

205. *See* Letter from United States Secretary of Labor W. Willard Wirtz to Speaker of the United States House of Representatives John W. McCormack, January 23, 1967, reprinted in BNA Daily Labor Report No. 20 — 1/30/67 at AA-1.

206. Opinion Letter of Acting Wage-Hour Administrator, 8 Lab. Rel. Rep. 401:5223 (January 7, 1969). In that letter, the Acting Wage-Hour Administrator opined that a state law providing only for fines of not less than $50 nor more than $100 for each wilful violation was not entitled to precedence.

Eklund v. Lubrizol Corp., 529 F.2d 247, 249 (6th Cir. 1976) ("Section 633(b) envisions a state authority equipped to investigate age discrimination claims, to mediate genuine disputes, to attempt to resolve disputes through voluntary compliance and, if necessary, to initiate administrative or judicial proceedings to secure compliance with the state age discrimination law."). *Accord.* Arnold v. Hawaiian Tel. Co., 11 CCH Employ. Prac. Dec. ¶10,786, 12 Fair Employ. Prac. Cas.

The fact that a state agency, found to have been specifically charged by the state's legislature with dealing with age discrimination in employment complaints under a state law prohibiting such discrimination, had a shortage in personnel and funding for investigating such complaints and followed a policy of referring all age discrimination claims of persons within the ADEA's protected age bracket to the Federal Wage and Hour Division without undertaking any investigation or attempt at conciliation of a claim pursuant to a tacit understanding with Federal officials was held insufficient to obviate the statutory requirement that a person complaining of age discrimination in

---

400 (D. Hawaii, June 30, 1975) n.o.r.; Vazquez v. Eastern Air Lines, 11 CCH Employ. Prac. Dec. ¶10,617, at 6574, 12 Fair Employ. Prac. Cas. 686, 691 (D.P.R., December 30, 1975) n.o.r. In Garces v. Sagner Int'l Inc., 534 F.2d 987 (1st Cir. 1976), the Court of Appeals held that Puerto Rico's laws dealing with age discrimination in employment did not satisfy the requirements of Section 14(b) of the ADEA so as to require deferral. The Court of Appeals noted that, while Puerto Rican law permitted either aggrieved individuals or the Secretary of Labor of the Commonwealth to file suit for damages or other relief against persons engaging in prohibited age discrimination in employment, there was no provision for administrative action such as investigation, mediation, or conciliation of claims of age discrimination. The Court of Appeals held that the underlying policy of the deferral procedure was to "allow time for the processes of conciliation to be fully explored through appropriate state machinery before resorting to litigation." 534 F.2d at 989. Since the Commonwealth Secretary of Labor was not required to seek administrative resolution of age discrimination claims and the only other alternative would be the pointless and wasteful formality of filing a lawsuit in the Commonwealth courts which would be abandoned after 60 days for an action under the ADEA, the Court of Appeals concluded that

> Puerto Rico has not made the kind of institutional commitment, assuring administrative exploration of all age discrimination claims prior to litigation, on which a duty to defer federal court action may be predicated. [534 F.2d at 990.]

Curry v. Continental Airlines, 513 F.2d 691 (9th Cir. 1975) (where the Court of Appeals reversed the trial court and held that the plaintiff had no obligation under the ADEA to first seek relief under state law where the state had a statute prohibiting age discrimination in employment but the only penalty for a violation of the statute was criminal prosecution of an alleged violator, there were no state personnel assigned to handling age discrimination complaints, and potential plaintiffs were advised by state authorities to take their complaints to local law enforcement officials or the Federal government).

connection with employment seek redress through state procedures before instituting an action under the ADEA.[207] The Court rejected what it termed a practical test or standard for construing Section 633(b). Noting that reference to state procedure would only delay action under the ADEA for 60 days, it stated that

> This court believes that Congress did not intend the courts to engage in a fact-finding judicial inquiry into whether or not a particular state agency is adequately funded and staffed to carry out its statutory duties and responsibilities merely for the purpose of determining whether the statutory prerequisites for filing suit have been satisfied.[208]

One court has held that an employee who was 59 years old when he was discharged allegedly in violation of the ADEA and 60 years old when he filed suit under the statute was required to first file a complaint with the appropriate state authority although the state law only protected persons under 60 years of age from age discrimination in employment.[209] This holding ignores the fact that damages for wrongful discharge under the ADEA have been held recoverable until either a plaintiff is offered reinstatement at the conclusion of a trial or reaches 65 years of age, whichever occurs first.[210] If a person will reach the maximum age limit under the applicable state law, which is lower than 65 years of age, before a trial or other state proceeding can be concluded and relief granted, then to require that person to first apply for relief under the state law before proceeding in Federal court under the ADEA

---

207. Arnold v. Hawaiian Tel. Co., 11 CCH Employ. Prac. Dec. ¶10,786, 12 Fair Employ. Prac. Cas. 400 (D. Hawaii, June 30, 1975) n.o.r.

208. 11 CCH Employ. Prac. Dec. ¶10,786, at 7306, 12 Fair Employ. Prac. Cas. at 403.

209. Rucker v. Great Scott Supermarkets, Inc., 10 CCH Employ. Prac. Dec. ¶10,508, 11 Fair Employ. Prac. Cas. 473 (E.D. Mich., November 13, 1974) (The Court erroneously refers to the applicable statutory provision as "Sec. 14(b) of the Fair Labor Standard Act. . . ." 10 CCH Employ. Prac. Dec. ¶10,508, at 6161, 11 Fair Employ. Prac. Cas. at 473) n.o.r., aff'd on another ground, 528 F.2d 393 (6th Cir. 1976).

210. See pp. 197-201, infra.

is both illogical and wasteful. Since the state authority could not grant to or seek for the person all the relief to which he is entitled under the ADEA and there is nothing in the statute requiring a person to accept lesser relief under state law, he should not have been required to seek relief under state law as a condition precedent to proceeding under the ADEA. This result can be achieved by reading the phrase "relief from such discriminatory practice" to mean relief substantially equivalent to that available under the ADEA. This would excuse a person who is less than 65 years of age but older than the maximum protected age under a particular state law from having to resort first to state law where he could not in any case obtain under that law all the relief to which he is entitled under the ADEA. Any other result would allow a state to unilaterally reduce the relief to which an individual is entitled under the ADEA.

The ADEA does not make it clear whether an individual must first resort to available state procedures before proceeding under the ADEA if the alleged discriminatory act takes place in a state with a statute entitled to primacy or whether an individual can choose to proceed under the ADEA initially and not look to the state procedures at all. The ADEA speaks only of the period "after proceedings have been commenced under the State law." It does not require by its terms that such a state proceeding must be commenced.[211] The legislative history of the ADEA is similarly vague.[212]

Despite the unclear language of the ADEA, the courts have almost uniformly held that the ADEA requires that an individual

---

211. This view has been adopted by the Court in Vazquez v. Eastern Airlines, 11 CCH Employ. Prac. Dec. ¶10,617, 12 Fair Employ. Prac. Cas. 686 (D.P.R., December 30, 1975) n.o.r. The Secretary of Labor unsuccessfully argued this position in an amicus brief in Goger v. H.K. Porter Co., 492 F.2d 13, 17-18 (3rd Cir. 1974) (Garth, C. J., concurring).

See also Levien, The Age Discrimination in Employment Act: Statutory Requirements and Recent Development, 13 Duq. L. Rev. 227, 232-34 (1974); and Note, State Deferral of Complaints Under the Age Discrimination in Employment Act, 51 Notre Dame Law. 492, 495 (1976) (citing Levien, supra).

212. See, e.g., H.R. Rep. No. 805, 6, 11-12, [1967] U.S. Code Cong. and Admin. News at 2218-19, 2224.

must first seek relief under state law if the alleged discriminatory act took place in a state with a statute under which relief from the claimed discrimination is available and that this requirement is jurisdictional so that failure to comply therewith mandates dismissal of a Federal court action brought under the ADEA.[213]

---

213. Curry v. Continental Airlines, 513 F.2d 691 (9th Cir. 1975); Arnold v. Hawaiian Tel. Co., 11 CCH Employ. Prac. Dec. ¶10,786, at 7307, 12 Fair Employ. Prac. Cas. 400,404 (D. Hawaii, June 30, 1975) n.o.r.; Balc v. United Steelworkers of America, AFL-CIO, 6 CCH Employ. Prac. Dec. ¶8948, 6 Fair Employ. Prac. Cas. 824 (W.D. Pa., October 19, 1973) n.o.r., aff'd without opinion, 503 F.2d 1398 (3rd Cir. 1974); Goger v. H.K. Porter Co., 5 CCH Employ. Prac. Dec. ¶8562, 5 Fair Employ. Prac. Cas. 695 (D.N.J., January 23, 1973) n.o.r., aff'd in part and vacated and remanded on other grounds, 492 F.2d 13 (3rd Cir. 1974); McGarvey v. Merck and Co., 359 F. Supp. 525 (D.N.J. 1973), vacated and remanded without opinion, 493 F.2d 1401 (3rd Cir. 1974), cert. denied, 419 U.S. 836 (1974); Garces v. Sagner Int'l, Inc., 12 Fair Employ. Prac. Cas. 569 (D.P.R., December 2, 1974) n.o.r., reversed on other grounds, 534 F.2d 987 (1st Cir. 1976); Negron v. Pan Am. World Airways, 12 Fair Employ. Prac. Cas. 569 (D.P.R., December 2, 1974) n.o.r., reversed on other grounds sub nom. Garces v. Sagner Int'l, Inc., 534 F.2d 987 (1st Cir. 1976); Rucker v. Great Scott Supermarkets, Inc., 10 CCH Employ. Prac. Dec. ¶10,508, 11 Fair Employ. Prac. Cas. 473 (E.D. Mich., November 13, 1974) n.o.r., aff'd on another ground, 528 F.2d 393 (6th Cir. 1976); Smith v. Crest Communities, Inc., 9 CCH Employ. Prac. Dec. ¶10,053, 8 Fair Employ. Prac. Cas. 1328 (W.D.Ky., November 21, 1974) n.o.r.; McGinley v. Burroughs Corp., 8 Fair Employ. Prac. Cas. 574 (E.D. Pa., June 21, 1974) n.o.r., and 407 F. Supp. 903, 908 (E.D. Pa. 1975); Acford v. Exxon Corp., 12 Fair Employ. Prac. Cas. 1500 (D. Conn., December 17, 1975) n.o.r.; Vaughn v. Chrysler Corp., 382 F. Supp. 143 (E.D. Mich. 1974). See also Opinion Letter of Acting Wage-Hour Administrator, 8 Lab. Rel. Rep. 401:5222 (January 7, 1969). Contra: Vazquez v. Eastern Airlines, 11 CCH Employ. Prac. Dec. ¶10,617, 12 Fair Employ. Prac. Cas. 686 (D.P.R., December 30, 1975) n.o.r.; Skoglund v. Singer Co., 403 F. Supp. 797 (D.N.H. 1975) (a contrary holding would not further the Congressional purpose of fostering state enforcement but would only deny plaintiff any remedy at all since resort to the state agencies was time barred). See generally Note, State Deferral of Complaints Under the Age Discrimination in Employment Act, 51 Notre Dame Law. 492 (1976) [suggesting that the majority view may be "ill-founded" insofar as it is based on an analogy to the similar provision in Title VII of the Civil Rights Act of 1964, 42 U.S.C. § 2000e-5(c) (1970)].

In Garces v. Sagner Int'l, Inc., 534 F.2d 987, 988 n. 6 (1st Cir. 1976), the Court of Appeals specifically reserved decision on the question of whether the state deferral requirement of the ADEA is jurisdictional.

The requirement that recourse be had to state procedures before a Federal action under the ADEA can be commenced has been held not to apply to actions brought by the Secretary of Labor.[214] Although that result is a practical one, it is not compelled by the statutory language which on its face includes all actions brought under the ADEA.[215]

An exception to the general requirement was created by the Court of Appeals in *Goger v. H. K. Porter Company*.[216] In that case, the plaintiff commenced her court action without resort to available state procedures only after her counsel was erroneously advised by a Department of Labor compliance officer that the Department's efforts to reach a satisfactory settlement had failed and that plaintiff was free to institute an action under the ADEA. The Court of Appeals excused the plaintiff's failure to seek relief first from the appropriate state agency based on the absence of judicial decisions construing the ADEA requirement that primary resort be had to state remedies where there is a qualifying state statute and the remedial purposes of ADEA. The Court of Appeals stated that

> In the future, however, we think the Congressional intent that state agencies be given the initial opportunity to act should be strictly followed and enforced.[217]

---

214. Dunlop v. Crown Cork & Seal Co., 405 F. Supp. 774 (D. Md. 1976). *See also* Vazquez v. Eastern Airlines, 11 CCH Employ. Prac. Dec. ¶10,617, at 6574 n.; 12 Fair Employ. Prac. Cas. 686, 688 n. 2 (D.P.R., December 30, 1975) *(dictum)* n.o.r.

215. *See* 29 U.S.C. §§ 626, 633(b) (1970).

216. 492 F.2d 13 (3rd Cir. 1974).

217. 492 F.2d at 17. The *Goger* exception was discussed in Vaughn v. Chrysler Corp., 382 F. Supp. 143, 146 (E.D. Mich. 1974), where the Court found the exception inapplicable to the case before it because

> there has been neither allegation or [*sic*] showing of detrimental reliance or the like which would influence the Court in the exercise of its equitable discretion.

The Court of Appeals' decision in *Goger* has been criticized insofar as it would require future plaintiffs to resort to state proceedings before commencing an action under the ADEA on the ground that the decision relies on an analogy to Title VII of the Civil Rights Act of 1964 which contains similar language to that contained in Section 14 of the ADEA. While the language of the two sections, 42 U.S.C. § 2000e-5(c) (1970) and 29 U.S.C. § 633 (1970), is nearly identical, it is argued that

A second exception to the requirement that available qualifying state procedures must be used before an action can be commenced under the ADEA was recognized by the Court in *Arnold v. Hawaiian Telephone Co.*[18] Citing *Goger* and *Vaughn,* the Court granted the plaintiff equitable relief from his failure to seek redress at the state level before instituting his action under the ADEA based upon a showing that (1) the Wage and Hour Division with which plaintiff filed two complaints alleging that he was subjected to age discrimination in connection with his employment never advised him that he should file a complaint with the state agency and had negotiated a favorable settlement for him with respect to the first complaint, (2) the Federal officials involved thought it unnecessary for plaintiff to file a complaint with the state agency, (3) if plaintiff had attempted to file a complaint with the state agency the state officials would have advised him to exhaust his Federal remedies under the ADEA, (4) Federal and state officials had an understanding with respect to that state policy which meant that no investigation or conciliation efforts would be made by state officials with respect to claims cognizable under the ADEA and plaintiff would not be advised by state or Federal officials of the necessity of resorting initially to the state agency, and (5) at the time that plaintiff was dismissed from his employment the law was unsettled with respect to the necessity for exhausting state procedures before seeking relief under the ADEA with the Secretary of Labor taking the position that there was no necessity for doing so. The Court emphasized that in the future the statutory requirement of prior resort to state procedures would be strictly followed citing the *Goger* Court's statement to the same effect. This suggests that it was the last factor set forth above, the unsettled state of the law, that was

---

the sections serve different functions and that the courts have construed the provision of Title VII, unlike that of the ADEA, and approved procedural regulations applicable thereto so as to preserve the rights of complainants who fail to seek initial relief under state law to seek relief under Federal law despite the procedural irregularity. Note, *State Deferral of Complaints Under the Age Discrimination in Employment Act,* 51 Notre Dame Law. 492, 496-98 (1976).

218. 11 CCH Employ. Prac. Dec. ¶10,786, at 7307, 12 Fair Employ. Prac. Cas. 400, 404 (D. Hawaii, June 30, 1975) n.o.r.

determinative for the Court since that was the only factor which had clearly changed between the time of the allegedly discriminatory act in *Arnold* and the Court's decision. Yet the other four factors referred to by the Court would certainly justify a court in exercising its equitable powers on behalf of an unsophisticated person such as the plaintiff in that case.

ii. Notice to Secretary of Labor. — Section 7(d) prohibits the commencement of a civil action under the ADEA by an individual until the individual has given the Secretary of Labor not less than sixty days' notice of an intent to file such an action. Such notice must be filed within 180 days after the alleged unlawful practice occurred, or, in a case where initial resort to state procedures is provided for by the ADEA, within 300 days after the alleged unlawful practice occurred or within thirty days after receipt by the individual of notice of termination of proceedings under state law, whichever is earlier.[219]

An unlawful practice under the ADEA occurs at a particular point in time and there are no continuing violations with respect to a particular individual, though there may be repeated violations.[220] It has been held that an individual's time to file the required notice of intent to sue began to run, in the case of an alleged wrongful discharge, not on either the date when she was first notified that she would be discharged on a specific future date or the date on which she last worked for the employer but rather on the subsequent date on which she was terminated for administrative purposes. The latter date was the same one first mentioned to the employee by her employer.[221] In that case, the

---

219. 29 U.S.C. § 626(d) (1970). *See generally* Eklund v. Lubrizol Corp., 529 F.2d 247 (6th Cir. 1976).

220. Woodburn v. LTV Aerospace Corp., 531 F.2d 750 (5th Cir. 1976) *(per curiam)* (to hold that a discriminatory discharge and failure to rehire, at a time when hiring by defendant continued, is a continuing violation for purposes of the 180 day notice requirement would almost eliminate any practical effect of the notice provision and frustrate the intent of Congress to encourage mediation and reconciliation); Law v. United Air Lines, 519 F.2d 170 (10th Cir. 1975) *(per curiam)*. *See also* Hiscott v. General Elec. Co., 521 F.2d 632 (6th Cir. 1975); Brohl v. Singer Co., 407 F. Supp. 936, 939 (M.D. Fla. 1976).

221. Moses v. Falstaff Brewing Corp., 525 F.2d 92 (8th Cir. 1975).

Court of Appeals properly noted that the defendant employer's argument that one of the earlier dates should be chosen furthered no substantial goal of the ADEA, that the liberal interpretation which should be given to remedial and humanitarian legislation such as the ADEA required that the statute's failure to specify when an alleged unlawful practice occurred was tantamount to a procedural ambiguity which should be construed in favor of the party seeking the protection of the ADEA, and that the date of official termination was more easily ascertainable and less subject to ambiguity than the date upon which oral notice was given to the employee of termination upon a subsequent date.

The 180 or 300 day notice provision would seem to require that notice to the Secretary of Labor follow a resort to state remedies. Were the procedure otherwise, both the state authorities and the Secretary might be simultaneously engaged with the alleged discriminator in duplicative efforts at resolution of a complaint. In addition, the alleged discriminator would be forced to deal with two agencies at the same time. The ADEA clearly contemplates that in such circumstances the Secretary become involved only after a state authority has had an opportunity to resolve a claim of age discrimination in employment where a complainant has resorted to such an authority in a state having a statute "prohibiting discrimination in employment because of age and establishing or authorizing a State authority to grant or seek relief from such discriminatory practice...." [222]

The statutory requirement that an individual give notice to the Secretary of Labor before institution of a civil action under the ADEA is, unlike the question of primary resort to state procedures,

---

222. 29 U.S.C. § 633(b) (1970). *Cf.* Address by Clarence T. Lundquist, Administrator, Wage and Hour and Public Contracts Division of United States Department of Labor, Federal Bar Association, May 16, 1968.

In case a person in a State where there is a State age discrimination law complains to us rather than the State authorities, or complains to both, we would follow the enforcement procedures outlined in the Act without referral of the complaint, or the finding of a violation, to any State agency unless or until we are at a point where all other remedies have failed and it becomes necessary to bring suit. [BNA Daily Labor Report 97—5/16/68, D-1, at D-3.]

on its face "a condition precedent to the bringing of [an] action by an individual. . . ." [223] The courts have, accordingly, held that the giving of the 60 day notice of intent to sue is a jurisdictional prerequisite and the failure to do so requires dismissal of a Federal court action brought under the ADEA.[224]

One court has, however, recognized an exception to the 60 day notice requirement where a claimant proves that his employer did not post the notice approved by the Secretary of Labor as required by the ADEA. In *Bishop v. Jelleff Associates, Inc.* [225] the Court held that the failure of the plaintiff-employees to file the required 60 day notice was excused by their employer's failure to post the required notice explaining the purposes of the ADEA in conspicuous places on its premises and that the employees should not be penalized by reason of the employer's failure to advise them of their rights as required by law. The Court based its decision upon the relative newness of the ADEA at the time the suit was instituted, the plaintiff-employees' overall lack of sophistication,

---

223. H.R. Rep. No. 805, 5, [1967] U.S. Code Cong. and Admin. News at 2218. The same report states that "persons intending to file civil actions under this act *must* give the Secretary of Labor 60 days' notice before doing so." *Id.* at 10, [1967] U.S. Code Cong. and Admin. News at 2223. (Emphasis added.)

224. Rucker v. Great Scott Supermarkets, Inc., 528 F.2d 393 (6th Cir. 1976); Law v. United Air Lines, 519 F.2d 170 (10th Cir. 1975) *(per curiam);* Balc v. United Steelworkers of America, AFL-CIO, 6 CCH Employ. Prac. Dec. ¶8948, 6 Fair Employ. Prac. Cas. 824 (W.D. Pa., October 19, 1973) n.o.r., *aff'd without opinion,* 503 F.2d 1398 (3rd Cir. 1974); Hayes v. Southern Pac. Co., 12 CCH Employ. Prac. Dec. ¶11,196, 13 Fair Employ. Prac. Cas. 753 (C. D. Cal., August 18, 1976) n.o.r.; McCorstin v. United States Steel Corp., 11 Fair Employ. Prac. Cas. 1478 (N.D. Ala., December 16, 1974) (members of a proposed class) n.o.r.; Acford v. Exxon Corp., 12 Fair Employ. Prac. Cas. 1500 (D. Conn., December 17, 1975) n.o.r.; Oshira v. Pan Am. World Airways, Inc., 378 F. Supp. 80 (D. Hawaii 1974); McGinley v. Burroughs Corp., 8 Fair Employ. Prac. Cas. 574 (E.D. Pa., June 21, 1974) n.o.r.; Vaughn v. Chrysler Corp., 382 F. Supp. 143 (E.D. Mich. 1974); Bishop v. Jelleff Associates, Inc., 7 CCH Employ. Prac. Dec. ¶9214, 7 Fair Employ. Prac. Cas. 510 (D.D.C., March 11, 1974) n.o.r.; Woodford v. Kinney Shoe Corp., 369 F. Supp. 911 (N.D. Ga. 1973); Burgett v. Cudahy Co., 361 F. Supp. 617 (D. Kan. 1973); Grossfield v. W. B. Saunders Co., 1 CCH Employ. Prac. Dec. ¶9941, 1 Fair Employ. Prac. Cas. 624 (S.D.N.Y., December 31, 1968) n.o.r.

225. 398 F. Supp. 579 (D.D.C. 1974).

the defendant-employer's failure to post any notice under the ADEA, and the plaintiff-employees' oral representation to members of the United States Department of Labor that the defendant-employer was discharging large numbers of elderly employees.

The decision of the *Bishop* court seems to be consistent with the remedial purposes of the ADEA and the notice posting requirement of the statute. However, since complaints must be made by employees untrained in law, the length of time the ADEA has been in effect should not be a relevant consideration.[226] This is even more significant with respect to the requirement that the notice to the Secretary of Labor be filed within either 180 days or 300 days of the alleged discriminatory act since, as is noted below,[227] failure to comply with that requirement would prevent an individual claiming to have been discriminated against in violation of the ADEA from suing at all while failure to comply with the 60 day notice requirement only delays the time when an individual can commence his court action. However, there are possibly conflicting decisions with respect to whether an employer's failure to post a notice eliminates the requirement that the Secretary be given notice within either 180 days or 300 days, as applicable, of the alleged discriminatory act.[228]

---

226. *See* Note, *Procedural Aspects of the Age Discrimination in Employment Act of 1967,* 36 U. Pitt. L. Rev. 914, 921 (1975).

227. *See* pp. 151-154, *infra.*

228. *Cf.* Gebhard v. GAF Corp., 59 F.R.D. 504 (D.D.C. 1973) (finding notice was posted), *with* Hiscott v. General Elec. Co., 8 CCH Employ. Prac. Dec. ¶9735, 8 Fair Employ. Prac. Cas. 1003 (N.D. Ohio, August 28 and October 11, 1974) (rejecting the decision in Bishop v. Jellef Associates, Inc., *supra,* as against the weight of authority and distinguishing it on the grounds that the ADEA was enacted 4½ years prior to the institution of the action, plaintiff was a professional person possessed of a higher degree of sophistication than the plaintiffs in *Bishop,* and plaintiff made no timely oral representations which could constitute notice, constructive or otherwise, to the Department of Labor relevant to defendant's employment practices) n.o.r., *aff'd,* 521 F.2d 632, 634 (6th Cir. 1975) ("[W]e find nothing in the Act nor its legislative history to indicate that compliance with the notice provision was intended to be tolled or excused by the employer's failure, as here, to post the informational notices.").

The House of Representatives' Report states that the purpose of the 60 day notice requirement "is to allow the Secretary to mediate the grievance." [229] In *Bishop v. Jelleff Associates, Inc.,*[230] the Court stated that

This provision is designed to afford the Secretary of Labor opportunity to invoke appropriate conciliatory and mediative action in order to avert litigation. It is also an apparent purpose of this provision to alert the Secretary of Labor to cases and situations which may have widespread implications for employees, as the Secretary is empowered to initiate proceedings to supersede pending litigation instituted under the Act.[231]

In *Burgett v. Cudahy Company,* the Court notes that

As is evident from the unambiguous language of the statute, the emphasis is on private settlement and the elimination of age discrimination without formal litigation. The purpose for requiring an individual to file notice of a violation prior to the commencement of an action is two-fold: first, it puts the Secretary of Labor on notice of possible violations of the Act so that he can investigate the claims in order to determine whether action should be taken; and second, it puts the alleged discriminator on notice that a complaint has been filed against him so that he can voluntarily rectify any discriminatory practice. It therefore serves to facilitate

---

229. H.R. Rep. No. 805, 5, [1967] U.S. Code Cong. and Admin. News at 2218. As the discussion at pp. 159-163, *infra*, notes, informal settlement of discrimination claims is emphasized by the ADEA since it achieves results with a minimal expenditure of the time of personnel and of resources.

230. 398 F. Supp. 579 (D.D.C. 1974).

231. 398 F. Supp. at 592. *See also* Vazquez v. Eastern Air Lines, 11 CCH Employ. Prac. Dec. ¶10,617, 12 Fair Employ. Prac. Cas. 686 (D.P.R., December 30, 1975) n.o.r., where the Court held that

The sole purpose of this requirement is to enable the Secretary to eliminate the alleged violation through informal method of conciliation, conference and persuasion, if that is possible, before suit is filed, and to ensure that the Secretary expends his conciliation resources only on alleged unlawful practices which are reasonably current. [11 CCH Employ. Prac. Dec. ¶10,617, at 6571, 12 Fair Employ. Prac. Cas. at 688];

Acford v. Exxon Corp., 12 Fair Employ. Prac. Cas. 1500, 1502 (D. Conn., December 17, 1975) n.o.r.

232. 361 F. Supp. 617 (D. Kan. 1973).

the avoidance of unnecessary and expensive litigation by encouraging voluntary compliance with the Act's provisions.[233] The statutory requirement that the notice to the Secretary of Labor be given either 180 days or 300 days, depending on whether or not resort to qualifying state procedures is available, after the occurrence of the alleged discriminatory incident has, like the 60-day requirement, been held to be jurisdictional and the failure of a complainant to serve a timely notice requires dismissal of a Federal court action brought under the ADEA.[234] As has been noted above,[235] one court has suggested that failure of an employer to post the required notice advising employees of their rights under the ADEA might excuse an employee's failure to file his notice of

---

233. 361 F. Supp. at 621.
234. Woodburn v. LTV Aerospace Corp., 531 F.2d 750 (5th Cir. 1976) *(per curiam);* Moses v. Falstaff Brewing Corp., 525 F.2d 92 (8th Cir. 1975); Ott v. Midland-Ross Corp., 523 F.2d 1367, 1370 (6th Cir. 1975) ("Consequently, compliance with the notice procedure must be pleaded. Fed. R. Civ. P. 8(a)(1) and 12(b)(1). "); Edwards v. Kaiser Aluminum & Chem. Sales, Inc., 515 F.2d 1195 (5th Cir. 1975); Eklund v. Lubrizol Corp., 529 F.2d 247 (6th Cir. 1976), *affirming* 12 Fair Employ. Prac. Cas. 364 (N.D. Ohio, March 20, 1975) n.o.r.; Powell v. Southwestern Bell Tel. Co., 494 F.2d 485 (5th Cir. 1974); Brohl v. Singer Co., 407 F. Supp. 936, 938 (M.D. Fla. 1976); Raynor v. Great Atlantic & Pacific Tea Co., 400 F. Supp. 357 (E.D. Va. 1975); Hughes v. Beaunit Corp., 12 CCH Employ. Prac. Dec. ¶11,092 (E.D. Tenn., May 19, 1976) (written notice filed on 181st day) n.o.r.; Hayes v. Southern Pac. Co., 12 CCH Employ. Prac. Dec. ¶11,196 (C.D. Cal., August 18, 1976) n.o.r.; Acford v. Exxon Corp., 12 Fair Employ. Prac. Cas. 1500 (D. Conn., December 17, 1975) (incorrectly stating in dicta that plaintiff's failure to resort to qualifying state procedure made 180 as opposed to 300 day period applicable) n.o.r.; Dartt v. Shell Oil Co., 9 CCH Employ. Prac. Dec. ¶10,205, 10 Fair Employ. Prac. Cas. 844 (N.D. Okla., February 6, 1975) n.o.r.; Hiscott v. General Elec. Co., 8 CCH Employ. Prac. Dec. ¶9735, 8 Fair Employ. Prac. Cas. 1003 (N.D. Ohio, August 28 and October 11, 1974) n.o.r., *aff'd,* 521 F.2d 632 (6th Cir. 1975); McGinley v. Burroughs Corp., 8 Fair Employ. Prac. Cas. 574 (E.D. Pa., June 21, 1974) n.o.r.; Blankenship v. Ralston Purina Co., 62 F.R.D. 35 (N.D. Ga. 1973); Woodford v. Kinney Shoe Corp., 369 F. Supp. 911 (N.D. Ga. 1973); Gebhard v. GAF Corp., 59 F.R.D. 504 (D.D.C. 1973); Price v. Maryland Cas. Co., 62 F.R.D. 614 (S.D. Miss. 1972); Cochran v. Ortho Pharmaceutical Co., 376 F. Supp. 302 (E.D. La. 1971). *Contra,* Skoglund v. Singer Co., 403 F. Supp. 797, 804 (D.N.H. 1975) ("Section 626(d) is not 'jurisdictional' in the strict sense and. . . is a requirement subject to equitable modifications.").
235. *See* pp. 148-149, *supra.*

intention to bring an action under the statute within the specified time period after the alleged discriminatory incident.[236]

---

236. Gebhard v. GAF Corp., 59 F.R.D. 504, 507 (D.D.C. 1973). *Accord,* Skoglund v. Singer Co., 403 F. Supp. 797 (D.N.H. 1975). *Contra,* Hiscott v. General Elec. Co., 8 CCH Employ. Prac. Dec. ¶9735, 8 Fair Employ. Prac. Cas. 1003 (N.D. Ohio, August 28 and October 11, 1974) n.o.r., aff'd, 521 F.2d 632 (6th Cir. 1975).

In Edwards v. Kaiser Aluminum & Chem. Sales, Inc., 515 F.2d 1195 (5th Cir. 1975), the Court of Appeals found Bishop v. Jelleff Associates, Inc., 398 F. Supp. 579 (D.D.C. 1974), "unpersuasive authority" and noted, further, that the plaintiff could no longer rely on the "newness" of the ADEA as in *Bishop* nor could he be considered "unsophisticated." The Court of Appeals did, however, state that in an appropriate case an employer's failure to post the required notice might be held to toll, but not waive, the running of the statutory 180 day period for filing of a notice of intent to sue based upon "equitable considerations." The case before it was held not to be such a case in light of plaintiff's failure to file within 180 days of discharge, of hiring his first attorney, or of obtaining actual knowledge of the ADEA.

Skoglund v. Singer Co., 12 CCH Employ. Prac. Dec. ¶11,041 (D.N.H., December 9, 1975) n.o.r., holding that plaintiff had failed to convince the Court that there were sufficient equitable considerations to mandate that the filing requirement be tolled based on findings that plaintiff's position with defendant was such that he should have known of the ADEA and could not claim that his ignorance was due solely to defendant's alleged failure to post the required notice and that plaintiff was manager of one of defendant's stores where a notice was posted for at least part of the time he managed it.

The possible ground for avoiding the effect of a failure to comply with the 180 day notice requirement of the ADEA noted by the Court of Appeals in Edwards v. Kaiser Aluminum & Chem. Sales, Inc., *supra,* was presented in Brohl v. Singer Co., 407 F. Supp. 936 (M.D.Fla. 1976). In *Brohl* the Court refused "to toll the jurisdictional time-periods expiration, relieving plaintiff of his obligation to comply with Sec. 626" despite the fact that plaintiff's employer had failed to post the required notices under the ADEA and plaintiff had alleged that he was unaware of his rights under the ADEA for 16 months after the allegedly discriminatory act. The Court held that those facts

> do not as a matter of law supply the authority for the Court to invent an exception to the statute's clear jurisdictional requirement. The Court will not rewrite the statute in order to create jurisdiction. It is the responsibility of the Court to interpret and apply the law, [citations omitted], not to rewrite it. Humanitarian and equitable arguments that would urge the Court to do virtually that are in the wrong forum. They should be addressed to the Congress that enacted the statute. [407 F. Supp. at 936.]

The *Brohl* Court's decision overlooks a court's inherent power to take into consideration equitable factors particularly when construing a remedial statute such as the ADEA, as was noted in *Edwards,* and the fact that Congress enacted both the 180 day notice requirement and the notice posting requirement which could

In *McGinley v. Burroughs Corporation,*[237] the plaintiff alleged two violations of the ADEA based upon his discharge from employment and his employer's failure to recall him, despite its promise to do so, while the employer retained and then hired and transferred younger persons into the position previously held by plaintiff. Plaintiff's termination occurred in October, 1971, the hirings of younger persons were alleged to have occurred in December, 1972 or January, 1973 and in March, 1973, and plaintiff's notification to the Secretary of Labor of his intention to sue occurred in October, 1973. The Court held that plaintiff's notification was not given within the applicable 300 day period with respect to the wrongful discharge cause of action and dismissed that claim upon defendant's motion to dismiss the complaint for lack of jurisdiction. However, the Court held that the notification was timely with respect to the cause of action based on defendant's failure to recall plaintiff based on plaintiff's allegation that defendant hired a younger person in December, 1972 rather than recalling plaintiff. In addition, the Court held that plaintiff's allegation that defendant willfully concealed the hirings of younger persons from him, which was assumed to be true for the purpose of deciding defendant's motion to dismiss, provided "equitable reasons" for holding that the jurisdictional prerequisites were satisfied where plaintiff asserted that he did not learn of the hirings until September, 1973.[238]

The purpose of requiring that notice of intent to sue must be filed with the Secretary within a specified period after the occurrence

---

only have been included in the ADEA in order to advise of their rights thereunder those for whose protection the statute was enacted.

See also Eklund v. Lubrizol Corp., 529 F.2d 247 (6th Cir. 1976), where the Court of Appeals rejected a request for equitable relief from plaintiff's failure to give the 180 day notice which was based on plaintiff's counsel's reasonable attempt to comply with the ADEA and the unsettled state of the judicial interpretations of the notice requirement at the relevant time.

237. 407 F. Supp. 903 (E.D. Pa. 1975).

238. *Id.* at 909-10. The Court noted that it did not have to decide whether the defendant's alleged willful concealment tolled the running of the 300 day requirement or, instead, resulted in plaintiff's cause of action "continuing up to the time of his discovery of the hirings." *Id.*

of an alleged discriminatory act was explained as follows in *Powell v. Southwestern Bell Telephone Company*,[239]

> it is logical that the 180 day notice was intended to insure that potential defendants would become aware of their status and the possibility of litigation reasonably soon after the alleged discrimination since the notice goes from the Secretary of Labor on to the employer involved. In turn this would promote the good faith negotiation of employers during the 60 day conciliation period and provide an opportunity for preservation of evidence and records for use at a trial necessitiated by failure of negotiation.***. [I]t gives notice to concerned parties that the plaintiff intends to sue and may do so within the applicable two or three year statute of limitations.[240]

It has been noted that the notice requirement

> benefits other employees ... by eliminating discriminatory practices and policies. Further, the notice alerts the Secretary of Labor to situations which affect other employees and allows him to determine whether agency litigation should be initiated. [Citations omitted.] It enhances employee/employer relations by encouraging voluntary rectification and precludes premature resort to the courts, conserving judicial resources.[241]

The ADEA does not specify what constitutes proper notice to the Secretary of Labor.[242] In an opinion letter, an Assistant Secretary of Labor advised that

> No particular form is necessary in order to notify the Secretary of Labor of an intent to file civil action under

---

239. 494 F.2d 485 (5th Cir. 1974).

240. 494 F.2d at 488. *See also* Moses v. Falstaff Brewing Corp., 525 F.2d 92, 94 (8th Cir. 1975); Edwards v. Kaiser Aluminum & Chem. Sales, Inc., 515 F.2d 1195, 1197-98 (5th Cir. 1975); Cochran v. Ortho Pharmaceutical Co., 376 F. Supp. 302, 303 (E.D. La. 1971), where the Court held that

> Congress has utilized this method of forcing complainants to speedily present their claims and allow a neutral outside agency an opportunity to mediate, conciliate, or arbitrate the matter while it is fresh.

241. Edwards v. Kaiser Aluminum & Chem. Sales, Inc., 515 F.2d 1195, 1198 (5th Cir. 1975).

242. *See* Raynor v. Great Atlantic & Pacific Tea Co., Inc., 400 F. Supp. 357, 358 (E.D. Va. 1975) (noting "the question of the nature of notice on which point § 626(d) is silent, leaving room for judicial interpretation.").

the Age Discrimination in Employment Act. Such notification should be provided in writing, however, and may be addressed either to the Department of Labor in Washington, D.C., or to the nearest office of the Wage and Hour and Public Contracts Division. . . .[243]

The foregoing pronouncement has not, however, concluded the question. Thus, some courts have held that written communications to the Secretary asserting claims of alleged discriminatory acts in violation of the ADEA which do not specifically set forth an intention to institute a civil action do not meet the statutory requirements.[244] On the other hand, in *Woodford v. Kinney Shoe Corporation*[245] the Court held that an

---

243. Opinion Letter of Assistant Secretary of Labor, 8 Lab. Rel. Rep. 401:5213 (August 26, 1968). There is a suggestion in Dartt v. Shell Oil Co., 9 CCH Employ. Prac. Dec. ¶10,205, 10 Fair Employ. Prac. Cas. 844 (N.D. Okla., February 6, 1975) n.o.r., that the filing of a notice of intent to sue with a local office of the Department of Labor rather than with the Secretary of Labor would not constitute compliance with the requirements of the ADEA. No reference is made by the Court to the foregoing opinion letter. In addition, though the Court makes reference to the notice required to be posted under the ADEA, it was apparently unaware that the form of notice adopted by the Secretary of Labor provided that

> If you feel you have been discriminated against in matters of hiring, discharge, compensation, or other phases of employment because of age contact the: U.S. Department of Labor Wage and Hour Division Local Address: [U.S. Department of Labor, Employment Standards Administration Publication 1289.]

In McCorstin v. United States Steel Corp., 11 Fair Employ. Prac. Cas. 1478, 1480 (N.D. Ala., December 16, 1974) n.o.r., the Court stated that "[t]he notice under § 626(d) must identify the plaintiffs sufficiently for the Secretary of Labor effectively to conciliate on their behalf."

244. *See, e.g.,* Hiscott v. General Elec. Co., 521 F.2d 632, 634 (6th Cir. 1975) (quoting letter from a Labor Department official to the same effect); Powell v. Southwestern Bell Tel. Co., 494 F.2d 485 (5th Cir. 1974) (notice requesting Secretary of Labor to commence litigation on complainant's behalf held insufficient); Acford v. Exxon Corp., 12 Fair Employ. Prac. Cas. 1500 (D. Conn., December 17, 1975) (neither oral complaint concerning anticipated acts of discrimination nor later complaint of discrimination were sufficient) n.o.r.; Dartt v. Shell Oil Co., 9 CCH Employ. Prac. Dec. ¶10,205, 10 Fair Employ. Prac. Cas. 844 (N.D. Okla., February 6, 1975) (complaint of age discrimination in employment to local office of Department of Labor held insufficient) n.o.r.; Grossfield v. W.B. Saunders Co., 1 CCH Employ. Prac. Dec. ¶9941, 1 Fair Employ. Prac. Cas. 624 (S.D.N.Y., December 31, 1968) n.o.r.

245. 369 F. Supp. 911 (N.D. Ga. 1973).

employee's right to file suit later is preserved by a timely report to the United States Department of Labor claiming age discrimination in employment "even if he does not in so many words declare to the Department his intent to file such action."[246] The Court based its determination on the following reasoning:

> The persons making complaints to the Department will in the most part not be lawyers; they should not be compelled to adhere to strict rules of pleading merely to preserve their right to come to court to enforce their right to be free of discrimination employment [sic] because of age. If they are to be able to enforce the Age Discrimination Act, their complaints should be construed not narrowly and technically, but broadly and liberally. Where the employee identifies himself and his employer and reports facts which, if true, would support a cause of action pursuant to the Act, the Labor Department should assume that the aggrieved employee will take whatever steps are necessary to enforce his rights, including court action; thus, an intent to file suit is implied in a complaint of age discrimination in employment.[247]

---

246. 369 F. Supp. at 915. *See also* Burgett v. Cudahy Co., 361 F. Supp. 617, 621 (D. Kan. 1973), where the Court referred to the opinion letter quoted above and noted that the notice is not required to meet any formal specifications but must contain the basic facts which will enable the Secretary of Labor to perform his functions, should be in writing properly addressed to the Secretary of Labor, should contain an identification of the parties involved, and should include a general description of the alleged discriminatory action. While the Court did not specify that the writing had to include a notice of intention to sue, the plaintiff's counsel in that case had, in fact, included such a provision in a letter to the Department of Labor.

247. 369 F. Supp. at 915. *Contra,* Dartt v. Shell Oil Co., 9 CCH Employ. Prac. Dec. ¶10,205, at 7914, 10 Fair Employ. Prac. Cas. 844, 848 (N.D. Okla., February 6, 1975) n.o.r., where the Court held that

> The filing of notice of intent to sue performs two functions. The prospective defendant is promptly notified of the possibility of litigation. And the Secretary is induced to promptly begin informal methods of conciliation, knowing that a civil action will proceed if he does not obtain results. It cannot be said that these functions are performed by the mere filing of a complaint of age discrimination with a local office of the Department of Labor. It does not appear that in the enforcement provisions of the ADEA applicable to the Secretary that there is any requirement of promptly notifying an employer that a complaint has been filed against it. Nor does it appear that there is any requirement that the Secretary promptly act on a complaint. Therefore, the mere

While this analysis is not strictly in conformity with the terms of the ADEA which speaks of "notice of intent to file such action," [248] it does reflect a realistic recognition of the level of knowledge and sophistication about the technical requirements of the ADEA of the individuals who are likely to assert claims thereunder. Clearly, a "broad and liberal" interpretation in this matter would advance the remedial purposes of the ADEA and not prejudice a potential defendant. Indeed, the Department of Labor could reasonably be required to inform a complainant advising it of an alleged act of discrimination of the necessity of setting forth an intention to commence a civil action in order to preserve his right to do so. This could be accomplished by a departmental regulation requiring that a form including a statement of intention to sue be sent for completion to all persons making inquiries about asserting a claim of, or complaining of, age discrimination in employment. An alternative solution would involve amending the ADEA to substitute "notice of an alleged discriminatory practice" for "notice of intent to file such action." No change would be required in the time periods and no prejudice would result to a person alleged to have acted in violation of the statute since he can reasonably expect that an individual unable to obtain satisfaction by informal means will resort to formal ones; that is, a civil action under the ADEA.

---

registration of a complaint of age discrimination with the local wage and hour division of the Department of Labor cannot be held by this Court to satisfy the notice requirement of 29 U.S.C. § 626(d).

The Court's formalistic approach to a remedial statute overlooks the significance of the fact, noted by the Court, that if there is no provision in the ADEA requiring the filing of a complaint of age discrimination in employment with the Secretary of Labor, as opposed to a notice of intention to sue, then a complaint of such age discrimination filed with the appropriate authorities can only be rationally interpreted as a notice of intention to sue. Since there is no statutory provision for the filing with the Department of Labor of a "complaint" of age discrimination in employment, upon the filing of such a "complaint" it should, strictly speaking, be rejected and the filing of a notice of intention to sue should be required in its place. To require a non-lawyer claiming to have been discriminated against in violation of the ADEA to comply with this technical distinction would serve only to create a trap for laymen and exalt procedure over substance. Such an interpretation would clearly not further the achievement of the statute's objectives.

248. 29 U.S.C. § 626(d) (1970).

Somewhat surprisingly, there is still uncertainty as to whether the notice to the Secretary of Labor must be in writing. The courts have, generally, held or assumed that a written notice is required [249] as has the Department of Labor.[250] However, the Court in *Woodford v. Kinney Shoe Corporation*[251] held that nothing in the ADEA expressly commanded that the notice be written and that the legislative history did not indicate that only written notice was intended by Congress.[252] The Court, further, stated that it was uncertain whether the Department of Labor opinion letter quoted above meant that only written notice was acceptable or that any type of notice was acceptable with written notice preferred.[253]

While the attitude of the *Woodford* Court with its emphasis on preserving rights can be appreciated, both the language of Section 7(d) of the ADEA requiring that "notice shall be filed" [254] and the

---

249. *See* Hughes v. Beaunit Corp., 12 CCH Employ. Prac. Dec. ¶11,092 (E.D. Tenn., May 19, 1976) n.o.r.; Burgett v. Cudahy Co., 361 F. Supp. 617, 621 (D. Kan. 1973); Grossfield v. W. B. Saunders Co., 1 CCH Employ. Prac. Dec. ¶9941, at 1349, 1 Fair Employ. Prac. Cas. 624, 625 (S.D.N.Y. December 31, 1968) n.o.r.

250. *See* pp. 154-155, *supra.*

251. 369 F. Supp. 911 (N.D. Ga. 1973).

252. 369 F. Supp. at 914.

253. *Id.*

254. 29 U.S.C. § 626(d) (1970). It would not seem logical to require an oral notice to be "filed." Such a notice would be "given". The requirement of "filing" has been held in other contexts to contemplate "the deposit of a writing with the proper official." City of Overland Park v. Nikias, 209 Kan. 643, 498 P.2d 56, 59 (Sup. Ct. 1972), and to exclude oral communications, Troska v. Industrial Comm'n, 14 Ariz. App. 400, 484 P.2d 12, 13 (Ct. App. 1971). The rationale behind this interpretation was succinctly described by the Court in Wrightsman Petroleum Co. v. United States, 92 Ct. Cl. 217, 238, 35 F. Supp. 86, 96 (1940), *cert. denied,* 313 U.S. 578 (1941), as follows:

> There is good reason for the requirement that the claim be in writing. It is common knowledge that the personnel in government departments is constantly changing. Many times several different employees work on a single case. Some of them have before them only such information as is contained in the files. For this reason, and because of the shortness of the memory of man, and for many other reasons, only a written claim is sufficient to meet the requirements of the statute and the need it intended to fill.

That Court held that the making of an oral claim was not sufficient compliance with a statute requiring the "filing" of a claim since "an oral claim cannot be filed. The claim must be in writing." *Id.*

practical requirement of a tangible, preferably signed, complaint before an investigation is commenced give support to an interpretation requiring that the notice be written. The suggestion made above to the effect that all persons making complaints of, or inquiries concerning the filing of a complaint of, age discrimination in employment to the Department of Labor be provided with a form to complete and submit would probably eliminate the problem.

iii. Notice to Alleged Discriminator. — Upon receipt of a notice of intent to sue, the United States Secretary of Labor is required by Section 7(d) of the ADEA to promptly notify all persons named therein as prospective defendants in the action.[255]

Although there are no cases in point, a failure by the Secretary of Labor to notify a prospective defendant might be held to be jurisdictional and require dismissal of an action brought by the Secretary of Labor before the giving of such notice.[256]

b. Preliminary Procedures for Individuals and the Secretary of Labor.

Conciliation, Conference, and Persuasion. Section 7(d) of the ADEA provides that, where a proceeding is initiated by an individual's filing a notice of intent to file an action under the statute with the Secretary of Labor, the Secretary is required to promptly seek to eliminate any alleged unlawful practice by informal methods of conciliation, conference, and persuasion.[257]

Similarly, where a legal action under the statute is to be commenced by the Secretary before he does so he is required by Section 7(b) to attempt to eliminate the discriminatory practice or practices alleged and effect voluntary compliance with the requirements of the ADEA through informal methods of conciliation, conference, and persuasion.[258]

---

255. 29 U.S.C. § 626(d) (1970).

256. *See* pp. 161-163, *infra*, noting that a similar result has been reached where the Secretary of Labor has notified a prospective defendant but has either failed to engage in informal methods of complaint resolution or has not engaged in meaningful efforts in that direction.

257. 29 U.S.C. § 626(d) (1970).

258. 29 U.S.C. § 626(b) (1970).

The importance of the informal approach to the elimination of discriminatory practices under the ADEA was emphasized in the House of Representatives' Report which states that

It is intended that the responsibility for enforcement vested in the Secretary of Labor ... be initially and exhaustively directed through informal methods of conciliation, conference, and persuasion and formal methods applied only in the ultimate sense.[259]

The courts have, similarly, recognized the primary position given to informal methods of settlement of claims of age discrimination in employment in violation of the ADEA.[260]

As both the legislative history of the ADEA and the courts have noted, the statutory requirement that the Secretary of Labor be given 60 days' notice of intention to sue before a civil action under the ADEA may be commenced is meant to give the Secretary an opportunity to obtain voluntary elimination of practices in violation of the statute through the informal methods of conciliation, conference, and persuasion.[261] Some courts have found a similar

---

259. H.R. Rep. No. 805, 5, [1967] U.S. Code Cong. and Admin. News, at 2218.

260. *See, e.g.,* Brennan v. Ace Hardware Corp., 362 F. Supp. 1156, 1160 (D. Neb. 1973), *aff'd,* 495 F. 2d 368, 374 (8th Cir. 1974); Brennan v. Approved Personnel Service, Inc., 8 CCH Employ. Prac. Dec. ¶9810, at 6393 (M.D.N.C., September 20, 1974) ("The Act requires that before the Secretary of Labor takes legal action to enforce provisions of the Act that he first warn the individual of his violations and give him a chance to correct his error. The Secretary first has a duty to encourage the individual to comply with the Act through methods of conciliation and persuasion.") n.o.r., *reversed on other grounds,* 529 F.2d 760 (4th Cir. 1975); McCorstin v. United States Steel Corp., 11 Fair Employ. Prac. Cas. 1478, 1480 (N.D. Ala., December 16, 1974) ("Informal conciliation is at the very heart of the Act.") n.o.r.; Burgett v. Cudahy Co., 361 F. Supp. 617, 621 (D. Kan. 1973) ("As is evident from the unambiguous language of the statute, the emphasis is on private settlement and the elimination of age discrimination without formal litigation."); Grossfield v. W.B. Saunders Co., 1 CCH Employ. Prac. Dec. ¶9941, at 1349, 1 Fair Employ. Prac. Cas. 624, 625 (S.D.N.Y., December 31, 1968) n.o.r.:

[I]n what has become a familiar pattern, Congress required that "informal methods," purposefully employed by the responsible agency, be exhausted before resort to the more formal and less flexible procedures of the courts would be permissible.

261. H.R. Rep. No. 805, 10, [1967] U.S. Code Cong. and Admin. News at 2223; McCorstin v. United States Steel Corp., 11 Fair Employ. Prac. Cas. 1478 (N.D. Ala., December 16, 1974) n.o.r.; Bishop v. Jelleff Associates, Inc., 398 F. Supp. 579 (D.D.C.

purpose in the provision of the ADEA requiring that the notice to the Secretary of Labor must be given within either 180 or 300 days of the occurrence of the allegedly discriminatory practice.[262] The courts have interpreted the provisions of the ADEA requiring an initial resort by the Secretary of Labor to informal methods of resolving complaints as mandatory [263] and have held that those methods must be "purposefully employed" [264] by the Secretary in "strong, affirmative attempts by the Secretary to effect compliance before resorting to legal action" [265] by the use of "exhaustive, affirmative action." [266] The ADEA's emphasis on the use of the informal methods of conciliation, conference, and persuasion has led two courts to hold that the requirement that the Secretary of Labor seek voluntary compliance before instituting suit is jurisdictional and a statutory precondition to bringing suit. Failure of the Secretary either to engage in the informal methods at all or to engage in meaningful efforts at informal resolution of complaints would, under this view, require dismissal of a civil action.[267] The philosophical basis for this

---

1974); Blankenship v. Ralston Purina Co., 62 F.R.D. 35, 42 (N.D. Ga. 1973); Burgett v. Cudahy Co., *supra;* Woodford v. Kinney Shoe Corp., 369 F. Supp. 911, 913 (N.D. Ga. 1973).

262. McCorstin v. United States Steel Corp., 11 Fair Employ. Prac. Cas. 1478, 1480 (N.D. Ala., December 16, 1974) n.o.r.; Cochran v. Ortho Pharmaceutical Co., 376 F. Supp. 302, 303 (E. D. La. 1971):

> Congress has utilized this method of forcing complainants to speedily present their claims and allow a neutral outside agency an opportunity to mediate, conciliate, or arbitrate the matter while it is fresh.

263. Brennan v. Weis Markets, 5 CCH Employ. Prac. Dec. ¶8519, 5 Fair Employ. Prac. Cas. 850 (M.D. Pa., March 22, 1973) n.o.r.

264. Grossfield v. W.B. Saunders Co., 1 CCH Employ. Prac. Dec. ¶9941, at 1349, 1 Fair Employ. Cas. 624, 625 (S.D.N.Y., December 31, 1968) n.o.r.

265. Brennan v. Ace Hardware Corp., 495 F.2d 368, 374 (8th Cir. 1974); McCorstin v. United States Steel Corp., 11 Fair Employ. Prac. Cas. 1478, 1480 (N.D. Ala., December 16, 1974) n.o.r.

266. Brennan v. Ace Hardware Corp., 495 F.2d 368, 374 (8th Cir. 1974).

267. Brennan v. Ace Hardware Corp., 362 F. Supp. 1156 (D. Neb. 1973), aff'd, 495 F.2d 368 (8th Cir. 1974); Brennan v. Weis Markets, 5 CCH Employ. Prac. Dec. ¶8519, 5 Fair Employ. Prac. Cas. 850 (M.D. Pa., March 22, 1973) (holding that the courts have the power to determine the adequacy of the Secretary of Labor's conciliation attempts) n.o.r. See also Hodgson v. Ideal Corrugated Box Co., 8 CCH Employ. Prac. Dec. ¶9805, 10 Fair Employ. Prac. Cas. 744 (N.D. W.Va., January

position was stated as follows by the Court of Appeals in *Brennan v. Ace Hardware Corporation*.[268]

Although the availability of and resort to courts allow for a method of resolving conflicts, the framework of a free people and the functioning of their government depends not essentially upon the courts, but upon the desire of the people to agree within the framework of their law and to compromise the differences outside the walls of a courtroom. The voluntary compliance provisions recognize this principle and also wisely perceive that conciliation is a difficult process in which exhaustive, affirmative action, in this situation initiated by the Secretary is demanded to achieve resolution without the necessity of legal action.

The Court of Appeals in that case noted that the lower court had the power to stay further proceedings in the action until the Secretary of Labor had engaged in meaningful efforts at conciliation of the dispute rather than dismissing it. However, the District Court's refusal to do so was held not to be an abuse of discretion.[269] It has, with some justification, been suggested that a stay rather than dismissal would be the most appropriate action in all such cases.[270]

31, 1974) n.o.r. *See* Brennan v. Approved Personnel Service, Inc., 529 F.2d 760 (4th Cir. 1975), *reversing*, 8 CCH Employ. Prac. Dec. ¶9810, at 6394 (M.D.N.C., September 20, 1974) n.o.r., where the District Court had denied injunctive relief in part on the ground that, while the Secretary of Labor may have made "certain formalistic efforts" to apprise the defendant of its violations of the ADEA, he did not use "proper" methods of conciliation and persuasion as required by the statute. *Cf.* Lundgren v. Continental Indus., Inc., 11 CCH Employ. Prac. Dec. ¶10,778 (N.D. Okla., March 16, 1976) (conciliation efforts by the Secretary of Labor are not a jurisdictional prerequisite to the filing of an action by an individual under the ADEA) n.o.r.

268. 495 F.2d, *supra*, at 375.

269. 495 F.2d at 376.

270. Note, *Procedural Aspects of the Age Discrimination in Employment Act of 1967*, 36 U. Pitt. L. Rev. 914, 929-30 (1975).

In Brennan v. Texas Instruments Inc., 12 CCH Employ. Prac. Dec. ¶10,983, 12 Fair Employ. Prac. Cas. 1724 (E. D. Ky., March 12, 1976) n.o.r., the District Court found that the Secretary of Labor had engaged in conciliation efforts with respect to some, but not all, of the alleged discriminatory acts engaged in by defendant. The Court held that, since the Secretary of Labor had fulfilled his statutory obligation to attempt to obtain voluntary compliance with the ADEA with respect

While the dismissal of a civil action based on a finding that the Secretary has failed to comply with the informal settlement effort requirements of the ADEA may seem harsh in the abstract, in practice it is not since the dismissal would not be on the merits and it is only in the rare case where the statute of limitations [271] has run that the action could not be reinstituted after the Secretary has made a proper effort to settle the matter by informal methods. Indeed, with the dismissal of the Secretary's action, a complainant would be free to commence his own action.

Furthermore, requiring initial resort to informal methods as mandated by the ADEA may promote settlements and avoid unnecessary litigation. Once an action has been commenced with the attendant publicity, positions tend to harden and settlement may become impossible since it may be seen as an admission of a violation of the ADEA.

L. STATUTE OF LIMITATIONS

A statute of limitations generally sets the time within which an action must be commenced after the event which is alleged to give rise to liability by the defendant to the plaintiff. The purposes of statutes of limitations were described as follows by the United States Supreme Court in *Burnett v. New York Central R. Co.,*[272]

> Statutes of limitations are primarily designed to assure fairness to defendants. Such statutes "promote justice by preventing surprises through the revival of claims that have been allowed to slumber until evidence has been lost, memories have faded, and witnesses have disappeared. The theory is that even if one has a just claim it is unjust not to put the adversary on notice to defend within the period of limitation and that the right to be free of stale claims in time comes to prevail over the right to prosecute them." Order of Railroad Tele-

---

to certain of the charges before the Court, the action would be stayed in the interest of judicial economy for sixty days while the Secretary of Labor attempted to effect voluntary compliance with the statute as to all allegations of age discrimination at defendant's plant.

271. The statute of limitations for actions brought under the ADEA is discussed on pp. 163-166, *infra.*

272. 380 U.S. 424, 428 (1965).

graphers v. Railway Express Agency, Inc., 321 U.S. 342, 348-49. Moreover, the courts ought to be relieved of the burden of trying stale claims when a plaintiff has slept on his rights.

The ADEA provides that any action to enforce a cause of action for violation of its provisions must be commenced within two years after the cause of action accrued; that is, after the allegedly discriminatory practice took place.[273] Every such action is forever barred unless commenced within two years after the cause of action accrued, except that a cause of action arising out of "a willful violation" may be commenced within three years after the cause of action accrued.[274]

The Secretary of Labor or an individual may commence an action under the ADEA at any time within the two year period, three years in the case of a willful violation, after the allegedly discriminatory act takes place provided that the required effort by the Secretary at conciliation, conference, and persuasion has been made and, in the case of an individual action, the 60 day waiting period after notice to the Secretary of Labor (given within the 180 day or 300 day period, as applicable, after the alleged unlawful practice occurred) has passed.[275]

---

273. Ott v. Midland-Ross Corp., 523 F.2d 1367 (6th Cir. 1975) (cause of action held to accrue under the ADEA on the date of alleged wrongful discharge in violation of the statute) n.o.r.

274. 29 U.S.C. § 626(e) (1970) *incorporating* 29 U.S.C. § 255 (1970).

The statute of limitations is an affirmative defense which must be pleaded by a defendant or it is waived. Fed. R. Civ. P. 8(c); Dunlop v. Westinghouse Elec. Corp., 11 CCH Employ. Prac. Dec. ¶10,814 (S.D. Fla., March 3, 1976) n.o.r.; 5 C. Wright and A. Miller, Federal Practice and Procedure § 1278 (1969).

275. Opinion Letter of Acting Wage-Hour Administrator, 8 Lab. Rel. Rep. 401:5223 (January 27, 1969).

There has been a determination by one court that no action can be maintained under the ADEA where an individual has failed to first seek relief under an appropriate state law and the shorter state statute of limitations for actions alleging age discrimination in employment has run. Smith v. Crest Communities, Inc., 9 CCH Employ. Prac. Dec. ¶10,053, 8 Fair Employ. Prac. Cas. 1328 (W.D. Ky., November 21, 1974) n.o.r. The Court of Appeals specifically reserved decision on that question in Curry v. Continental Airlines, 513 F.2d 691, 694 n. 3 (9th Cir. 1975).

In *Ott v. Midland-Ross Corp.*[276] the Court of Appeals held that neither the subsequent administrative efforts of the Secretary to settle a dispute nor the sixty day waiting period after an individual files a notice of intent to sue before he may file a civil action toll the running of the statute of limitations after a cause of action under the ADEA has accrued.

The Court of Appeals in *Ott,* further, held that an employer's failure or refusal to remedy a prior unlawful practice under the ADEA does not start the statute of limitations running again. However, if an individual is fraudulently induced not to assert his rights under the statute by the acts of a covered person then, the Court of Appeals held, he

> must bring suit within a reasonable time after discovery, or within a reasonable time after he should have discovered the actions of the defendant that induced him to delay filing suit.[277]

The two or three year statute of limitations is separate and distinct from the 180 or 300 day notice requirement although both are measured from the same date — the occurrence of the allegedly discriminatory act in violation of the ADEA. The former period fixes the time within which a civil action must be commenced while the latter fixes the time within which notice must be given to the Secretary of Labor.[278]

In determining when an action is commenced by the Secretary of Labor for the purposes of the statute of limitations, it is considered to be commenced in the case of an individual claimant on the date when the complaint is filed if he is specifically named as a party plaintiff in the complaint, or, if his name did not so appear, on the subsequent date on which his name is added as a party plaintiff in such action.[279]

---

276. 523 F.2d 1367 (6th Cir. 1975).
277. *Id.* at 1370.
278. Powell v. Southwestern Bell Tel. Co., 494 F. 2d 485, 487 (5th Cir. 1974).
279. 29 U.S.C. § 626(b) (1970) *incorporating* 29 U.S.C. § 216(c) (Supp. V 1975).

The "willful" violations of the ADEA which are subject to a three year statute of limitations have been described as follows:

> Generally, willful violations have been found only where there has been a bad faith evasion of the Act and definite knowledge of its applicability.[280]

M. DEFENSE BASED ON ADMINISTRATIVE ACTION

In any action or proceeding based on any act or omission alleged to violate the ADEA, an employer is not subject to any liability or punishment for or on account thereof if the employer pleads and proves that the act or omission complained of was in good faith conformity with and in reliance on any written administrative regulation, order, ruling, approval, or interpretation of the Administrator of the Wage and Hour Division of the Department of Labor or the Secretary of Labor or any Federal officer utilized by him in the administration of the ADEA, or any administrative practice or enforcement policy thereof with respect to the class of employers to which the employer belongs.[281] Such a defense, if established, is a bar to the action or proceeding notwithstanding that after the subject act or omission such administrative regulation, order, ruling, approval, interpretation, practice, or enforcement policy is modified or rescinded or is determined by judicial authority to be invalid or of no legal effect.[282]

---

280. Bishop v. Jelleff Associates, Inc., 398 F. Supp. 579, 593 (D.D.C. 1974).

In Dunlop v. Westinghouse Elec. Corp., 11 CCH Employ. Prac. Dec. ¶10,814 (S.D. Fla., March 3, 1976) n.o.r., the Court, relying on cases decided under the Fair Labor Standards Act, held that

> In order to establish willfulness, it is sufficient to show that the employer acted in the knowledge that his conduct was governed by the Fair Labor Standards Act [sic]. A violation is willful if "the employer knew or suspected that his actions might violate the FLSA." ***. Moreover, the defendant has the burden of proving that the willful provision which extends the statute of limitations to three years is not applicable. [11 CCH Employ. Prac. Dec. ¶10,814, at 7403.]

281. 29 U.S.C. § 626(e) (1970) *incorporating* 29 U.S.C. § 259 (1970). Although the incorporated section refers only to "employer," the courts can be expected to include employment agencies and labor organizations in applying it to the ADEA. The language of the incorporated section would require a defendant seeking to avail itself of the provision to assert the relevant facts as an affirmative defense under Fed. R. Civ. P. 8 (c).

282. 29 U.S.C. § 626(e) (1970) *incorporating* 29 U.S.C. § 259 (1970).

This provision protects employers, employment agencies, and labor organizations covered by the ADEA which act in compliance with interpretations of the statute by those charged with its enforcement and encourages voluntary compliance with those interpretations without constant resort to the courts for authoritative determinations. As has been noted above, the interpretations of the ADEA by the Secretary of Labor and the Administrator of the Wage and Hour Division of the Department of Labor are given weight by, but are not binding upon, the courts.[283]

N. CIVIL ACTIONS UNDER THE ADEA BY INDIVIDUALS

Section 7(b) of the ADEA provides that it shall be enforced in accordance with the powers, remedies, and procedures set forth in specified sections of the Fair Labor Standards Act of 1938.[284] Those provisions permit the Wage-Hour Administrator and the Secretary of Labor, for the purpose of carrying out their respective functions and duties under the ADEA, with the consent and cooperation of state agencies charged with the administration of state labor laws to utilize the services of state and local agencies and their employees and to reimburse such state and local agencies and their employees for services rendered for such purposes.[285]

As has been noted above,[286] any person entitled to the protection of the ADEA aggrieved by a violation of the statute may bring a civil action in any court of competent jurisdiction for such legal or equitable relief as will effectuate the purposes of the ADEA, subject to the termination of a person's right to bring such action upon the commencement of an action by the United States Secretary of Labor to enforce the rights of such person under the statute.[287] Such an action may be maintained against any person, including an employer, an employment agency, or a labor organization covered by the ADEA, who is alleged to have violated

---

283. *See* notes 5 and 6, *supra.*
284. 29 U.S.C. § 626(b) (1970) *incorporating* 29 U.S.C. §§ 211(b), 216(b), (c), (d), (e), 217 (1970 & Supp. V 1975).
285. 29 U.S.C. § 211(b) (1970).
286. Pp. 137-138, *supra.*
287. 29 U.S.C. § 626(c) (1970).

the provisions of the statute to recover amounts owing to a person as a result of a violation of the statute and, in cases of willful violations of the ADEA, an additional equal amount as liquidated damages.[288]

Such an action may be maintained in any Federal or state court of competent jurisdiction by any one or more persons entitled to the protection of the ADEA for and on behalf of himself or themselves and others similarly situated.[289] No person can be made a party plaintiff to any such action unless he has given his consent in writing to become such a party and such consent is filed in the court in which such action is brought.[290]

The court in such an action is required, in addition to any judgment awarded to the plaintiff or plaintiffs, to allow a successful plaintiff both a reasonable attorney's fee to be paid by the defendant and costs of the action.[291]

The right of an individual or individuals to bring an action under the ADEA, and the right of any person to become a party plaintiff to any such action, terminates upon the filing of a complaint by the Secretary of Labor in an action in which restraint is sought of any further delay in the payment of amounts owing to such person or persons as a result of a violation of the ADEA by a person liable therefor under the provisions of the statute.[292]

There has been some dispute as to whether the institution of an action under the ADEA by the Secretary terminates only the right of an individual on whose behalf the Secretary has brought an action to thereafter commence his own action or terminates, as well, the right of an individual to further prosecute his previously

---

288. 29 U.S.C. § 626(b) (1970) *incorporating* 29 U.S.C. § 216(b) (Supp. V 1975).

289. 29 U.S.C. § 216(b) (Supp. V 1975). The incorporated statutory provision uses the word "employee" to describe the persons entitled to bring an action. When applied to the ADEA, the word must be read to include all persons entitled to the protection of the statute. *See* Blankenship v. Ralston Purina Co., 62 F.R.D. 35, 38, 39 (N.D. Ga. 1973).

290. 29 U.S.C. § 216(b) (Supp. V 1975).

291. *Id.*

292. *Id.*

commenced action. The statutory language would seem to contemplate only the former since it provides that

> the right of any person to *bring* such action shall terminate upon the commencement of an action by the Secretary to enforce the right of such employee under this chapter.[293] (Emphasis added.)

Since no reference is made to "prosecute," as opposed to "bring," in Section 7(c), the Secretary of Labor should be placed under the same restraints as an individual. He should be prohibited from commencing an action seeking relief for an individual after that individual has begun his own action in compliance with the provisions of the ADEA. Where the Secretary commences an action under the statute on behalf of persons similarly situated to the plaintiff in a previously commenced action, consolidation of the two actions would be appropriate.[294]

While the commencement of an action by the Secretary of Labor under the ADEA terminates the statutory right of an individual whose claim of age discrimination forms the basis for the Secretary's action to thereafter commence an action on his own behalf, it may not foreclose that individual, or others claiming to have been discriminated against by the defendant, from participating in the action brought by the Secretary. Those

---

293. 29 U.S.C. § 626(c) (1970).

294. The questions discussed in the text were presented in Brennan v. McDonnell Douglas Corp., 519 F.2d 718 (8th Cir. 1975), but the Court of Appeals did not find it necessary to answer them holding, instead, that the Secretary of Labor, whose action had been dismissed below after denial of his motion to consolidate his action with a previously commenced individual action, could intervene in the prior action.

There is unfortunate dicta in Bishop v. Jelleff Associates, Inc., 398 F. Supp. 579, 592 (D.D.C. 1974), suggesting, without analysis or citation of authority, that

> the Secretary [of Labor] is empowered to initiate proceedings to supersede pending litigation instituted under the Act.

Similarly, in Lundgren v. Continental Indus., Inc., 11 CCH Employ. Prac. Dec. ¶10,778 (N.D. Okla., March 16, 1976) n.o.r., the Court stated in unsupported dicta that

> subsection (c) [of Section 7] provides that if after an individual institutes action, the Secretary thereafter institutes action, the individual shall immediately terminate such action and the Secretary shall enforce the right of the employee under the Act. [11 CCH Employ. Prac. Dec. ¶10,778, at 7277.]

169

individuals may seek to intervene in the Secretary's action under Federal Rule of Civil Procedure 24. One writer has suggested that under a statutory scheme such as that contained in the ADEA once the government has commenced an action and, thereby, prevented an individual from prosecuting his own action the individual should be allowed to intervene in the government action to raise, for example, new claims.[295]

The Secretary of Labor is authorized to supervise the payment of the amounts owing to a person as a result of a violation of the ADEA and the agreement of any person to accept such payment constitutes, upon payment in full, a waiver by such person of any right he may have under the statute to sue for damages for the violation and, where applicable, an additional equal amount as liquidated damages.[296]

O. CIVIL ACTIONS UNDER THE ADEA BY SECRETARY OF LABOR

The Secretary of Labor may bring an action in any court of competent jurisdiction to recover the amounts owing to a person as a result of a violation of the ADEA and, if the violation was willful, an equal amount as liquidated damages.[297]

The right to bring an action by or on behalf of any person entitled to the protection of the ADEA and of any such person to become a party plaintiff to any such action terminates upon the filing of a complaint by the Secretary in an action in which a recovery is sought of the amounts owing to such a person under the statute or of liquidated or other damages owing to such individual against a person who is subject to the provisions of the ADEA unless such action is dismissed without prejudice on motion of the Secretary.[298] Any sums thus recovered by the Secretary on behalf of an

---

295. Note, *Intervention in Government Enforcement Actions,* 89 Harv. L. Rev. 1174, 1179 and n. 16, 1192-93 (1976).

296. 29 U.S.C. § 216(c) (Supp. V 1975).

297. *Id.*

298. *Id. See* pp. 168-170, *supra,* for a discussion of the termination of an individual's right to bring an action under the ADEA resulting from the institution of an action by the Secretary of Labor.

individual are required to be held in a special deposit account and to be paid, on order of the Secretary of Labor, directly to the individual or individuals affected. Any such sums not paid to an employee because of inability to do so within a period of three years must be transferred into the Treasury of the United States.[299]

P. INJUNCTIVE PROCEEDINGS

The United States district courts, including those for the Districts of the Canal Zone, the Virgin Islands, and Guam, have jurisdiction, for cause shown, to restrain violations of the ADEA, including the restraint of any withholding of payment of amounts owing to persons as a result of a violation of the statute found by a court to be due to individuals thereunder, except for sums which individuals are barred from recovering at the time of the commencement of the action to restrain the violation by virtue of the statute of limitations.[300]

The major issues which have arisen in connection with litigation under the ADEA involve: (1) class actions and consent to suit, (2) the availability of jury trials, (3) the proper burden of proof, (4) methods of proof, and (5) the damages and costs available where a violation of the ADEA is proven. Those issues are discussed in the following sections.

Q. CLASS ACTIONS AND CONSENTS TO SUIT

A "class action" is a lawsuit in which one or more persons are named as plaintiffs or defendants representing themselves and, by court direction, others similarly situated who, though they do not actively participate in the litigation, are bound by the court's determination as though they were named therein. The justifications for allowing class actions include eliminating the necessity for multiple parties and litigations and permitting persons with similar claims which are not large enough individually to justify commencing an action to aggregate their claims and seek relief in a single action which is justifiable on a cost basis.

---

299. *Id.*
300. 29 U.S.C. § 626(b) (1970) *incorporating* 29 U.S.C. § 217 (1970).

As has been noted by the Court in *Blankenship v. Ralston Purina Company*,[301] the Federal courts have recognized that the class action is particularly adaptable to situations involving discrimination, in general, and to situations involving discrimination in employment, in particular. The typical class action in a Federal court is governed by Rule 23 of the Federal Rules of Civil Procedure which sets forth the prerequisites which a court must find present in a particular case before it can permit the action to be maintained as a class action.[302] The ADEA incorporates a provision of the Fair Labor Standards Act of 1938 dealing specifically with representative actions.[303]

---

301. 62 F.R.D. 35, 38, 39 (N.D. Ga. 1973).
302. Rule 23(a) provides that

> One or more members of a class may sue or be sued as representative parties on behalf of all only if (1) the class is so numerous that joinder of all members is impracticable, (2) there are questions of law or fact common to the class, (3) the claims or defenses of the representative parties are typical of the claims or defenses of the class, and (4) the representative parties will fairly and adequately protect the interests of the class.

Rule 23(b) provides, in part, that

> An action may be maintained as a class action if the prerequisites of subdivision (a) are satisfied, and in addition:
> (1) the prosecution of separate actions by or against individual members of the class would create a risk of
> (A) inconsistent or varying adjudications with respect to individual members of the class which would establish incompatible standards of conduct for the party opposing the class, or
> (B) adjudications with respect to individual members of the class which would as a practical matter be dispositive of the interests of the other members not parties to the adjudications or substantially impair or impede their ability to protect their interests; or
> (2) the party opposing the class has acted or refused to act on grounds generally applicable to the class, thereby making appropriate final injunctive relief or corresponding declaratory relief with respect to the class as a whole; or
> (3) the court finds that the questions of law or fact common to the members of the class predominate over any questions affecting only individual members, and that a class action is superior to other available methods for the fair and efficient adjudication of the controversy.

303. 29 U.S.C. § 216(b), (c) (Supp. V 1975) *incorporated by* 29 U.S.C. § 626(b) (1970).

Section 216(b) provides in relevant part that an

> [a]ction . . . may be maintained . . . by any one or more employees for and in behalf of himself or themselves and other employees similarly

THE FEDERAL AGE DISCRIMINATION IN EMPLOYMENT ACT

Three questions have arisen with respect to representative actions under the ADEA: (1) whether both Section 216 of the Fair Labor Standards Act of 1938 and Rule 23 of the Federal Rules of Civil Procedure apply to such actions or just the former; (2) whether all members of the class or just the named parties plaintiff must file with the court written consents to their becoming a party plaintiff; and (3) whether all members of the class or just the named parties plaintiff must comply with the provisions of the ADEA requiring the giving of timely notice of intention to sue to the Secretary of Labor and, where appropriate, initial resort to state remedies.

The legislative history of the ADEA does not provide any assistance in answering the foregoing questions and the courts have divided in dealing with them. Thus, some courts have held that a person seeking to bring a class action under the ADEA must comply with the provisions of both Section 216 of the Fair Labor Standards Act of 1938 and Rule 23 of the Federal Rules of Civil Procedure,[304] while other courts have held that a plaintiff seeking to maintain an action under the statute individually and

---

situated. No employee shall be a party plaintiff to any such action unless he gives his consent in writing to become such a party and such consent is filed in the court in which such action is brought.

Section 216(c) provides, *inter alia*, that

In determining when an action is commenced by the Secretary of Labor ... for the purposes of the statutes of limitations ..., it shall be considered to be commenced in the case of any individual claimant on the date when the complaint is filed if he is specifically named as a party plaintiff in the complaint, or if his name did not so appear, on the subsequent date on which his name is added as a party plaintiff in such action.

304. Blankenship v. Ralston Purina Co., 62 F.R.D. 35 (N.D. Ga. 1973); Gebhard v. GAF Corp., 59 F.R.D. 504 (D.D.C. 1973); Bishop v. Jelleff Associates, Inc., 5 CCH Employ. Prac. Dec. ¶7995, 4 Fair Employ. Prac. Cas. 1262 (D.D.C., August 1, 1972) n.o.r. *See also* Comment, *Class Actions Under the Age Discrimination in Employment Act: The Question is "Why not?"*, 23 Emory L.J. 831 (1974), arguing that Section 216 of the Fair Labor Standards Act of 1938 and the ADEA should be interpreted so as to permit class actions under the ADEA and to require, in effect, compliance only with the provisions of Rule 23. The author's arguments are properly disposed of by the Court of Appeals in Lachapelle v. Owens-Illinois, Inc., 513 F.2d 286, 289 n. 10 (5th Cir. 1975) (*per curiam*).

173

representatively need comply only with Section 216 and that Rule 23 is inapplicable to representative actions under the ADEA.[305]

There has also been a divergence of opinion as to whether or not each member of the class must file a consent to being made a party plaintiff to a class action under the ADEA.[306]

Similarly, the courts have divided on the question of whether each class member must have filed a notice with the Secretary of Labor and, in appropriate cases, exhausted his state remedies.[307]

---

305. Cooke v. Reynolds Metals Co., 65 F.R.D. 539 (E.D. Va. 1975); Lachapelle v. Owens-Illinois, Inc., 64 F.R.D. 96 (N.D. Ga. 1974), aff'd per curiam, 513 F.2d 286 (5th Cir. 1975); McGinley v. Burroughs Corp., 407 F. Supp. 903, 911 (E.D. Pa. 1975); Burgett v. Cudahy Co., 361 F. Supp. 617 (D. Kan. 1973); Hull v. Continental Oil Co., 58 F.R.D. 636 (S.D. Tex. 1973); Price v. Maryland Cas. Co., 62 F.R.D. 614 (S.D. Miss. 1972). See also Doctor v. Seaboard Coast Line R.R., 540 F.2d 699, 710 n. 37 (4th Cir. 1976) (dictum). where the Court of Appeals noted that "it is generally held that class certification under the Act is inappropriate."

See also Roshto v. Chrysler Corp., 67 F.R.D. 28, 29 (E.D. La. 1975), where the Court noted the conflict and that "the emerging majority view suggests that § 216(b) is exclusive, providing for the only type of class action permissible under the Act." The Court held that it did not have to reach the question because, although the plaintiff had originally filed the action as a Rule 23 class action, she subsequently amended her complaint "to reflect that its class action aspects were brought under § 216(b)."

306. Class members not required to each file consents: Blankenship v. Ralston Purina Co., supra, at 41 ("provided that their grievances fall within the charges filed by the party plaintiff"). Class members each required to file consents: Cooke v. Reynolds Metals Co., supra; Lachapelle v. Owens-Illinois, Inc., supra; Burgett v. Cudahy Co., supra; Hull v. Continental Oil Co., supra; Price v. Maryland Cas. Co., supra; Bishop v. Jelleff Associates, Inc., supra; Roshto v. Chrysler Corp., supra.

307. Each member of the class must file a timely notice with the Secretary of Labor: McCorstin v. United States Steel Corp., 11 Fair Employ. Prac. Cas. 1478 (N.D. Ala., December 16, 1974) n.o.r. Each member of the class must file a timely notice with the Secretary of Labor unless the condition is affirmatively waived by the defendant: Price v. Maryland Cas. Co., supra. Only the plaintiff representative must comply with the notice requirement and exhaust administrative remedies: Blankenship v. Ralston Purina Co., supra; Burgett v. Cudahy Co., supra; Bishop v. Jelleff Associates, Inc., supra. See also Gebhard v. GAF Corp., supra, indicating agreement with the latter position. In Cooke v. Reynolds Metals Co., supra, the Court specifically reserved ruling on whether class members filing consents with the Court must have filed individual notices of intent to sue with the Secretary of Labor. A person cannot be the representative of a class if he has failed to comply with the notice requirement: Dartt v. Shell Oil Co., 9 CCH Employ. Prac. Dec. ¶10,205, 10 Fair Employ. Prac. Cas. 844 (N.D. Okla., February 6, 1975) n.o.r.

The answers to the questions of whether an action under the ADEA may be maintained on behalf of a class without a finding of compliance with the provisions of Rule 23 of the Federal Rules of Civil Procedure, whether each party plaintiff must file a consent with the court, and whether all class members must file a timely notice with the Secretary and exhaust state procedures where applicable cannot be determined from the statute and must, therefore, be found in the purposes of the ADEA and general principles of statutory interpretation.

The Federal Rules of Civil Procedure provide that, in cases where a class action is allowed because of the existence of predominating common questions of law and fact, the members of the class must be given notice of the determination and of their membership in the class and advised that they can request exclusion from the class, in which case they will not be bound by the judgment of the court.[308] Section 216 of the Fair Labor Standards Act contains no provisions for notice to class members or for an opportunity to "opt out" of the class.[309] Accordingly, since most class actions under the ADEA will be based on common questions of law or fact, fairness and due process would seem to require that class members be advised of the pendency of a class action on behalf of a class of which they are members, which would among other things avoid the institution of separate actions for identical relief based on lack of knowledge of the prior action, and that they be permitted to exclude themselves from the action if they desire. This result could be accomplished either by making Rule 23 applicable to class actions under the ADEA or by requiring each class member to file a consent with the court under Section 216.[310]

Since the ADEA specifically adopts the "procedures provided in" Section 216,[311] those specific procedures should be applied in lieu

---

308. Fed. R. Civ. P. 23(c) (2).

309. 29 U.S.C. § 216(b) (Supp. V 1975); Roshto v. Chrysler Corp., 67 F.R.D. 28, 29 (E.D. La. 1975); Burgett v. Cudahy Co., 361 F. Supp. 617, 622 (D. Kan. 1973).

310. *See* McGinley v. Burroughs Corp., 407 F. Supp. 903, 911 (E.D. Mich. 1975) (holding that class actions under the ADEA are governed by Section 216 and not Rule 23 and refusing to permit a Rule 23 type notice to proposed class members in order to give them an opportunity to "opt in" to the action).

311. 29 U.S.C. § 626(b) (1970).

of the general provisions of the Federal Rules of Civil Procedure in accordance with the normal rules of statutory interpretation. It would seem, therefore, that a class action under the ADEA may be maintained where compliance with Section 216 of the Fair Labor Standards Act is shown, without the necessity of compliance with Rule 23, on behalf of all persons filing consents with the court.[312] This is consistent with the provision of Section 216(b) that no employee can be a party plaintiff unless he consents thereto in a writing filed with the court.[313] This cannot logically refer simply to the originally named plaintiffs as suggested by one court[314] since no attorney can bring an action on behalf of a specific person in that person's name without their directing him to do so. Thus, the written consent requirement must refer to persons in addition to the original plaintiff or plaintiffs. Similarly, Section 216(c) provides that an action brought by the Secretary of Labor is commenced for purposes of the statute of limitations with respect to persons other than the original plaintiff or plaintiffs when their names are added as party plaintiffs and not when the action is first

---

312. McGinley v. Burroughs Corp., 407 F. Supp. 903 (E.D. Mich. 1975). *See generally* Schmidt v. Fuller Brush Co., 527 F.2d 532 (8th Cir. 1975) (*per curiam*) (FLSA).

313. The use of the word "employee" in Section 216 should not be read to make the procedures for representative actions set forth therein inapplicable to actions under the ADEA by persons alleging that they were denied employment or discharged from employment in violation of the statute. It would be illogical to read a section of the Fair Labor Standards Act which is incorporated into the ADEA by reference as requiring one procedure for class actions by employees and a second procedure, that set forth in Rule 23, for actions by persons who were denied employment or discharged from employment. Indeed, one action could conceivably include persons from two or all three of those categories. In addition, the Fair Labor Standards Act applies only to employees unlike the ADEA so that it is to be expected that the terminology of the incorporated provisions of the former statute may not exactly fit the latter. [For examples of such modifications of the provisions of the Fair Labor Standards Act incorporated into the ADEA, *see* Section 7(b) of the ADEA, 29 U.S.C. § 626(b) (1975).] *But see* Gilfix, *First Hired-First Fired: Age Discrimination in Employment,* 50 Cal. State Bar J. 462, 465 n. 28 (1975), where the author takes a contrary position.

314. *See* Blankenship v. Ralston Purina Co., 62 F.R.D. 35, 39-40 (N.D. Ga. 1973).

filed as is the case in Rule 23 class actions.[315] As was noted in *Hull v. Continental Oil Company,*[316]

> The cases interpreting § 216(b) of Title 29 have uniformly required the filing of such consents. See, Montalvo v. Tower Life Bldg., 426 F.2d 1135 (5th Cir. 1970). A person who does not file a consent can neither benefit from nor be bound by any judgment in the suit. Sims v. Parke Davis & Co., 334 F. Supp. 774 (D. Mich. 1971). Some courts have even stated that this type action is not a "class action" within Rule 23, F.R. Civ. P., but is a form of permissive joinder. See, Fink v. Oliver Iron Mining Co., 65 F. Supp. 316 (D. Minn. 1941) and Schimerowski v. Iowa Beef Packers, Inc., 196 N.W. 2d 551 (Iowa 1972). This proposition was accepted in another form by the court in Maguire v. Trans World Airlines, Inc., 55 F.R.D. 48 (S.D.N.Y. 1972), where it held that a "class action" under the Fair Labor Standards Act is statutory and independent of class actions under Rule 23, and did not require leave of court as did actions under the rule to enforce class actions under Title VII, 42 U.S.C. § 2000e.

The Court in *Bishop v. Jelleff Associates, Inc.*[317] was clearly correct in holding that, while the consents of members of the class need not be filed simultaneously with the complaint since most members of the class will probably not be aware of the filing of the action, "fairness and due process require that defendants be put on notice as to the names of plaintiffs within a reasonable time." This procedure could be implemented by court order after the filing of a class action under the ADEA as was done in the *Bishop* case.[318] Adoption of that procedure would avoid the

---

315. *See* American Pipe and Constr. Co. v. Utah, 414 U.S. 538, *rehearing denied,* 415 U.S. 952 (1974).

316. 58 F.R.D. 636, 637 (S.D. Tex. 1973).

317. 5 CCH Employ. Prac. Dec. ¶7995, at 6659, 4 Fair Employ. Prac. Cas. 1262 (D.D.C., August 1, 1972) n.o.r.

318. The Court in *Bishop* gave plaintiffs forty-five days from the date of its decision to file consents. In Roshto v. Chrysler Corp., 67 F.R.D. 28, 30 (E.D. La. 1975), the Court granted defendant's motion to fix a cut-off date for the filing of consents by new plaintiffs by ordering prospectively that the action be dismissed without prejudice as to all potential plaintiffs who did not file written consents with

problem of lack of identification of class members, and that of class members who await the court's decision before formally joining the action, referred to by the Court in *Blankenship v. Ralston Purina Company.*[319]

The fact that notice is not required to be given to class members under Section 216(b), as it is under Rule 23 on due process grounds, should not, however, be used as a basis for preventing a plaintiff in a class action under the ADEA from sending notice of the action to potential class members, as one court has done.[320] Unless a plaintiff can communicate with other potential plaintiffs there will be few class actions under the ADEA. To deny the plaintiff in an action under the ADEA the ability to give notice to other potential plaintiffs would deny those potential plaintiffs an opportunity to "opt in" to the action and, as has been noted above, may result in the institution of separate actions for identical relief based on lack of knowledge of a prior action. The efficacy of class actions in cases of employment discrimination militates in favor of allowing all those procedures which promote elimination of discrimination in the most efficient manner and provide knowledge of their rights to the relatively unsophisticated objects of such discrimination.

While the requirement that a person seeking to bring an action under the ADEA file notice of his intention to sue within 180 or 300 days after the alleged violation of the statute and at least 60 days before the action is commenced so that the Secretary of Labor can attempt to settle the matter by informal methods would seem to require that each class member file a notice so as to permit the Secretary of Labor to attempt to resolve each individual's complaint, the provision in Section 216(b) that all class members

---

the Court in conformity with Section 216(b) at least thirty days prior to trial of the action. The Court noted that

> This procedure will allow sufficient time for potential class members to opt in should they so desire and at the same time should afford the defendant adequate time to prepare its defenses [against each plaintiff who might join plaintiff Roshto].

319. 62 F.R.D. 35, 39-40 and n. 2 (N.D. Ga. 1973). *See also* Note, *Proving Discrimination Under the Age Discrimination in Employment Act,* 17 Ariz. L. Rev. 495, 500 (1975) (suggesting that due process and fairness require that a defendant in a suit under the ADEA receive notice of all the plaintiffs' names within a "reasonable time").

320. Roshto v. Chrysler Corp., 67 F.R.D. 28 (E.D. La. 1975).

be "similarly situated" should obviate the necessity for the filing of individual notices. As the Court held in *Burgett v. Cudahy Company,*

> If an individual properly complies with the Act's provisions and provides the Secretary with notice of a practice which either inherently discriminates against a class of individuals intended to be protected by the Act or allegedly has adversely affected a number of "similarly situated" employees, the purposes of the Act's notice filing provision are fulfilled. Both the Secretary and the alleged discriminator are put on notice that the complaint encompasses a pattern or practice of discrimination transcending an isolated individual claim, and they should act accordingly. To require each individual aggrieved party to file an essentially identical claim or notice would serve no useful purpose other than the promotion of a futile charade.[321]

The Court in *McCorstin v. United States Steel Corp.* [322] made no reference to Section 216(b) of the Fair Labor Standards Act in denying class action status because of the effect permitting the action would have on conciliation procedures in a case where class members had not filed individual notices of intent to sue.

R. AVAILABILITY OF JURY TRIAL

While the ADEA does not specify whether a jury trial is available in an action brought under the statute, it has been held by the courts that the right to a jury trial depends upon whether the issues to be tried can be characterized as "legal" or "equitable" under the

---

321. 361 F. Supp. 617, 624-25 (D. Kan. 1973). *Accord,* Blankenship v. Ralston Purina Co., 62 F.R.D. 35, 42 (N.D. Ga. 1973); Note, *Procedural Aspects of the Age Discrimination in Employment Act of 1967,* 36 U. Pitt. L. Rev. 914, 925-26 (1975). One writer has supported the view that only the original plaintiff should be required to comply with the ADEA's notice of intention requirement on the grounds that the original plaintiff's notice gives both the Secretary of Labor and the prospective defendant timely notice of the complaint and that requiring each class member to give notice may be wasteful of administrative resources. Note, *Proving Discrimination Under the Age Discrimination in Employment Act,* 17 Ariz. L. Rev. 495, 500 (1975).

322. 11 Fair Employ. Prac. Cas. 1478, 1480 (N.D. Ala., December 16, 1974) n.o.r.

Seventh Amendment to the United States Constitution [323] and whether the action is brought by the United States Secretary of Labor or an individual and whether injunctive relieve or damages is sought.[324] Thus, the courts have allowed, or suggested the availability of, jury trials in actions brought by individuals for damages.[325]

One court in an extensive examination of the applicable law has held that an individual plaintiff has the right to a jury trial on the issue of lost wages and benefits but that the issues of the award of liquidated damages and attorney's fees and costs under the ADEA are within the discretion of the court and that there is, accordingly, no right to a jury trial with respect to those issues.[326] A second court disagreed only with respect to the issue of liquidated damages which it held was to be determined by the jury.[327] In addition, that Court held that a claim for reinstatement was a request for equitable relief and was not, therefore, triable to a jury.

---

323. *See* Cleverly v. Western Elec. Co., 69 F.R.D. 348, 350 (W.D. Mo. 1975).

324. *See generally* Wallace, *Age Discrimination in Employment Under Federal Law,* 9 Ga. State Bar J. 114, 127-28 (1972).

325. *See* Wilson v. Sealtest Foods Div. of Kraftco Corp., 501 F.2d 84, 86 and n. 4 (5th Cir. 1974), *petitions for rehearing denied,* 10 CCH Employ. Prac. Dec. ¶10,399, 11 Fair Employ. Prac. Cas. 128 (5th Cir., Dec. 13, 1974) *(per curiam)* n.o.r.; Rogers v. Exxon Research and Engineering Co., 404 F. Supp. 324 (D.N.J. 1975); Woodford v. Kinney Shoe Corp., 369 F. Supp. 911, 916 (N.D. Ga. 1973) ("Ordinarily, the question of whether a defendant was the employer of a plaintiff in an age discrimination case is a question of fact which is to be decided by the jury."); Monroe v. Penn-Dixie Cement Corp., 335 F. Supp. 231, 233 (N.D. Ga. 1971). *But see* Laugesen v. Anaconda Co., 510 F.2d 307, 312 n. 2 (6th Cir. 1975), where the Court of Appeals in reviewing a decision in a jury trial under the ADEA noted that the question of the availability of a jury trial was not before it.

326. Chilton v. National Cash Register Co., 370 F. Supp. 660, 666 (S.D. Ohio 1974). *See also* Rogers v. Exxon Research and Eng'r Co., 404 F. Supp. 324, 334 (D.N.J. 1975) (issue of willfulness in connection with deciding whether liquidated damages should be awarded is for the court not the jury); Monroe v. Penn-Dixie Cement Corp., *supra,* at 234, n. 3 (indicating in *dictum* that the determination of whether to grant liquidated damages is for the judge not the jury). *Contra,* O'Connell v. Ford Motor Co., 11 CCH Employ. Prac. Dec. ¶10,753, 11 Fair Employ. Prac. Cas. 1474 (E.D. Mich., September 23, 1975) (claim for back pay not triable to a jury) n.o.r.

327. Cleverly v. Western Elec. Co., 69 F.R.D. 348 (W.D. Mo. 1975). The *Cleverly* Court's determination with respect to the issue of liquidated damages is the better reasoned of the two decisions.

On the other hand, the courts have held that there is no right to a jury trial in actions brought under the ADEA by the Secretary of Labor to enjoin violations of the statute and to obtain back wages for an individual by means of an injunction under Section 217 of the Fair Labor Standards Act of 1938 which provides for restraint of any further withholding of lost wages and other benefits.[328] Since the Secretary is suing in such a case in the place of an individual who is prohibited from bringing an action once the Secretary has commenced one,[329] a jury trial should be available to the Secretary and, through him, the complainant. Any other view would make the question of the availability of a jury trial turn on the purely fortuitous event of whether the Secretary brings an action during the 60 day period after notice of intention to sue or thereafter before the complainant does.

The foregoing determinations must be measured against the United States Supreme Court's most recent interpretation of the right to jury trial under the Seventh Amendment to the United States Constitution. In *Curtis v. Loether*,[330] the Supreme Court had before it the question of whether a jury trial was available in an action pursuant to Section 812 of the Civil Rights Act of 1968 dealing with fair housing.[331] The Supreme Court held that

> The Seventh Amendment does apply to actions enforcing statutory rights, and requires a jury trial upon demand, if the statute creates legal rights and remedies,

---

328. Hodgson v. Bowman, 4 CCH Employ. Prac. Dec. ¶7601, 4 Fair Employ. Prac. Cas. 165 (E.D. Tenn., December 7, 1971) n.o.r.; Brennan v. International Harvester Co., 7 CCH Employ. Prac. Dec. ¶9171 (N.D. Ill., February 21, 1971) n.o.r. To the same effect *see* Chilton v. National Cash Register Co., *supra*, at 664 (*dictum*).

See also O'Connell v. Ford Motor Co., 11 CCH Employ. Prac. Dec. ¶10,753, 11 Fair Employ. Prac. Cas. 1474 (E.D. Mich., September 23, 1975) n.o.r., where the Court denied a jury trial in an individual action in which the plaintiff sought "equitable relief" enjoining defendant from failing to pay plaintiff compensation and directing that plaintiff be made whole by appropriate back pay. The Court relied upon the cases decided under Section 217 of the Fair Labor Standards Act which authorizes the Secretary of Labor to seek injunctive relief similar to that sought by the plaintiff.

329. *See* 29 U.S.C. § 626(c) (1970).

330. 415 U.S. 189 (1974).

331. 42 U.S.C. § 3612 (1970).

enforceable in an action for damages in the ordinary courts of law.[332]

* * *

[W]hen Congress provides for enforcement of statutory rights in an ordinary civil action in the district courts, where there is obviously no functional justification for denying the jury trial right, a jury trial must be available if the action involves rights and remedies at law.[333]

The foregoing holdings would seem to support the right to a jury trial in actions for damages under the ADEA and one court has so interpreted them.[334] If an individual seeks both equitable relief, in the form of an injunction against violations of the ADEA, and damages, then there is a right to a jury trial with respect to the legal claim for damages and all issues common to the legal and equitable claims.[335]

S. BURDEN OF PROOF

The phrase "burden of proof" refers to the obligation of a party to an action to produce evidence sufficient to support a finding in his favor by the judge or jury and to prevent a finding in favor of the adverse party. The burden of proof does not remain on one party throughout a trial but rather switches from one party to another depending upon the claims asserted by the plaintiff and the defenses set forth by the defendant.

The general guidelines for the burden of proof in ADEA cases

---

332. 415 U.S. at 194.

333. 415 U.S. at 195.

334. Wilson v. Sealtest Foods Div. of Kraftco Corp., 501 F.2d 84, 86 n. 4 (5th Cir. 1974), *petitions for rehearing denied,* 10 CCH Employ. Prac. Dec. ¶10,399, 11 Fair Employ. Prac. Cas. 128 (5th Cir., December 13, 1974) (*per curiam*) n.o.r. *But see* Laugesen v. Anaconda Co., 510 F.2d 307, 312 n. 2 (6th Cir. 1975).

335. *See* Curtis v. Loether, 415 U.S. 189, 196 n. 11 (1974). *Accord,* Cleverly v. Western Elec. Co., 69 F.R.D. 348, 350 (W.D. Mo. 1975).

have been formulated as follows in the leading case of *Hodgson v. First Federal Savings and Loan Association.*[336]

> In discrimination cases the law with respect to burden of proof is well-settled. The plaintiff is required only to make out a prima facie case of unlawful discrimination at which point the burden shifts to the defendant to justify the existence of any disparities. [Citations omitted.] Once the plaintiff has made out his prima facie case we look to the defendant for an explanation since he is in a position to know whether he failed to hire a person for reasons which would exonerate him.[337]

Subsequently, in *Bittar v. Air Canada* [338] the Fifth Circuit Court of Appeals, although citing *inter alia* its earlier decision in *Hodgson v. First Federal Savings and Loan Association,* reformulated the applicable rule as follows:

> Upon ... a prima facie showing by the plaintiff, there is a shift, but not in the burden of proof. Only the burden of going forward with the evidence shifts to the defendant-employer. [Citations omitted.] Once the

---

336. 455 F.2d 818 (5th Cir. 1972). *Followed in* O'Connell v. Ford Motor Co., 11 CCH Employ. Prac. Dec. ¶10,753, 11 Fair Employ. Prac. Cas. 1471 (E.D. Mich., September 23, 1975) n.o.r.; Bishop v. Jelleff Associates, Inc., 398 F. Supp. 579, 593 (D.D.C. 1974); Schulz v. Hickok Mfg. Co., 358 F. Supp. 1208, 1213 (N.D. Ga. 1973); Hodgson v. Sugar Cane Growers Coop., 5 CCH Employ. Prac. Dec. ¶8618, at 7813, 5 Fair Employ. Prac. Cas. 1136, 1138 (S.D. Fla., April 4, 1973) n.o.r.; Hodgson v. Tamiami Trail Tours, Inc., 4 CCH Employ. Prac. Dec. ¶7795, at 6050, 4 Fair Employ. Prac. Cas. 728, 731 (S.D. Fla., March 31, 1972) n.o.r.

337. 455 F.2d at 822. The same standards would apply, for example, to a case alleging wrongful discharge in violation of the ADEA [Brennan v. Goodyear Tire & Rubber Co., 10 CCH Employ. Prac. Dec. ¶10,562, at 6332, 11 Fair Employ. Prac. Cas. 589, 590 (M.D. Fla., May 8, 1975) ("Plaintiff has proved a prima facie case of violation of the" ADEA "as to the Reed discharge and defendant has failed to carry its burden of showing that said discharge was within the exception of 'good cause'.") n.o.r.; Bishop v. Jelleff Associates, Inc., *supra;* Schulz v. Hickok Mfg. Co., 358 F. Supp., *supra,* at 1213 ("[P]laintiff has clearly made out a strong prima facie case. . . . The law is well settled that in discrimination cases the burden then shifts to the defendant to establish that the discharge was for reasonable non-discriminatory reasons."); Hodgson v. Sugar Cane Growers Coop., *supra*] and, presumably, to one alleging that an advertisement violates the statute. *See* Levien, *The Age Discrimination in Employment Act: Statutory Requirements and Recent Developments,* 13 Duq. L. Rev. 227, 236-38 (1974).

338. 512 F.2d 582 (5th Cir. 1975) (*per curiam*).

defendant-employer comes forward with evidence that the plaintiff was discharged because of reasonable factors other than age, the plaintiff must still bear the burden of establishing a case of discrimination by a preponderance of the evidence.[339]

The plaintiff in a case brought under the ADEA has, therefore, the initial burden of proving a prima facie case if he is to avoid dismissal of his claim and shift the burden of proof, or going forward with the evidence under *Bittar,* to the defendant.

What constitutes a prima facie case was discussed indirectly by the Court in *Bishop v. Jelleff Associates, Inc.,*[340] which held that

> Although there have been no decisions which define a prima facie case, the Court construes the statute as requiring the plaintiff to show more than simply the fact that he was within the protected age group and that he was adversely affected by an employment decision.[341]

The Acting Wage-Hour Administrator, in response to an inquiry as to the prima facie evidence of age discrimination necessary to support a complaint under the ADEA, stated that

> In general, the evidence must be sufficient, standing alone and uncontradicted, to support a conclusion that the act has been violated; and what evidence will suffice would depend on what activity prohibited by section 4 of the act is alleged to have taken place.[342]

In *O'Connell v. Ford Motor Co.*[343] the Court, noting the absence of detailed and definitive guidelines concerning the proofs

---

339. 512 F.2d at 582-83.

340. 398 F. Supp. 579 (D.D.C. 1974).

341. 398 F. Supp. at 593. *Accord,* Wilson v. Sealtest Foods Div. of Kraftco Corp., 501 F.2d 84, 86 (5th Cir. 1974), *petitions for rehearing denied,* 10 CCH Employ. Prac. Dec. ¶10,399, 11 Fair Employ. Prac. Cas. 128 (5th Cir., Dec. 13, 1974) (per curiam) n.o.r. *See also* Laugesen v. Anaconda Co., 510 F.2d 307, 313 n. 4 (6th Cir. 1975) ("we do not believe that Congress intended automatic presumptions to apply whenever a worker is replaced by another of a different age.").

342. Opinion Letter of Acting Wage-Hour Administrator, 8 Lab. Rel. Rep. 401:5222 (January 7, 1969).

343. 11 CCH Employ. Prac. Dec. ¶10,753, 11 Fair Employ. Prac. Cas. 1471 (E.D. Mich., September 23, 1975) n.o.r.

necessary to sustain the burdens allocated under prior ADEA cases, adopted

> a three-step test, which requires plaintiff to prove a prima facie case of employment discrimination. One manner of satisfying that burden is to show: (i) that plaintiff is over 40, which is the target age of the ADEA; (ii) that he applied and was qualified for a job; (iii) that he was rejected; and (iv) that the defendant continued to seek applicants with plaintiff's qualifications. The burden then shifts to defendant to "articulate some legitimate non-discriminatory reason" for the refusal to promote. 29 U.S.C. § 623(f) codifies that burden by allowing employment decisions on the basis of a bona fide occupational qualification, business necessity, seniority, or good cause. Thirdly, the complainant must be given an opportunity to prove that an otherwise valid reason might be used as a pretext for discrimination.[344]

Examples of evidence sufficient to constitute a prima facie case of a violation of the ADEA would include proof that a plaintiff is within the protected age bracket and that the defendant has: filled the opening for which the plaintiff was qualified with a younger person with similar qualifications;[345] told the plaintiff that he is being discharged or not being hired because of his age;[346] placed an advertisement either explicitly or by use of words or phrases eliminating or discouraging persons between 40 and 65 from applying for a particular position;[347] or engaged in a pattern of never hiring persons within the protected age bracket.[348] Conversely, it has been held that, where the plaintiff failed to introduce any evidence that the defendant employer had actual knowledge of the complainant's approximate age or that would suggest or imply that the employer had any reason to be aware

---

344. 11 CCH Employ. Prac. Dec. ⁋10,753, at 7162, 11 Fair Employ. Prac. Cas. at 1472.

345. O'Connell v. Ford Motor Co., *supra.*

346. *See, e.g.,* Hodgson v. Poole Truck Line, Inc., 4 CCH Employ. Prac. Dec. ⁋7668, 4 Fair Employ. Prac. Cas. 265 (S.D. Ala., January 13, 1972) n.o.r.

347. *See* cases discussed pp. 91-97, *supra.*

348. *See, e.g.,* Hodgson v. First Fed. Sav. and Loan Ass'n, 455 F.2d 818, 822-23 (5th Cir. 1972); Hodgson v. Poole Truck Line, Inc., *supra.*

of the age of the complainant, the fact that the complainant's appearance was such that it should have been obvious to the employer that the complainant was over 40 years of age was not enough to place upon the employer the burden of establishing by evidence the details of the reasons for the complainant's discharge.[349]

Once the plaintiff has carried his burden of proving a prima facie case, the burden has been held to shift to the defendant. Then the

> defendant is required to carry the burden of convincing the court that it discharged plaintiff for reasons other than age.
> * * *. Thus defendant has the burden of proving that plaintiff was discharged because of reasonable factors other than age or for cause. Failure to carry that burden must result in judgment for plaintiff.[350]

An exception to the foregoing rule has been recognized in *Laugesen v. Anaconda Company*[351] where the Court of Appeals held in a jury case that the burden of proof was initially upon the plaintiff to prove he was discharged because of age and that, absent an admission by the defendant or a state of facts so clear that no reasonable person could disagree or an admission and reliance upon one of the statutory exceptions to the prohibitions of the ADEA as an affirmative defense, where the defendant's defense was that it did not discriminate on account of age but acted based on other factors the burden of proof remained with the plaintiff throughout the trial and never shifted to the defendant. The decision must be considered in light of the fact that the case involved a jury trial and the Court of Appeals found that plaintiff's

---

349. Hodgson v. Earnest Machine Prods., Inc., 479 F.2d 1133 (6th Cir. 1973) (*per curiam*).

350. Schulz v. Hickok Mfg. Co., 358 F. Supp. 1208, 1214 (N.D. Ga. 1973). Similarly, in Bishop v. Jelleff Associates, Inc. 398 F. Supp. 579, 593 (D.D.C. 1974), the Court stated that

> In construing the Act, the Court concludes that when the burden shifts to the defendant, such burden is discharged by the employer showing that its conduct was not motivated by age bias and was "reasonable" or rational.

351. 510 F.2d 307 (6th Cir. 1975). *Accord,* Bittar v. Air Canada, 512 F.2d 582 (5th Cir. 1975) (*per curiam*).

evidence "was at best equivocal" and "presented no more than a jury question." [352]

A second exception to the foregoing statement of the defendant's burden of proof in a case under the ADEA has been applied in the bus driver cases.[353] Thus, in *Hodgson v. Greyhound Lines, Inc.*[354] the defendant admitted refusing to hire persons within the protected age bracket based on their age but asserted that it was entitled to rely on the exception for bona fide occupational qualifications. The District Court applied the standard set forth in *Hodgson v. First Federal Savings and Loan Association.*[355] The Court of Appeals reversed holding that, like the airline industry, the essence of Greyhound's business is the safe transportation of its passengers. To establish its defense it was held necessary for Greyhound to establish that the essence of its operations would be endangered by hiring drivers over forty years of age. The Court, further, held that due to compelling concerns for safety it was not necessary for Greyhound to show that all or substantially all bus driver applicants over forty could not perform safely. Instead,

> Greyhound must demonstrate that it has a rational basis in fact to believe that elimination of its maximum hiring age will increase the likelihood of risk of harm to its passengers. Greyhound need only demonstrate however a minimal increase in risk of harm for it is enough to show that elimination of the hiring policy might jeopardize the life of one more person than might otherwise occur under the present hiring practice.[356]

Interestingly, the same result was reached by the District Court in *Hodgson v. Tamiami Trail Tours, Inc.*[357] which purported to follow the *First Federal Savings and Loan Association* case. The Fifth Circuit Court of Appeals affirmed the District Court's

---

352. 510 F.2d, *supra,* at 312.

353. *See* pp. 100-107, *supra.*

354. 499 F.2d 859 (7th Cir. 1974), *cert. denied sub. nom.* Brennan v. Greyhound Lines, 419 U.S. 1122 (1975), *reversing* 354 F. Supp. 230 (N.D. Ill. 1973).

355. 354 F. Supp. at 232.

356. 499 F.2d, *supra,* at 863.

357. 4 CCH Employ. Prac. Dec. ¶7795, 4 Fair Employ. Prac. Cas. 728 (S.D. Fla., March 31, 1972) n.o.r.

determination.[358] The Fifth Circuit reviewed the Seventh Circuit's decision in the *Greyhound* case and, while agreeing with the result reached in that case, held that the Seventh Circuit had misinterpreted the Fifth Circuit decisions describing the burden of a defendant relying upon a bona fide occupational qualification defense in an employment discrimination case.[359]

Ultimately, of course, the plaintiff bears the burden of convincing the trier of the facts, be it judge or jury, by a preponderance of the evidence that he was discriminated against by the defendant because of age in violation of the ADEA if he is to prevail. A plaintiff need not prove that age was the sole ground for a defendant's action. Even if more than one factor affected a defendant's decision to act, a plaintiff who is within the protected age bracket and who is otherwise qualified, for example, for a position or a referral can recover if one factor was his age and it in fact made a difference in the determination of whether or not a challenged action would be taken.[360]

There is, as should be clear from the foregoing, no requirement that a plaintiff in an action under the ADEA prove that the defendant acted with an intent to discriminate in order to prevail. Proof of a violation and the absence of any valid defense is all that is required.[361]

---

358. 531 F.2d 224 (5th Cir. 1976).

359. *See*, pp. 105-107, *supra.*

360. Laugesen v. Anaconda Co., 510 F.2d 307, 310, 317 (6th Cir. 1975). *See also* Brennan v. Reynolds & Co., 367 F. Supp. 440, 444 (N.D. Ill. 1973) ("[E]ven when age is but one of a number of causes for discharge, the finding must be that the discharge was not for 'good cause', within the meaning of 621"); Opinion Letter of Acting Wage-Hour Administrator (WH-302), 2 CCH Employ. Prac. Guide ¶5334, at 3643 (April 24, 1975) ("Generally, the Act prohibits employers from basing any employment decision on the factor of age.").

361. The fact that Congress set forth specific defenses in the ADEA but did not include the absence of an intent to discriminate among those defenses and provided for liquidated damages for willful violations and compensatory damages for all violations in the statute has been pointed to as supporting the conclusion that no proof of discriminatory intent is required. Note, *Proving Discrimination Under the Age Discrimination in Employment Act,* 17 Ariz. L. Rev. 495, 503-504 (1975); Kovarsky and Kovarsky, *Economic, Medical and Legal Aspects of the Age Discrimination Laws in Employment,* 27 Vand. L. Rev. 839, 881 (1974). *But see*

On the other hand, the defendant, once a prima facie case has been made out by plaintiff, bears the burden of proving either that he acted as he did not because of the plaintiff's age but for a rational, reasonable reason or that his actions fall within one of the exceptions to the prohibitions of the statute.[362]

The court developed guidelines for allocating the burdens of proof in an action under the ADEA have been the object of some criticism because they serve to deny a plaintiff relief where he is unable to prove a *prima facie* case. Thus, one writer has suggested that a more practical approach would be to place the ultimate burden of persuasion on the defendant with the plaintiff required simply to prove that he was within the protected age bracket when the allegedly discriminatory act occurred in order to switch the burden of proof to the defendant to provide an explanation since the latter is in a position to know whether, for example, he failed to hire or discharged the plaintiff for permissible reasons under the ADEA.[363]

That writer suggests that the proposal would modify only the current burden of proof of the plaintiff who is required to make a prima facie case of unlawful discrimination before the burden of going forward and explaining his actions shifts to the defendant.[364]

Wilson v. Sealtest Foods Div. of Kraftco Corp., 501 F.2d 84, 86 (5th Cir. 1974), *petitions for rehearing denied,* 10 CCH Employ. Prac. Dec. ¶10,399, 11 Fair Employ. Prac. Cas. 128 (5th Cir., Dec. 13, 1974) *(per curiam)* n.o.r.; and pp. 191-192 and note 370, *infra.*

With the possible exception of the *Wilson* case, the courts have not required a showing of specific intent to discriminate. See Haslam, *Age Discrimination in Campus Employment,* 4 Human Rights 321, 326, 327 (1975). Even in the *Wilson* case, the Court of Appeals indicated that the existence or absence of an impermissible intent could be determined by viewing the evidence as a whole, including that which would be adduced during the presentation of defendant's case. The Court of Appeals, thus, rejected any suggestion that a plaintiff had any obligation to show the existence of an intent to discriminate in order to make out a *prima facie* case.

362. See, e.g., Wilson v. Sealtest Foods Div. of Kraftco Corp., 501 F.2d 84, 86-87 (5th Cir. 1974), *petitions for rehearing denied,* 10 CCH Employ. Prac. Dec. ¶10,399, 11 Fair Employ. Prac. Cas. 128 (5th Cir., Dec. 13, 1974) *(per curiam)* n.o.r.; Billingsley v. Service Tech. Corp., 6 CCH Employ. Prac. Dec. ¶8874, 6 Fair Employ. Prac. Cas. 404 (S.D. Tex., April 5 and 24, 1973) n.o.r.

363. Note, *The Age Discrimination in Employment Act of 1967: A Practical Application,* XXIV Baylor L. Rev. 601, 607-608 (1972).

364. *Id.* at 608.

The argument for a revised burden of proof for the plaintiff in an ADEA case is stated as follows:

> The Age Discrimination in Employment Act of 1967 was enacted in order to ensure full employment opportunities for those persons aged 40 through 65. Although it was conceived with the best motives, the interpretation of its application, viewed through *Hodgson v. First Federal Savings and Loan Association,* places an undue burden of proof on the aggrieved party who has been denied employment in favor of a younger applicant, but has little, if any, affirmative proof that the sole reason for not hiring him was his age. As viewed within the presently utilized procedure, if conciliatory conferences fail, the federal courts would not have the opportunity to probe the employer's explanation for denying employment to the applicant because the plaintiff would not have sufficient evidence to establish a prima facie case of age discrimination against the employer. In this regard, the real purposes of the Act are subverted since age discrimination, is unique in that, absent evidence of blatant discrimination, the applicant can produce little, if any, evidence of why he was denied employment. For this reason, the ultimate burden of persuasion should be placed on the defendant-employer since he is the only person who can provide an explanation as to why the applicant was denied employment, for reasons other than his age.[365]

The foregoing view has much to commend it although it does ignore the availability of pre-trial discovery by means of which a plaintiff can obtain evidence, both documentary and testimonial, from a defendant which may well aid in assembling a prima facie case and will allow the plaintiff to learn the defendant's case before the trial begins. In addition, there is no reference to the right of a plaintiff to call a defendant to testify during plaintiff's case [366] nor is recognition given to the possibility discussed below of a plaintiff proving a prima facie case by showing a pattern or

---

365. *Id.* at 608-609. As has been noted above, however, it has been held that an aggrieved party does not have to prove "that the sole reason for not hiring him was his age." *See* p. 188 and note 360, *supra.*

366. *See, e.g.,* Laugesen v. Anaconda Co., 510 F.2d 307 (6th Cir. 1975).

practice of age discrimination by a defendant.[367] It should be noted, however, that there has been some support in the case law for the views quoted above.

In *Wilson v. Sealtest Foods Division of Kraftco Corp.,*[368] the District Court had granted the defendant's motion for a directed verdict at the close of the plaintiff's case presumably finding that the plaintiff had failed to prove a prima facie case of age discrimination. On appeal, the Court of Appeals reversed, holding that plaintiff's showing that he was within a protected class, was asked to take early retirement against his will, was doing apparently satisfactory work, and was replaced by a younger person would not permit dismissal at the close of plaintiff's case since a minimal showing of those factors justified some explanation on the part of the employer.[369]

The Court of Appeals reasoned that

> The Age Discrimination in Employment Act requires that the complainant prove the employer discharged him or her because of such individual's age. It is possible that in the presentation of the employer's case, further evidence relating more directly to the requisite specific intent to discriminate might be adduced during cross-examination by Appellant. We cannot foreclose this possibility. It may be that the company in this case had an impermissible intent when discharging the Appellant which can only be judged from viewing the evidence as a whole.[370]

---

367. See pp. 192-195, *infra.*

368. 501 F.2d 84 (5th Cir. 1974), *petitions for rehearing denied,* 10 CCH Employ. Prac. Dec. ¶10,399, 11 Fair Employ. Prac. Cas. 128 (5th Cir., Dec. 13, 1974) *(per curiam)* n.o.r.

369. *But see* Donnelly v. Exxon Research & Eng'r Co., 11 CCH Employ. Prac. Dec. ¶10,860, 12 Fair Employ. Prac. Cas. 417 (D.N.J., October 30, 1974) n.o.r., *aff'd without opinion,* 521 F.2d 1398 (3rd Cir. 1975) (holding that a *prima facie* case was not made out using the same standards).

370. 501 F.2d, *supra,* at 86. The reference by the Court of Appeals to "the requisite specific intent to discriminate" is unfortunate and erroneous since, as has been noted above at p. 188, *supra,* no such requirement exists under the ADEA. *See* Note, *Proving Discrimination Under the Age Discrimination in Employment Act,* 17 Ariz. L. Rev. 495, 503-504 (1975); Kovarsky and Kovarsky, *Economic, Medical and Legal Aspects of the Age Discrimination Laws in Employment,* 27 Vand. L. Rev. 839, 881 (1974).

The approach seems to accord proper recognition both to the burden a plaintiff must ultimately bear and to the fact that the defendant is likely to have exclusive knowledge of the relevant facts including the motivation for his actions. The Court of Appeals was, however, careful to note that

> Should the evidence at the end of the Appellee's case be such that it is without contradiction that the company in fact was forced simply to choose one man over another and that the choice was not at all tainted with the impermissible criteria of age — then the District Court would be correct in directing a verdict for the Appellee at the end of all the evidence.[371]

T. METHODS OF PROOF

Proof of age discrimination in employment or of a defense to a claim of such discrimination can take many forms. The simplest proof would be required in cases alleging age discrimination in advertising where the advertisements themselves would constitute the basic proof. Similarly, the basic proof would be a relatively simple matter in cases where there is documentary evidence of age discrimination [371a] or testimony as to statements indicating such discrimination.[372]

However, in cases where there is neither documentary nor testimonial evidence of unfavorable consideration of an individual's age in connection with his employment, the difficulty is greatly increased for a plaintiff seeking to bear his burden of proof. Plaintiffs have responded to the problem, with the general approval of the courts, by relying upon statistical evidence to show a general pattern or practice of age discrimination in employment by a defendant with an inference drawn therefrom that a specific plaintiff has been subjected to such discrimination under the

---

371. 501 F.2d, *supra,* at 87.

371a. *See, e.g.,* Brennan v. Ace Hardware Corp., 362 F. Supp. 1156 (D. Neb. 1973), *aff'd,* 495 F. 2d 368 (8th Cir. 1974); Hodgson v. First Fed. Sav. and Loan Ass'n, 455 F.2d 818 (5th Cir. 1972); Hodgson v. Poole Truck Line, Inc., 4 CCH Employ. Prac. Dec. ¶7668, 4 Fair Employ. Prac. Cas. 265 (S.D. Ala., January 13, 1972) n.o.r.

372. *See, e.g.,* Schulz v. Hickok Mfg. Co., 358 F. Supp. 1208 (N.D. Ga. 1973); Hodgson v. Sugar Cane Growers Coop., 5 CCH Employ. Prac. Dec. ¶8618, 5 Fair Employ. Prac. Cas. 1136 (S.D. Fla., April 4, 1973) n.o.r.

pattern or practice.[373] Thus, in *Hodgson v. First Federal Savings and Loan Association* [374] the Court of Appeals stated that

> We note that the undisputed documentary evidence introduced by the Secretary [of Labor] established that for a period of more than a year after the effective date of the Age Discrimination Act not a single person within the protected age group was hired by the defendant for the job of teller. Of thirty-five persons hired as tellers or teller trainees during that period all were younger than forty and all but three were under thirty.[375]

---

373. *See generally* Note, *Beyond the Prima Facie Case in Employment Discrimination Law: Statistical Proof and Rebuttal,* 89 Harv. L. Rev. 387 (1975); Note, *Evidence: Statistical Proof in Employment Discrimination Cases,* 28 Okla. L. Rev. 885 (1975); Gilfix, *First Hired-First Fired: Age Discrimination in Employment,* **50 Cal. State Bar J.** 462, 511-12 (1975); Comment, *Statistical Evidence in Employment Discrimination Litigation: Selection of the Available Population, Problems, and Proposals,* 29 Sw. L. J. 859 (1975) (Title VII of the Civil Rights Act of 1964); Montlack, *Using Statistical Evidence to Enforce the Laws Against Discrimination,* 22 Cleveland State L. Rev. 259 (1973) (discussing the use of statistics in cases under Title VII of the Civil Rights Act of 1964 and the Ohio laws against discrimination). Some courts have, in the absence of specific authority, allowed the use of statistics in age discrimination cases by analogy to cases under Title VII. *See, e.g.,* Laugesen v. Anaconda Co., 510 F.2d 307 (6th Cir. 1975) (holding that the use of statistics is permissible in an individual as well as a class action under the ADEA as evidence of a general pattern of age discrimination or the absence thereof with the weight to be accorded to the statistics an issue for the jury); Hodgson v. Ideal Corrugated Box Co., 8 CCH Employ. Prac. Dec. ¶9805, at 6371, 10 Fair Employ. Prac. Cas. 744, 749 (N.D. W. Va., January 31, 1974) n.o.r.; Schulz v. Hickok Mfg. Co., 358 F. Supp. 1208, 1213 (N.D.Ga. 1973).

But see Dunlop v. Westinghouse Elec. Corp., 11 CCH Employ. Prac. Dec. ¶10,814 (S.D. Fla., March 3, 1976) n.o.r., where the Court denied, subject to reconsideration upon presentation of supporting "competent authority", the Secretary of Labor's discovery requests for information concerning all persons whose employment was terminated during a specified period by defendant's elevator divisions and all personnel records of all employees of those divisions during the same period. The Secretary of Labor unsuccessfully argued that, although the case involved only the claim of one specified individual, the complaint sought full restitution and reinstatement for any individual damaged by defendant's discrimination and that the requested discovery would, with respect to the named individual, strengthen his case if it showed a pattern of practice and the full extent of defendant's illegal retirement and termination practices.

374. 455 F.2d 818 (5th Cir. 1972).

375. *Id.* at 822-23.

The Court of Appeals held that "these statistics by themselves would perhaps support a finding that defendant had violated the Act. ..."[376] With respect to the individual complainant, the Court of Appeals held that

> Certainly the fact that Mrs. Hall applied for a job at a time when defendant was pursuing a practice of age discrimination in hiring is relevant to the question whether she herself was a victim of unlawful discrimination. That fact furnishes a strong, though not conclusive, inference that Mrs. Hall was rejected for employment, at least with respect to the job of teller, because of her age.[377]

The justification for permitting the use of statistics in discrimination cases was described as follows by the New York Court of Appeals in *State Division of Human Rights v. Kilian Manufacturing Corporation*[378]

> Discrimination today is rarely so obvious, or its practices so overt that recognition of the fact is instant and conclusive. "One intent on violating the Law against Discrimination cannot be expected to declare or announce his purpose. Far more likely is it that he will pursue his discriminatory practices in ways that are devious, by methods, subtle and elusive — for we deal with an area in which 'subtleties of conduct * * * play no small part.' (Cf. Labor Bd. v. Express Pub. Co., 312 U.S. 426, 437.)" (Matter of Holland v. Edwards, 307 N.Y. 38, 45.) Statistics are valuable and often demonstrate more than the testimony of witnesses, "and they should be given proper effect by the courts" (Jones v. Lee Way Motor Frgt., 431 F.2d 245, 247, cert. den. 401 U.S. 954).

Closely related to, and sometimes combined with, the statistical approach is the use of historical evidence of a defendant's actions towards specific persons other than the plaintiff or plaintiffs to

---

376. *Id.* at 823.

377. *Id. See also* Schulz v. Hickok Mfg. Co., 358 F. Supp. 1208, 1213 (N.D. Ga. 1973), where the Court held that "statistics are not conclusive proof of an employer's reasons for any particular discharge; they are relevant simply on the question of motive."

378. 35 N.Y.2d 201, 209-10, 318 N.E.2d 770, 774, 360 N.Y.S. 2d 603, 609 (1974), *appeal dismissed,* 420 U.S. 915 (1975).

show the presence or absence of a pattern or practice of age discrimination.[379]

Indeed, one court has considered the presence of multiple plaintiffs who may show a pattern or policy of age discrimination a relevant consideration in determining whether to permit an action under the ADEA to proceed as a class action. The Court in *Bishop v. Jelleff Associates, Inc.,*[380] stated that

> Although each plaintiff may have been terminated at a different time by a different agent and allegedly for different reasons, the evidence as a whole may show a broad policy of discrimination, which policy each plaintiff suing alone would be unable to prove.

U. REMEDIES FOR VIOLATION OF THE ADEA

After a finding by judge or jury of a violation of the ADEA, the appropriate relief must be fashioned to redress the defendant's wrong.

Section 7(b) of the ADEA provides that it is to be enforced in accordance with the powers, remedies, and procedures provided in specified sections of the Fair Labor Standards Act of 1938.[381] In an action to enforce the ADEA, a court has jurisdiction to grant such legal or equitable relief as may be appropriate to effectuate its purposes, including without limitation, judgments compelling employment, reinstatement or promotion, or enforcing the defendant's liability for amounts owing to a person as a result of a violation of the ADEA.[382] In addition, the ADEA provides for the

---

379. *See, e.g.,* Bishop v. Jelleff Associates, Inc., 398 F. Supp. 579 (D.D.C. 1974); Hodgson v. Ideal Corrugated Box Co., 8 CCH Employ. Prac. Dec. ¶9805, 10 Fair Employ. Prac. Cas. 744 (N.D. W.Va., January 31, 1974) n.o.r.; Schulz v. Hickok Mfg. Co., 358 F. Supp. 1208, 1212 (N.D. Ga. 1973) ("[E]vidence of the defendant's behavior in similar cases is decidedly relevant to the court's determination of the reasons behind plaintiff's discharge."); Billingsley v. Service Tech. Corp., 6 CCH Employ. Prac. Dec. ¶8874, 6 Fair Employ. Prac. Cas. 404 (S.D. Tex., April 5 and 24, 1973) n.o.r.; Hodgson v. Poole Truck Line, Inc., 4 CCH Employ. Prac. Dec. ¶7668, 4 Fair Employ. Prac. Cas. 265 (S.D. Ala., January 13, 1972) n.o.r.

380. 5 CCH Employ. Prac. Dec. ¶7995, at 6659, 4 Fair Employ. Prac. Cas. 1262 (D.D.C., August 1, 1972) n.o.r.

381. 29 U.S.C. § 626(b) (1970).

382. *Id.*

payment of liquidated damages as defined in the Fair Labor Standards Act in cases of willful violations of the statute.[383]

The United States district courts are given jurisdiction, for cause shown, to restrain violations of the ADEA including the restraint of any withholding of payment of amounts found by a court to be due to a person as a result of a violation of the statute, except for sums which persons are barred from recovering at the time of the commencement of the action to restrain the violations by reason of the statute of limitations.[384]

The following discussion reviews the remedies available under the ADEA and their applicability to specific violations of the statute.

1. *Reinstatement and Compelled Employment.* "Reinstatement" is obviously only available in cases of wrongful discharge and has been ordered in such cases,[385] while "compelled employment" is available in cases of wrongful refusal to hire although it has apparently not as yet been used by the courts.

Where, between the time of wrongful discharge and the reinstatement order, the position formerly held by the plaintiff has been eliminated or filled by another person, a problem is presented. One court has ordered that in such an eventuality the plaintiff was to be given the position with the defendant employer which is most comparable to the one from which he was wrongfully discharged.[386] This resolution of the problem is acceptable so long as the alternative position is equal in responsibility, salary,

---

383. *Id.* "Liquidated damages" are defined as an amount equal to the amounts owing to a person as a result of a violation of the ADEA, 29 U.S.C. § 216(b) (Supp. V 1975) *incorporated by* 29 U.S.C. § 626(b) (1970).

384. 29 U.S.C. § 217 (1970) *incorporated by* 29 U.S.C. § 626(b) (1970). The remedy of an injunction restraining any withholding of payment of amounts owing to a person as a result of a violation of the ADEA, as opposed to a direct order for the payment of such amounts, has been employed in cases where the Secretary of Labor sues on behalf of a complainant rather than the complainant suing on his own behalf. *See, e.g.,* Hodgson v. First Fed. Sav. and Loan Ass'n, 455 F.2d 818 (5th Cir. 1972); Hodgson v. Poole Truck Line, Inc., 4 CCH Employ. Prac. Dec. ¶7668, 4 Fair Employ. Prac. Cas. 265 (S.D. Ala., January 13, 1972) n.o.r.

385. *See, e.g.,* Schulz v. Hickok Mfg. Co., 358 F. Supp. 1208 (N.D. Ga. 1973); Hodgson v. Sugar Cane Growers Coop., 5 CCH Employ. Prac. Dec. ¶8618, 5 Fair Employ. Prac. Cas. 1136 (S.D. Fla., April 4, 1973) n.o.r.

386. Schulz v. Hickok Mfg. Co., *supra.*

benefits, and promotion opportunities to the plaintiff's prior position. If not, an alternative solution must be found which might include: creation of a new position meeting the foregoing requirements; return of the person presently filling the position to his previous position if he was promoted to replace plaintiff; or, if the person filling the position was hired to replace the plaintiff, the discharge of that person. The latter two alternatives, though harsh, recognize that the person filling the position obtained it only because of the plaintiff's having been wrongfully discharged.

Regardless of the manner in which a plaintiff is reinstated, he is entitled to be credited with all pension and retirement benefits to which he would have been entitled had he never been discharged.[387]

The significance of reinstatement goes beyond the fact that it is the most complete remedy for a wrongful discharge. It has, as is noted below, been used as a means of determining when a plaintiff's right to back wages terminates.

2. *Damages.* The method for determining monetary damages depends upon the nature of the violation the ADEA found.

a. WRONGFUL DISCHARGE. The damages recoverable for wrongful discharge are the lost wages or back pay which is

> measured by the difference between the salary an employee would have received but for a violation of the Act and the salary actually received from other employment, less unemployment benefits.[388]

---

387. Bishop v. Jelleff Associates, Inc., 398 F. Supp. 579, 597 (D.D.C. 1974).
388. Bishop v. Jelleff Associates, Inc., 398 F. Supp. 579, 597 (D.D.C. 1974). *Accord,* Hodgson v. Ideal Corrugated Box Co., 8 CCH Employ. Prac. Dec. ¶9805, 10 Fair Employ. Prac. Cas. 744 (N.D. W.Va., January 31, 1974) n.o.r.; Schulz v. Hickok Mfg. Co., 358 F. Supp. 1208 (N.D. Ga. 1973); Monroe v. Penn-Dixie Cement Corp., 335 F. Supp. 231 (N.D. Ga. 1971) (*dictum*).

The Court in Hodgson v. Ideal Corrugated Box Co., *supra,* 8 CCH Employ. Prac. Dec. ¶9805, at 6373, 10 Fair Employ. Prac. Cas. at 751-52, seems to have assumed that damages in the form of back wages are recoverable in an action under the ADEA only for willful violations of the statute. This is clearly incorrect since the willfulness requirement applies only to the recovery of "liquidated damages" which is an additional sum equal to the amount to which a person is otherwise entitled for a violation of the ADEA. 29 U.S.C. § 626(b) (1970) *incorporating* 29 U.S.C. § 216(b) (Supp. V 1975); Bishop v. Jelleff Associates, Inc., *supra;* Billingsley v. Service Tech. Corp., 6 CCH Employ. Prac. Dec. ¶8874, at 5720, 6 Fair Employ. Prac. Cas. 404, 410 (S.D. Tex., April 5 and 24, 1973) (*dictum*) n.o.r.

In determining the amount of back pay to which a person is entitled,

> The relevant period for measuring back pay begins with the time of the loss of employment as a result of the violation and ends when the affected employee accepts or declines reinstatement.[389]

The reasons for terminating a plaintiff's right to damages at the time he is given the opportunity by the court to be reinstated include the fact that any computation of damages thereafter would be a highly speculative estimation of his future employment experience and the fact that if the plaintiff had accepted reinstatement he would have no further damages and he cannot be permitted to enlarge his damages voluntarily.[390]

An exception to the normal rule for determining the amount of back wages to which a successful plaintiff is entitled has been recognized where the plaintiff has reached 65 years of age prior to the time that it is determined that he is entitled to reinstatement. Since the ADEA only provides protection for persons aged 40 to 65, after a person reaches 65 years of age his right to recover additional back wages terminates inasmuch as he could thereafter have legally been discharged by reason of his age.[391]

---

389. Bishop v. Jelleff Associates, Inc., *supra*, at 597. *Accord*, Schulz v. Hickok Mfg. Co., *supra;* Monroe v. Penn-Dixie Cement Corp., *supra, (dictum)*.
But see Brennan v. Goodyear Tire & Rubber Co., 10 CCH Employ. Prac. Dec. ¶10,562, 11 Fair Employ. Prac. Cas. 589 (M.D. Fla., May 8, 1975) (back wages measured from date of discharge to the time of trial) n.o.r.

390. Monroe v. Penn-Dixie Cement Corp., *supra*, at 235 *(dictum). See also* Price v. Maryland Cas. Co., 391 F. Supp. 613, 621 (S.D. Miss. 1975) ("The Court considers any such projected salary for years following the trial of this case inapplicable.") *(dictum);* Note, *Proving Discrimination Under the Age Discrimination in Employment Act,* 17 Ariz. L. Rev. 495, 501-502 and n. 53 (1975) (the parties then stand in the same position as though the court had ordered the reinstatement of the plaintiff and he had simultaneously quit for non-discriminatory reasons).

391. Billingsley v. Service Tech. Corp., 6 CCH Employ. Prac. Dec. ¶8874, at 5720, 6 Fair Employ. Prac. Cas. 404, 410 (S.D. Tex., April 5 and 24, 1973) n.o.r.
A similar result has been suggested where an employer ceases business between the date of the violation of the ADEA and the date of trial. That is, unless the employee can show that he suffered damages after the employer's cessation of business as a result of the wrongful discharge not suffered by the employer's other employees, the employer should not be liable for damages after it ceases to engage

The back pay or lost wages to which a plaintiff is entitled includes not only the amount he would have received in salary had he not been wrongfully discharged but also all other monetary benefits which he would have received had he remained in the defendant's employ to the date he is given an opportunity to choose to be reinstated including, for example, increased pension benefits which would normally have vested prior to the decision; [392] any disability benefits to which he would have been entitled; [393] and reimbursement for health, life and other insurance premiums actually paid for by the plaintiff which would have been paid for by the defendant employer but for the discharge.[394]

---

in business. Note, *Proving Discrimination Under the Age Discrimination in Employment Act*, 17 Ariz. L. Rev. 495, 502 (1975).

392. Bishop v. Jelleff Associates, Inc., 398 F. Supp. 579, 597 (D.D.C. 1974); Monroe v. Penn-Dixie Cement Corp., 335 F. Supp. 231, 234-35 (N.D. Ga. 1971) *(dictum)*. *Contra*, Hodgson v. Ideal Corrugated Box Co., 8 CCH Employ. Prac. Dec. ¶9805, at 6374, 10 Fair Employ. Prac. Cas. 744, 752 (N.D. W.Va., January 31, 1974) n.o.r., where the Court held that pension contributions and bonuses were too contingent and speculative to be included. This view is contrary to the purposes of the remedy which include returning the wronged plaintiff to the position he would have occupied had he not been discharged. If there is, in fact, a conjectural or speculative element in any of the items of benefits which the plaintiff was denied, then the employer defendant should be made to bear that burden since it is the one found guilty of having violated the ADEA and can reasonably be held to have assumed the risk when it wrongfully discharged the plaintiff.

Where a plaintiff rejects reinstatement or cannot be reinstated because, for example, he has obtained other employment or become disabled then the defendant employer can be required to grant to the plaintiff such rights as he would have been entitled to under a pension plan if he had retired on the date he rejects reinstatement or could have done so before becoming disabled. Bishop v. Jelleff Associates, Inc., *supra*.

393. Bishop v. Jelleff Associates, Inc., *supra*. Similarly, a plaintiff who has been wrongfully discharged or his estate should be entitled to recover any other health or insurance benefits provided for employees by the defendant employer to which he or his estate would have been entitled had he not been discharged. It is not unfair to place this burden on the defendant employer who chose to act and can properly be held liable for all damages to the plaintiff flowing therefrom. *Contra*, Hodgson v. Ideal Corrugated Box Co., *supra*, 8 CCH Employ. Prac. Dec. ¶9805, at 6373, 10 Fair Employ. Prac. Cas. at 752, holding that hospital and medical insurance was "something that the Court cannot involve itself with." If the Court was referring to the amount of premiums for such insurance which plaintiffs paid for themselves after discharge or benefits they would have been entitled to then the decision would appear to be incorrect.

394. *But see* Hodgson v. Ideal Corrugated Box Co., *supra*.

There must be deducted from the back pay and other benefits described above the amount of any wages earned by the plaintiff after his discharge and before the date he is given an opportunity to choose to be reinstated together with such things as the value of benefits received in connection with such other employment, any unemployment benefits received by the plaintiff,[395] and severance pay received as a result of the discharge.[396] There should, in addition, be deducted from the back pay and other benefits to which a plaintiff would otherwise be entitled an amount equal to that portion of the pay and other benefits which would have accrued from the time the plaintiff voluntarily retired from a subsequent job to the date he is given an opportunity to be reinstated.[397]

Of course, remuneration received by a plaintiff after his discharge for activities which he could or did engage in while employed by the defendant employer should not be deducted from the back pay to which the plaintiff is entitled to the extent that the activities could have been pursued while employed by the defendant employer and would not have been inconsistent therewith. Thus, for example, in *Laugesen v. Anaconda Company* [398] the plaintiff argued on appeal that the District Court erred in setting off the amount he earned teaching and lecturing after his discharge. The Court of Appeals held that

Any remuneration that Laugesen received following his discharge should be set off from the damages only to the extent that it actually mitigated his losses. If Laugesen had received such sums during his employment at

395. *See, e.g.,* Brennan v. Goodyear Tire & Rubber Co., 10 CCH Employ. Prac. Dec. ¶10,562, 11 Fair Employ. Prac. Cas. 589 (M.D. Fla., May 8, 1975) (between date of discharge and time of trial) n.o.r.; Bishop v. Jelleff Associates, Inc., *supra;* Hodgson v. Ideal Corrugated Box Co., *supra;* Schulz v. Hickok Mfg. Co., 358 F. Supp. 1208 (N.D. Ga. 1973); Billingsley v. Service Tech. Corp., 6 CCH Employ. Prac. Dec. ¶8874, 6 Fair Employ. Prac. Cas. 404 (S.D. Tex., April 5 and 24, 1973) n.o.r.

396. *See, e.g.,* Laugesen v. Anaconda Co., 510 F.2d 307 (6th Cir. 1975); Schulz v. Hickok Mfg. Co., *supra.*

397. *See* Hodgson v. Ideal Corrugated Box Co., *supra,* 8 CCH Employ. Prac. Dec. ¶9805, at 6373, 10 Fair Employ. Prac. Cas. at 752. The plaintiff should, however, be given an opportunity to prove that he would not have retired if he had not been discharged from his position with the defendant employer. If the plaintiff carries this burden then no deduction based on his retirement should be made.

398. 510 F.2d 307 (6th Cir. 1975).

Anaconda, and could have expected to continue to receive them, a set-off should be allowed only to the extent that the amount actually received exceeded that which Laugesen would have received had he been employed at Anaconda during the period in question. Only that amount may be set off as mitigation of damages.[399]

b. REFUSAL TO HIRE. The measure of damages in a case of a wrongful refusal to hire should be the same as that in a case of wrongful discharge except that in the former case the basic damages would be determined by the difference between what the plaintiff applicant would have received in wages and benefits had he been hired and the amount he, in fact, received in wages and benefits from other employment.[400] Since, as has been noted above, the ADEA empowers a court to compel the employment of a complainant, the appropriate time period for measuring damages would be that between the date the defendant prospective employer refused to hire the plaintiff, or is deemed to have done so if it failed to respond to plaintiff's application for employment, and the date the court gives the plaintiff an option to be employed by the defendant.[401]

c. REFUSAL TO REFER. The refusal by an employment agency or labor organization to refer a person within the protected age bracket to a potential employer because of his age presents particular problems because the applicant is thereby denied not employment but only an opportunity to be interviewed by the potential employer and a court cannot, therefore, know whether the applicant would have been accepted or rejected by the employer as an individual or from the group of persons applying for the position on non-discriminatory grounds. In addition, there is the possibility that more persons have been wrongfully denied referral because of age than there were positions open so that not all of the wronged applicants could have obtained a job in any case.

---

399. *Id.* at 317-18.
400. Brennan v. Ace Hardware Corp., 495 F.2d 368, 373 (8th Cir. 1974) *(dictum).*
401. There have not, apparently, been any decisions under the ADEA compelling the employment of a person who was refused employment in violation of the statute.

The only reported decision involving a wrongful refusal to refer is *Brennan v. Hughes Personnel, Inc.*[402] In that case the defendant employment agency refused to refer anyone over 35 years of age at the direction of its client, the potential employer. The Court properly rejected the defendant's argument that its refusal to refer persons over 35 years of age was only compliance with its client's direction holding that the defendant was on notice that it was being asked to commit an illegal act which it did not have to but did accede to as a result of which it profited.

The Court first held that

> where a violation of the Act is proved, and where there is a substantial connection between that violation and the failure of a person to obtain the job which she is seeking through the employment agency, as a result of a violation of the Act by the agency, then the employee [*sic*] is entitled to recover the unpaid minimum wages to which she would have been entitled had the referral agency referred her to the prospective employer.[403]

This seems to be the proper basic rule of damages under the ADEA, although it might be modified to provide that, in a case where there are more persons who are wrongfully not referred because of their age than openings, the minimum wages for the available positions should be divided among those potential applicants qualified to fill the jobs and serious about seeking them. This calculation would recognize the fact that with fewer openings than serious, qualified potential applicants not all of them could, in any case, obtain a position.[404] It would also place a rational maximum limit on damages which would be particularly important where there are many applicants wrongfully not referred for one position or a few positions.

It should be noted that the Court in the *Hughes Personnel, Inc.* case failed to give consideration to a special problem which exists

402. 8 CCH Employ. Prac. Dec. ¶9571 (W.D. Ky., May 22, 1974) n.o.r., *amended,* 8 CCH Employ. Prac. Dec. ¶9679 (W.D. Ky., June 25, 1974) n.o.r.

403. 8 CCH Employ. Prac. Dec. ¶9571, at 5475-76.

404. It would probably be necessary, where the maximum referral age is below 40 years, to add into the calculation the applicants who are below the minimum protected age of 40.

in determining an appropriate cut-off date for damages in cases such as that one where a covered employment agency acting as such violates the ADEA by, for example, not referring a person in the protected age bracket when there has either not been any involvement by an employer or an employer has been involved but has not been named as a party to the action. In such cases, the remedy of compelling employment is not available either to actually terminate the accrual of an individual's damages when such employment is accepted or to act as such a termination date when compelled employment is rejected by an individual. Clearly, an employment agency cannot be expected to pay an individual either lost wages or the difference between lost wages and the income actually received by the individual indefinitely. Although fixing the termination date as the date upon which judgment is entered in an action might be argued to encourage individuals to delay commencing an action in order to increase their damages, that date is the most logical one and is consistent with that used in employer cases. In addition, most individuals who are unable to either obtain any other employment or employment at an equal or greater salary than the jobs for which they were wrongfully not referred are likely to be interested in obtaining as rapid a recovery as possible.

Despite the holding quoted above and a specific finding that one of the wrongfully rejected potential appicants was qualified for the position, was desirous of acquiring it, and would have done so had it not been for defendant's illegal action, the Court in the *Hughes Personnel, Inc.* case held that, since there were two openings and three claimants,

> the Court believes that in this case it would be equitable and realistic to award damages based upon the profits which the defendant would have secured had it placed two of the three ladies in employment . . . .[405]

Since the Court found that the defendant employment agency did place two persons under 35 in the position in question with its client, it awarded as damages an amount equal to the profits which the defendant received from placing those two persons.

---

405. 8 CCH Employ. Prac. Dec. ¶9571, *supra*, at 5476.

In explaining its determination, the Court conceded that Section 7(b) of the ADEA

> does, at first blush, seem to command the Court to award unpaid minimum wages or unpaid overtime compensation [sic], and not to consider any other criteria, but the last sentence of that statute, which allows the Court to grant such legal or equitable relief as is appropriate to effectuate the purposes of this chapter, would seem to give the Court leeway to award damages along the lines proposed by the plaintiff, rather than to compel the Court to enter a larger verdict based on the unpaid minimum wages.
>
> Since there were only two positions open and the Court is allowing damages to only two of the three ladies who applied for the position of quality control inspector, the Court has decided that Mrs. Swallow and Mrs. Daugherty are entitled to the recovery of damages, inasmuch as they were the ones who were most concerned with obtaining the job and who made the most efforts to secure other employment.[406]

The Court's interpretation of the ADEA's provision on damages is subject to criticism since it does not, in fact, "effectuate the purposes" of the statute. It neither makes the complainant whole nor does it act as a deterrent to future violations. Thus, one of the complainants who the Court found it "could reasonably award. . .$3,800"[407] on the basis of lost back wages received only $72.[408] The defendant, on the other hand, lost only its profits on the placement of persons under 35. The ADEA's reference to "appropriate" relief should not be read to *permit* the awarding of damages equal to lost wages and benefits but rather to *require* such damages to be awarded and to permit modification of that formula only in special circumstances such as those where there

---

406. 8 CCH Employ. Prac. Dec. ¶9571, at 5477. On reconsideration, the Court found that the defendant placed seven not two people under 35 years of age with its client in the same position and ordered the three claimants to divide defendant's profits between them equally. No indication is given as to whether the amount of the defendant's profits was increased accordingly. 8 CCH Employ. Prac. Dec. ¶9679 (W.D. Ky., June 25, 1974) n.o.r.

407. 8 CCH Employ. Prac. Dec. ¶9571, at 5476.

408. 8 CCH Employ. Prac. Dec. ¶9679, at 5851.

are more applicants for a position who are discriminated against because of age than there are positions available.[409]

d. OTHER VIOLATIONS. The damages recoverable under the ADEA by persons who are the object of acts prohibited by the statute other than those discussed above have not been the subject of court decisions. However, the proper method for determining damages in those cases can generally be determined by analogy to the guidelines described above for cases involving wrongful discharge or wrongful refusal to refer because of age.

Thus, for example, an employer's unlawful discrimination between employees with respect to compensation, terms, conditions, or privileges of employment because of age can be compensated for by damages equal to the detriment suffered by the employee discriminated against together with promotion, if appropriate, just as a wrongful discharge would be ameliorated by the payment of lost wages and benefits and reinstatement. Similarly, damages for a discriminatory advertisement for a specific position could properly be treated like a refusal to refer by a division of the amount of wages and benefits offered for the position between the qualified, serious potential applicants where there is a specific claimant or claimants or identifiable persons who made inquiries despite the terms of the advertisement. Where, however, the advertisement which is discriminatory is one seeking job applicants in general rather than one referring to specific positions, the damages of any person reading it are probably so speculative that injunctive relief rather than damages may be more appropriate.

3. *Liquidated Damages.* Section 7(b) of the ADEA permits the recovery of "liquidated damages" in cases of "willful" violations of the statute.[409a]

---

409. The decision in Brennan v. Hughes Personnel, Inc., *supra,* is properly criticized for misreading Congressional intent with respect to the penultimate sentence of Section 7(b) of the ADEA so as to permit rather than to prevent a reduction of the damages to which an individual is otherwise entitled under the statute in Note, *Proving Discrimination Under the Age Discrimination in Employment Act,* 17 Ariz. L. Rev. 495, 502-503 n. 56 (1975).

409a. 29 U.S.C. § 626(b) (1970).

"Liquidated damages" are defined as an additional amount equal to the amounts owing to a person as a result of a violation of the ADEA.[410] Thus, in a case where a willful violation of the statute is found the defendant is liable to the injured party for twice the latter's actual damages incurred by reason of the defendant's violation of the statute.

The incorporated provisions of the Fair Labor Standards Act of 1938 permit the recovery of liquidated damages in actions brought by individuals [411] and those brought by the Secretary of Labor.[412]

While there is no statutory definition of "willful", the term is commonly used in statutes and has been defined as follows in one case under the ADEA:

> it means violations which are intentional, knowingly and voluntarily made as distinguished from accidental, innocent or for good reason acts.
> The Court believes that willful goes beyond conduct that can be characterized as careless, or unknowing, or unintentional.[413]

The applicable statutory language, providing that a person found to have willfully violated the ADEA "shall" be liable to the injured person for amounts owing as a result of a violation and "an additional equal amount as liquidated damages," [414] clearly indicates that the payment of liquidated damages in cases involving willful violations of the statute is mandatory rather than discretionary.[415]

---

410. 29 U.S.C. § 216(b) (Supp. V 1975) *incorporated by* 29 U.S.C. § 626(b) (1970).

411. *Id.*

412. 29 U.S.C. § 216(c) (Supp. V 1975).

413. Hodgson v. Ideal Corrugated Box Co., 8 CCH Employ. Prac. Dec. ¶9805, at 6373, 10 Fair Employ. Prac. Cas. 744, 751 (N.D. W.Va., January 31, 1974) n.o.r. *See also* Rogers v. Exxon Research and Eng'r Co., 404 F. Supp. 324, 334-35 (D.N.J. 1975); Bishop v. Jelleff Associates, Inc., 398 F. Supp. 579, 593 (D.D.C. 1974), defining "willful" violations of the ADEA as those involving "bad faith evasion of the Act and definite knowledge of its applicability" in connection with a determination of whether to apply the two or three year statute of limitations.

414. 29 U.S.C. § 216(b) (Supp. V 1975).

415. *See* Note, *Proving Discrimination Under the Age Discrimination in Employment Act,* 17 Ariz. L. Rev. 495, 501-502 n. 50 (1975).

In one case under the ADEA, the Court charged the jury that, in addition to lost wages resulting from wrongful involuntary retirement in violation of the statute, the deceased employee's estate could recover

compensation for alleged pain, suffering, mental anguish and physical injury . . . suffered as a proximate result of the age discrimination practiced against him by the defendant.

* * *

Now, I tell you that a plaintiff who is awarded a verdict is entitled to fair and reasonable compensation for his pain and suffering, discomfort and distress sustained as a result of discrimination practiced against him by a defendant. The measure of damages is what a reasonable man or woman would consider to be adequate and just under all the circumstance of the case to compensate the plaintiffs . . . .[416]

The Court reasoned that the ADEA essentially established a new statutory tort which brought into play the full panoply of usual tort remedies to compensate injured parties for their provable damages including those for pain and suffering.[417] The Court went on to note that

In measuring the wrong done and ascertaining the appropriate remedy here, the Court is aware that the most pernicious effect of age discrimination is not to the pocketbook, but to the victim's self-respect. As in this case, the out-of-pocket loss occasioned by such discrimination is often negligible in comparison to the

---

416. Rogers v. Exxon Research & Eng'r Co., 404 F. Supp. 324 (D.N.J., February 4, 1975). Court's instructions to jury and jury's verdicts excerpted in 2 CCH Employ. Prac. Guide ¶5311, at 3580. The jury returned a verdict for $750,000 for pain, suffering, and mental anguish.

The punitive possibilities in allowing damages for pain and suffering without specific statutory authority is exemplified by the fact that the Court subsequently lowered the recovery, with plaintiffs' approval, from $750,000 to $200,000 because the original award was excessive and improperly "manifested the jury's outrage at the defendant's conduct and its desire to award the maximum permissible recovery to plaintiffs." Rogers v. Exxon Research and Eng'r Co., 404 F. Supp. 324, 338 (D.N.J. 1975).

417. Rogers v. Exxon Research and Eng'r Co., 404 F. Supp. 324, 327-28 (D.N.J. 1975).

physiological and psychological damage caused by the employer's unlawful conduct.[418]

The Court's instruction permitting the jury to return a damage verdict for pain, suffering, and mental anguish resulting from a violation of the ADEA is without support in the statute. It would, in fact, appear to be contrary to the ADEA's provision governing damages which provides for the recovery by a successful plaintiff of amounts owing to him as a result of a violation of the statute, and liquidated damages in cases of willful violations. The reference to "[a]mounts owing" strongly suggests that damages should be limited to pecuniary losses suffered because of a violation of the ADEA.[419] Since the existence of a Federal cause of action based on age discrimination in connection with employment is solely a creation of the Congress which provided remedies for violations of the statute, the courts should be loath to engraft thereon a right to recover additional types of damages for violations of the statute not specifically provided for by the Congress.[420]

4. *Permanent Injunctive Relief.* Permanent injunctive relief under the ADEA, unlike either preliminary injunctive relief which only restrains threatened or existing violations of the statute until a decision is rendered on the merits at a trial or a final injunction against the restraint of any withholding of payment of funds owing to a person for a violation of the ADEA,[421] prohibits violations of the statute *in futuro.*

Since permanent injunctive relief does not remedy past or existing violations of the ADEA, it is generally involved in actions by the Secretary of Labor and class actions rather than individual actions under the statute. The ADEA specifically authorizes a court to grant equitable relief,[422] which includes an injunction, and

---

418. 404 F. Supp. at 329.

419. *See* Monroe v. Penn-Dixie Cement Corp., 335 F. Supp. 231, 234-35 n. 3 (N.D. Ga. 1971) *(dictum).*

420. The "amounts owing" language in Section 7(b) of the ADEA led the Court in Rogers v. Exxon Research and Eng'r Co., *supra,* 404 F. Supp. at 333, 334, 335, to limit the liquidated damages doubling provision to the pecuniary losses proved by plaintiff excluding the damages allowed for pain and suffering.

421. 29 U.S.C. § 217 (1970) *incorporated by* 29 U.S.C. § 626(b) (1970).

422. 29 U.S.C. § 626(b) (1970).

incorporates a provision of the Fair Labor Standards Act of 1938 granting the Federal district courts jurisdiction, for cause shown, to restrain violations of the statute.[423]

Once there has been a finding of a violation of the ADEA, the decision as to whether to grant injunctive relief against future violations has been held to rest primarily within the judicial discretion of the trial court.[424] It has been held that permanent injunctive relief is appropriate where there has been a finding that the defendant has engaged in a pattern, practice, or policy of age discrimination in employment in violation of the ADEA.[425]

Two questions have arisen with respect to permanent injunctive relief. The first relates to the appropriate breadth of permanent injunctive relief and the second to whether such relief should be granted where the defendant's violation of the ADEA has been ended prior to judgment.

The permanent injunctions which have been issued by courts in cases under the ADEA can be divided into three general categories: those limited to the specific violation found in a particular case,[426] those limited to prohibited practices of the type found in a particular case,[427] and general injunctions prohibiting any acts of

---

423. *Id. incorporating* 29 U.S.C. § 217 (1970).

424. Hodgson v. First Fed. Sav. and Loan Ass'n, 455 F.2d 818, 825 (5th Cir. 1972).

425. *See, e.g.,* Brennan v. International Harvester Co., 7 CCH Employ. Prac. Dec. ¶9294 (N.D. Ill., March 27, 1974) n.o.r.; Hodgson v. Poole Truck Line, Inc., 4 CCH Employ. Prac. Dec. ¶7668, 4 Fair Employ. Prac. Cas. 265 (S.D. Ala., January 13, 1972) n.o.r.

426. *See* Hodgson v. Career Counsellors Int'l, Inc., 5 CCH Employ. Prac. Dec. ¶7983, 5 Fair Employ. Prac. Cas. 129 (N.D. Ill., September 28, 1972) (enjoining notices or advertisements or classifications or referrals containing the term "girl" or the phrase "young girl") n.o.r. *Contra,* Hodgson v. First Fed. Sav. and Loan Ass'n, 455 F.2d 818 (5th Cir. 1972), *reversing on this ground and affirming on other grounds* 3 CCH Employ. Prac. Dec. ¶8066, 3 Fair Employ. Prac. Cas. 16 (S.D. Fla., December 3, 1970) (enjoining violation of provisions of ADEA in hiring bank tellers) n.o.r.

427. *See, e.g.,* Hodgson v. Approved Personnel Service, Inc., 529 F.2d 760, 765 (4th Cir. 1975) ("The Department is entitled to an injunction only against future conduct which actually violates Section 4(e) of the Act."); Hodgson v. Great Am. Disct. and Credit Co., 336 F. Supp. 1355 (M.D. Ala. 1972) (enjoining "further violation of the provisions of 29 U.S.C. § 623(e)"); Hodgson v. Western Textile Co., 7 CCH Employ. Prac. Dec. ¶9383 (N.D. Ill., April 26, 1974) (noting prior injunction against printing or publishing any notice or advertisement indicating any preference, limitation, specification, or discrimination based on age) n.o.r.

employment discrimination based on age in violation of the ADEA.[428]

Once a court has found a violation of the ADEA, the most appropriate relief to avoid future violations by the defendant is a general permanent injunction prohibiting the defendant from engaging in any practices which the statute makes unlawful. The most thorough consideration has been given to this question by the Court of Appeals in *Hodgson v. First Federal Savings and Loan Association.*[429] In that case, the District Court had found a violation of the ADEA in connection with a failure to hire an applicant for a position as bank teller and ordered, *inter alia,* that the defendant be restrained from violating the provisions of the statute with regard to the hiring of tellers. The Court of Appeals reversed as to the scope of the injunction holding that

> we find no legal justification in compartmentalizing an employer corporation in order to warrant an injunction against illegal employment practices to be applied only as to the particular job category in which the violation occurred. When confronted by a situation such as this courts should not be loath to issue injunctions of general applicability. See Wirtz v. Ocala Gas Company, 336 F.2d 236 (CA5, 1964). The aim of such an .injunction is remedial, not punitive. McComb v. Jacksonville Paper Company, 336 U.S. 187, 69 S. Ct. 497, 93 L. Ed. 599 (1949).[430]

The Court of Appeals, further, noted that a general injunction is not burdensome since it simply requires the defendant to obey the law and that it is an effective device for enforcement of the ADEA since the Department of Labor should not be charged with the

---

428. *See, e.g.,* Hodgson v. First Fed. Sav. and Loan Ass'n, *supra;* Brennan v. Goodyear Tire & Rubber Co., 10 CCH Employ. Prac. Dec. ¶10,562, 11 Fair Employ. Prac. Cas. 589 (M.D. Fla., May 8, 1975) n.o.r.; Hodgson v. Ideal Corrugated Box Co., 8 CCH Employ. Prac. Dec. ¶9805, 10 Fair Employ. Prac. Cas. 744 (N.D. W.Va., January 31, 1974) n.o.r.; Hodgson v. Sugar Cane Growers Coop., 5 CCH Employ. Prac. Dec. ¶8618, 5 Fair Employ. Prac. Cas. 1136 (S.D. Fla. April 4, 1973) n.o.r.
429. 455 F.2d 818 (5th Cir. 1972).
430. *Id.* at 826.

responsibility of checking back on past violators to make certain they are obeying the law.

> Having once made out a case of unlawful discrimination, we think the government should not have to bear this administrative burden. This consideration, balanced against the minimal inconvenience to the defendant, weighs heavily in favor of enforcement by an injunction of general applicability without reference to specific jobs.[431]

In addition, the existence of a general permanent injunction against a defendant's violating the ADEA allows the Secretary of Labor to bring a future violation of the statute before a court, by means of a contempt proceeding based on the defendant's violation of the injunction, more quickly than is normally possible.[432]

One court, despite a finding that the defendant had violated the ADEA, refused to grant an injunction against future violations because the defendant had previously terminated its unlawful acts.[433] However, the same reasoning that supports the issuance of a broad permanent injunction also militates in favor of the issuance of a permanent injunction against a defendant found to have violated the ADEA even if the defendant has complied with the statute since the violation occurred. As the Court of Appeals noted in *Mitchell v. Pidcock*,[434]

> The injunctive processes are a means of effecting general compliance with national policy as expressed by Congress, a public policy judges too must carry out — actuated by the spirit of the law and not begrudgingly as if it were a newly imposed fiat of a presidium.

5. *Attorney's Fees and Costs.* In addition to any judgment awarded to a successful plaintiff in an action under the ADEA, the

---

431. *Id.* at 826-27. *Accord,* Hodgson v. Approved Personnel Service, Inc., 529 F.2d 760 (4th Cir. 1975), *reversing,* 8 CCH Employ. Prac. Dec. ¶9810, 11 Fair Employ. Prac. Cas. 683 (M.D. N.C., September 20, 1974) n.o.r.

432. *See, e.g.,* Hodgson v. Western Textile Co., 7 CCH Employ. Prac. Dec. ¶9383 (N.D. Ill., April 26, 1974) n.o.r.

433. Brennan v. C/M Mobile, Inc., 8 CCH Employ. Prac. Dec. ¶9532, 8 Fair Employ. Prac. Cas. 551 (S.D. Ala., March 6, 1974) n.o.r.

434. 299 F.2d 281, 287 (5th Cir. 1962) (Fair Labor Standards Act of 1938).

court is required to allow him a reasonable attorney's fee and costs of the action to be paid by the defendant.[435] The Courts have, with one exception, implemented this provision.[436]

There is no provision allowing a successful defendant to recover its attorney's fees and costs. Since attorney's fees are not recoverable by either party in the United States in the absence of a statutory provision providing therefor, it is expected that successful defendants will not be able to do so.[437] However, costs are recoverable by the prevailing party [438] and they have been allowed to successful defendants in actions under the ADEA.[439]

---

435. 29 U.S.C. § 216(b) (Supp. V 1975) *incorporated by* 29 U.S.C. § 626(b) (1970). *See* Alyeska Pipeline Service Co. v. Wilderness Society, 421 U.S. 240, 261 n. 34 (1975), where the Supreme Court noted in *dictum* that the incorporated provision of the Fair Labor Standards Act is "mandatory in terms of awarding attorneys' fees. . . .".

436. Brennan v. Ace Hardware Corp., 495 F.2d 368 (8th Cir. 1974) *(dictum)*; Lachapelle v. Owens-Illinois, Inc., 64 F.R.D. 96, 99 (N.D. Ga. 1974) *(dictum)*, *aff'd on other grounds*, 513 F.2d 286 (5th Cir. 1975) *(per curiam)*; Rogers v. Exxon Research and Eng'r Co., 404 F. Supp. 324, 334, 338 (D. N.J. 1975); Brennan v. Goodyear Tire & Rubber Co., 10 CCH Employ. Prac. Dec. ¶10,562, 11 Fair Employ. Prac. Cas. 589 (M.D. Fla., May 8, 1975) n.o.r.; Bishop v. Jelleff Associates, Inc., 398 F. Supp. 579, 597 (D.D.C. 1974); Chilton v. National Cash Register Co., 370 F. Supp. 660 (S.D. Ohio, 1974); Schulz v. Hickok Mfg. Co., 358 F. Supp. 1208 (N.D. Ga. 1973); Monroe v. Penn-Dixie Cement Corp., 335 F. Supp. 231 (N.D. Ga. 1971) *(dictum)*. *Contra*, Stringfellow v. Monsanto Co., 320 F. Supp. 1175, 1181 (W.D. Ark. 1970) *(dictum)*, where the Court apparently overlooked the incorporated provision of the Fair Labor Standards Act of 1938. In Brennan v. Ace Hardware Corp., *supra*, at 374 n. 11, the Court noted that the plaintiff was unsuccessful in Stringfellow v. Monsanto Co. and interpreted that Court's statement to mean that an unsuccessful plaintiff could not recover attorney's fees and costs.

437. *See* Alyeska Pipeline Service Co. v. Wilderness Society, 421 U.S. 240, 264 n. 37 (1975), where the Supreme Court stated in *dictum* that Congress had specified in the Fair Labor Standards Act provision incorporated in the ADEA "that only one of the litigants can be awarded fees."

438. Rule 54(d) of the Fed. R. Civ. P.

439. *See, e.g.,* Leach v. Hilti, Inc., 414 F. Supp. 3 (E.D. Mo. 1975); Price v. Maryland Cas. Co., 391 F. Supp. 613 (S.D. Miss. 1975); Moses v. Falstaff Brewing Corp., 13 Fair Employ. Prac. Cas. 347 (E.D. Mo., June 15, 1976) n.o.r.; Smith v. Crest Communities, Inc., 9 CCH Employ. Prac. Dec. ¶10,053, 8 Fair Employ. Prac. Cas. 1328 (W.D. Ky., November 21, 1974) n.o.r.; Hinote v. Dworshak Dam Constructors, 6 CCH Employ. Prac. Dec. ¶8892 (D. Idaho, July 13, 1973) n.o.r.; Billingsley v. Service Tech. Corp., 6 CCH Employ. Prac. Dec. ¶8874, 6 Fair Employ. Prac. Cas. 404 (S.D. Tex., April 5 and 24, 1973) n.o.r.; Hodgson v. Tamiami Trail Tours, Inc.,

6. *Interest on Damages.* The ADEA contains no provision specifying the extent to which interest is recoverable on monetary damages awarded in an action under the statute, if at all. One court has ordered the payment of interest on the damages awarded in an action brought under the ADEA from the date of judgment until payment of the damages.[440] The award of post-judgment interest is not uncommon. A more difficult question is whether a plaintiff can recover pre-judgment interest.

Some courts have awarded pre-judgment interest in ADEA cases.[441] Such a determination is consistent with the fact that the damages awarded are for lost wages and benefits which the plaintiff has been denied the use of by reason of the defendant's illegal act. Clearly, between the plaintiff and the defendant the former has the greater claim to the monies which could have been earned on the wages and benefits wrongfully denied to the plaintiff by the defendant.

---

4 CCH Employ. Prac. Dec. ¶7795, 4 Fair Employ. Prac. Cas. 728 (S.D. Fla., March 31, 1972) n.o.r.; Hodgson v. Great Am. Disct. and Credit Co., 336 F. Supp. 1355 (M.D. Ala. 1972).

But see Donnelly v. Exxon Research & Eng'r Co., 11 CCH Employ. Prac. Dec. ¶10,860, 12 Fair Employ. Prac. Cas. 417 (D. N.J., October 30, 1974) n.o.r., *aff'd without opinion*, 521 F.2d 1398 (3rd Cir. 1975) (denying costs to either party upon the granting of defendant's motion for a judgment dismissing the action at the close of plaintiff's case); Klopp v. Civil Serv. Comm'n, 11 CCH Employ. Prac. Dec. ¶10,878 (C.D. Cal., October 29, 1975) (ordering each party to bear its own costs upon dismissal of the action based on the fact that plaintiff was not within the protected age bracket) n.o.r.

440. Brennan v. Hughes Personnel, Inc., 8 CCH Employ. Prac. Dec. ¶9679 (W.D. Ky., June 25, 1974) n.o.r.

441. *See* Rogers v. Exxon Research and Eng'r Co., 404 F. Supp. 324, 338 (D. N.J. 1975) ("judgment in the amount of $260,000 plus interest"); Brennan v. Goodyear Tire & Rubber Co., 10 CCH Employ. Prac. Dec. ¶10,562, at 6332, 11 Fair Employ. Prac. Cas. 589, 590 (M.D. Fla., May 8, 1975) ("interest since the date of discharge at six percent per annum" "computed from the end of each calendar quarter until paid.") n.o.r.; Hodgson v. Poole Truck Line, Inc., 4 CCH Employ. Prac. Dec. ¶7668, 4 Fair Employ. Prac. Cas. 265 (S.D. Ala., January 13, 1972) (awarding interest on damages from August 21, 1969 until payment where plaintiff applied for employment with the defendant on June 28, 1969, was wrongfully denied employment by reason of his age on June 30, 1969, brought suit in 1970, and the case was submitted for decision on January 7, 1972) n.o.r.; Hodgson v. Sugar Cane Growers Coop., 5 CCH Employ. Prac. Dec. ¶8618, at 7814, 5 Fair Employ. Prac. Cas. 1136, 1138 (S.D. Fla., April 4, 1973) (providing for "recovery of back wages, together with interest at six percent per annum.") n.o.r.

213

Interest on lost wages and benefits should be determined from the date each element thereof would normally have been paid but for the defendant's illegal act and not from the date of the wrong [442] at which point no damages could have accrued.

V. AGE DISCRIMINATION IN FEDERAL GOVERNMENT EMPLOYMENT

As has been previously noted, the ADEA excludes from its definition of "employer" the United States or a corporation wholly owned by the Government of the United States [443] and excludes an agency of the United States from its definition of "employment agency." [444] As a result, employees of and applicants for employment with the Federal government have been excluded from the protection of and resort to the procedures provided by the ADEA.[445]

However, the Fair Labor Standards Amendments of 1974 [446] added a new Section 15 to the ADEA specifically covering age discrimination in Federal government employment.[447] The amendment provides that all personnel actions affecting employees or applicants for employment, other than with respect to aliens outside the limits of the United States, in military departments; [448] executive agencies,[449] including employees and applicants for employment who are paid from nonappropriated funds; in the United States Postal Service and the Postal Rate Commission; in those units in the government of the District of Columbia having positions in the competitive service; in those units

---

442. *Cf.* Hodgson v. Poole Truck Line, Inc., *supra. But see* Brennan v. Goodyear Tire & Rubber Co., *supra.*

443. 29 U.S.C. § 630(b) (Supp. V 1975).

444. 29 U.S.C. § 630(c) (Supp. V 1975).

445. *See* Opinion Letter of Wage-Hour Administrator, 8 Lab. Rel. Rep. 401:5212 (August 12, 1968); Opinion Letter of Wage-Hour Administrator, 8 Lab. Rel. Rep. 401:5202 (July 5, 1968).

446. Pub. L. No. 93-259, §§ 1-29 (April 8, 1974).

447. 29 U.S.C. § 633a (Supp. V 1975).

448. As defined in 5 U.S.C. § 102 (1970).

449. As defined in 5 U.S.C. § 105 (1970). The Veterans Administration is an executive agency subject to the ADEA — Bevans v. Nugent, 12 CCH Employ. Prac. Dec. ¶11,123 (S.D.N.Y., July 28, 1976) n.o.r.

of the legislative and judicial branches of the Federal Government having positions in the competitive service; and in the Library of Congress shall be made free from any discrimination based on age.[450]

Except as otherwise provided therein, the Federal Civil Service Commission is authorized to enforce the provisions of the amendment through appropriate remedies, including reinstatement or hiring of employees with or without back pay, as will effectuate the policies of the section.[451] The Civil Service Commission is required to issue such rules, regulations, orders, and instructions as it deems necessary and appropriate to carry out its responsibilities under the section.[452] The Civil Service Commission is, further, made responsible for reviewing and evaluating the operation of all agency programs designed to carry out the policy of the section, periodically obtaining and publishing (on at least a semiannual basis) progress reports from each department, agency, or unit covered by the section; required to consult with and solicit the recommendations of interested individuals, groups, and organizations relating to nondiscrimination in employment on account of age; and required to provide for the acceptance and processing of complaints of discrimination in Federal employment on account of age.[453]

The head of each covered department, agency, or unit is required to comply with the rules, regulations, orders, and instructions issued by the Civil Service Commission under the ADEA which are to include a provision requiring that an employee or applicant for employment be notified of any final action taken on any complaint of discrimination filed by him thereunder.[454]

The amendment also provides that the Civil Service Commission may establish reasonable exemptions to the provisions of the section but only when the Civil Service Commission has established a maximum age requirement on the basis of a determination that

450. 29 U.S.C. § 633a(a) (Supp. V 1975).
451. 29 U.S.C. § 633a(b) (Supp. V 1975).
With respect to employment in the Library of Congress, the Librarian of Congress rather than the Civil Service Commission is to exercise the authority granted by the Section. 29 U.S.C. § 633a(b) (Supp. V 1975).
452. 29 U.S.C. § 633a(b) (Supp. V 1975).
453. Id.
454. Id.

age is a bona fide occupational qualification necessary to the performance of the duties of the position.[455]

Any person aggrieved may bring a civil action in any Federal district court of competent jurisdiction for such legal or equitable relief as will effectuate the purposes of the ADEA.[456] However, when an individual has not filed a complaint concerning age discrimination with the Civil Service Commission, no civil action may be commenced by him until he has given the Commission not less than thirty days' notice of an intent to file such action. Such notice must be filed within 180 days after the alleged unlawful practice occurred.[457]

Upon receiving a notice of intent to sue, the Civil Service Commission is required to promptly notify all persons named therein as prospective defendants in the action and take any appropriate action to assure the elimination of any unlawful practice.[458]

The section also provides that nothing contained therein relieves any Government agency or official of the responsibility of assuring nondiscrimination on account of age in employment as required under any provision of Federal law.[459]

The inclusion of the amendment covering age discrimination in Federal employment in the ADEA limits the protection afforded by the amendment to individuals at least forty years of age but less than sixty-five years of age.[460]

W. RECORDKEEPING

Section 7(a) of the ADEA grants to the Secretary of Labor the power to require the keeping of records necessary or appropriate

---

455. *Id.*
456. 29 U.S.C. § 633a(c) (Supp. V 1975).
457. 29 U.S.C. § 633a(d) (Supp. V 1975).
458. *Id.*
459. 29 U.S.C. § 633a(e) (Supp. V 1975).
460. 29 U.S.C. § 631 (Supp. V 1975). Bevans v. Nugent, 12 CCH Employ. Prac. Dec. ¶11,123, at 5195-96 (S.D.N.Y., July 28, 1976) n.o.r. The Court in *Bevans* left for future resolution the plaintiff's assertion that to construe Section 15 of the ADEA to apply only to Federal government employees between 40 and 65 years of age would render the section unconstitutional under the "rational basis test" used by the United States Supreme Court in Massachusetts Bd. of Retirement v. Murgia, 427 U.S. 307 (1976) *(per curiam)*.

for the administration of the statute.[461] In accordance with this mandate, the Secretary of Labor has issued regulations requiring employers, employment agencies, and labor organizations to keep designated records.[462] The records kept pursuant to these regulations serve not only to make available to the Secretary of Labor information concerning older persons in the work force but also to provide the Secretary of Labor with statistical data in connection with investigations of claims of age discrimination in employment, particularly where a complainant charges the existence of a pattern or practice of age discrimination. As has been previously noted,[463] such statistics may be introduced at a trial to aid in the proof of a *prima facie* case of a violation of the ADEA. While an individual plaintiff may not have access to such records prior to the commencement of an action alleging a violation of the ADEA, thereafter an individual plaintiff may in the course of pre-trial discovery obtain such information where relevant.

No particular order or form of records is required, only that the records kept contain in some form the information specified in the regulations. If the required information is available in records kept for other purposes or can be obtained readily by recomputing or extending data recorded in some other form, no further records are required to be made or kept on a routine basis by the regulations.[464]

1. *Employers.* Every employer subject to the provisions of the ADEA is required to make and keep for three years payroll or other records for each of his employees containing their name, address, date of birth, occupation, rate of pay, and compensation earned each week.[465]

Every covered employer who, in the regular course of his business, makes, obtains, or uses any personnel or employment records related to the following is required to keep them for a period of one year from the date of the personnel action to which any records relate: job applications, resumes, or any other form of employment inquiry whenever submitted to the employer in

---

461. 29 U.S.C. § 626(a) (1970); 29 C.F.R. § 850.1 (1974). *See also* 29 U.S.C. § 628 (1970), authorizing the Secretary of Labor to issue such rules and regulations as he may consider necessary or appropriate for carrying out the ADEA.

462. 29 C.F.R. §§ 850.1-850.7, 850.11 (1974).

463. *See* pp. 192-195, *supra.*

464. 29 C.F.R. § 850.2 (1974).

465. 29 C.F.R. § 850.3(a) (1974).

response to his advertisement or other notice of existing or anticipated job openings, including records pertaining to the failure or refusal to hire any individual; promotion, demotion, transfer, selection for training, layoff, recall, or discharge of any employee; job orders submitted by the employer to an employment agency or labor organization for recruitment of personnel for job openings; test papers completed by applicants or candidates for any position which disclose the results of any employer-administered aptitude or other employment test considered by the employer in connection with any personnel action; the results of any physical examination where such examination is considered by the employer in connection with any personnel action; and any advertisements or notices to the public or to employees relating to job openings, promotions, training programs, or opportunities for overtime work.[466]

Every covered employer is also required to keep on file any employee benefit plans such as pension and insurance plans, as well as copies of any seniority systems and merit systems which are in writing, for the full period the plan or system is in effect, and for at least one year after its termination. If the plan or system is not in writing, the employer is required to keep on file a memorandum fully outlining the terms of such plan or system and the manner in which it has been communicated to the affected employees, together with notations relating to any changes or revisions therein for the full period the plan or system is in effect, and for at least one year after its termination.[467]

An exception is made to the foregoing employer record retention regulation in the case of application forms and other preemployment records of applicants for positions which are, and are known by applicants to be, of a temporary nature. All such records which are required to be kept by the regulation need only be retained for a period of 90 days from the date of the personnel action to which they relate.[468]

A second exception applies when an enforcement action is commenced under the ADEA regarding a particular applicant or employee, the Wage-Hour Administrator is authorized to require

466. 29 C.F.R. § 850.3(b)(1) (1974).
467. 29 C.F.R. § 850.3(b)(2) (1974).
468. 29 C.F.R. § 850.3(b)(3) (1974).

the employer to retain any record required to be kept under the regulations which is relative to such action until the final disposition thereof.[469]

2. *Employment Agencies.* Every employment agency subject to the provisions of the ADEA which, in the regular course of its business, makes, obtains, or uses, any records related to the following is required to keep them for a period of one year from the date of the action to which the records relate: placements; referrals, where an individual is referred to an employer for a known or reasonably anticipated job opening; job orders from employers seeking individuals for job openings; job applications, resumes, or any other form of employment inquiry or record of any individual which identifies his qualifications for employment, whether for a known job opening at the time of submission or for future referral to an employer; test papers completed by applicants or candidates for any position which disclose the results of any agency-administered aptitude or other employment test considered by the agency in connection with any referrals; and advertisements or notices relative to job openings.[470]

An exception is made to the foregoing employment agency record retention regulation in the case of application forms and other preemployment records of applicants for positions which are, and are known by applicants to be, of a temporary nature. All such records which are required to be kept by the regulation need only be retained for a period of 90 days from the date of the making or obtaining of the record involved.[471]

A second exception applies when an enforcement action is commenced under the ADEA regarding a particular applicant. The Wage-Hour Administrator is authorized to require the employment agency to retain any record required to be kept under the regulations which is relative to such action until the final disposition thereof.[472]

Whenever an employment agency has an obligation as an employer or a labor organization under the ADEA, the employment

---

469. 29 C.F.R. § 850.3(b)(4) (1974).
470. 29 C.F.R. § 850.4(a)(1) (1974).
471. 29 C.F.R. § 850.4(a)(2) (1974).
472. 29 C.F.R. § 850.4(a)(3) (1974).

agency must also comply with the recordkeeping requirements for employers or labor organizations, as appropriate.[473]

In the only reported decision dealing with recordkeeping, the Court rejected the Secretary of Labor's position and held that it was not illegal for an employment agency subject to the provisions of the ADEA to maintain in its corporate files records and notations referring to age characteristics of applicants for employment

> since the statute refers to printing or publishing of notices or advertisements relating to referral, and does not prohibit the keeping of intra-corporate records which contain such information, which would be prohibited if placed on notices designed for the general public or in newspapers or other advertisements.[474]

It should be noted that the recordkeeping regulations applicable to covered employers [475] and labor organizations,[476] but not those covering employment agencies, require that records of dates of birth be kept. The absence of a requirement that employment agencies keep records of the age of applicants, placements, and referrals makes it extremely difficult to prove a pattern, practice, or policy of age discrimination by an employment agency.

3. *Labor Organizations.* Every labor organization subject to the provisions of the ADEA is required to keep current records identifying its members by name, address, and date of birth,[477] and to keep for a period of one year from the making thereof a record of the name, address, and age of any individual seeking membership in the organization.[478]

---

473. 29 C.F.R. § 850.4(b) (1974).

474. Brennan v. Hughes Personnel, Inc., 8 CCH Employ. Prac. Dec. ¶9571, at 5475 (W. D. Ky., May 22, 1974) n.o.r., *amended on other grounds,* 8 CCH Employ. Prac. Dec. ¶9679 (W.D. Ky., June 25, 1974) n.o.r.

475. 29 C.F.R. § 850.3(a)(3) (1974).

476. 29 C.F.R. § 850.5(a) (1974).

477. 29 C.F.R. § 850.5(a) (1974).

478. 29 C.F.R. § 850.5(b) (1974). An "individual seeking membership" is considered to be a person who files an application for membership or who, in some other manner, indicates a specific intention to be considered for membership, but does not include any individual who is serving for a stated limited probationary period prior to permanent employment and formal union membership. A person who merely makes an inquiry about the labor organization or, for example, about its general program, is not considered to be an individual seeking membership in a labor organization. *Id.*

An exception to the foregoing provides that when an enforcement action is commenced under the ADEA regarding a labor organization the Wage-Hour Administrator is authorized to require the labor organization to retain any record required to be kept under the regulations which is relative to such action until the final disposition thereof.[479]

Whenever a covered labor organization has an obligation as an employer or as an employment agency under the ADEA, the labor organization must also comply with the recordkeeping requirements for employers or employment agencies, as appropriate.[480]

4. *Inspection of Records.* The records required to be kept by the Secretary of Labor's regulations are required to be kept safe and accessible at the place of employment or business at which the individual to whom they relate is employed or has applied for employment or membership, or at one or more established central recordkeeping offices.[481]

All records required to be kept by the regulations must be made available for inspection and transcription by authorized representatives of the Wage-Hour Administrator during business hours generally observed by the office at which they are kept or in the community generally. Where records are maintained at a central recordkeeping office pursuant to the regulations, such records must be made available at the office at which they would otherwise be required to be kept within 72 hours following a request from the Wage-Hour Administrator or his authorized representative.[482]

Every person required to maintain records under the ADEA must make such extension, recomputation, or transcriptions of his records and must submit such reports concerning actions taken and classifications of individuals set forth in records as the Wage-Hour Administrator or his authorized representative may request in writing.[483]

---

479. 29 C.F.R. § 850.5(c) (1974).
480. 29 C.F.R. § 850.5(d) (1974).
481. 29 C.F.R. § 850.6(a) (1974).
482. 29 C.F.R. § 850.6(b) (1974).
483. 29 C.F.R. § 850.7 (1974).

5. *Recordkeeping Exceptions.* Each employer, employment agency, or labor organization subject to the provisions of the ADEA which for good cause wishes to maintain records in a manner other than that required by the regulations, or to be relieved of preserving certain records for the period or periods prescribed in the regulations, may submit in writing a petition to the Wage-Hour Administrator requesting such relief setting forth the reasons therefor and proposing alternative recordkeeping or record-retention procedures.[484]

If, on review of the petition and after completion of any necessary or appropriate investigation supplementary thereto, the Wage-Hour Administrator finds that the alternative procedure proposed, if granted, will not hamper or interfere with the enforcement of the ADEA and will be of equivalent usefulness in its enforcement, the Wage-Hour Administrator is authorized to grant the petition subject to such conditions as he may determine appropriate and subject to revocation.[485]

Whenever any relief from the recordkeeping and record-retention regulations granted to any person is sought to be revoked for failure to comply with the conditions of the Wage-Hour Administrator, that person must be notified in writing of the facts constituting such failure and afforded an opportunity to achieve or demonstrate compliance.[486]

The submission of a petition or any delay of the Wage-Hour Administrator in acting upon such a petition does not relieve any employer, employment agency, or labor organization from any obligations to comply with the recordkeeping, record-retention regulations. However, the Wage-Hour Administrator is required to give notice of the denial of any petition with due promptness.[487]

X. EXEMPTIONS FROM THE ADEA

Section 9 of the ADEA authorizes the Secretary of Labor to establish such reasonable exemptions "to and from any or all provisions" of the ADEA "as he may find necessary and proper in the public interest." [488] This power to establish exemptions is

484. 29 C.F.R. § 850.11(a) (1974).
485. 29 C.F.R. § 850.11(b) (1974).
486. *Id.*
487. 29 C.F.R. § 850.11(c) (1974).
488. 29 U.S.C. § 628 (1970).

potentially very important since the way in which it is exercised might well determine the effectiveness of the statute in dealing with age discrimination in employment.

The Secretary of Labor's regulations covering administrative exemptions from the provisions of the ADEA recognize the significance of the power and provide that it will be exercised with caution and due regard for the remedial purpose of the ADEA to promote employment of older persons based on their ability rather than age and to prohibit arbitrary age discrimination in employment. Specifically, the regulations provide that administrative action consistent with that statutory purpose may be taken under the section of the ADEA authorizing it, with or without a request therefor, when found necessary and proper in the public interest in accordance with the statutory standards.[489]

No formal procedures are prescribed for requesting an exemption, but a request therefor must be submitted in writing to the Wage-Hour Administrator. The regulation, further, provides that a reasonable exemption from the ADEA's provisions will be granted only if it is decided, after notice of the proposed exemption is published in the Federal Register giving all interested persons an opportunity to present data, views, or arguments, that a strong and affirmative showing has been made that such exemption is in fact necessary and proper in the public interest.[490]

The only exemption from the provisions of the ADEA granted to date exempts from all prohibitions of the ADEA all activities and programs under Federal contracts or grants, or carried out by state public employment services, designed exclusively to provide employment for, or to encourage the employment of, persons with special employment problems, including employment activities and programs under the Manpower Development and Training Act of 1962, as amended, and the Economic Opportunity Act of 1964, as amended, for persons among the long-term unemployed, handicapped, members of minority groups, older workers, or youth.[491] The Wage-Hour Administrator is given authority to decide questions concerning the application of the exemption.[492]

---

489. 29 C.F.R. § 850.15(b) (1974).
490. Id.
491. 29 C.F.R. § 850.16(a) (1974).
492. Id.

Any employer, employment agency, or labor organization whose activities are exempt from the prohibitions of the ADEA by reason of the foregoing exemption is required to maintain and preserve records containing the same information and data that is required of non-exempt employers, employment agencies, and labor organizations under the recordkeeping, record-retention regulations.[493]

Y. STUDY OF INVOLUNTARY RETIREMENT

Section 5 of the ADEA directs the Secretary of Labor to undertake an appropriate study of institutional and other arrangements giving rise to involuntary retirement, and to report his findings and any appropriate legislative recommendations to the President of the United States and the United States Congress.[494]

Involuntary retirement, which is permitted under the ADEA when it is pursuant to a bona fide employee benefit plan such as a retirement or pension plan,[495] represents a major problem facing older workers.[496]

Although the Secretary of Labor has not yet submitted his report on involuntary retirement, summaries of preliminary studies have been included in the Secretary of Labor's annual reports to Congress under the ADEA.[497]

---

493. 29 C.F.R. § 850.16(b) (1974).

494. 29 U.S.C. § 624 (1970).

495. 29 U.S.C. § 623(b)(2) (1970). *See* pp. 125-129, *supra.*

496. *See* Kaplan, *Too Old to Work: The Constitutionality of Mandatory Retirement Plans,* 44 So. Cal. L. Rev. 150 (1971).

497. Employment Standards Administration, U.S. Dep't of Labor, *A Report Covering Activities Under the Act During 1976,* at 29-37 (1977); Employment Standards Administration, U.S. Dep't of Labor, *A Report Covering Activities Under the Act During 1975,* at 23-26, A-3 to A-7 (1976); Employment Standards Administration, U.S. Dep't of Labor, *A Report Covering Activities Under the Act During 1974,* at 23-27 (1975); Employment Standards Administration, U.S. Dep't of Labor, *A Report Covering Activities Under the Act During 1973,* at 16-41 (1974); Employment Standards Administration, U.S. Dep't of Labor, *A Report Covering Activities Under the Act During 1972,* at 11-14 (1973); Employment Standards Administration, U.S. Dep't of Labor, *A Report Covering Activities Under the Act During 1971,* at 6-11 (1972).

Z. CRIMINAL PENALTIES

Any person who forcibly resists, opposes, impedes, intimidates or interferes with a duly authorized representative of the Secretary of Labor while he is engaged in the performance of his duties can under Section 10 of the ADEA be punished by a fine of not more than $500 or by imprisonment for not more than one year, or by both. However, no person can be imprisoned under this provision unless he has previously been convicted thereunder.[498]

AA. ANNUAL REPORTS TO CONGRESS

The Secretary of Labor is required by Section 13 of the ADEA to submit annually in January a report to the United States Congress covering his activities for the preceding year under the ADEA and to include such information, data, and recommendations for further legislation in connection with the matters covered by the ADEA as he may find advisable.[499]

The Secretary of Labor's annual reports are also required to contain an evaluation and appraisal by the Secretary of the effect of the minimum and maximum ages established by the statute, together with his recommendations thereon to the Congress. In making his evaluation and appraisal, the Secretary of Labor is required to take into consideration any changes which may have occurred in the general age level of the population, the effect of the ADEA upon workers not covered by its provisions, and such other factors as he may deem pertinent.[500]

---

498. 29 U.S.C. § 629 (1970).

499. 29 U.S.C. § 632 (1970).

500. *Id.* The Secretary of Labor was required by the ADEA to recommend to the United States Congress within six months after the effective date of the statute any measures he deemed desirable to change the lower or upper age limits set forth in the ADEA. 29 U.S.C. § 622(b) (1970). By letter dated November 27, 1968, Secretary of Labor Willard Wertz made the required report to Congress in which he concluded that

> The age limits presently included in the statute encompass approximately half of all persons 25 years of age or older and almost three-fifths of the labor force 25 years of age or older. Any broadening of the age span might limit the effectiveness of the statute in promoting the interests of the older worker. Changes in the age limits would therefore seem to be inappropriate. [CCH [Transfer Binder — New Developments, Aug. 1968 — April, 1969] Lab. L. Rep. ¶8054, at 6088.]

BB. APPROPRIATIONS

As originally enacted, the ADEA contained a provision authorizing the appropriation of such sums, not in excess of $3 million for any fiscal year, as might be necessary to carry out the statute.[501] In 1974, that provision was amended to authorize the appropriation of up to $5 million for any fiscal year.[502]

The funds actually expended have, in fact, never approached the amounts authorized.[503]

501. Pub. L. No. 90-202, § 16, 81 Stat. 608 (December 15, 1967).

502. Pub. L. No. 93-259, § 28(a) (5), 88 Stat. 74 (April 8, 1974); 29 U.S.C. § 634 (Supp. V 1975).

503. *Improving the Age Discrimination Law* at 13: 1969-$500,000; 1970-$530,000; 1971-$1,450,000; 1972-$1,362,000; 1973 (estimate)-$1,441,000; 1974 (requested)-$1,451,000.

Chapter 8

THE ADEA IN RETROSPECT

The ADEA has been in effect for approximately nine years. Through June 20, 1976, 77,983 establishments were investigated under the ADEA of which 58,861 or approximately 75 percent were found to be in compliance with the statute and 18,008 establishments or approximately 23 percent were found not to be in compliance with the ADEA. Through December 31, 1976, the United States Secretary of Labor had instituted 306 court actions alleging violations of the ADEA. The following table sets forth a detailed summary of the investigations undertaken by the United States Department of Labor under the ADEA and results thereof:

	JUNE 21, 1968– JUNE 20, 1969 1969A	JUNE 21, 1969– JUNE 20, 1970B	JUNE 21, 1970– JUNE 20, 1971C	JUNE 21, 1971– JUNE 20, 1972D	JUNE 21, 1972– JUNE 20, 1973E	JUNE 21, 1973– JUNE 20, 1974F	JUNE 21, 1974– JUNE 20, 1975G	JUNE 21, 1975– JUNE 20, 1976H	TOTALS
I. Unduplicated Number of Establishments Investigated under ADEA	25,291	10,956	6,846	6,067	6,856	7,535	6,555	7,877	77,983
A. Found in compliance with ADEA	24,291	8,622	4,080	3,633	3,923	4,578	4,462	5,272	58,861
B. Found in noncompliance with ADEA	497	2,216	2,522	2,185	2,933	2,957	2,093	2,605	18,008
1. Employers-noncompliance	475	2,249	2,414	2,489	2,725	2,344	1,563	NR	—
a. Refuse to hire	159	592	683	818	843	544	434	NR	—
b. Discharge	12	78	110	186	180	NR	354	NR	—
c. Promotional bars	17	212	265	339	NR	NR	NR	NR	—
d. Terms and conditions of employment	22	NR	NR	NR	NR	NR	NR	NR	—
e. Illegal employment advertising	231	1,207	1,180	1,003	1,559	1,800	775	833	8,588
f. Other	34	160	176	143	143	NR	NR	NR	—
2. Employment agencies-noncompliance	160	712	936	516	393	340	96	104	—
a. Failure to refer	31	229	325	186	112	53	NR	28	—
b. Illegal employment advertising	88	434	585	295	276	287	96	70	2,131
c. Other	41	49	26	35	5	NR	NR	6	—
3. Labor organizations—noncompliance	5	1	4	1	5	2	0	NR	—
a. Exclusion	2	1	NR	NR	NR	NR	NR	NR	—
b. Bars to referral	2	0	3	1	2	1	NR	NR	—
c. Other	1	0	1	0	1	NR	NR	6	—
d. Illegal Advertising	NR	NR	NR	NR	1	1	0	2	—
e. Discharge	NR	NR	NR	NR	1	NR	NR	NR	—

	(1)	(2)	(3)	(4)	(5)	(6)	(7)
4. State and local governments—noncompliance	—	—	—	—	85	216	301
a. Refuse to hire	—	—	—	—	37	94	131
b. Illegal employment advertising	—	—	—	—	25	54	79
c. Discharge	—	—	—	—	7	21	28
d. Other	—	—	—	—	16	47	63
II. Results of Conciliation, Conference, and Persuasion Efforts of Secretary of Labor							
1. Employers							
a. Agreement to correct	335	1,771	1,941	1,930	NR	NR	NR
b. Refusal to correct	31	96	117	151	NR	NR	NR
c. Possible future noncompliance	107	382	356	408	NR	NR	NR
2. Employment agencies							
a. Agreement to correct	152	673	840	463	NR	NR	NR
b. Refusal to correct	4	1	34	21	NR	NR	NR
c. Possible future noncompliance	24	38	62	32	NR	NR	NR
3. Labor organizations							
a. Agreement to correct	4	1	4	1	NR	NR	NR
b. Refusal to correct	1	0	0	0	NR	NR	NR
c. Possible future noncompliance	0	0	0	0	NR	NR	NR
4. State and local governments							
a. Agreement to correct	—	—	—	—	NR	NR	NR

229

	1969	1970	1971	1972	1973	1974	1975	1976	
b. Refusal to correct	—	—	—	—	—	—	NR	NR	—
c. Possible future noncompliance	—	—	—	—	—	—	NR	NR	—
III. Legal Actions Commenced By Secretary of Labor Under ADEA	1	NR(22)	50	63	46	47	30	47	306

NR.—Not Reported

A. Wage and Labor Standards Administration, U.S. Dep't of Labor, *A Report Covering Activities In Connection With The Act During 1969* at 6, 10, 11 (1970). ("1969 Report")

B. Workplace Standards Administration, U.S. Dep't of Labor, *A Report Covering Activities In Connection With The Act During 1970* at 9, 11 (1971). ("1970 Report")

C. Employment Standards Administration, U.S. Dep't of Labor, *A Report Covering Activities Under The Act During 1971* at 3, 14, 16 (1972). ("1971 Report")

D. Employment Standards Administration, U.S. Dep't of Labor, *A Report Covering Activities Under The Act During 1972* at 7, 17, 19 (1973). ("1972 Report")

E. Employment Standards Administration, U.S. Dep't of Labor, *A Report Covering Activities Under The Act During 1973* at vii, 9, 10 , 45 (1974). ("1973 Report")

F. Employment Standards Administration, U.S. Dep't of Labor, *A Report Covering Activities Under The Act During 1974* at vii, 9-11, 32 (1975). ("1974 Report")

G. Employment Standards Administration, U.S. Dep't of Labor, *A Report Covering Activities Under The Act During 1975* at vii 8, 9, 12 (1976). ("1975 Report")

H. Employment Standards Administration, U.S. Dep't of Labor, *A Report Covering Activities Under The Act During 1976* at 10-13, 41-42 (1977). ("1976 Report")

Although the Secretary of Labor's annual reports to Congress do not report the same statistics each year, some indication of the actual and potential impact of the ADEA on older workers can be obtained from the following table:

	JUNE 21, 1968– JUNE 20, 1969A	JUNE 21, 1969– JUNE 20, 1970B	JUNE 21, 1970– JUNE 20, 1971C	JUNE 21, 1971– JUNE 20, 1972D	JUNE 21, 1972– JUNE 20, 1973E	JUNE 21, 1973– JUNE 20, 1974F	JUNE 21 1974– JUNE 20, 1975I	JUNE 21, 1975– JUNE 20, 1976I	TOTALS
I. Number of Establishments Covered by ADEA	NR	NR	685,000	685,000	800,000	1,000,000	1,000,000	1,000,000	—
II. Number of Persons Covered by ADEA	NR	NR	43,000,000	43,000,000	46,000,0000	60,000,000	64,000,000	66,000,000	—
III. Number of Complaints Received by Secretary of Labor	1,031H	1,344H	1,658H	1,862H	2,208H	3,040H	4,717	5,121	20,981
IV. Results of Investigations:									
A. Monetary									
1. Amounts found owing	$39,875G	$129,514G	$738,074	$1,650,039	$1,866,226G	$6,315,484	$6,574,000	8,631,432	25,944,644
2. Number of persons entitled to payments	48G	131G	655	964	1,031	1,648	2,350	1,908	8,735
3. Amount of income restored	NR	NR	NR	NR	662,324G	2,507,448I	1,676,171	3,491,658	—
4. Number of persons to whom income restored	NR	NR	NR	NR	304	637	728	742	—
5. Number of persons discriminated against	NR	NR	NR	NR	14,386G	3,800G	5,540	12,951	—
B. Nonmonetary									
1. Job opportunities for older workers made available by									

								TOTALS
elimination of dis-criminatory prac-tices	NR	NR	500,000	119,000	106,000	39,667	84,207	27,217	31,964 —
2. Persons aided	NR	NR	NR	NR	NR	8,849I	2,744	3,376	2,351 —

NR—Not Reported

A 1969 Report, at 5.
B 1970 Report, at 3.
C 1971 Report, at 1, 3.
D 1972 Report, at vii, 7.
E 1973 Report, at vii, 10.
F 1974 Report, at vii, 11.
G Id., at 7.
H Id., at 8.
I 1975 Report, at 5.
J 1976 Report, at 3, 7, 8.

The foregoing tables show that the ADEA has had a substantial impact both with respect to the opening of employment opportunities for older workers in general which, in its absence, would have been closed to them simply because of their age and the protection of the jobs and job opportunities of specific older workers.

The first years after the passage of the ADEA were marked by an attack on the more obvious forms of age discrimination in employment prohibited for the first time on a national basis by the statute. Thereafter, the emphasis switched to more subtle forms of discrimination based, in part, on complaints by individuals resulting from a greater awareness on the part of older workers of the protections afforded by the statute.[1]

In addition to the results achieved by means of informal contacts and litigation, a third means of eliminating unlawful age discrimination in employment is the settlement agreement entered into either prior to or after the commencement of a legal action by the Secretary of Labor. It was reported in 1974 that of the nearly 200 suits theretofore filed under the ADEA by the Secretary of Labor

> a majority have been settled and settled to the satisfaction of the government with relief to the individual affected by the discrimination.[2]

The most sizable settlement after the commencement of litigation was achieved in *Brennan v. Western Operations, Inc. (Division of Standard Oil Company of California)*[3] where the

---

1. *See* U.S. Senate, Special Committee on Aging, *Improving the Age Discrimination Law — A Working Paper,* 93d Cong. 1st Sess., at 2 (September 1973) (hereinafter *Improving the Age Discrimination Law*).

> In 1969, there were 1,031 complaints received by the U.S. Department of Labor from individuals who felt themselves discriminated against because of age. In fiscal 1972, there were 1,862 for an increase of over 80 percent for the three-year period.

2. Statement of Karen Ann Clauss, Assistant Solicitor of United States Department of Labor — August 7, 1973, in Report of 1973 Proceedings of Section of Labor Relations Law of the American Bar Association at 136 (1974).

3. Civil Action No. C-74-1039 (N.D. Cal., May 15, 1974), excerpts from settlement agreement reprinted in 96 BNA Daily Labor Rep. — 5/16/74, G-1. *See also* N.Y. Times, May 17, 1974, p. 1 ("Oil Concern to Pay Age — Bias Settlement").

parties entered into a consent judgment providing, *inter alia*, that the defendant be permanently enjoined from violating the prohibitions of the ADEA; make offers of reinstatement to 120 of its previously terminated employees and reinstate those who desired employment to their former job or one of similar status, pay and location; pay a total of $2 million, subject to limited reductions, to approximately 160 persons to compensate them for lost wages and benefits during the period from the date of their termination to the date of the judgment; and adjust upward the monthly pension payment to be paid to specified persons to reflect the amount they would have received had they remained on the defendant's payroll through the date of judgment.

The importance of the *Western Operations, Inc.* case is not limited to the individuals involved. As one writer has noted, the Wage-Hour Division of the United States Department of Labor

> Pulled out all the publicity stops to spread the word about its recent consent decree with the Standard Oil Company of California, in which the company agreed to ante up $2-million in back pay to workers let out because of age. Highlighted in the press briefings (so that the lesson would not be lost on occupants of executive row) was the fact that among those who were ordered reinstated were top-drawer personnel (division managers in the $40,000-a-year bracket).[4]

Just four months before the entry of the foregoing consent judgment, the Secretary of Labor had noted in his annual report to Congress that

> There is currently a pressing need for dramatic litigation cases as a reinforcement to our administrative efforts. Such cases have widespread impact on employers, employment agencies, and labor organizations in that the potential costliness of noncompliance is brought home, and their sensitivity to the need for voluntary efforts heightened.[5]

Although it involved less money than the *Western Operations, Inc.* case, a possibly more significant settlement from the

4. Stessin, *The Ax and Older Workers*, N.Y. Times, June 23, 1974, § 3, p. 3.
5. Employment Standards Administration, U.S. Dep't of Labor, *A Report Covering Activities Under the Act During 1973* at 8 (1974).

standpoint of the future was reached before the initiation of litigation between the Department of Labor and the Friendly Ice Cream Corporation. Without admitting a violation of the ADEA, the company agreed, *inter alia*, to pay to the Department of Labor $40,000, before those deductions required by law, for disbursement to those who suffered age discrimination, in settlement of all claims of past age discrimination by those accepting payment from the fund; to review its practices, policies, and restrictions based on age which may be in violation of the ADEA; to establish, maintain, and apply to all employees and applicants for employment on a continuing basis minimal hiring and employment standards, practices and procedures which are not unlawfully discriminatory under the statute; and, most importantly, to develop an "Affirmative Action Program" designed to ensure compliance with the ADEA, including a minimum percentage hiring goal for persons within the protected age bracket, subject to review and approval by the Department of Labor prior to implementation and to supervision thereafter.[6]

While the use of affirmative action programs has become common under Title VII of the Civil Rights Act of 1964, the settlement involving the Friendly Ice Cream Corporation is the first reported use of the device in connection with the ADEA. The advantage of such an approach is that it provides a means to attempt to overcome the results of past discrimination and to make sure that past unlawful actions are corrected and not repeated. Care must, of course, be taken to assure that an affirmative action program does not result in discrimination against persons outside the protected age bracket. While such persons are not protected by the ADEA, the statute should not be permitted to become a means for discriminating against persons because of their age.

While there have been major advancements in the protection of older workers under the ADEA, the achievements have not been as great as they could have been, in large part because of a lack of personnel and a failure to appropriate and spend the authorized

---

6. Agreement between Friendly Ice Cream Corp. and U.S. Department of Labor, 2 CCH Employ. Prac. Guide ¶5198 (November 29, 1973).

funds. As was noted in a 1973 working paper prepared for the Special Committee on Aging of the United States Senate:

In fiscal 1969 there were only 46 positions allotted to the new nationwide program launched against age discrimination. Although $3 million was authorized to be appropriated, only $500,000 of this sum was utilized. Today, five years later, there are only 69 positions for fiscal 1974 and less than $1.5 million budgeted. In the regions, furthermore, there are no specific individuals assigned to ADEA. Instead, the man-hours authorized by the budgeted positions are allocated among the compliance officers working on ADEA cases.[7]

Despite the foregoing, experience under the ADEA has proven both the need for legal protection of older workers and the effectiveness of the statute in dealing with the covered forms of age discrimination in employment. As was noted in the United States Senate working paper,

Clearly, no employee should remain in a position if he or she cannot meet its demands and the law recognizes this fact.

But equally clearly, no employee should be forced to quit or retire early simply because of reaching a certain age.

Such judgments should be made on the basis of facts, not blanket assumptions.

ADEA was enacted, not only to enforce the law, but to provide the facts that would help change attitudes. Much more remains to be done in the way of education, and improving ADEA generally.[8]

---

7. *Improving the Age Discrimination Law* at 13. *See also* note 503, at p. 226 *supra.*

8. *Improving the Age Discrimination Law* at (iii).

Chapter 9

THE FUTURE AND THE ADEA

There are two major areas in which changes in the ADEA would further the objectives of the statute — elimination of the exception authorizing involuntary retirement of employees regardless of age if done pursuant to a bona fide retirement plan [1] and elimination of the upper limit of 65 years of age on the protected age bracket.

A. INVOLUNTARY RETIREMENT

The Secretary of Labor has not yet completed and submitted the study required by Section 5 of the ADEA on institutional and other arrangements giving rise to involuntary retirement which he is directed to submit together with his findings and appropriate legislative recommendations to the President of the United States and the United States Congress.[2]

Even in the absence of the Secretary of Labor's study, it has been recognized that

> This exception has proven difficult to administer because of the complexities involved in determining if an employee is being terminated because of age discrimination (and only incidentally is eligible for some retirement benefit) or if he or she is being retired early according to the plan's stipulations. The problem is compounded by the wide variations in the provisions of pension plans.[3]

An economist in the Division of General Compensation Structures of the Bureau of Labor Statistics of the United States Department of Labor has concluded, after reviewing pension provisions in force in 1967 and 1971 that may force older workers to retire or that limit their employment opportunities after retirement to determine what changes had occurred after passage of the ADEA, that while one purpose of the statute was to discourage such provisions the ADEA had not, in fact, done so.[4]

---

1. See pp. 125-129, supra.
2. 29 U.S.C. § 624 (1970), and p. 224, supra.
3. Improving the Age Discrimination Law at 15-16. See also id., at 18.
4. Davis, Pension Provisions Affecting The Employment Of Older Workers, 96(4) Monthly Labor Rev. (April, 1973).

A representative of the Department of Labor has stated that the Department's interpretation of the ADEA as permitting involuntary retirement "is under re-examination and could be changed."[5]

With respect to the defenses afforded persons subject to the provisions of the ADEA by the exception for bona fide employee benefit plans such as retirement, pension, or insurance plans, there would appear to be no justification for permitting involuntary retirement except in cases where there is either another exception under the statute available or there is a single fixed age applicable to all employees without exception for compulsory as opposed to voluntary retirement. It can be expected that such a requirement would cause the management of a covered employer or labor organization to either require mandatory retirement at an age related to the employer's or labor organization's needs or eliminate mandatory retirement entirely.

B. MAXIMUM AGE LIMIT

The adoption of a maximum age limit, restricting the protection afforded by the ADEA to persons below a certain age, is contrary to the objective of eliminating arbitrary age discrimination in employment against older workers and denies protection to those most in need of it.

As has previously been noted,[6] the choice of age 65 was based on historical precedent fixing that age for the commencement of governmental retirement benefits and the use of that age in prior state laws dealing with age discrimination in employment. However, some states have placed no such upper age limit in their statutes without, apparently, any untoward results. In view of the increasing longevity of the population of the United States and the relatively few extra persons who would be brought within the coverage of the ADEA by an elimination of the present upper age limit, the statute should be so amended.[7]

---

5. Statement of Karen Ann Clauss, Assistant Solicitor of United States Department of Labor — August 7, 1973, in Report of 1973 Proceedings of Section of Labor Relations Law of the American Bar Association at 137 (1974).

6. *See* pp. 83-85, *supra.*

7. *See* Comment, *Age Discrimination and the Over-Sixty-Five Worker,* 3 Cumberland-Samford L. Rev. 333 (1972); Gilfix, *First Hired — First Fired: Age Discrimination in Employment,* 50 Cal. State Bar J. 462, 512 (1975).

THE FUTURE AND THE ADEA

A bill was introduced in the United States Senate on September 28, 1973 which would have amended the ADEA to extend the protection of the statute to "individuals who are forty years of age or older." [8] No action was taken on that bill.[9]

On February 3, 1975, two bills were introduced in the United States House of Representatives which would have amended the ADEA to expand its coverage to include all "individuals who are at least forty years of age." [10]

During 1975, fourteen bills were introduced in Congress to remove the upper age limit from the ADEA.[11] In 1976, twelve such bills were introduced.[12]

8. S. 2499, 93d Cong., 1st Sess. (1973).

9. The House of Delegates of the American Bar Association disapproved a recommendation of its Family Law Section that the ABA support the proposed amendment of the ADEA. Summary of Action of the House of Delegates of the American Bar Association — 1974 Annual Meeting at 11.

10. H.R. 2588, 2589, 94th Cong., 1st Sess. (1975).

11. Employment Standards Administration, U.S. Dep't of Labor, *A Report Covering Activities Under the Act During 1975* at 19 (1976).

12. Employment Standards Administration, U.S. Dep't of Labor, *A Report Covering Activities Under the Act During 1976* at 27 (1977).

Chapter 10

CONCLUSION

It would now seem clear that discrimination based on age in its various manifestations, (like discrimination based on race, religion and sex) will, in the first instance, be attacked in the courts and legislatures of the United States with changes in the attitudes of the population toward older persons following the legal and legislative lead.

With a predictable acceleration in the challenges to all types of age discrimination [1] as a result of an increase in the percentage of older persons in the population and the completion of the formal structure necessary to combat the other major forms of discrimination, the successes and failures of the attack on age discrimination in employment, as the first full-scale national legal and legislative attempt to deal with a form of age discrimination, will take on increasing significance as the other types of age discrimination are challenged. If the mistakes are to be avoided and the successes repeated, a study of the current multi-faceted attempt to eliminate certain forms of age discrimination in employment in the United States has more than academic interest.

This book has attempted to provide a broad but detailed study of the attempt to deal on a national level with age discrimination in employment in the United States.

---

1. *See generally* Note, *Discrimination Against The Elderly: A Prospectus of the Problem,* VII Suffolk L. Rev. 917 (1973), identifying employment, income, housing and health care as major areas of discrimination. *See also* In re Adoption of Michelle Lee T., 44 Cal. App. 3d 699, 117 Cal. Rptr. 856 (Ct. App. 1975), and cases cited therein, reversing determination of trial court which had denied petition of proposed parents aged 71 and 55 to adopt two year old child solely on the basis of their age.

Appendix A.

1. FEDERAL AGE DISCRIMINATION IN EMPLOYMENT ACT OF 1967 (29 U.S.C. §§ 621-634)

§ 2. Congressional statement of findings and purpose.

§ 3. Education and research program; recommendation to Congress.

§ 4. Prohibition of age discrimination.
  (a) Employer practices.
  (b) Employment agency practices.
  (c) Labor organization practices.
  (d) Opposition to unlawful practices; participation in investigations, proceedings, or litigation.
  (e) Printing or publication of notice or advertisement indicating preference, limitation, etc.
  (f) Lawful practices; age an occupational qualification; other reasonable factors; seniority system; employee benefit plans; discharge or discipline for good cause.

§ 5. Study by Secretary of Labor; reports to President and Congress.

§ 6. Administration.
  (a) Delegation of functions; appointment of personnel; technical assistance.
  (b) Cooperation with other agencies, employers, labor organizations, and employment agencies.

§ 7. Recordkeeping, investigation, and enforcement.
  (a) Attendance of witness; investigations, inspections, records, and homework regulations.
  (b) Enforcement; prohibition of age discrimination under fair labor standards; unpaid minimum wages and unpaid overtime compensation; liquidated damages; judicial relief; conciliation, conference, and persuasion.
  (c) Civil actions; persons aggrieved; jurisdiction; judicial relief; termination of individual action upon commencement of action by Secretary.
  (d) Same; notice to Secretary; timeliness; conciliation, conference, and persuasion.
  (e) Statute of limitations; reliance in future on administrative rulings, etc.

§ 8. Notices to be posted.

§ 9. Rules and regulations; exemptions.

§ 10. Criminal penalties.

§ 11. Definitions.

§ 12. Age limits.

§ 13. Annual report to Congress.

§ 14. Federal-State relationship.
  (a) Federal action superseding State action.
  (b) Limitation of Federal action upon commencement of State proceedings.

§ 15. Nondiscrimination on account of age in Federal Government employment.
  (a) Federal agencies affected.

(b) Enforcement by Civil Service Commission and by Librarian of Congress in the Library of Congress; remedies; rules, regulations, orders, and instructions of Commission; compliance by Federal agencies; powers and duties of Commission; notification of final action on complaint of discrimination; exemptions; bona fide occupational qualification.

(c) Civil actions; jurisdiction; relief.

(d) Same; notice to Commission; time of notice; Commission notification of prospective defendants; Commission elimination of unlawful practices.

(e) Duty of Government agency or official.

§ 17. Authorization of appropriations.

§ 2. Congressional statement of findings and purpose.

(a) The Congress hereby finds and declares that —

(1) in the face of rising productivity and affluence, older workers find themselves disadvantaged in their efforts to retain employment, and especially to regain employment when displaced from jobs;

(2) the setting of arbitrary age limits regardless of potential for job performance has become a common practice, and certain otherwise desirable practices may work to the disadvantage of older persons;

(3) the incidence of unemployment, especially long-term unemployment with resultant deterioration of skill, morale, and employer acceptability is, relative to the younger ages, high among older workers; their numbers are great and growing; and their employment problems grave;

(4) the existence in industries affecting commerce, of arbitrary discrimination in employment because of age, burdens commerce and the free flow of goods in commerce.

(b) It is therefore the purpose of this chapter to promote employment of older persons based on their ability rather than age; to prohibit arbitrary age discrimination in employment; to help employers and workers find ways of meeting problems arising from the impact of age on employment. [29 U.S.C. § 621]

APPENDIX A

§ 3. Education and research program; recommendation to Congress.

(a) The Secretary of Labor shall undertake studies and provide information to labor unions, management, and the general public concerning the needs and abilities of older workers, and their potentials for continued employment and contribution to the economy. In order to achieve the purposes of this chapter, the Secretary of Labor shall carry on a continuing program of education and information, under which he may, among other measures —

(1) undertake research, and promote research, with a view to reducing barriers to the employment of older persons, and the promotion of measures for utilizing their skills;

(2) publish and otherwise make available to employers, professional societies, the various media of communication, and other interested persons the findings of studies and other materials for the promotion of employment;

(3) foster through the public employment service system and through cooperative effort the development of facilities of public and private agencies for expanding the opportunities and potentials of older persons;

(4) sponsor and assist State and community informational and educational programs.

(b) Not later than six months after the effective date of this chapter, the Secretary shall recommend to the Congress any measures he may deem desirable to change the lower or upper age limits set forth in section 631 of this title. [29 U.S.C. § 622]

§ 4. Prohibition of age discrimination.

(a) Employer practices.

It shall be unlawful for an employer —

(1) to fail or refuse to hire or to discharge any individual or otherwise discriminate against any individual with respect to his compensation, terms, conditions, or privileges of employment, because of such individual's age;

(2) to limit, segregate, or classify his employees in any way which would deprive or tend to deprive any individual of

employment opportunities or otherwise adversely affect his status as an employee, because of such individual's age; or

(3) to reduce the wage rate of any employee in order to comply with this chapter.

(b) Employment agency practices.

It shall be unlawful for an employment agency to fail or refuse to refer for employment, or otherwise to discriminate against, any individual because of such individual's age, or to classify or refer for employment any individual on the basis of such individual's age.

(c) Labor organization practices.

It shall be unlawful for a labor organization —

(1) to exclude or to expel from its membership, or otherwise to discriminate against, any individual because of his age;

(2) to limit, segregate, or classify its membership, or to classify or fail or refuse to refer for employment any individual, in any way which would deprive or tend to deprive any individual of employment opportunities, or would limit such employment opportunities or otherwise adversely affect his status as an employee or as an applicant for employment, because of such individual's age;

(3) to cause or attempt to cause an employer to discriminate against an individual in violation of this section.

(d) Opposition to unlawful practices; participation in investigations, proceedings, or litigation.

It shall be unlawful for an employer to discriminate against any of his employees or applicants for employment, for an employment agency to discriminate against any individual, or for a labor organization to discriminate against any member thereof or applicant for membership, because such individual, member or applicant for membership has opposed any practice made unlawful by this section, or because such individual, member or applicant for membership has made a charge, testified, assisted or participated in any manner in an investigation, proceeding, or litigation under this chapter.

(e) Printing or publication of notice or advertisement indicating preference, limitation, etc.

It shall be unlawful for an employer, labor organization, or employment agency to print or publish, or cause to be printed or published, any notice or advertisement relating to employment by such an employer or membership in or any classification or referral for employment for such a labor organization, or relating to any classification or referral for employment by such an employment agency, indicating any preference, limitation, specification, or discrimination, based on age.

(f) Lawful practices; age an occupational qualification; other reasonable factors; seniority system; employee benefit plans; discharge or discipline for good cause.

It shall not be unlawful for an employer, employment agency, or labor organization —

(1) to take any action otherwise prohibited under subsections (a), (b), (c), or (e) of this section where age is a bona fide occupational qualification reasonably necessary to the normal operation of the particular business, or where the differentiation is based on reasonable factors other than age;

(2) to observe the terms of a bona fide seniority system or any bona fide employee benefit plan such as a retirement, pension, or insurance plan, which is not a subterfuge to evade the purposes of this chapter, except that no such employee benefit plan shall excuse the failure to hire any individual; or

(3) to discharge or otherwise discipline an individual for good cause. [29 U.S.C. § 623]

§ 5. Study by Secretary of Labor; reports to President and Congress.

The Secretary of Labor is directed to undertake an appropriate study of institutional and other arrangements giving rise to involuntary retirement, and report his findings and any appropriate legislative recommendations to the President and to the Congress. [29 U.S.C. § 624]

§ 6. Administration.

The Secretary shall have the power —

(a) Delegation of functions; appointment of personnel; technical assistance.

to make delegations, to appoint such agents and employees, and to pay for technical assistance on a fee for service basis, as he deems necessary to assist him in the performance of his functions under this chapter;

(b) Cooperation with other agencies, employers, labor organizations, and employment agencies.

to cooperate with regional, State, local, and other agencies, and to cooperate with and furnish technical assistance to employers, labor organizations, and employment agencies to aid in effectuating the purposes of this chapter. [29 U.S.C. § 625]

§ 7. Recordkeeping, investigation, and enforcement.

(a) Attendance of witnesses; investigations, inspections, records, and homework regulations.

The Secretary shall have the power to make investigations and require the keeping of records necessary or appropriate for the administration of this chapter in accordance with the powers and procedures provided in sections 209 and 211 of this title.

(b) Enforcement; prohibition of age discrimination under fair labor standards; unpaid minimum wages and unpaid overtime compensation; liquidated damages; judicial relief; conciliation, conference, and persuasion.

The provisions of this chapter shall be enforced in accordance with the powers, remedies, and procedures provided in sections 211(b), 216 (except for subsection (a) thereof), and 217 of this title, and subsection (c) of this section. Any act prohibited under section 623 of this title shall be deemed to be a prohibited act under section 215 of this title. Amounts owing to a person as a result of a violation of this chapter shall be deemed to be unpaid minimum wages or unpaid overtime compensation for purposes of sections

216 and 217 of this title: *Provided*, That liquidated damages shall be payable only in cases of willful violations of this chapter. In any action brought to enforce this chapter the court shall have jurisdiction to grant such legal or equitable relief as may be appropriate to effectuate the purposes of this chapter, including without limitation judgments compelling employment, reinstatement or promotion, or enforcing the liability for amounts deemed to be unpaid minimum wages or unpaid overtime compensation under this section. Before instituting any action under this section, the Secretary shall attempt to eliminate the discriminatory practice or practices alleged, and to effect voluntary compliance with the requirements of this chapter through informal methods of conciliation, conference, and persuasion.

(c) Civil actions; persons aggrieved; jurisdiction; judicial relief; termination of individual action upon commencement of action by Secretary.

Any person aggrieved may bring a civil action in any court of competent jurisdiction for such legal or equitable relief as will effectuate the purposes of this chapter: *Provided*, That the right of any person to bring such action shall terminate upon the commencement of an action by the Secretary to enforce the right of such employee under this chapter.

(d) Same; notice to Secretary: timeliness; conciliation, conference, and persuasion.

No civil action may be commenced by any individual under this section until the individual has given the Secretary not less than sixty days' notice of an intent to file such action. Such notice shall be filed —

(1) within one hundred and eighty days after the alleged unlawful practice occurred, or

(2) in a case to which section 633(b) of this title applies, within three hundred days after the alleged unlawful practice occurred or within thirty days after receipt by the individual of notice of termination of proceedings under State law, whichever is earlier.

Upon receiving a notice of intent to sue, the Secretary shall promptly notify all persons named therein as prospective defendants in the action and shall promptly seek to eliminate any alleged unlawful practice by informal methods of conciliation, conference, and persuasion.

(e) Statute of limitations; reliance in future on administrative rulings, etc.

Sections 255 and 259 of this title shall apply to actions under this chapter. [29 U.S.C. § 626]

§ 8. Notices to be posted.

Every employer, employment agency, and labor organization shall post and keep posted in conspicuous places upon its premises a notice to be prepared or approved by the Secretary setting forth information as the Secretary deems appropriate to effectuate the purposes of this chapter. [29 U.S.C. § 627]

§ 9. Rules and regulations; exemptions.

In accordance with the provisions of subchapter II of chapter 5 of Title 5, the Secretary of Labor may issue such rules and regulations as he may consider necessary or appropriate for carrying out this chapter, and may establish such reasonable exemptions to and from any or all provisions of this chapter as he may find necessary and proper in the public interest. [29 U.S.C. § 628]

§ 10. Criminal penalties.

Whoever shall forcibly resist, oppose, impede, intimidate or interfere with a duly authorized representative of the Secretary while he is engaged in the performance of duties under this chapter shall be punished by a fine of not more than $500 or by imprisonment for not more than one year, or by both: *Provided, however,* That no person shall be imprisoned under this section except when there has been a prior conviction hereunder. [29 U.S.C. § 629]

APPENDIX A

§ 11. Definitions.

For the purposes of this chapter —

(a) The term "person" means one or more individuals, partnerships, associations, labor organizations, corporations, business trust, legal representatives, or any organized groups of persons.

(b) The term "employer" means a person engaged in an industry affecting commerce who has twenty or more employees for each working day in each of twenty or more calendar weeks in the current or preceding calendar year: *Provided*, That prior to June 30, 1968, employers having fewer than fifty employees shall not be considered employers. The term also means (1) any agent of such a person, and (2) a State or political subdivision of a State and any agency or instrumentality of a State or a political subdivision of a State, and any interstate agency, but such term does not include the United States, or a corporation wholly owned by the Government of the United States.

(c) The term "employment agency" means any person regularly undertaking with or without compensation to procure employees for an employer and includes an agent of such a person; but shall not include an agency of the United States.

(d) The term "labor organization" means a labor organization engaged in an industry affecting commerce, and any agent of such an organization, and includes any organization of any kind, any agency, or employee representation committee, group, association, or plan so engaged in which employees participate and which exists for the purpose, in whole or in part, of dealing with employers concerning grievances, labor disputes, wages, rates of pay, hours, or other terms or conditions of employment, and any conference, general committee, joint or system board, or joint council so engaged which is subordinate to a national or international labor organization.

(e) A labor organization shall be deemed to be engaged in an industry affecting commerce if (1) it maintains or operates a hiring hall or hiring office which procures employees for an employer or procures for employees opportunities to work for an employer, or (2) the number of its members (or, where it is a labor organization composed of other labor organizations or their representatives, if the aggregate number of the members of such other labor organization) is fifty or more prior to July 1, 1968, or twenty-five or more on or after July 1, 1968, and such labor organization —

(1) is the certified representative of employees under the provisions of the National Labor Relations Act, as amended, or the Railway Labor Act, as amended; or

(2) although not certified, is a national or international labor organization or a local labor organization recognized or acting as the representative of employees of an employer or employers engaged in an industry affecting commerce; or

(3) has chartered a local labor organization or subsidiary body which is representing or actively seeking to represent employees of employers within the meaning of paragraph (1) or (2); or

(4) has been chartered by a labor organization representing or actively seeking to represent employees within the meaning of paragraph (1) or (2) as the local or subordinate body through which such employees may enjoy membership or become affiliated with such labor organization; or

(5) is a conference, general committee, joint or system board, or joint council subordinate to a national or international labor organization, which includes a labor organization engaged in an industry affecting commerce within the meaning of any of the preceding paragraphs of this subsection.

(f) The term "employee" means an individual employed by any employer except that the term "employee" shall not include any person elected to public office in any State or political subdivision of any State by the qualified voters thereof, or any person chosen by such officer to be on such officer's personal staff, or an appointee on the policymaking level or an immediate adviser with respect to the exercise of the constitutional or legal powers of the office. The exemption set forth in the preceding sentence shall not include employees subject to the civil service laws of a State government, governmental agency, or political subdivision.

(g) The term "commerce" means trade, traffic, commerce, transportation, transmission, or communication among the several States; or between a State and any place outside thereof; or within the District of Columbia, or a possession of the United States; or between points in the same State but through a point outside thereof.

APPENDIX A

(h) The term "industry affecting commerce" means any activity, business, or industry in commerce or in which a labor dispute would hinder or obstruct commerce or the free flow of commerce and includes any activity or industry "affecting commerce" within the meaning of the Labor-Management Reporting and Disclosure Act of 1959.

(i) The term "State" includes a State of the United States, the District of Columbia, Puerto Rico, the Virgin Islands, American Samoa, Guam, Wake Island, the Canal Zone, and Outer Continental Shelf lands defined in the Outer Continental Shelf Lands Act. [29 U.S.C. § 630]

§ 12. Age limits.

The prohibitions in this chapter shall be limited to individuals who are at least forty years of age but less than sixty-five years of age. [29 U.S.C. § 631]

§ 13. Annual report to Congress.

The Secretary shall submit annually in January a report to the Congress covering his activities for the preceding year and including such information, data and recommendations for further legislation in connection with the matters covered by this chapter as he may find advisable. Such report shall contain an evaluation and appraisal by the Secretary of the effect of the minimum and maximum ages established by this chapter, together with his recommendations to the Congress. In making such evaluation and appraisal, the Secretary shall take into consideration any changes which may have occurred in the general age level of the population, the effect of the chapter upon workers not covered by its provisions and such other factors as he may deem pertinent. [29 U.S.C. § 632]

§ 14. Federal-State relationship.

(a) Federal action superseding State action.

Nothing in this chapter shall affect the jurisdiction of any agency of any State performing like functions with regard to discriminatory employment practices on account of age except that upon commencement of action under this chapter such action shall supersede any State action.

(b) Limitation of Federal action upon commencement of State proceedings.

In the case of an alleged unlawful practice occurring in a State which has a law prohibiting discrimination in employment because of age and establishing or authorizing a State authority to grant or seek relief from such discriminatory practice, no suit may be brought under section 626 of this title before the expiration of sixty days after proceedings have been commenced under the State law, unless such proceedings have been earlier terminated: *Provided,* That such sixty-day period shall be extended to one hundred and twenty days during the first year after the effective date of such State law. If any requirement for the commencement of such proceedings is imposed by a State authority other than a requirement of the filing of a written and signed statement of the facts upon which the proceeding is based, the proceeding shall be deemed to have been commenced for the purposes of this subsection at the time such statement is sent by registered mail to the appropriate State authority. [29 U.S.C. § 633]

§ 15. Nondiscrimination on account of age in Federal Government employment.

(a) Federal agencies affected.

All personnel actions affecting employees or applicants for employment (except with regard to aliens employed outside the limits of the United States) in military departments as defined in section 102 of Title 5, in executive agencies as defined in section 105 of Title 5 (including employees and applicants for employment who are paid from nonappropriated funds), in the United States Postal Service and the Postal Rate Commission, in those units in the government of the District of Columbia having positions in the competitive service, and in those units of the legislative and judicial branches of the Federal Government having positions in the competitive service, and in the Library of Congress shall be made free from any discrimination based on age.

256

APPENDIX A

(b) Enforcement by Civil Service Commission and by Librarian of Congress in the Library of Congress; remedies; rules, regulations, orders, and instructions of Commission; compliance by Federal agencies; powers and duties of Commission; notification of final action on complaint of discrimination; exemptions: bona fide occupational qualification.

Except as otherwise provided in this subsection, the Civil Service Commission is authorized to enforce the provisions of subsection (a) of this section through appropriate remedies, including reinstatement or hiring of employees with or without backpay, as will effectuate the policies of this section. The Civil Service Commission shall issue such rules, regulations, orders, and instructions as it deems necessary and appropriate to carry out its responsibilities under this section. The Civil Service Commission shall —

(1) be responsible for the review and evaluation of the operation of all agency programs designed to carry out the policy of this section, periodically obtaining and publishing (on at least a semiannual basis) progress reports from each department, agency, or unit referred to in subsection (a) of this section;

(2) consult with and solicit the recommendations of interested individuals, groups, and organizations relating to nondiscrimination in employment on account of age; and

(3) provide for the acceptance and processing of complaints of discrimination in Federal employment on account of age.

The head of each such department, agency, or unit shall comply with such rules, regulations, orders, and instructions of the Civil Service Commission which shall include a provision that an employee or applicant for employment shall be notified of any final action taken on any complaint of discrimination filed by him thereunder. Reasonable exemptions to the provisions of this section may be established by the Commission but only when the Commission has established a maximum age requirement on the basis of a determination that age is a bona fide occupational qualification necessary to the performance of the duties of the position. With respect to employment in the Library of Congress,

257

authorities granted in this subsection to the Civil Service Commission shall be exercised by the Librarian of Congress.

(c) Civil actions; jurisdiction; relief.

Any person aggrieved may bring a civil action in any Federal district court of competent jurisdiction for such legal or equitable relief as will effectuate the purposes of this chapter.

(d) Same; notice to Commission; time of notice; Commission notification of prospective defendants; Commission elimination of unlawful practices.

When the individual has not filed a complaint concerning age discrimination with the Commission, no civil action may be commenced by any individual under this section until the individual has given the Commission not less than thirty days' notice of an intent to file such action. Such notice shall be filed within one hundred and eighty days after the alleged unlawful practice occurred. Upon receiving a notice of intent to sue, the Commission shall promptly notify all persons named therein as prospective defendants in the action and take any appropriate action to assure the elimination of any unlawful practice.

(e) Duty of Government agency or official.

Nothing contained in this section shall relieve any Government agency or official of the responsibility to assure nondiscrimination on account of age in employment as required under any provision of Federal law. [29 U.S.C. § 633a]

§ 17. Authorization of appropriations.

There are hereby authorized to be appropriated such sums, not in excess of $5,000,000 for any fiscal year, as may be necessary to carry out this chapter. [29 U.S.C. § 634]

APPENDIX A

2. RELATED STATUTES
(29 U.S.C. §§209, 211, 216, 217, 255, 259)

§ 209. Attendance of witnesses.
§ 211. Investigations, inspections, records, and homework regulations.
§ 216. Penalties; civil and criminal liability; injunction proceedings terminating right of action; waiver of claims;

actions by Secretary of Labor; limitation of actions; savings provision.
§ 217. Injunction proceedings.
§ 255. Statute of limitations.
§ 259. Reliance in future on administrative rulings, etc.

§ 209. Attendance of witnesses.

For the purpose of any hearing or investigation provided for in this chapter, the provisions of sections 49 and 50 of Title 15 (relating to the attendance of witnesses and the production of books, papers, and documents), are made applicable to the jurisdiction, powers, and duties of the Administrator, the Secretary of Labor, and the industry committees.

§ 211. Investigations, inspections, records, and homework regulations.

(a) The Administrator or his designated representatives may investigate and gather data regarding the wages, hours, and other conditions and practices of employment in any industry subject to this chapter, and may enter and inspect such places and such records (and make such transcriptions thereof), question such employees, and investigate such facts, conditions, practices, or matters as he may deem necessary or appropriate to determine whether any person has violated any provision of this chapter, or which may aid in the enforcement of the provisions of this chapter. Except as provided in section 212 of this title and in subsection (b) of this section, the Administrator shall utilize the bureaus and divisions of the Department of Labor for all the investigations and inspections necessary under this section. Except as provided in section 212 of this title, the Administrator shall bring all actions under section 217 of this title to restrain violations of this chapter.

(b) With the consent and cooperation of State agencies charged with the administration of State labor laws, the Administrator and the Secretary of Labor may, for the purpose of carrying out their

259

respective functions and duties under this chapter, utilize the services of State and local agencies and their employees and, notwithstanding any other provision of law, may reimburse such State and local agencies and their employees for services rendered for such purposes.

(c) Every employer subject to any provision of this chapter or of any order issued under this chapter shall make, keep, and preserve such records of the persons employed by him and of the wages, hours, and other conditions and practices of employment maintained by him, and shall preserve such records for such periods of time, and shall make such reports therefrom to the Administrator as he shall prescribe by regulation or order as necessary or appropriate for the enforcement of the provisions of this chapter or the regulations or orders thereunder.

(d) The Administrator is authorized to make such regulations and orders regulating, restricting, or prohibiting industrial homework as are necessary or appropriate to prevent the circumvention or evasion of and to safeguard the minimum wage rate prescribed in this chapter, and all existing regulations or orders of the Administrator relating to industrial homework are continued in full force and effect.

§ 216. Penalties; civil and criminal liability; injunction proceedings terminating right of action; waiver of claims; actions by Secretary of Labor; limitation of actions; savings provision.

(a) Any person who willfully violates any of the provisions of section 215 of this title shall upon conviction thereof be subject to a fine of not more than $10,000, or to imprisonment for not more than six months, or both. No person shall be imprisoned under this subsection except for an offense committed after the conviction of such person for a prior offense under this subsection.

(b) Any employer who violates the provisions of section 206 or section 207 of this title shall be liable to the employee or employees affected in the amount of their unpaid minimum wages, or their unpaid overtime compensation as the case may be, and in an additional equal amount as liquidated damages. Action to recover such liability may be maintained against any employer (including

APPENDIX A

a public agency) in any Federal or State court of competent jurisdiction by any one or more employees for and in behalf of himself or themselves and other employees similarly situated. No employee shall be a party plaintiff to any such action unless he gives his consent in writing to become such a party and such consent is filed in the court in which such action is brought. The court in such action shall, in addition to any judgment awarded to the plaintiff or plaintiffs, allow a reasonable attorney's fee to be paid by the defendant, and costs of the action. The right provided by this subsection to bring an action by or on behalf of any employee, and the right of any employee to become a party plaintiff to any such action, shall terminate upon the filing of a complaint by the Secretary of Labor in an action under section 217 of this title in which restraint is sought of any further delay in the payment of unpaid minimum wages, or the amount of unpaid overtime compensation, as the case may be, owing to such employee under section 206 or section 207 of this title by an employer liable therefor under the provisions of this subsection.

(c) The Secretary is authorized to supervise the payment of the unpaid minimum wages or the unpaid overtime compensation owing to any employee or employees under section 206 or 207 of this title, and the agreement of any employee to accept such payment shall upon payment in full constitute a waiver by such employee of any right he may have under subsection (b) of this section to such unpaid minimum wages or unpaid overtime compensation and an additional equal amount as liquidated damages. The Secretary may bring an action in any court of competent jurisdiction to recover the amount of unpaid minimum wages or overtime compensation and an equal amount as liquidated damages. The right provided by subsection (b) of this section to bring an action by or on behalf of any employee and of any employee to become a party plaintiff to any such action shall terminate upon the filing of a complaint by the Secretary in an action under this subsection in which a recovery is sought of unpaid minimum wages or unpaid overtime compensation under sections 206 and 207 of this title or liquidated or other damages provided by this subsection owing to such employee by an employer liable under the provisions of subsection (b) of this section, unless such action is dismissed without prejudice on motion of the Secretary. Any sums thus recovered by the Secretary of Labor on behalf of an employee pursuant to this subsection shall be held in a special deposit account and shall be paid, on order of the Secretary of Labor, directly to the employee or employees affected. Any such sums not paid to an employee because of inability to do so within a period of three years shall be covered into the Treasury of the United States as miscellaneous receipts. In determining when an action is commenced by the Secretary of Labor under this subsection for the purposes of the statutes of limitations provided in section 255(a) of this title, it shall be considered to be commenced in the case of any individual claimant on the date when the complaint is filed if he is specifically named as a party plaintiff in the complaint, or if his name did not so appear, on the subsequent date on which his name is added as a party plaintiff in such action.

(d) In any action or proceeding commenced prior to, on, or after August 8, 1956, no employer shall be subject to any liability or punishment under this Act or the Portal-to-Portal Act of 1947 on account of his failure to comply with any provision or provisions of such Acts (1) with respect to work heretofore or hereafter performed in a workplace to which the exemption in section 213 (f) of this title is applicable, (2) with respect to work performed in Guam, the Canal Zone or Wake Island before the effective date of this amendment of subsection (d), or (3) with respect to work performed in a possession named in section 206 (a) (3) of this title at any time prior to the establishment by the Secretary, as provided therein, of a minimum wage rate applicable to such work.

(e) Any person who violates the provisions of section 212 of this title, relating to child labor, or any regulation issued under that section, shall be subject to a civil penalty of not to exceed $1,000 for each such violation. In determining the amount of such penalty, the appropriateness of such penalty to the size of the business of the person charged and the gravity of the violation shall be considered. The amount of such penalty, when finally determined, may be —

(1) deducted from any sums owing by the United States to the person charged;

(2) recovered in a civil action brought by the Secretary in any

262

court of competent jurisdiction, in which litigation the Secretary shall be represented by the Solicitor of Labor; or

(3) ordered by the court, in an action brought for a violation of section 215(a)(4) of this title, to be paid to the Secretary.

Any administrative determination by the Secretary of the amount of such penalty shall be final, unless within fifteen days after receipt of notice thereof by certified mail the person charged with the violation takes exception to the determination that the violations for which the penalty is imposed occurred, in which event final determination of the penalty shall be made in an administrative proceeding after opportunity for hearing in accordance with section 554 of Title 5, and regulations to be promulgated by the Secretary. Sums collected as penalties pursuant to this section shall be applied toward reimbursement of the costs of determining the violations and assessing and collecting such penalties, in accordance with the provisions of section 9a of this title.

§ 217. Injunction proceedings.

The district courts, together with the United States District Court for the District of the Canal Zone, the District Court of the Virgin Islands, and the District Court of Guam shall have jurisdiction, for cause shown, to restrain violations of section 215 of this title, including in the case of violations of section 215(a)(2) of this title the restraint of any withholding of payment of minimum wages or overtime compensation found by the court to be due to employees under this chapter (except sums which employees are barred from recovering, at the time of the commencement of the action to restrain the violations, by virtue of the provisions of section 255 of this title.

§ 255. Statute of limitations.

Any action commenced on or after May 14, 1947, to enforce any cause of action for unpaid minimum wages, unpaid overtime compensation, or liquidated damages, under the Fair Labor Standards Act of 1938, as amended, the Walsh-Healey Act, or the Bacon-Davis Act —

(a) if the cause of action accrues on or after May 14, 1947 — may be commenced within two years after the cause of action accrued, and every such action shall be forever barred unless commenced within two years after the cause of action accrued, except that a cause of action arising out of a willful violation may be commenced within three years after the cause of action accrued;

(b) if the cause of action accrued prior to May 14, 1947 — may be commenced within whichever of the following periods is the shorter: (1) two years after the cause of action accrued, or (2) the period prescribed by the applicable State statute of limitations; and, except as provided in paragraph (c) of this section, every such action shall be forever barred unless commenced within the shorter of such two periods;

(c) if the cause of action accrued prior to May 14, 1947, the action shall not be barred by paragraph (b) of this section if it is commenced within one hundred and twenty days after May 14, 1947 unless at the time commenced it is barred by an applicable State statute of limitations;

(d) with respect to any cause of action brought under section 216(b) of this title against a State or a political subdivision of a State in a district court of the United States on or before April 18, 1973, the running of the statutory periods of limitation shall be deemed suspended during the period beginning with the commencement of any such action and ending one hundred and eighty days after the effective date of the Fair Labor Standards Amendments of 1974, except that such suspension shall not be applicable if in such action judgment has been entered for the defendant on the grounds other than State immunity from Federal jurisdiction.

§ 259. Reliance in future on administrative rulings, etc.

(a) In any action or proceeding based on any act or omission on or after May 14, 1947, no employer shall be subject to any liability or punishment for or on account of the failure of the employer to pay minimum wages or overtime compensation under the Fair Labor Standards Act of 1938, as amended, the Walsh-Healey Act, or the Bacon-Davis Act, if he pleads and proves that the act or omission complained of was in good faith in conformity with and in reliance on any written administrative regulation, order, ruling, approval, or interpretation, of the agency of the United States specified in subsection (b) of this section, or any administrative practice or enforcement policy of such agency with respect to the class of employers to which he belonged. Such a defense, if established, shall be a bar to the action or proceeding, notwithstanding that after such act or omission, such administrative regulation, order, ruling, approval, interpretation, practice, or enforcement policy is modified or rescinded or is determined by judicial authority to be invalid or of no legal effect.

(b) The agency referred to in subsection (a) of this section shall be —

(1) In the case of the Fair Labor Standards Act of 1938, as amended — the Administrator of the Wage and Hour Division of the Department of Labor;

(2) in the case of the Walsh-Healey Act — the Secretary of Labor, or any Federal officer utilized by him in the administration of such Act; and

(3) in the case of the Bacon-Davis Act — the Secretary of Labor.

Appendix B.

REGULATIONS OF THE UNITED STATES SECRETARY OF LABOR PROMULGATED PURSUANT TO SECTIONS 7(a), 8, AND 9 OF THE FEDERAL AGE DISCRIMINATION IN EMPLOYMENT ACT OF 1967 (29 C.F.R. PARTS 850, 860)

SUBCHAPTER C — AGE DISCRIMINATION IN EMPLOYMENT

PART 850 — RECORDS TO BE MADE OR KEPT RELATING TO AGE; NOTICES TO BE POSTED; ADMINISTRATIVE EXEMPTIONS

Subpart A — General

Sec.
850.1   Purpose and scope.

Subpart B — Records To Be Made or Kept Relating to Age; Notices To Be Posted

850.2   Forms of records.
850.3   Records to be kept by employers.
850.4   Records to be kept by employment agencies.
850.5   Records to be kept by labor organizations.

Sec.
850.6   Availability of records for inspection.
850.7   Transcriptions and reports.
850.8—850.9 [Reserved]
850.10 Notices to be posted.
850.11 Petitions for recordkeeping exceptions.

Subpart C — Administrative Exemptions

850.15 Administrative exemptions: procedures.
850.16 Specific exemptions.

AUTHORITY: The provisions of this Part 850 issued under sec. 7, 81 Stat. 604; 29 U.S.C. 626; sec. 11, 52 Stat. 1066, as amended, 29 U.S.C. 211.

SOURCE: The provisions of this Part 850 appear at 34 F.R. 19193, Dec. 4, 1969, unless otherwise noted.

SUBPART A — GENERAL

§ 850.1   Purpose and scope.

(a) Section 7 of the Age Discrimination in Employment Act of 1967 (hereinafter referred to in this part as the Act) empowers the Secretary of Labor to require the keeping of records which are necessary or appropriate for the administration of the Act in accordance with the powers contained in section 11 of the Fair Labor Standards Act of 1938. Subpart B of this part sets forth the recordkeeping and posting requirements which are prescribed by the Secretary of Labor for employers, employment agencies, and labor organizations which are subject to the Act. Reference should be made to section 11 of the Act for definitions of the terms "employer", "employment agency", and "labor organization". General interpretations of the Act and of this part are published in Part 860 of this chapter. This part also reflects pertinent delegations of the Secretary of Labor's duties to the Administrator of the Wage and Hour Division.

(b) Subpart C of this part sets forth the Department of Labor's rules under section 9 of the Act providing that the Secretary of Labor may establish reasonable exemptions to and from any or all provisions of the Act as he may find necessary and proper in the public interest.

SUBPART B — RECORDS TO BE MADE OR KEPT RELATING TO AGE; NOTICES TO BE POSTED

§ 850.2 Forms of records.

No particular order or form of records is required by the regulations in this Part 850. It is required only that the records contain in some form the information specified. If the information required is available in records kept for other purposes, or can be obtained readily by recomputing or extending data recorded in some other form, no further records are required to be made or kept on a routine basis by this Part 850.

§ 850.3 Records to be kept by employers.

(a) Every employer shall make and keep for 3 years payroll or other records for each of his employees which contain:

(1) Name;

(2) Address;

(3) Date of birth;

(4) Occupation;

(5) Rate of pay, and

(6) Compensation earned each week.

(b) (1) Every employer who, in the regular course of his business, makes, obtains, or uses, any personnel or employment records related to the following, shall, except as provided in subparagraphs (3) and (4) of this paragraph, keep them for a period of 1 year from the date of the personnel action to which any records relate:

(i) Job applications, resumes, or any other form of employment inquiry whenever submitted to the employer in response to his advertisement or other notice of existing or anticipated job openings, including records pertaining to the failure or refusal to hire any individual,

(ii) Promotion, demotion, transfer, selection for training, layoff, recall, or discharge of any employee,

(iii) Job orders submitted by the employer to an employment agency or labor organization for recruitment of personnel for job openings,

(iv) Test papers completed by applicants or candidates for any position which disclose the results of any employer-administered aptitude or other employment test considered by the employer in connection with any personnel action,

(v) The results of any physical examination where such examination is considered by the employer in connection with any personnel action,

(vi) Any advertisements or notices to the public or to employees relating to job openings, promotions, training programs, or opportunities for overtime work.

(2) Every employer shall keep on file any employee benefit plans such as pension and insurance plans, as well as copies of any seniority systems and merit systems which are in writing, for the full period the plan or system is in effect, and for at least 1 year after its termination. If the plan or system is not in writing, a memorandum fully outlining the terms of such plan or system and the manner in which it has been communicated to the affected employees, together with notations relating to any changes or revisions thereto, shall be kept on file for a like period.

(3) In the case of application forms and other preemployment records of applicants for positions which are, and are known by applicants to be, of a temporary nature, every record required to be kept under subparagraph (1) of this paragraph shall be kept for a period of 90 days from the date of the personnel action to which the record relates.

(4) When an enforcement action is commenced under section 7 of the Act regarding a particular applicant or employee, the Administrator may require the employer to retain any record required to be kept under subparagraph (1), (2), or (3) of this paragraph which is relative to such action until the final disposition thereof.

§ 850.4 Records to be kept by employment agencies.

(a) (1) Every employment agency which, in the regular course of its business, makes, obtains, or uses, any records related to the following, shall, except as provided in subparagraphs (2) and (3) of this paragraph, keep them for a period of 1 year from the date of the action to which the records relate:

(i) Placements;

(ii) Referrals, where an individual is referred to an employer for a known or reasonably anticipated job opening;

(iii) Job orders from employers seeking individuals for job openings;

(iv) Job applications, resumes, or any other form of employment inquiry or record of any individual which identifies his qualifications for employment, whether for a known job opening at the time of submission or for future referral to an employer;

(v) Test papers completed by applicants or candidates for any position which disclose the results of any agency-administered aptitude or other employment test considered by the agency in connection with any referrals;

(vi) Advertisements or notices relative to job openings.

(2) In the case of application forms and other preemployment records of applicants for positions which are, and are known by applicants to be, of a temporary nature, every record required to be kept under subparagraph (1) of this paragraph shall be kept for a period of 90 days from the date of the making or obtaining of the record involved.

(3) When an enforcement action is commenced under section 7 of the Act regarding a particular applicant, the Administrator may require the employment agency to retain any record required to be kept under subparagraph (1) or (2) of this paragraph which is relative to such action until the final disposition thereof.

(b) Whenever an employment agency has an obligation as an "employer" or a "labor organization" under the Act, the employment agency must also comply with the recordkeeping requirements set forth in § 850.3 or § 850.5, as appropriate.

§ 850.5 Records to be kept by labor organizations.

(a) Every labor organization shall keep current records identifying its members by name, address, and date of birth.

(b) Every labor organization shall, except as provided in paragraph (c) of this section, keep for a period of 1 year from the making thereof, a record of the name, address, and age of any individual seeking membership in the organization. An individual seeking membership is considered to be a person who files an application for membership or who, in some other manner, indicates a specific intention to be considered for membership, but does not include any individual who is serving for a stated limited probationary period prior to permanent employment and formal union membership. A person who merely makes an inquiry about the labor organization or, for example, about its general program, is not considered to be an individual seeking membership in a labor organization.

(c) When an enforcement action is commenced under section 7 of the Act regarding a labor organization, the Administrator may require the labor organization to retain any record required to be kept under paragraph (b) of this section which is relative to such action until the final disposition thereof.

(d) Whenever a labor organization has an obligation as an "employer" or as an "employment agency" under the Act, the labor organization must also comply with the recordkeeping requirements set forth in § 850.3 or § 850.4, as appropriate.

§ 850.6 Availability of records for inspection.

(a) *Place records are to be kept.* The records required to be kept by this part shall be kept safe and accessible at the place of employment or business at which the individual to whom they relate is employed or has applied for employment or membership, or at one or more established central recordkeeping offices.

(b) *Inspection of records.* All records required by this part to be kept shall be made available for inspection and transcription by

271

authorized representatives of the Administrator during business hours generally observed by the office at which they are kept or in the community generally. Where the records are maintained at a central recordkeeping office pursuant to paragraph (a) of this section, such records shall be made available at the office at which they would otherwise be required to be kept within 72 hours following request from the Administrator or his authorized representative.

§ 850.7 Transcriptions and reports.

Every person required to maintain records under the Act shall make such extension, recomputation or transcriptions of his records and shall submit such reports concerning actions taken and limitations and classifications of individuals set forth in records as the Administrator or his authorized representative may request in writing.

§§ 850.8 — 850.9 [Reserved]

§ 850.10 Notices to be posted.

Every employer, employment agency, and labor organization which has an obligation under the Age Discrimination in Employment Act of 1967 shall post and keep posted in conspicuous places upon its premises the notice pertaining to the applicability of the Act prescribed by the Secretary of Labor or his authorized representative. Such a notice must be posted in prominent and accessible places where it can readily be observed by employees, applicants for employment and union members.

§ 850.11 Petitions for recordkeeping exceptions.

(a) *Submission of petitions for relief.* Each employer, employment agency, or labor organization who for good cause wishes to maintain records in a manner other than required in this part, or to be relieved of preserving certain records for the period or periods prescribed in this part, may submit in writing a petition to the Administrator requesting such relief setting forth the reasons therefor and proposing alternative recordkeeping or record-retention procedures.

(b) *Action on petitions.* If, on review of the petition and after completion of any necessary or appropriate investigation supplementary thereto, the Administrator shall find that the alternative procedure proposed, if granted, will not hamper or interfere with the enforcement of the Act, and will be of equivalent usefulness in its enforcement, the Administrator may grant the petition subject to such conditions as he may determine appropriate and subject to revocation. Whenever any relief granted to any person is sought to be revoked for failure to comply with the conditions of the Administrator, that person shall be notified in writing of the facts constituting such failure and afforded an opportunity to achieve or demonstrate compliance.

(c) *Compliance after submission of petitions.* The submission of a petition or any delay of the Administrator in acting upon such petition shall not relieve any employer, employment agency, or labor organization from any obligations to comply with this part. However, the Administrator shall give notice of the denial of any petition with due promptness.

SUBPART C — ADMINISTRATIVE EXEMPTIONS

§ 850.15 Administrative exemptions; procedures.

(a) Section 9 of the Act provides that, "In accordance with the provisions of subchapter II of chapter 5, of title 5, United States Code, the Secretary of Labor * * * may establish such reasonable exemptions to and from any or all provisions of this Act as he may find necessary and proper in the public interest."

(b) The authority conferred on the Secretary by section 9 of the Act to establish reasonable exemptions will be exercised with caution and due regard for the remedial purpose of the statute to promote employment of older persons based on their ability rather than age and to prohibit arbitrary age discrimination in employment. Administrative action consistent with this statutory purpose may be taken under this section, with or without a request therefor, when found necessary and proper in the public interest in accordance with the statutory standards. No formal procedures have been prescribed for requesting such action. However, a reasonable exemption from the Act's provisions will be granted only if it is decided, after notice published in the FEDERAL REGISTER giving all interested persons an opportunity to present data, views, or arguments, that a strong and affirmative showing has been made that such exemption is in fact necessary and proper in the public interest. Request for such exemption shall be submitted in writing to the Administrator.

§ 850.16 Specific exemptions.

(a) Pursuant to the authority contained in section 9 of the Act and in accordance with the procedure provided therein and in § 850.15(b), it has been found necessary and proper in the public interest to exempt from all prohibitions of the Act all activities and programs under Federal contracts or grants, or carried out by the public employment services of the several States, designed exclusively to provide employment for, or to encourage the employment of, persons with special employment problems, including employment activities and programs under the Manpower Development and Training Act of 1962, as amended, and the Economic Opportunity Act of 1964, as amended, for persons among the long-term unemployed, handicapped, members of minority groups, older workers, or youth. Questions concerning the application of this exemption shall be referred to the Administrator for decision.

(b) Any employer, employment agency, or labor organization the activities of which are exempt from the prohibitions of the Act under paragraph (a) of this section shall maintain and preserve records containing the same information and data that is required of employers, employment agencies, and labor organizations under §§ 850.3, 850.4, and 850.5, respectively.

PART 860 — INTERPRETATIONS

Sec.
860.1   Purpose of this part.
860.20   Geographical   scope   of coverage.
860.30   Definitions.
860.31   "Employer."
860.35   "Employment agency."
860.36   Employment   agencies   — prohibitions.
860.50   "Compensation,   terms, conditions, or privileges of employment * * *"

Sec.
860.75   Wage   rate   reduction prohibited.
860.91   Discrimination within the age bracket of 40-65.
860.92   Help   wanted   notices   or advertisements.
860.95   Job applications.
860.102 Bona   fide   occupational qualifications.

APPENDIX B

Sec.

860.103 Differentiations based on reasonable factors other than age.

860.104 Differentiations based on reasonable factors other than age — Additional examples.

Sec.

860.105 Bona fide seniority systems.

860.106 Bona fide apprenticeship programs.

860.110 Involuntary retirement before age 65.

860.120 Costs and benefits under employee benefit plans.

AUTHORITY: The provisions of this part are issued under 81 Stat. 602; 29 U.S.C. 620, 5 U.S.C. 301, Secretary's Order No. 10-68, and Secretary's Order No. 11-68.

§ 860.1 Purpose of this part.

This part is intended to provide an interpretative bulletin on the Age Discrimination in Employment Act of 1967 like Subchapter B of this title relating to the Fair Labor Standards Act of 1938. Such interpretations of this Act are published to provide "a practical guide to employers and employees as to how the office representing the public interest in its enforcement will seek to apply it" (Skidmore v. Swift & Co., 323 U.S. 134, 138). These interpretations indicate the construction of the law which the Department of Labor believes to be correct, and which will guide it in the performance of its administrative and enforcement duties under the Act unless and until it is otherwise directed by authoritative decisions of the Courts or concludes, upon reexamination of an interpretation, that it is incorrect.
[33 F.R. 9172, June 21, 1968]

§ 860.20 Geographical scope of coverage.

The prohibitions in section 4 of the Act are considered to apply only to performance of the described discriminatory acts in places over which the United States has sovereignty, territorial jurisdiction, or legislative control. These include principally the geographical areas set forth in the definition of the term "State" in section 11(i). There, the term State is defined to include "a State of the United States, the District of Columbia, Puerto Rico, the Virgin Islands, American Samoa, Guam, Wake Island, the Canal Zone, and Outer Continental Shelf lands defined in the Outer Continental Shelf Lands Act." Activities within such geographical areas which are discriminatory against protected individuals or

employees are within the scope of the Act even though the activities are related to employment outside of such geographical areas.
[34 F.R. 322, Jan. 9, 1969]

§ 860.30 Definitions.

Considering the purpose of the proviso to section 7(c) of the Act as indicated in the reports of both the Senate and House Committees (see S. Rept. No. 723, 90th Cong., 1st Sess., and H. Rept. No. 805, 90th Cong., 1st Sess.) it was clearly the intent of Congress that the term "employee" in that proviso should apply to any person who has a right to bring an action under the Act, including an applicant for employment.
[34 F.R. 9708, June 21, 1969]

§ 860.31 "Employer."

Section 11(b) defines "employer" to mean "* * * a person engaged in an industry affecting commerce who has 25 or more employees for each working day in each of 20 or more calendar weeks in the current or preceding calendar year: * * * The term also means any agent of such a person, but such term does not include the United States, a corporation wholly owned by the Government of the United States, or a State or political subdivision thereof."
[37 F.R. 13345, July 7, 1972]

§ 860.35 "Employment agency."

(a) Section 11(c) defines "employment agency" to mean "any person regularly undertaking with or without compensation to procure employees for an employer and includes an agent of such a person; but shall not include an agency of the United States, or an agency of a State or political subdivision of a State, except that such term shall include the United States Employment Service and the system of State and local employment services receiving Federal assistance."

(b) As long as an employment agency regularly procures employees for at least one covered employer, it qualifies under section 11(c) as an employment agency with respect to all of its activities whether they be for covered or noncovered employers.
[37 F.R. 13345, July 7, 1972]

APPENDIX B

§ 860.36 Employment agencies — prohibitions.

(a) Section 4(b) provides that "It shall be unlawful for an employment agency to fail or refuse to refer for employment, or otherwise to discriminate against, any individual because of such individual's age, or to classify or refer for employment any individual on the basis of such individual's age."

(b) Since a covered employment agency is subject to the prohibitions of the Act even when acting on behalf of noncovered employers (see § 860.35(b)), it may not discriminate contrary to the statute with respect to any referrals it makes.

(c) The prohibitions of section 4(b) apply not only to the referral activities of a covered employment agency but also to the agency's own employment practices, regardless of the number of employees the agency may have. This is so because section 4(b) makes it unlawful for a covered employment agency "otherwise to discriminate against" any individual between 40 and 65 because of age. To illustrate, a covered employment agency's use of an age preference of "not over 35" in an advertisement seeking employees for itself is unlawful since such preference discriminates against individuals in the 40 to 65 age bracket.
[37 F.R. 13345, July 7, 1972]

§ 860.50 "Compensation, terms, conditions, or privileges of employment * * *".

(a) Section 4(a)(1) of the Act specifies that it is unlawful for an employer "to fail to [sic] refuse to hire or to discharge any individual or otherwise discriminate against any individual with respect to his compensation, terms, conditions, or privileges of employment, because of such individual's age;"

(b) The term "compensation" includes all types and methods of remuneration paid to or on behalf of or received by an employee for his employment.

(c) The phrase "terms, conditions, or privileges of employment" encompasses a wide and varied range of job-related factors including, but not limited to, job security, advancement, status, and benefits. The following are examples of some of the more common terms, conditions, or privileges of employment: The many and varied employee advantages generally regarded as being within

277

the phrase "fringe benefits," promotion, demotion or other disciplinary action, hours of work (including overtime), leave policy (including sick leave, vacation, holidays), career development programs, and seniority or merit systems (which govern such conditions as transfer, assignment, job retention, layoff and recall). An employer will be deemed to have violated the Act if he discriminates against any individual within its protection because of age with respect to any terms, conditions, or privileges of employment, such as the above, unless a statutory exception applies.
[33 F.R. 12227, Aug. 30, 1968]

§ 860.75   Wage rate reduction prohibited.

Section 4(a) (3) of the Act provides that where an age-based wage differential is paid in violation of the statute, the employer cannot correct the violation by reducing the wage rate of any employee. Thus, for example, in a situation where it has been determined that an employer has violated the Act by paying a 62-year-old employee a prohibited wage differential of 50 cents an hour less than he is paying a 30-year-old worker, in order to achieve compliance with the Act he must raise the wage rate of the older employee to equal that of the younger worker. Furthermore, the employer's obligation to comply with the statute cannot be avoided by transferring either the older or the younger employee to other work since the transfer itself would appear discriminatory under the particular facts and circumstances.
[34 F.R. 322, Jan. 9, 1969]

§ 860.91   Discrimination within the age bracket of 40-65.

(a) Although section 4 of the Act broadly makes unlawful various types of age discrimination by employers, employment agencies, and labor organizations, section 12 limits this protection to individuals who are at least 40 years of age but less than 65 years of age. Thus, for example it is unlawful in situations where this Act applies, for an employer to discriminate in hiring or in any other way by giving preference because of age to an individual 30 years old over another individual who is within the 40-65 age bracket limitation of section 12. Similarly, an employer will have violated the Act, in situations where it applies, when one individual

278

within the age bracket of 40-65 is given job preference in hiring, assignment, promotion or any other term, condition, or privilege of employment, on the basis of age, over another individual within the same age bracket.

(b) Thus, if two men apply for employment to which the Act applies, and one is 42 and the other 52, the personnel officer or employer may not lawfully turn down either one on the basis of his age; he must make his decision on the basis of other factors, such as the capabilities and experience of the two individuals. The Act, however, does not restrain age discrimination between two individuals 25 and 35 years of age.

[33 F.R. 9172, June 21, 1968]

§ 860.92 **Help wanted notices or advertisements.**

(a) Section 4(e) of the Act prohibits "an employer, labor organization, or employment agency" from using printed or published notices or advertisements indicating any preference, limitation, specification, or discrimination, based on age.

(b) When help wanted notices or advertisements contain terms and phrases such as "age 25 to 35," "young," "boy," "girl," "college student," "recent college graduate," or others of a similar nature, such a term or phrase discriminates against the employment of older persons and will be considered in violation of the Act. Such specifications as "age 40 to 50," "age over 50," or "age over 65" are also considered to be prohibited. Where such specifications as "retired person" or "supplement your pension" are intended and applied so as to discriminate against others within the protected group, they too are regarded as prohibited, unless one of the exceptions applies.

(c) However, help wanted notices or advertisements which include a term or phrase such as "college graduate," or other educational requirement, or specify a minimum age less than 40, such as "not under 18," or "not under 21," are not prohibited by the statute.

(d) The use of the phrase "state age" in help wanted notices or advertisements is not, in itself, a violation of the statute. But because the request that an applicant state his age may tend to deter older applicants or otherwise indicate a discrimination based on age, employment notices or advertisements which include the phrase "state age," or any similar term, will be closely scrutinized to assure that the request is for a permissible purpose and not for purposes proscribed by the statute.

(e) There is no provision in the statute which prohibits an individual seeking employment through advertising from specifying his own age.

[33 F.R. 9172, June 21, 1968 as amended at 34 F.R. 9708, June 21, 1969]

§ 860.95 Job applications.

(a) The term "job applications," within the meaning of the recordkeeping regulations under the Act (Part 850 of this chapter), refers to all inquiries about employment or applications for employment or promotion including, but not limited to, resumes or other summaries of the applicant's background. It relates not only to preemployment inquiries but to inquiries by employees concerning terms, conditions, or privileges of employment as specified in section 4 of the statute. As in the case with help wanted notices or advertisements (see § 860.92), a request on the part of an employer, employment agency, or labor organization for information such as "Date of Birth" or "State Age" on an employment application form is not, in itself, a violation of the Age Discrimination in Employment Act of 1967. But because the request that an applicant state his age may tend to deter older applicants or otherwise indicate a discrimination based on age, employment application forms which request such information in the above, or any similar phrase, will be closely scrutinized to assure that the request is for a permissible purpose and not for purposes proscribed by the statute. That the purpose is not proscribed by the statute should be made known to the applicant, as by a reference on the application form to the statutory prohibition in language to the following effect: "The Age Discrimination in Employment Act of 1967 prohibits discrimination on the basis of age with respect to individuals who are at least 40 but less than 65 years of age."

(b) An employer may limit the active period of consideration of an application so long as he treats all applicants alike regardless of age. Thus, for example, if the employer customarily retains employment applications in an active status for a period of 60 days, he will be in compliance with the Act if he so retains those of individuals in the 40 to 65 age group for an equal period of consideration as those of younger persons. Further, there is no objection to the employer advising all applicants of the above practice by means of a legend on his application forms as long as this does not suggest any limitation based on age. If it develops, however, that such a legend is used as a device to avoid consideration of the applications of older persons, or otherwise discriminate against them because of age, there would then appear to be a violation of the Act. It should be noted that this position in no way alters the recordkeeping requirements of the Act which are set forth in Part 850 of this chapter.

[33 F.R. 12227, Aug. 20, 1968 as amended at 34 F.R. 9708, June 21, 1969]

§ 860.102 Bona fide occupational qualifications.

(a) Section 4(f) (1) of the Act provides that "It shall not be unlawful for an employer, employment agency, or labor organization * * * to take any action otherwise prohibited under subsections (a), (b), (c), or (e) of this section where age is a bona fide occupational qualification reasonably necessary to the normal operation of the particular business * * *."

(b) Whether occupational qualifications will be deemed to be "bona fide" and "reasonably necessary to the normal operation of the particular business", will be determined on the basis of all the pertinent facts surrounding each particular situation. It is anticipated that this concept of a bona fide occupational qualification will have limited scope and application. Further, as this is an exception it must be construed narrowly, and the burden of proof in establishing that it applies is the responsibility of the employer, employment agency, or labor organization which relies upon it.

(c) The following are illustrations of possible bona fide occupational qualifications.

(d) Federal statutory and regulatory requirements which provide compulsory age limitations for hiring or compulsory retirement, without reference to the individual's actual physical condition at the terminal age, when such conditions are clearly imposed for the safety and convenience of the public. This exception would apply, for example, to airline pilots within the jurisdiction of the Federal Aviation Agency. Federal Aviation Agency regulations do not permit airline pilots to engage in carrier operations, as pilots, after they reach age 60.

(e) A bona fide occupational qualification will also be recognized in certain special, individual occupational circumstances, e.g., actors required for youthful or elderly characterization or roles, and persons used to advertise or promote the sale of products designed for, and directed to appeal exclusively to, either youthful or elderly consumers.

[33 F.R. 9172, June 21, 1968]

§ 860.103 Differentiations based on reasonable factors other than age.

(a) Section 4(f) (1) of the Act provides that "It shall not be unlawful for an employer, employment agency, or labor organization * * * to take any action otherwise prohibited under subsections (a), (b), (c), or (e) of this section * * * where the differentiation is based on reasonable factors other than age; * * *"

(b) No precise and unequivocal determination can be made as to the scope of the phrase "differentiation based on reasonable factors other than age." Whether such differentiations exist must be decided on the basis of all the particular facts and circumstances surrounding each individual situation.

(c) It should be kept in mind that it was not the purpose or intent of Congress in enacting this Act to require the employment of anyone, regardless of age who is disqualified on grounds other than age from performing a particular job. The clear purpose is to insure that age, within the limits prescribed by the Act, is not a determining factor in making any decision regarding hiring, dismissal, promotion or any other term, condition, or privilege of employment of an individual.

(d) The reasonableness of a differentiation will be determined on an individual, case by case basis, not on the basis of any general or class concept, with unusual working conditions given weight according to their individual merit.

(e) Further, in accord with a long chain of decisions of the Supreme Court of the United States with respect to other remedial labor legislation, all exceptions such as this must be construed narrowly, and the burden of proof in establishing the applicability of the exception will rest upon the employer, employment agency or labor union which seeks to invoke it.

(f) Where the particular facts and circumstances in individual situations warrant such a conclusion, the following factors are among those which may be recognized as supporting a differentiation based on reasonable factors other than age:

(1) (i) Physical fitness requirements based upon preemployment or periodic physical examinations relating to minimum standards for employment: *Provided, however,* That such standards are reasonably necessary for the specific work to be performed and are uniformly and equally applied to all applicants for the particular job category, regardless of age.

(ii) Thus, a differentiation based on a physical examination, but not one based on age, may be recognized as reasonable in certain job situations which necessitate stringent physical requirements due to inherent occupational factors such as the safety of the individual employees or of other persons in their charge, or those occupations which by nature are particularly hazardous: For example, iron workers, bridge builders, sandhogs, underwater demolition men, and other similar job classifications which require rapid reflexes or a high degree of speed, coordination, dexterity, endurance, or strength.

(iii) However, a claim for a differentiation will not be permitted on the basis of an employer's assumption that every employee over a certain age in a particular type of job usually becomes physically unable to perform the duties of that job. There is medical evidence, for example, to support the contention that such is generally not the case. In many instances, an individual at age 60 may be physically capable of performing heavy-lifting on a job, where as another individual of age 30 may be physically incapable of doing so.

(2) Evaluation factors such as quantity or quality of production, or educational level, would be acceptable bases for differentiation when, in the individual case, such factors are shown to have a valid

relationship to job requirements and where the criteria or personnel policy establishing such factors are applied uniformly to all employees, regardless of age.

(g) The foregoing are intended only as examples of differentiations based on reasonable factors other than age, and do not constitute a complete or exhaustive list or limitation. It should always be kept in mind that even in situations where experience has shown that most elderly persons do not have certain qualifications which are essential to those who hold certain jobs, some may have them even though they have attained the age of 60 or 64, and thus discrimination based on age is forbidden.

(h) It should also be made clear that a general assertion that the average cost of employing older workers as a group is higher than the average cost of employing younger workers as a group will not be recognized as a differentiation under the terms and provisions of the Act, unless one of the other statutory exceptions applies. To classify or group employees solely on the basis of age for the purpose of comparing costs, or for any other purpose, necessarily rests on the assumption that the age factor alone may be used to justify a differentiation — an assumption plainly contrary to the terms of the Act and the purpose of Congress in enacting it. Differentials so based would serve only to perpetuate and promote the very discrimination at which the Act is directed.

[33 F.R. 9173, June 21, 1968]

§ 860.104 Differentiations based on reasonable factors other than age — Additional examples.

(a) *Employment of Social Security recipients.* (1) It is considered discriminatory for an employer to specify that he will hire only persons receiving old age Social Security insurance benefits. Such a specification could result in discrimination against other individuals within the age group covered by the Act willing to work under the wages and other conditions of employment involved, even though those wages and conditions may be peculiarly attractive to Social Security recipients. Similarly, the specification of Social Security recipients cannot be used as a convenient reference to persons of sufficient age to be eligible for old age benefits. Thus, where two persons apply for a job, one age 56, and the other age 62 and receiving Social Security benefits, the employer may not lawfully give preference in hiring to the older individual solely because he is receiving such benefits.

(2) Where a job applicant under age 65 is unwilling to accept the number or schedule of hours required by an employer as a condition for a particular job, because he is receiving Social Security benefits and is limited in the amount of wages he may earn without losing such benefits, failure to employ him would not violate the Act. An employer's condition as to the number or schedule of hours may be "a reasonable factor other than age" on which to base a differentiation.

(b) *Employee testing.* The use of a validated employee test is not, of itself, a violation of the Act when such test is specifically related to the requirements of the job, is fair and reasonable, is administered in good faith and without discrimination on the basis of age, and is properly evaluated. A vital factor in employee testing as it relates to the 40-65-age group protected by the statute is the "test-sophistication" or "test-wiseness" of the individual. Younger persons, due to the tremendous increase in the use of tests in primary and secondary schools in recent years, may generally have had more experience in test-taking than older individuals and, consequently, where an employee test is used as the sole tool or the controlling factor in the employee selection procedure, such younger persons may have an advantage over older applicants who may have had considerable on-the-job experience but who due to age, are further removed from their schooling. Therefore, situations in which an employee test is used as the sole tool or the controlling factor in the employee selection procedure will be carefully scrutinized to ensure that the test is for a permissible purpose and not for purposes prohibited by the statute.

(c) *Refusal to hire relatives of current employees.* There is no provision in the Act which would prohibit an employer, employment agency, or labor organization from refusing to hire individuals within the protected age group not because of their age but because they are relatives of persons already employed by the firm or organization involved. Such a differentiation would appear to be based on "reasonable factors other than age."

[34 F.R. 322, Jan. 9, 1969, as amended at 34 F.R. 9709, June 21, 1969]

§ 860.105 Bona fide seniority systems.

Section 4(f) (2) of the Act provides that "It shall not be unlawful for an employer, employment agency, or labor organization * * * to observe the terms of a bona fide seniority system * * * which is not a subterfuge to evade the purposes of this Act * * *."

(a) Though a seniority system may be qualified by such factors as merit, capacity, or ability, any bona fide seniority system must be based on length of service as the primary criterion for the equitable allocation of available employment opportunities and prerogatives among younger and older workers. In this regard it should be noted that a bona fide seniority system may operate, for example, on an occupational, departmental, plant, or company wide unit basis.

(b) Seniority systems not only distinguish between employees on the basis of their length of service, they normally afford greater rights to those who have the longer service. Therefore, adoption of a purported seniority system which gives those with longer service lesser rights, and results in discharge or less favored treatment to those within the protection of the Act, may, depending upon the circumstances, be a "subterfuge to evade the purposes" of the Act. Furthermore, a seniority system which has the effect of perpetuating discrimination which may have existed on the basis of age prior to the effective date of the Act will not be recognized as "bona fide."

(c) Unless the essential terms and conditions of an alleged seniority system have been communicated to the affected employees and can be shown to be applied uniformly to all of those affected, regardless of age, it will also be regarded as lacking the necessary bona fides to qualify for the exception.

(d) It should be noted that seniority systems which segregate, classify, or otherwise discriminate against individuals on the basis of race, color, religion, sex, or national origin, are prohibited under Title VII of the Civil Rights Act of 1964, where that Act otherwise applies. Neither will such systems be regarded as "bona fide" within the meaning of section 4(f) (2) of the Age Discrimination in Employment Act of 1967.

[33 F.R. 12227, Aug. 30, 1968]

APPENDIX B

§ 860.106   Bona fide apprenticeship programs.

Age limitations for entry into bona fide apprenticeship programs were not intended to be affected by the Act. Entry into most apprenticeship programs has traditionally been limited to youths under specified ages. This is in recognition of the fact that apprenticeship is an extension of the educational process to prepare young men and women for skilled employment. Accordingly, the prohibitions contained in the Act will not be applied to bona fide apprenticeship programs which meet the standards specified in §§ 521.2 and 521.3 of this chapter.

[34 F.R. 323, Jan. 9, 1969]

§ 860.110   Involuntary retirement before age 65.

(a) Section 4(f) (2) of the Act provides that "It shall not be unlawful for an employer, employment agency, or labor organization * * * to observe the terms of * * * any bona fide employee benefit plan such as a retirement, pension, or insurance plan, which is not a subterfuge to evade the purposes of this Act, except that no such employee benefit plan shall excuse the failure to hire any individual * * *." Thus, the Act authorizes involuntary retirement irrespective of age, provided that such retirement is pursuant to the terms of a retirement or pension plan meeting the requirements of section 4(f) (2). The fact that an employer may decide to permit certain employees to continue working beyond the age stipulated in the formal retirement program does not, in and of itself, render an otherwise bona fide plan invalid insofar as the exception provided in section 4(f) (2) is concerned.

(b) This exception does not apply to the involuntary retirement before 65 of employees who are not participants in the employer's retirement or pension program. It should be noted that section 5 of the Act directs the Secretary of Labor to undertake an appropriate study of institutional and other arrangements giving rise to involuntary retirement, and report his findings and any appropriate legislative recommendations to the President and to Congress.

[34 F.R. 9709, June 21, 1969]

§ 860.120 Costs and benefits under employee benefit plans.

(a) Section 4(f) (2) of the Act provides that it is not unlawful for an employer, employment agency, or labor organization "to observe the terms of * * * any bona fide employee benefit plan such as a retirement, pension, or insurance plan, which is not a subterfuge to evade the purposes of this Act, except that no such employee benefit plan shall excuse the failure to hire any individual * * *." Thus, an employer is not required to provide older workers who are otherwise protected by the law with the same pension, retirement or insurance benefits as he provides to younger workers, so long as any differential between them is in accordance with the terms of a bona fide benefit plan. For example, an employer may provide lesser amounts of insurance coverage under a group insurance plan to older workers than he does to younger workers, where the plan is not a subterfuge to evade the purposes of the Act. A retirement, pension, or insurance plan will be considered in compliance with the statute where the actual amount of payment made, or cost incurred, in behalf of an older worker is equal to that made or incurred in behalf of a younger worker, even though the older worker may thereby receive a lesser amount of pension or retirement benefits, or insurance coverage. Further, an employer may provide varying benefits under a bona fide plan to employees within the age group protected by the Act, when such benefits are determined by a formula involving age and length of service requirements.

(b) Profit-sharing plans: Not all employee benefit plans but only those similar to the kind enumerated in section 4(f) (2) of the Act come within this provision and a profit-sharing plan as such would not appear to be within its terms. However, where it is the essential purpose of a plan financed from profits to provide retirement benefits for employees, the exception may apply. The "bona fides" of such plans will be considered on the basis of all the particular facts and circumstances.

(c) Forfeiture clauses in retirement programs: Clauses in retirement programs which state that litigation or participation in any manner in a formal proceeding by an employee will result in the forfeiture of his rights are unlawful insofar as they may be applied to those who seek redress under the Act. This is by reason

of section 4(d) which provides that it "shall be unlawful for an employer to discriminate against any of his employees * * * because such individual * * * has made a charge, testified, assisted, or participated in any manner in an investigation, proceeding, or litigation under this Act."
[34 F.R. 9709, June 21, 1969]

Appendix C.

NOTICE PREPARED BY THE UNITED STATES SECRETARY OF LABOR PURSUANT TO SECTION 8 OF THE FEDERAL AGE DISCRIMINATION IN EMPLOYMENT ACT OF 1967

(WAGE AND HOUR DIVISION PUBLICATION 1289)

Persons 40-65 Years Note!

The Federal Age Discrimination in Employment Act prohibits arbitrary age discrimination in employment by:

Private Employers of 20 or more persons

Federal, State, and Local Governments, without regard to the number of employees in the employing unit

Employment Agencies serving such employers

Labor Organizations with 25 or more members

Certain exceptions are provided.

If you feel you have been discriminated against because of age, contact the nearest office of the Wage and Hour Division, U. S. Department of Labor. It is important to contact the Division promptly.

If you wish to bring a court action yourself, you must first notify the Secretary of Labor of your intent to do so. This notice should be filed promptly, but in no event later than *180* days after the alleged unlawful practice occurred.

Questions on State age discrimination laws should be directed to State authorities. These laws may affect the *180* day time limit noted above.

Questions on Federal employment should be directed to the U. S. Civil Service Commission, Washington, D. C. 20415.

U. S. Department of Labor
Employment Standards Administration
Wage and Hour Division

☆ U.S. GOVERNMENT PRINTING OFFICE: 1976 O--207-399

WH Publication 1289 (Rev. 5/76)

Appendix D.

SUMMARY OF PROVISIONS UNDER STATE LAWS PERTAINING TO DISCRIMINATION IN EMPLOYMENT BECAUSE OF AGE AS OF FEBRUARY 1, 1976 [EMPLOYMENT STANDARDS ADMINISTRATION, UNITED STATES DEPARTMENT OF LABOR, REPORT COVERING ACTIVITIES UNDER THE FEDERAL AGE DISCRIMINATION IN EMPLOYMENT ACT OF 1967 DURING 1975 SUBMITTED TO CONGRESS IN 1976 IN ACCORDANCE WITH SECTION 13 OF THE ACT 32-58 (JANUARY 30, 1976)]

293

| State | Coverage | | Exclusions and exemptions | Prohibited practices | Penalties | Enforcement agency |
	Law applies to—	Age limits*				
Alabama	No law.					
Alaska	Employers; labor organizations; employment agencies.	None	Nonprofit social clubs; fraternal, charitable, educational, or religious organizations, associations, or corporations; domestic service.	*Employer:* To refuse or bar from employment; to discriminate in compensation, terms, conditions or privileges of employment. *Employer and employment agency:* To advertise, publish or to use application forms which suggest age limitations. *Labor organization:* To exclude, expel or discriminate in any way. *All three:* To discharge, expel, or otherwise discriminate against a person who has opposed unlawful practices, filed a charge, testified, or assisted in any proceeding under the law. *Any person:* To print, publish, broadcast, or otherwise circulate a statement, inquiry, or advertisement directly expressing a limitation, specification, or discrimination. *State, employer, labor orga-*	Up to $500 fine, up to 30 days in jail, or both.	Commission for Human Rights

* Age limits refer to birthdays.

State	Coverage Law applies to—	Coverage Age limits*	Exclusions and exemptions	Prohibited practices	Penalties	Enforcement agency
				nization, and employment agency: Failure to maintain confidential age records required by civil rights agencies for administrative and statistical evaluation.		
American Samoa	No law.					
Arizona	No law.					
Arkansas	No law.					
California	Employers; State and local governments; labor organizations; employment agencies.	40 to 64	Employers of fewer than 5; domestic service, family employment; nonprofit social clubs, fraternal, educational or religious associations or corporations.	To refuse to hire or employ, to discharge, dismiss, reduce, suspend or demote	Up to $500 fine, up to 6 months in jail, or both.	Department of Industrial Relations
Canal Zone	No law.					
Colorado	Any person, firm, association, or corporation conducting business in the State.	18 to 60	None	To discharge.	No less than $100 or more than $250 fine.	None

*Age limits refer to birthdays.

295

State	Law applies to—	Coverage Age limits*	Exclusions and exemptions	Prohibited practices	Penalties	Enforcement agency
Connecticut	Employers; State and political subdivisions; employment agencies; labor organizations.	None	Employers of fewer than 3; domestic service; family employment.	*Employer:* To refuse, bar, or discharge from employment; to discriminate in compensation, terms, conditions or privileges of employment. *Labor organization:* To exclude, expel or discriminate in any way. *Employment agency:* To fail or refuse to classify properly or refer or otherwise discriminate. *All three:* To advertise in such a manner that restricts employment so as to discriminate; discriminate for opposing unfair practices, filing a complaint or testifying or assisting in proceedings. *Person:* To aid, abet, incite, compel, or coerce the doing or attempting to do an unlawful act under the law.	Contempt of court citations.	Commission on Human Rights and Opportunities
Delaware	Employers; State and political subdivisions; employment	40 to 65	Employers of fewer than 4; domestic service; agriculture; fam-	*Employer:* To refuse, bar or discharge from employment; to discriminate in compensation, terms, conditions, or	Contempt of court citations.	Department of Labor

*Age limits refer to birthdays.

296

State	Law applies to—	Coverage Age limits*	Exclusions and exemptions	Prohibited practices	Penalties	Enforcement agency
	agencies; labor organizations; joint labor-management committees.		ily employment; any employee residing in the personal residence of the employer.	privileges of employment. *Employment agency:* To fail or refuse to refer for employment or otherwise discriminate. *Labor organization:* To exclude, expel or discriminate in any way. *Employer, labor organization, joint labor-management committee:* To discriminate in apprenticeship, or other training and retraining, including on-the-job training programs.		
District of Columbia	Employers; employment agencies; labor organizations; government agency.	18 to 65	Domestic service; family employment; working in or about employer's household; religious or political organizations or any organizations operated for charitable or educational purposes;	*Employer:* To fail or refuse to hire; to discharge or otherwise discriminate in compensation, terms, conditions, or privileges of employment, including promotion; to limit, segregate, or classify; to deprive of opportunities or otherwise adversely affect employment status. *Employment agency:* To fail or refuse to refer for employment,	Up to $300 fine, up to 10 days in jail, or both.	Office of Human Rights and Commission on Human Rights

*Age limits refer to birthdays.

297

| State | Coverage | | Exclusions and exemptions | Prohibited practices | Penalties | Enforcement agency |
	Law applies to—	Age limits*				
			professional associations.	or to classify or refer for employment, or otherwise discriminate. *Labor organization*: To exclude, expel, or otherwise discriminate; to limit, segregate, classify, fail or refuse to refer for employment. *All three*: To discriminate for complaints or assistance in complaints; to print or publish notices or advertisement indicating age preference; to discriminate in admission to or employment in apprenticeship or other training or retraining programs. *Person*: To aid, abet, incite, compel or coerce for doing or attempting to do an unlawful act under the law; to retaliate.		
Florida	State or counties.	None	None	To discriminate.	None	None
Georgia	Persons, firms, associations, or corporations.	40 to 65	None	*Employer*: To refuse to hire, employ, license, or bar or discharge from employment.	Not less than $100 or more than $250 fine.	None

*Age limits refer to birthdays.

State	Coverage Law applies to—	Coverage Age limits*	Exclusions and exemptions	Prohibited practices	Penalties	Enforcement agency
Guam	Employers; employment agencies; labor organizations.	None	None	*Employer:* To refuse to hire; to bar or discharge from employment; to discriminate in compensation, terms, conditions, or privileges of employment. *Employer and employment agency:* To advertise, print, circulate material or use application forms which suggest limitations, specifications or discrimination. *Labor organization:* To exclude, expel, or otherwise discriminate. *All three:* To discriminate because of complaint or assistance in complaints. *Person:* To aid in or cause forbidden discrimination practices.	Not more than $200 fine for first offense, not more than $500 fine for second and subsequent offenses, or up to 90 days in jail, or both.	Department of Labor
Hawaii	Employers; employment agencies; labor organizations.	None	None	*Employer:* To refuse, bar, or discharge from employment; to discriminate in compensation, terms, conditions or privileges of employment. *Employer and employment agency:* To print or circulate	First conviction, up to $200 fine, subsequent convictions, up to $500 fine, up to 90 days in jail, or both.	Department of Labor and Industrial Relations

*Age limits refer to birthdays.

299

State	Coverage		Exclusions and exemptions	Prohibited practices	Penalties	Enforcement agency
	Law applies to—	Age limits*				
				any statement, advertisement, or publication, or use any job application or make preemployment inquiry expressing limitations, specifications or discrimination. *Employer or labor organization*: To refuse to enter into an apprenticeship agreement. *Labor organization*: To exclude, expel or discriminate in any way. *All three*: To discharge, expel, or otherwise discriminate for opposition to any practice forbidden by this act, for filing a complaint, testifying or assisting in proceedings. *Person*: To aid, abet, incite, compel or coerce the doing or attempting to do any practices forbidden by this act.		
Idaho	Employers.	Under 60	None	To refuse to hire, bar, or discharge or to otherwise discriminate in compensation,	Not less than $100 or more than $500 fine,	Commissioner of Labor

*Age limits refer to birthdays.

300

State	Coverage		Exclusions and exemptions	Prohibited practices	Penalties	Enforcement agency
	Law applies to —	Age limits*				
Illinois	Employers; governmental units in State; labor organizations.	Over 45	None	hire, tenure, terms, conditions or privileges of employment. *Employer:* To refuse, bar, or discharge from employment; to discriminate in compensation, terms, conditions, or privileges of employment; to utilize any employment agency, placement service, training school or center, labor organization or any other source of unreasonable discrimination. *Labor organization:* To limit, segregate or classify; to in any way affect adversely wages, hours, or conditions of employment. *Employer and labor organization:* To discharge, expel or otherwise discriminate for opposing unlawful employment practices; or filing a charge, testifying, participation or as-	up to 30 days in jail, or both.	None
					Not less than $50 or more than $100 fine.	

*Age limits refer to birthdays.

State	Law applies to—	Coverage Age limits*	Exclusions and exemptions	Prohibited practices	Penalties	Enforcement agency
				sistance in proceedings under the law.		
Indiana	Employers; labor organizations; State and political subdivisions.	40 to 65	Nonprofit social, fraternal, charitable, educational, religious or sectarian organizations, associations or corporations; domestic service; farm labor.	Employer: To dismiss, refuse to employ or rehire, to discharge for furnishing evidence in connection with a complaint. Labor organization: To deny full and equal membership rights; to fail or refuse to classify or refer for employment.	None	Commissioner of Labor
	Employers; employment agencies; labor organizations; State and political subdivisions.	None	Employers of fewer than 4; family employment; domestic service; employees rendering personal service to employer; religious institutions.	Employer: To refuse to hire, accept, register, classify, or refer; to discharge or otherwise discriminate. Labor organization: To refuse to hire or admit for membership, to expel or otherwise discriminate. Employer, employment agency and labor organization: To advertise or in any other manner indicate or	Contempt of court citations.	Civil Rights Commission

*Age limits refer to birthdays.

State	Coverage		Exclusions and exemptions	Prohibited practices	Penalties	Enforcement agency
	Law applies to—	Age limits*				
				publicize not welcome, objectionable, not acceptable, or not solicited for employment or membership. *Person:* To aid, abet, compel, or coerce to engage in unfair practices; to discriminate for opposing or obeying practices, or filing a complaint, testifying or assisting in proceedings under the law.		
Kansas	No law.					
Kentucky	Employers; employment agencies; labor organizations; licensing agency (public and private); joint labor-management committees; State and political subdivisions.	40 to 65	Employers of fewer than 8; domestic service; family employment.	*Employer:* To fail or refuse to hire or discharge or otherwise discriminate in compensation, terms, conditions, or privileges of employment; to limit, segregate, or classify; to deprive of employment opportunities or otherwise adversely affect employment status. *Employment agency:* To fail or refuse to refer to employment or otherwise dis-	Contempt of court citations.	Commission on Human Rights

*Age limits refer to birthdays.

State	Coverage		Exclusions and exemptions	Prohibited practices	Penalties	Enforcement agency
	Law applies to—	Age limits*				
				criminate; to classify or refer on the basis of age; to refuse, bar, or terminate licensing to individuals. *Labor organization:* To exclude or expel or otherwise discriminate; to limit, segregate, or classify or refuse to refer so as to deprive of employment opportunities or otherwise affect status; to cause or attempt to cause an employer to discriminate. *Employer, labor organization, licensing agency or employment agency:* To print or publish notice or advertisement indicating preference, limitations, specifications or discrimination of any kind. *Licensing agency:* To refuse to license, or to bar or terminate from licensing. *Employer, labor organization, joint labor-management committee:* To discriminate in		

*Age limits refer to birthdays.

304

State	Law applies to—	Coverage Age limits*	Exclusions and exemptions	Prohibited practices	Penalties	Enforcement agency
				admission or employment in apprenticeship or other training programs. *Person:* To retaliate for opposition to unlawful practice or for making a charge, filing a complaint, testifying, assisting or participating in any investigation under the law; to aid, abet, incite, compel or coerce to engage in an unlawful practice; to resist or interfere with the Commission on Human Rights or its representatives in performance of its duty under the act.		
Louisiana	Employers	Under 50	Employers of fewer than 25; bus drivers.[1]	To adopt rules for discharge or rejection of applications for employment.	Up to $500 fine, up to 90 days in jail or both.	None
Maine	Employers; employment agencies; labor organizations; State agencies.	None	Nonprofit religious or fraternal corporations or associations employing own	*Employer and labor organization:* To fail or refuse to hire, to discharge or otherwise discriminate in hiring, tenure, promotion, transfer,	Damages, not more than $100 for first unlawful act; not more than $250 for	Human Rights Commmission

*Age limits refer to birthdays.

[1]Louisiana: An attorney general's opinion declared that bus drivers are engaged in hazardous work, therefore exempt.

State	Law applies to—	Coverage Age limits*	Exclusions and exemptions	Prohibited practices	Penalties	Enforcement agency
			members; family employment.	compensation, terms, conditions, or privileges; to use employment agency which discriminates. *Employment agency:* To fail or refuse to classify properly, or to refer, or otherwise discriminate; to comply with an employer's request, if request indicates no full and equal employment opportunities will be afforded. *Labor organization:* To exclude from apprenticeship or membership or to deny full and equal membership rights; to discriminate in representation; or in grievance whether or not authorized by contract, collective agreement or, bylaws or constitution; to fail or refuse to classify or refer for employment. *All three:* To discriminate because of opposition to any	second; not more than $1,000 for third and subsequent violations.	

*Age limits refer to birthdays.

State	Law applies to—	Coverage Age limits*	Exclusions and exemptions	Prohibited practices	Penalties	Enforcement agency
				violation of the act; or to make a charge, give testimony or assistance in proceedings under the act. *Person*: To aid, abet, coerce, incite, compel to perform unlawful acts under the law; obstruct or prevent from complying with act; punish, penalize for seeking to exercise civil rights.		
Maryland	Employers; employment agencies; labor organizations; joint labor-management committees; State.	None	Employers of fewer than 15; private clubs; religious corporations.	*Employer:* To fail or refuse to hire, to discharge or otherwise discriminate in compensation, terms, conditions, or privileges of employment; to limit, segregate, or classify employees to deprive of employment opportunities or otherwise adversely affect status. *Employment agency:* To refuse or fail to refer or to classify or refer for employment. Labor organization: To exclude, expel or otherwise	Contempt of court citations.	Commission on Human Relations

*Age limits refer to birthdays.

307

State	Law applies to—	Coverage Age limits*	Exclusions and exemptions	Prohibited practices	Penalties	Enforcement agency
				discriminate; to limit, segregate or classify; to cause employer to discriminate. *Employer, employment, agency, Labor organization:* To discriminate for opposition to unlawful practices, filed charges, testimony, or assistance in any proceeding under the law; to print or publish any notice or advertisement indicating preference, limitation, specification or other discrimination. *Employer, labor organization, joint labor-management committee:* To discriminate in admission to or employment in any training program.		
Massachusetts	Employers; State and political subdivisions; employment agencies; labor organizations.	40 to 65	Employer of fewer than 6; nonprofit social, religious, fraternal clubs, organizations, associations, or	*Employer:* To refuse, bar, or discharge from employment; to discriminate in compensation, terms, conditions, or privileges of employment. *Employer and employment*	Up to $500 fine, up to one year in jail, or both.	Commission Against Discrimination

* Age limits refer to birthdays.

| State | Coverage | | Exclusions and exemptions | Prohibited practices | Penalties | Enforcement agency |
	Law applies to—	Age limits*				
			corporations; domestic service; family employment.	*agency:* To print or circulate any statement, advertisement, or publication or to use an application form or to make any inquiry or record expressing limitations, specifications, or discrimination. *Labor organization:* To exclude, expel or discriminate in any way. *Person, employer, labor organization, employment agency:* To discharge, expel or otherwise discriminate for opposition to any practice forbidden by law, or for filing a complaint, testifying or assisting in any proceeding; to aid, abet, incite, compel or coerce a person to do or attempt an act forbidden by this law.		
Michigan	Employers; State and civil or political subdivisions; employment agencies; labor organizations.	18 to 60	Employers of fewer than 8; domestic service.	*Employer:* To refuse or to otherwise discriminate in hiring, tenure, terms, conditions, or privileges of employment. *Employment agency:* To fail	Contempt of court citations; not less than $100 or more than $500 fine	Civil Rights Commission

* Age limits refer to birthdays.

State	Law applies to—	Coverage Age limits*	Exclusions and exemptions	Prohibited practices	Penalties	Enforcement agency
				or refuse to properly classify, refer or otherwise discriminate. *Labor organization:* To discriminate, limit, segregate, or qualify in any way; to adversely affect employment status. wages, hours, or conditions of work. *All three:* To, prior to employment or admission to membership, print or publish any notice or advertisement indicating preference, limitation, specification, or discrimination; to establish or announce a policy of denying or limiting opportunities, through a quota system or otherwise; to utilize in recruitment or hiring an agency, service, school or any other labor-referring source known to discriminate.	for failure to post required notices.	
Minnesota	No law.					
Mississippi	No law.					
Missouri	No law.					

*Age limits refer to birthdays.

310

State	Coverage Law applies to—	Coverage Age limits*	Exclusions and exemptions	Prohibited practices	Penalties	Enforcement agency
Montana	Employers; labor organizations; joint labor-management committees; employment agencies; State and political subdivisions.	None	Nonprofit fraternal, charitable or religious associations or corporations.	*Employer:* To refuse employment; to discriminate in compensation or in terms, conditions or privileges of employment. *Labor organization or joint labor-management committee:* To exclude or expel from its membership, apprenticeship, or training program; or to discriminate in any way against a member or applicant. *Employment agency:* To fail or refuse to classify or otherwise discriminate. *Employer or employment agency:* To print, circulate a discriminatory statement, advertisement, publication, or job application. *Person:* To discharge, expel, blacklist, or otherwise discriminate for opposing any forbidden practice, or for filing a complaint, testifying or assisting in any proceeding un-	Up to $500 fine, or up to 6 months in jail, or both.	Commission for Human Rights

*Age limits refer to birthdays.

311

State	Coverage		Exclusions and exemptions	Prohibited practices	Penalties	Enforcement agency
	Law applies to—	Age limits*				
				der the law. *State, employer, labor organization, employment agency*: To fail to maintain records required by civil rights agencies for administrative and statistical evaluation.		
Nebraska	Employers; labor organizations.	40 to 65	Employers of fewer than 25; peace officers; firefighters.	*Employer*: To refuse to hire, discharge or otherwise discriminate in terms, conditions, or privileges of employment; to utilize any labor organization or employment agency which discriminates. *Labor organization*: To discriminate or to limit, segregate or classify membership. *Employer and labor organization*: To discharge, expel, or discriminate for opposing, filing charges, testifying or assisting in proceedings.	Up to $100 fine, up to 30 days in jail, or both, for second or subsequent convictions.	Equal Opportunity Commission
Nevada	Employers; employment agencies; labor organizations.	None	Employers of fewer than 15; private member-	*Employer*: To refuse to hire, to discharge or to otherwise discriminate in compensa-	Contempt of court citations.	Equal Rights Commission

*Age limits refer to birthdays.

312

State	Coverage		Exclusions and exemptions	Prohibited practices	Penalties	Enforcement agency
	Law applies to—	Age limits*				
	izations; joint labor-management committees; State and political subdivisions.		ship clubs; religious corporations, associations, or societies.	tion, terms, conditions or privileges of employment; to limit, segregate or classify employees; to deprive of employment opportunities or otherwise adversely affect status. *Employment agency*: To refer or to classify on basis of age or otherwise discriminate. *Labor organization*: To exclude, expel or otherwise discriminate; to limit, segregate, classify or refuse to refer; to cause employer to discriminate. *All three*: To discriminate because of complaints or assistance in complaints; to advertise indicating preference, limitation, specification, or discrimination. *Employer, labor organization, or joint labor-management committee*: To discriminate in admission, or employment in any apprenticeship or other training program.		

*Age limits refer to birthdays.

State	Law applies to—	Coverage Age limits*	Exclusions and exemptions	Prohibited practices	Penalties	Enforcement agency
New Hampshire	Employers; State and political subdivisions; employment agencies.	Less than 65	Employers of fewer than 6; family employment; domestic service; and nonprofit social, fraternal, charitable, educational, or religious associations or corporations.	*Employer:* To refuse, bar, discharge or otherwise discriminate in compensation, terms, conditions or privileges of employment. *Employer and employment agency:* To print and circulate any material, to use application forms, or to make inquiries or records with limitation, specification or discrimination. *Person:* To discriminate against persons who oppose forbidden practices, file a complaint, testify or assist in any proceeding under the law; to aid, abet, incite, compel or coerce a person to do or attempt an act forbidden by this law.	Up to $500 fine, up to 6 months in jail, or both.	Commission for Human Rights
New Jersey	Employers; employment agencies; labor organizations.	Over 21	Nonprofit social clubs, fraternal, charitable, educational, or religious organizations, associations, associ-	*Employer:* To refuse, bar, or discharge from employment or to discriminate in compensation, terms, conditions, or privileges of employment. *Employer and employment*	Up to $500 fine, up to one year in jail, or both.	Division on Civil Rights

*Age limits refer to birthdays.

314

State	Coverage		Exclusions and exemptions	Prohibited practices	Penalties	Enforcement agency
	Law applies to —	Age limits*				
			ations, or corporations; domestic service; family employment.	*agency*: To advertise, print or circulate any material, or use application forms which suggest age limitaations. *Labor organization*: To exclude, expel or discriminate in any way; to discriminate against persons in apprenticeship or other training programs. *Person*: To take reprisals for opposition to any practices or acts forbidden under the law or because of testimony, complaint, or assistance in any proceedings under the law; to aid, abet, incite, compel, or coerce discrimination.		
New Mexico	Employers; State and political subdivisions.	None	Employers of fewer than 4.	*Employer*: To refuse to hire or to promote, to discharge or demote, or to discriminate in matters of compensation. *Person and employer*: To aid, abet, incite, compel or coerce the doing of any act forbid-	Damages up to $1,000.	Human Rights Commission

*Age limits refer to birthdays.

315

State	Law applies to—	Coverage Age limits*	Exclusions and exemptions	Prohibited practices	Penalties	Enforcement agency
				den by the law; to engage in threats, reprisals, or discrimination for opposition to unlawful practices, for filing a complaint, testifying or participating in any proceeding under the law.		
New York	Employers; employment agencies; labor organizations; licensing agencies.	18 to 65	Employers of fewer than 4; domestic service; family employment.	*Employer:* To refuse, bar, or discharge from employment; to discriminate in compensation, terms, conditions, or privileges of employment. *Employment agency:* To discriminate in receiving, classifying, disposing or otherwise acting upon applications for service, or in referring applicants to employers. *Employer, employment agency and licensing agency:* To advertise, publish or use application forms which suggest age limitations. *Labor organization:* To exclude, expel or discriminate in any	Up to $500 fine, up to one year in jail, or both.	Division of Human Rights

*Age limits refer to birthdays.

316

State	Law applies to—	Coverage Age limits*	Exclusions and exemptions	Prohibited practices	Penalties	Enforcement agency
				way. *Licensing agency, employer:* To refuse to hire, employ or license and to discriminate in promotion, compensation or terms, conditions, or privileges of employment. *Employer, employment agency, licensing agency:* To encourage or compel the accomplishment of any forbidden action under the law, or because individual has opposed, complained, testified or assisted in any proceeding.		
North Carolina	State, and political subdivisions.	40 to 65	None	*Department or agency:* To deny equal employment opportunity.	None	None
North Dakota[1]	Employers.	40 to 65	None	To refuse to hire, employ, or license; to bar or discharge.	Up to $25 fine, up to one day in jail, or both.	None

* Age limits refer to birthdays.
[1] North Dakota: Under the personnel system law, age discrimination is prohibited in all appointments and promotions in the State classified service.

State	Law applies to—	Coverage Age limits*	Exclusions and exemptions	Prohibited practices	Penalties	Enforcement agency
Ohio[2]	Employers; State and political subdivisions.	None	Employers with gross annual sales of less than $95,000; baby-sitters, live-in companions. Certain employees of political subdivisions: Police, fire protection agencies, or students in part-time or seasonal work.	Employer: To discriminate in payment of wages or against persons complaining, instituting or testifying in proceedings.	Minor misdemeanor.	Department of Industrial Relations
Oklahoma[3]	State	40 to 65	None	To discriminate.	None	None
Oregon	Employers; State and political subdivisions; employment agencies; labor organizations.	18 to 65	Domestic service; family employment; nonprofit religious institutions; correctional institutions; State and city police, sheriff-	Employer: To refuse, bar, discharge, dismiss, reduce, suspend, or demote. Employer employment agency: To advertise, publish, use application forms, or make inquiry about prospective employment which suggest limita-	Up to $500 fine, up to one year in jail, or both.	Bureau of Labor (except for public employment)

*Age limits refer to birthdays.

[2]Ohio: In 1975, Ohio added age discrimination to its equal pay law, reported in the table, which deals only with discrimination in pay. Under another law dealing with age discrimination in other employment conditions, an employer is prohibited from refusing an opportunity for an interview or from discharging persons 40 to 65; there is no enforcement agency designated under this law.

[3]Oklahoma: A resolution declares it to be the legislative intent and purpose that departments and agencies of the State government conform as nearly as practicable to the Federal "Age Discrimination in Employment Act."

State	Law applies to—	Coverage Age limits*	Exclusions and exemptions	Prohibited practices	Penalties	Enforcement agency
			ifts; employees of Liquor Control Commission and State Agriculture Department; firefighters; weighmasters of the State Department of Transportation.	tions, specifications or discrimination. *Employer, employment agency, labor organization:* To discharge, expel or discriminate against persons who oppose forbidden practice, complain, testify, or assist in any proceeding under the law; to encourage or compel any forbidden action. *Public employer:* To disqualify or discriminate in any civil service entrance, appointment, or promotion; to refuse to hire or reemploy; or to bar, discharge, reduce, suspend or demote.		
Outer Continental Shelf Lands	No law.					
Pennsylvania	Employers; State and political subdivisions; employment agencies; labor organizations.	40 to 65	Employers of fewer than 4; domestic service; family employment; agriculture live-in workers.	*Employer:* To refuse, bar, discharge from employment or to otherwise discriminate in compensation, hire, tenure, terms, conditions, or privileges of employment. *Employment*	Not less than $100 nor more than $500 fine, not more than 30 days in jail, or both.	Human Relations Commission

*Age limits refer to birthdays.

319

State	Law applies to—	Coverage Age limits*	Exclusions and exemptions	Prohibited practices	Penalties	Enforcement agency
				agency: To fail or refuse to classify properly, refer, or to otherwise discriminate. *Employer, employment agency, and labor organization:* To advertise, publish or use application forms that suggest limitations, specifications or discrimination. *Labor organization:* To exclude, expel or discriminate in any way. *All three:* To discriminate against any person who has opposed forbidden practice or has made a charge, testified or assisted in any investigation or proceeding under the law; to aid, abet, incite, compel or coerce the doing of an unlawful act under the law; to deny or limit employment or membership through a quota system; to confine or limit recruitment or hiring to an employee-referring source		

*Age limits refer to birthdays.

320

State	Law applies to—	Coverage Age limits*	Exclusions and exemptions	Prohibited practices	Penalties	Enforcement agency
				serving persons in predominantly the same age group. *Any individual:* To publish any advertisement expressing preferences or limitations for a prospective employer.		
Puerto Rico	Employers; agencies and instrumentalities of the Commonwealth operated as private businesses or enterprises; employment agencies; labor organizations.	30 to 65	None	*Employer:* To discharge, suspend, demote, reduce the salary, impose more burdensome working conditions, or refuse to employ or reemploy, to advertise, publish, or use application forms which suggest age limitations. *Employment agency:* To make inquiries, establish limitations or exclusions; to publish or circulate statement, advertisement or notice expressing limitations or exclusions. *Labor organization:* To limit, divide, or classify membership.	Various civil and criminal penalties including double damages, up to $1,000 fine, up to 90 days in jail, or both.	Department of Labor
Rhode Island	Employers; State and political sub-	45 to 65	Nonprofit social clubs; fraternal,	*Employer:* To dismiss or refuse to employ or rehire; to	None	Department of Labor

*Age limits refer to birthdays.

321

State	Coverage — Law applies to—	Coverage — Age limits*	Exclusions and exemptions	Prohibited practices	Penalties	Enforcement agency
	divisions; employment agencies; labor organizations.		charitable, educational or religious organizations, associations, or corporations; domestic service; farm labor.	discharge for furnishing evidence on a complaint. *Employment agency:* To fail or refuse to classify or refer. *Employer and employment agency:* To advertise, publish, or use application forms, to make inquiry which expresses intent to dismiss, or refuse to employ or rehire. *Labor organization:* To deny full and equal membership, or fail or refuse to classify or refer for employment.		
South Carolina	State and political subdivisions.	None	None	*Department or agency:* To fail or refuse to hire, bar, discharge; to advertise, publish or use application forms suggesting age limitations. *Person:* To aid, abet, incite, compel or coerce the doing of a forbidden act; to retaliate, discharge, expel or discrimi-	None	Human Affairs Commission

*Age limits refer to birthdays.

322

State	Law applies to—	Coverage Age limits*	Exclusions and exemptions	Prohibited practices	Penalties	Enforcement agency
				nate because person has opposed, filed a complaint, testified or assisted in any investigation, proceeding, or hearing.		
South Dakota	No law					
Tennessee	State.	18 to 65	None	To discriminate.	None	None
Texas	State and political subdivisions.	21 to 65	Law enforcement personnel; peace officers; firefighters; institutions of higher education.	To deny employment.	None	None
Utah	Employers; employment agencies; labor organizations; joint apprenticeship committees; vocational school.	40 to 65	Family employment.	*Employer:* To refuse to hire or promote, discharge or demote, or discriminate in compensation. *Employment agency:* To refuse to list, classify, or refer; to comply with an employer's discriminatory request. *Labor organization:* To exclude, or expel from membership or otherwise discriminate. *Employer, labor organization, joint ap-*	None	Industrial Commissior

*Age limits refer to birthdays.

323

State	Law applies to—	Coverage Age limits*	Exclusions and exemptions	Prohibited practices	Penalties	Enforcement agency
				prenticeship committee and vocational school: To deny or withhold admission or participation in training programs; discriminate in terms, conditions, or privileges. All five: To print, circulate, advertise, publish or to use application forms expressing discrimination. Person: To aid, abet, incite, compel or coerce the doing of a forbidden act; to obstruct or prevent compliance; or to commit a discriminatory act.		
Vermont	No law.					
Virginia	No law.					
Virgin Islands	Employers; employment agencies.	None	None	Employer: To refuse to hire; to bar or discharge from employment; to discriminate in compensation, terms, conditions, or privileges of employment. Employer and employment agency: To adver-	Up to $200 fine for first offense; up to $500 for second and subsequent offenses.	Department of Labor

* Age limits refer to birthdays.

324

State	Law applies to—	Coverage Age limits*	Exclusions and exemptions	Prohibited practices	Penalties	Enforcement agency
				tise, publish, or use application forms which suggest age limitations.	Misdemeanor.	
Wake Island	No law.					
Washington	Employers; State and political subdivisions; employment agencies; labor organizations; licensing agencies.	40 to 65	Employers of fewer than 8; nonprofit religious or sectarian organizations; domestic service; family employment.	*Employer and licensing agency:* To refuse, discharge, or bar from employment or licensing; to discriminate in compensation or other terms, or conditions of employment. *Employer, licensing agency and employment agency:* To advertise, publish or use application forms, make inquiry suggesting limitations, specifications or discrimination. *Labor organization:* To deny membership or full membership rights, expel or discriminate in any way. *All three:* To expel or otherwise discriminate against a person because he has opposed a forbidden practice or because he		Human Rights Commission

*Age limits refer to birthdays.

325

State	Law applies to—	Coverage Age limits*	Exclusions and exemptions	Prohibited practices	Penalties	Enforcement agency
				has filed a charge, testified or assisted in any proceeding under the law.		
West Virginia	Employers; State and political subdivisions; employment agencies; labor organizations; joint labor-management committees.	40 to 65	Employers of fewer than 12; private clubs; family employment; domestic service.	*Employer:* To discriminate with respect to compensation, hire, tenure, terms, conditions, or privileges of employment. *Employment agency:* To fail or refuse to classify properly, refer for employment or otherwise discriminate. *Labor organization:* To deny full and equal membership rights or otherwise discriminate in hiring, tenure, terms, conditions or privileges of employment. *All three:* To elicit information, keep records, use forms, print or publish advertisements showing preference, limitation, specification or discrimination; to deny or limit employment or	Not less than $100 or more than $500 fine, up to 30 days in prison, or both.	Human Rights Commission

* Age limits refer to birthdays.

326

State	Law applies to—	Coverage Age limits*	Exclusions and exemptions	Prohibited practices	Penalties	Enforcement agency
				membership through a quota system; to engage in reprisal or otherwise discriminate against individual who has opposed a forbidden practice, filed a complaint, testified or assisted in any proceeding under the law. *Employer, labor organization, employment agency or joint labor-management committee:* To select trainees on any basis other than qualifications; to discriminate in right to be admitted to and to participate in the pursuit of such training, in terms, conditions or privileges of such program; to print or publish any statement, advertisement or publication which expresses discrimination or any intent to discriminate.		
Wisconsin	Employers; licensing agencies;	40 to 65	Nonprofit social clubs; fraternal,	*Employer, labor organization and licensing agency:* To	*None*	Department of Industry, Labor

State	Law applies to—	Coverage Age limits*	Exclusions and exemptions	Prohibited practices	Penalties	Enforcement agency
	employment agencies; labor organizations. organizations.		or religious associations; family employment; hazardous occupations; law enforcement or firefighting personnel.	refuse to hire, employ, admit, license, bar, or terminate or to discriminate in promotion, compensation, or in terms, conditions or privileges of employment. *Employer, employment agency and licensing agency:* To advertise, publish or use application forms which suggest age limitations or to discharge or otherwise discriminate against person who has opposed discriminatory practices or because he has made a complaint, testified or assisted in any proceeding under the law.		and Human Relations
Wyoming	No law.					

*Age limits refer to birthdays.
Note: Data for American Samoa, Wake Island, the Canal Zone, and the Outer Continental Shelf Lands are as of February 1, 1974.

328

TABLE OF CASES

References are to page numbers.

A

Ace Hardware Corp., Brennan v., ... 81, 160, 161, 162,
92, 200, 212

Acford v. Exxon Corp., ... 143, 148, 150, 151, 155

Air Canada, Bittar v., ... 134, 183, 184, 186

Air Line Pilots Ass'n Int'l, v. Quesada, ... 43, 54

Allgeyer v. Louisiana, ... 38

Alyeska Pipeline Serv. Co. v. Wilderness Soc'y, ... 212

American Airlines v. State Comm'n for Human Rights, ... 85

American Hardware Mut. Ins. Co., Hodgson v., ... 75, 118, 128

American Pipe and Constr. Co. v. Utah, ... 177

Anaconda Co., Laugesen v., ... 180, 182, 184, 186,
188, 190, 193, 200

Apprenticeship and Training Council, Judson v., ... 130

Approved Personnel Services, Inc., Brennan v., ... 92, 94, 160,
162

Approved Personnel Services, Inc., Hodgson v., ... 94, 209, 211

Armstrong v. Howell, ... 46

Arnold v. Hawaiian Tel. Co., ... 139, 141, 143, 145, 146

Aronstam v. Cushman, ... 47

B

Balc v. United Steelworkers of America, AFL-CIO, ... 143, 148

Baldwin-Whitehall School Dist., Frantz v., ... 46

Barsky v. Board of Regents, ... 39

Baskin v. University of Conn., ... 64

Beaunit Corp., Hughes v., ... 151, 155

Bevans v. Nugent, ... 214, 216

Billingsley v. Service Tech. Corp., . . 189, 195, 197, 198, 200, 212

Bishop v. Jelleff Associates, Inc., . . . 85, 114, 138, 148, 149, 150,
152, 160, 166, 169, 173, 174, 177,
183, 184, 186, 195, 197, 198,
199, 200, 206, 212

Bittar v. Air Canada, ... 134, 183, 184, 186

Blankenship v. Ralston Purina Co., ... 151, 161, 168, 172, 173, 174, 176, 178, 179
Board of Educ. of Salt Lake City, Usery v., ... 80
Board of Educ. of West Haven v. Commission on Civil Rights of the State of Conn., ... 64
Board of Regents, Barsky v., ... 39
Bouffier v. Frank, ... 47
Bowman, Hodgson v., ... 181
Brennan v. Ace Hardware Corp., ... 81, 160, 161, 162, 192, 200, 212
Brennan v. Approved Personnel Services, Inc., ... 92, 94, 160, 162
Brennan v. C/M Mobile, Inc., ... 92, 211
Brennan v. Goodyear Tire & Rubber Co., ... 183, 198, 200, 210, 212, 213, 214
Brennan v. Greyhound Lines, ... 100
Brennan v. Hughes Personnel, Inc., ... 75, 89, 92, 94, 202, 203, 205, 213, 220
Brennan v. International Harvester Co., ... 181, 209
Brennan v. McDonnell Douglas Corp., ... 169
Brennan, National League of Cities v., ... 80, 81
Brennan v. Paragon Employment Agency, Inc., ... 75, 76, 82, 89, 92, 93, 94, 116
Brennan v. Reynolds & Co., ... 133, 188
Brennan v. Root, ... 75, 82
Brennan v. Taft Broadcasting Co., ... 121, 129
Brennan v. Texas Instruments, Inc., ... 162
Brennan v. Weis Markets, ... 161
Brennan v. Western Operations, Inc., ... 234, 235
Brohl v. Singer Co., ... 146, 151, 152
Brotherhood of Locomotive Firemen and Engineers, Flowers v., ... 41
Brown and Williamson Tobacco Corp. and Int'l Assoc. of Machinists and Aerospace Workers, Local Number 681, .. 130
Bullock v. Carter, ... 55
Burge, Remick v., ... 64
Burgett v. Cudahy Co., ... 150, 155, 158, 160, 161, 174, 175, 179
Burnett v. New York Central R.R., ... 163

Burroughs Corp., McGinley v., ... 143, 148, 151, 153, 174, 175, 176

Butchers' Union Co. v. Crescent City Co., ... 38

C

California, Oyama v., ... 55
Cannon v. Guste, ... 50
Cannon v. University of Chicago, ... 82
Career Counsellors Int'l Inc., Hodgson v., ... 75, 92, 209
Carter, Bullock v., ... 55
Cenla Community Action Comm., Inc., Hines v., ... 39, 40
Chew v. Quesada, ... 42
Chilton v. National Cash Register Co., ... 180, 181, 212
Chrysler Corp., Roshto v., ... 174, 175, 177, 178
Chrysler Corp., Thompson v., ... 124
Chrysler Corp., Vaughn v., ... 39, 143, 144, 145, 148
City of Dallas, Corey v., ... 39
City of Overland Park v. Nikias, ... 158
Civil Service Comm'n, Klapp v., ... 85, 213
Cleverly v. Western Elec. Co., ... 180, 182
Clinchfield R.R., Goodin v., ... 41
C/M Mobile, Inc., Brennan v., ... 92, 211
Cochran v. Ortho Pharmaceutical Co., ... 151, 154, 161
Commission on Civil Rights of the State of Conn., Board of Educ. of West Haven v., ... 64
Commonwealth of Mass. Bd. of Retirement, Murgia v., ... 50, 51, 127
Community Unit School Dist. No. 7, Champaign County, Ill., Kennedy v., ... 46
Connecticut Commission on Human Rights and Opportunities, University of Conn. v., ... 64
Continental Airlines, Curry v., ... 140, 143, 164
Continental Indus., Inc., Lundgren v., ... 162, 169
Continental Oil Co., Hull v., ... 174, 177
Conwed Corp., Surrisi v., ... 134, 135
Cooke v. Reynolds Metals Co., ... 174
Cookson v. Lewiston School Dist. No. 1, ... 47, 48, 66
Corey v. City of Dallas, ... 39

Crescent City Co., Butchers' Union Co. v., ... 38
Crest Communities, Inc., Smith v., ... 143, 164, 212
Crown Cork & Seal Co., Dunlop v., ... 144, 164, 166
Cudahy Co., Burgett v., ... 150, 155, 158, 160, 161,
                                                    174, 175, 179
Curry v. Continental Airlines, ... 140, 143, 164
Curtis v. Loether, ... 181, 182
Cushman, Aronstam v., ... 47

D

Dallas, City of, Corey v., ... 39
Dandridge v. Williams, ... 56
Dartt v. Shell Oil Co., ... 151, 155, 156, 174
DeLoraine v. MEBA (Marine Engineers' Beneficial Ass'n)
    Pension Trust, ... 121
Diaz v. Pan Am World Airways, Inc., ... 105, 106
Doctor v. Seaboard Coast Line R.R, ... 174
Donnelly v. Exxon Research v. Eng'r Co., ... 74, 111, 122,
                                                    126, 191, 213
Duke Power Co., Griggs v., ... 75
Dunlop v. Crown Cork & Seal Co., ... 144, 164, 166
Dunlop v. Westinghouse Elec. Corp., ... 193
Dworshak Dam Constrs., Hinote v., ... 116, 212

E

Earnest Machine Prods., Inc., Hodgson v., ... 186
Eastern Air Lines, Vasquez v., ... 140, 142, 143, 144, 150
Edwards v. Kaiser Aluminum & Chem. Sales, Inc., ... 136, 151,
                                                    152, 154
Eklund v. Lubrizol Corp., ... 139, 146, 151, 153
Entenmann's Bakery, Williams v., ... 63
Exxon Corp., Acford v., ... 143, 148, 150, 151, 155
Exxon Research & Eng'r Co., Donnelly v., ... 74, 111, 122, 126,
                                                    191, 213
Exxon Research and Eng'r Co., Rogers v., ... 77, 180, 206, 207,
                                                    208, 212, 213

F

Falstaff Brewing Corp., Moses v., .. 134, 135, 146, 151, 154, 212
First Fed. Sav. & Loan Ass'n, Hodgson v., .. 183, 185, 187, 192, 193, 196, 209, 210
Florida, McLaughlin v., ... 55
Flowers v. Brotherhood of Locomotive Firemen and En-
 ginemen, ... 41
Ford Motor Co., O'Connell v., ... 180, 181, 183, 184, 185
Frank, Bouffier v., ... 47
Frantz v. Baldwin-Whitehall School Dist., ... 46
Fuller Brush Co., Schmidt v., ... 176

G

GAF Corp., Gebhard v., ... 149, 152, 173, 174
Garces v. Sagner Int'l, Inc., ... 140, 143
Gardner v. Nation, ... 46
Garrison, Gault v., ... 50
Gault v. Garrison, ... 50
Gebhard v. GAF Corp., ... 149, 152, 173, 174
General Elec. Co., Hiscott v., ... 146, 149, 151, 152, 155
Georgia Southern & Florida Ry., Lamon v., ... 41
Ghezzi, Rubino v., ... 47, 50
Gill v. Union Carbide Corp., ... 115
Goger v. H. K. Porter Co., ... 142, 143, 144, 145
Goodin v. Clinchfield R.R., ... 41
Goodyear Tire & Rubber Co., Brennan v., ... 183, 198, 200, 210, 212, 213, 214
Graham v. Richardson, ... 55
Great Am. Discount and Credit Co., Hodgson v., ... 209, 213
Great Atlantic & Pacific Tea Co., Raynor v., ... 151, 154
Great Scott Supermarkets, Rucker v., ... 141, 143, 148
Greyhound Lines, Brennan v., ... 100
Greyhound Lines, Hodgson v., ... 100, 102, 103, 105, 106, 107, 187
Griggs v. Duke Power Co., ... 75
Grossfield v. W. B. Saunders Co., ... 126, 148, 155, 158, 160, 161
Guste, Cannon v., ... 50

H

Hampton v. Mow Sun Wong, ... 38
Hart v. United Steelworkers of America, ... 75, 83, 85, 113
Hawaiian Tel. Co., Arnold v., ... 139, 141, 143, 145, 146
Hayes v. Southern Pac. Co., ... 74, 148, 151
Hickok Mfg. Co., Schulz v., ... 183, 186, 192, 193, 194, 195, 196,
    197, 198, 200, 212
Hilti, Inc., Leach v., ... 134, 212
Hines v. Cenla Community Action Comm., Inc., ... 39, 40
Hinote v. Dworshak Dam Constrs., ... 116, 212
Hiscott v. General Elec. Co., ... 146, 149, 151, 152, 155
H.K. Porter Co., Goger v., ... 142, 143, 144, 145
Hodgson v. American Hardware Mut. Ins. Co., ... 75, 118, 128
Hodgson v. Approved Personnel Service, Inc., ... 94, 209, 211
Hodgson v. Bowman, ... 181
Hodgson v. Career Counsellors Int'l Inc., ... 75, 92, 209
Hodgson v. Earnest Machine Prods., Inc., ... 186
Hodgson v. First Fed. Sav. & Loan Ass'n of Broward
    County, ... 183, 185, 187, 192, 193, 196, 209, 210
Hodgson v. Great Am. Discount and Credit Co., ... 209, 213
Hodgson v. Greyhound Lines, ... 100, 102, 103, 105, 106, 107, 187
Hodgson v. Ideal Corrugated Box Co., ... 161, 193, 195, 196,
    199, 200, 206, 210
Hodgson v. Poole Truck Line, Inc., ... 81, 185, 192, 195, 196,
    209, 213, 214
Hodgson v. Sugar Cane Growers Coop., .. 183, 192, 196, 210, 213
Hodgson v. Tamiami Trail Tours, Inc., .. 75, 100, 101, 103, 105,
    106, 107, 183, 187, 212
Hodgson v. Western Textile Co., ... 92, 209, 211
Howell, Armstrong v., ... 46
Hughes v. Beaunit Corp., ... 151, 155
Hughes Personnel, Inc., Brennan v., ... 75, 89, 92, 94, 202,
    203, 205, 213, 220
Hull v. Continental Oil Co., ... 174, 177

I

Ideal Corrugated Box Co., Hodgson v., ... 161, 193, 195, 196,
    199, 200, 206, 210

Industrial Comm'n, Troska v., ... 158
In re Adoption of Michelle Lee T., ... 243
International Harvester Co., Brennan v., ... 181, 209

J

Jelleff Associates, Inc., Bishop v., ... 85, 114, 138, 148, 149, 150,
                                         152, 160, 166, 169, 173, 174,
                                         177, 183, 184, 186, 195, 197,
                                         198, 199, 200, 206, 212
Johnson v. United States Steel Corp., ... 66
Jones v. Martin, ... 41
Judson v. Apprenticeship and Training Council, ... 130

K

Kaiser Aluminum & Chem. Sales, Inc., Edwards v., ... 136, 151,
                                                    152, 154
Kansas, Oklahoma and Gulf Ry., McMullans v., ... 41
Kennedy v. Community Unit School Dist. No. 7, Champaign
   County, Ill., ... 46
Kilian Mfg. Corp., State Div. of Human Rights v., ... 194
Kincaid v. United Steelworkers of America, ... 85
Kingston v. McLaughlin, ... 47
Kinney Shoe Corp., Woodford v., ... 79, 148, 151, 155, 158,
                                         161, 180
Klapp v. Civil Service Comm'n, ... 85, 213

L

Lachapelle v. Owens-Illinois, Inc., ... 173, 174, 212
Lamon v. Georgia Southern & Florida Ry., ... 41
Laugesen v. Anaconda Co., ... 180, 182, 184, 186, 188,
                                        190, 193, 200
Law v. United Air Lines, ... 148
Leach v. Hilti, Inc., ... 134, 212
Lewis v. Tuscon School Dist. No. 1, ... 47
Lewiston School Dist. No. 1, Cookson v., ... 47, 48, 66
Liebmann, New State Ice Co. v., ... 39
Loether, Curtis v., ... 181, 182

Louisiana, Allgeyer v., ... 38
LTV Aerospace Corp., Woodburn v., ... 146, 151
Lubrizol Corp., Eklund v., ... 139, 146, 151, 153
Lundgren v. Continental Indus., Inc., ... 162, 169
Lynn, Weisbrod v., ... 49, 50

M

Martin, Jones v. 41
Maryland Cas. Co., Price v., ... 116, 151, 174, 198, 212
Massachusetts Bd. of Retirement v. Murgia, ... 216
McCorstin v. U.S. Steel Corp., ... 148, 155, 160, 161, 174, 179
McDonnell Douglas Corp., Brennan v., ... 169
McGarvey v. Merch and Co., ... 143
McGinley v. Burroughs Corp., . 143, 148, 151, 153, 174, 175, 176
McIlvaine v. Pennsylvania, ... 50
McIlvaine v. Pennsylvania State Police, ... 46, 50
McLaughlin v. Florida, ... 55
McLaughlin, Kingston v., ... 47
McMullans v. Kansas, Oklahoma and Gulf Ry., ... 41
MEBA (Marine Engineers' Beneficial Ass'n), DeLoraine v.,.. 121
Merch and Co., McGarvey v., ... 143
Midland-Ross Corp., Ott v., ... 91, 151, 164, 165
Mitchell v. Pidcock, ... 211
Monroe v. Penn-Dixie Cement Corp., ... 74, 180, 197, 198,
                                                  199, 208, 212
Monsanto Co., Stringfellow v., ... 114, 115, 212
Moses v. Falstaff Brewing Corp., ... 134, 135, 146, 151, 154, 212
Mow Sun Wong, Hampton v., ... 38
Murgia v. Commonwealth of Mass. Bd. of Retirement, .. 50, 51,
                                                  127
Murgia, Massachusetts Bd. of Retirement v., ... 216

N

National Cash Register Co., Chilton v., ... 180, 181, 212
National League of Cities v. Brennan, ... 80, 81
National League of Cities v. Usery, ... 80
National League of Professional Baseball Clubs, Steiner v.,.. 121,
                                                  128

Nation, Gardner v., ... 46
Negron v. Pan Am World Airways, ... 143
New State Ice Co. v. Liebmann, ... 39
New Viceroy Restaurant, Smith v., ... 100
New York Central R.R., Burnett v., ... 163
Nikias, City of Overland Park v., ... 158
Norfolk and Western Ry., Ricks v., ... 41
Nugent, Bevans v., ... 214, 216

O

O'Connell v. Ford Motor Co., ... 180, 181, 183, 184, 185
O'Donnell v. Shaffer, ... 43
Oklahoma ex rel. Williamson, Skinner v., ... 55
Order of Railroad Telegraphers v. Railway Express Agency,
    Inc., ... 164
Ortho Pharmaceutical Co., Cochran v., ... 151, 154, 161
Oshira v. Pan Am Airways, ... 148
Ott v. Midland-Roll Corp., ... 91, 151, 164, 165
Overland Park, City of v. Nikias, ... 158
Owens-Illinois, Inc., Lachapelle v., ... 173, 174, 212
Oyama v. California, ... 55

P

Pan Am Airways, Oshira v., ... 148
Pan Am World Airways, Inc., Diaz v., ... 105, 106
Pan Am World Airways, Negron v., ... 143
Paragon Employment Agency, Inc., Brennan v., ... 75, 76, 82,
                                          89, 92, 93, 94, 116
Penn-Dixie Cement Corp., Monroe v., ... 74, 180, 197, 198,
                                          199, 208, 212
Pennsylvania, McIlvaine v., ... 50
Pennsylvania State Police, McIlvaine v., ... 46, 50
Pidcock, Mitchell v., ... 211
Pike, Talbot v., ... 51
Pittsburgh Comm'n on Human Relations, Pittsburgh Press
    Co. v., ... 64
Pittsburgh Press Co. v. Pittsburgh Comm'n on Human Rela-
    tions, ... 64

Poole Truck Line, Inc., Hodgson v., ... 81, 185, 192, 195, 196, 209, 213, 214
Porter, H.K., Co., Goger v., ... 142, 143, 144, 145
Powell v. Southwestern Bell Tel. Co., ... 151, 154, 155, 165
Price v. Maryland Cas. Co., ... 116, 151, 174, 198, 212

Q

Quesada, Air Line Pilots Ass'n Int'l v., ... 43, 54
Quesada, Chew v., ... 42

R

Raich, Truax, ... 38
Railway Express Agency, Inc., Order of Railroad Telegraphers v., ... 164
Ralston Purina Co., Blankenship v., ... 151, 161, 168, 172, 173, 174, 176, 178, 179
Raynor v. Great Atlantic & Pacific Tea Co., ... 151, 154
Remick v. Burge, ... 64
Retail Clerks Int'l Ass'n, Retail Clerks Union, Local 770 v., ... 41
Retail Clerks Union, Local 770 v. Retail Clerks Int'l Ass'n, ... 41
Reynolds & Co., Brennan v., ... 133, 188
Reynolds Metals Co., Cooke v., ... 174
Rhodes, Williams v., ... 55
Richardson, Graham v., ... 55
Ricks v. Norfolk and Western Ry., ... 41
Roe v. Wade, ... 55
Rogers v. Exxon Research and Eng'r Co., ... 77, 180, 206, 207, 208, 212, 213
Root, Brennan v., ... 75, 82
Roshto v. Chrysler Corp., ... 174, 175, 177, 178
Rubino v. Ghezzi, ... 47, 50
Rucker v. Great Scott Supermarkets, Inc., ... 141, 143, 148

S

Sagner Int'l, Inc., Garces v., ... 140, 143
Saunders, W.B., Co., Grossfield v., ... 126, 148, 155, 158, 160, 161

Schmidt v. Fuller Brush Co., ... 176

Schulz v. Hickok Mfg. Co., ... 183, 186, 192, 193, 194, 195,
196, 197, 198, 200, 212

Seaboard Coast Line R.R., Doctor v., ... 174

Sealtest Foods Div. of Kraftco Corp., Wilson v., ... 180, 182,
184, 189, 191

Service Tech. Corp., Billingsley v., ... 189, 195, 197, 198,
220, 212

Shaffer, O'Donnell v., ... 43

Shapiro v. Thompson, ... 40, 55

Shell Oil Co., Dartt v., ... 151, 155, 156, 174

Singer Co., Brohl v., ... 146, 151, 152

Singer Co., Skoglund v., ... 135, 138, 143, 151, 152

Skinner v. Oklahoma ex rel. Williamson, ... 55

Skoglund v. Singer Co., ... 135, 138, 143, 151, 152

Smith v. Crest Communities, Inc., ... 143, 164, 212

Smith v. New Viceroy Restaurant, ... 100

Southern Bell Tel. & Tel. Co., Weeks v., ... 105, 106

Southern Pac. Co., Hayes v., ... 74, 148, 151

Southwestern Bell Tel. Co., Powell v., ... 151, 154, 155, 165

State Comm'n for Human Rights, American Airlines v., ... 85

State Div. of Human Rights v. Kilian Mfg. Corp., ... 194

Steiner v. National League of Professional Baseball Clubs, ... 121,
128

Stringfellow v. Monsanto Co., ... 114, 115, 212

Sugar Cane Growers Coop. of Fla., Hodgson v., ... 183, 192, 196,
210, 213

Surrisi v. Conwed Corp., ... 134, 135

T

Taft Broadcasting Co., Brennan v., ... 121, 129

Talbot v. Pike, ... 51

Tamiami Trail Tours, Inc., Hodgson v., .. 75, 100, 101, 103, 105,
106, 107, 183, 187, 212

Texas Instruments, Inc., Brennan v., ... 162

Thompson v. Chrysler Corp., ... 124

Thompson, Shapiro v., ... 40, 55

Troska v. Industrial Comm'r, ... 158

Truax v. Raich, ... 38
Tuscon School Dist., No. 1, Lewis v., ... 47

U

Union Carbide Corp., Gill v., ... 115
United Air Lines, Law v., ... 148
United States Steel Corp., Johnson v., ... 66
United States, Wrightsman Petroleum Co. v., ... 158
United Steelworkers of America, AFL-CIO, Balc v., ... 143, 148
United Steelworkers of America, Hart v., ... 75, 83, 85, 113
United Steelworkers of America, Kincaid v., ... 85
University of Chicago, Cannon v., ... 82
University of Conn., Baskin v., ... 64
University of Conn. v. Connecticut Comm'n on Human
    Rights and Opportunities, ... 64
Usery v. Board of Educ. of Salt Lake City, ... 80
Usery, National League of Cities v., ... 80
U.S. Steel Corp., McCorstin v., ... 148, 155, 160, 161, 174, 179
Utah, American Pipe and Construction Co. v., ... 177

V

Vasquez v. Eastern Air Lines, ... 140, 142, 143, 144, 150
Vaughn v. Chrysler Corp., ... 39, 143, 144, 145, 148

W

Wade, Roe v., ... 55
Walsh, Weiss v., ... 44
W.B. Saunders Co., Grossfield v., .. 126, 148, 155, 158, 160, 161
Weeks v. Southern Bell Tel. & Tel. Co., ... 105, 106
Weisbrod v. Lynn, ... 49, 50
Weis Markets, Brennan v., ... 161
Weiss v. Walsh 44
Western Elec. Co., Cleverly v., ... 180, 182
Western Operations, Inc., Brennan v., ... 234, 235
Western Textile Co., Hodgson v., ... 92, 209, 211
Westinghouse Elec. Corp., Dunlop v., ... 193
Wilderness Soc'y, Alyeska Pipeline Serv. Co. v., ... 212

Williams, Dandridge v., ... 56
Williams v. Entenmann's Bakery, ... 63
Williams v. Rhodes, ... 55
Wilson v. Sealtest Foods Div. of Kraftco Corp., .. 180, 182, 184,
189, 191
Woodburn v. LTV Aerospace Corp., ... 146, 151
Woodford v. Kinney Shoe Corp., ... 79, 148, 151, 155,
158, 161, 180
Wrightsman Petroleum Co. v. United States, ... 158

Index

A

ADVERTISING.
Prohibited practices under federal age discrimination in employment act, pp. 91 to 97.

AGE DISCRIMINATION IN EMPLOYMENT ACT.
Federal law.
See FEDERAL AGE DISCRIMINATION IN EMPLOYMENT ACT.

AGING.
Attitudinal aspects, pp. 15 to 17.
Functional age, pp. 27 to 31.
Physical aspects, pp. 13 to 15.

APPROPRIATIONS.
Administration of federal age discrimination in employment act, p. 226.

ATTORNEYS.
Fees and costs, pp. 211, 212.

C

CIVIL ACTIONS.
Class actions.
Procedure, pp. 171 to 179.
Constitutional and equitable grounds.
See LEGAL CHALLENGES TO AGE DISCRIMINATION IN EMPLOYMENT.
Enforcement of federal act.
See ENFORCEMENT.
Injunctions.
Procedure, p. 171.

CIVIL SERVICE.
Protection from discrimination, pp. 214 to 216.

CLASS ACTIONS.
Procedure, pp. 171 to 179.

COMPENSATION.
Prohibited employer practices under federal age discrimination in employment act, p. 86.

CRIMINAL PENALTIES.
Obstruction of secretary of labor during performance of his duties under federal age discrimination in employment act, p. 225.

D

DAMAGES.
  Violations of federal age discrimination in employment act.
    See FEDERAL AGE DISCRIMINATION IN EMPLOYMENT ACT.
DEFENSES.
  Enforcement of federal age discrimination in employment act, pp. 166, 167.
DISCHARGE.
  Damages for wrongful discharge, pp. 197 to 201.
  Lawful practices under federal age discrimination in employment act, pp.
    133, 134.
DISCIPLINE.
  Discharge.
    See DISCHARGE.
  Lawful practices under federal age discrimination in employment act, pp.
    133, 134.
DISCRIMINATION IN EMPLOYMENT.
  Older workers.
    See FEDERAL AGE DISCRIMINATION IN EMPLOYMENT ACT.

E

EDUCATION.
  Federal age discrimination in employment act. pp. 77, 78.
EMPLOYEE.
  Federal age discrimination in employment act.
    Definition in act, pp. 82, 83.
EMPLOYER.
  Federal age discrimination in employment act.
    Definition in act, p. 79.
  Recordkeeping. pp. 217 to 219.
    Exceptions, p. 218.
      Generally, p. 222.
    Inspection, p. 221.
EMPLOYMENT AGENCIES.
  Federal age discrimination in employment act.
    Definition in act, pp. 81, 82.
  Prohibited practices under federal age discrimination in employment act, pp.
    88 to 90.
  Recordkeeping. pp. 219, 220.
    Exceptions, p. 219.
      Generally, p. 222.
    Inspection, p. 221.
  Refusal to refer.
    Damages awarded to applicants, pp. 201 to 205.

EMPLOYMENT AGENCIES—Cont'd
State challenges to age discrimination.
See LEGAL CHALLENGES TO AGE DISCRIMINATION IN
EMPLOYMENT.
ENFORCEMENT.
Federal age discrimination in employment act.
Civil actions.
By individuals.
Generally, pp. 167 to 170.
Preliminary procedure, pp. 137 to 159.
By secretary of labor.
Generally, p. 170.
Class actions.
Procedure, pp. 171 to 179.
Injunctions.
Procedure, p. 171.
Jury trials.
Availability, pp. 179 to 182.
Prerequisites generally, pp. 137 to 170.
Class actions.
Procedure, pp. 171 to 179.
Complaints, pp. 135, 136.
Conciliation, conference, and persuasion.
Required as prerequisite to civil actions, pp. 159 to 163.
Defenses, pp. 166, 167.
Injunctions.
Procedure, p. 171.
Investigations by secretary of labor, pp. 136, 137.
Statistics and commentary, pp. 227 to 237.
Investigations by wage and hour division, p. 135.
Limitations, pp. 163 to 166.
Notice to alleged discriminator.
Secretary of labor required to give, p. 159.
Notice to secretary of labor.
Prerequisite to commencement of civil action, pp. 146 to 159.
Secretary of labor.
Actions brought by secretary.
Automatic termination of complainant's right to bring action, pp. 137,
138, 168 to 170.
Investigations, pp. 136, 137.
State-federal relationship, pp. 138 to 146.
Complainant required to seek relief first under state law where
available, pp. 142, 143.
Exceptions, pp. 144, 145.
Statute of limitations, pp. 163 to 166.

EVIDENCE.
Proof.
See PROOF.

F

FAIR EMPLOYMENT PRACTICES STATUTES.
State challenges to age discrimination.
See LEGAL CHALLENGES TO AGE DISCRIMINATION IN
EMPLOYMENT.

FEDERAL AGE DISCRIMINATION IN EMPLOYMENT ACT.
Age limits.
Maximum age limit, pp. 240, 241.
Appropriation of funds for administration, p. 226.
Criminal penalties.
Obstruction of secretary of labor, p. 225.
Date of enactment, p. 73.
Definitions, pp. 79 to 83.
Education, pp. 77, 78.
Effective date, pp. 73, 74.
Employee.
Defined, p. 82.
Employer.
Defined, p. 79.
Employment agency.
Defined, p. 81.
Enforcement procedures.
See ENFORCEMENT.
Exemptions.
Generally, pp. 222 to 224.
Funds for administration, p. 226.
Jurisdiction.
Age limits, pp. 83 to 85.
Labor organization.
Defined, p. 83.
Lawful practices.
Apprenticeship programs.
Bona fide programs, pp. 129 to 131.
Benefit plans.
Bona fide employee plans, pp. 117 to 125.
Discharge or other discipline for good cause, pp. 133, 134.
Job applications, pp. 131, 132.
Pension and retirement plans.
Bona fide employee plans, pp. 124 to 129.

FEDERAL AGE DISCRIMINATION IN EMPLOYMENT ACT—Cont'd
Lawful practices—Cont'd
  Qualifications.
    Bona fide occupational requirements, pp. 99 to 108.
      Defendant's burden of proof, p. 187.
      "Reasonable necessity" to operation of employer's business.
      Statutory construction, pp. 106 to 108.
  Reasonable factors other than age.
    Basis of differentiations.
      Burden of proof, p. 110.
      Construction of exception, p. 110.
      Educational level, p. 111.
      Family relationship to persons already employed, p. 113.
      Physical fitness requirements, p. 110.
      Production levels, p. 111.
      Quantity of work, p. 111.
      Scope of exception.
        Determination on case-by-case basis, p. 109.
  Seniority systems.
    Bona fide systems, p. 117.
Person.
  Defined, p. 79.
Prohibited practices.
  Advertising practices, pp. 91 to 97.
  Employer practices.
    Exception.
      Business judgment of employer, p. 114.
Purposes, pp. 76, 77.
  Business judgment of employers.
    Act not intended to abrogate or diminish, p. 114.
Research, pp. 77, 78.
Retrospect on administration of act, pp. 227 to 237.
State laws.
  Influence upon act, pp. 74, 75.
Violations.
  Remedies.
    Class actions.
      Procedure, pp. 171 to 179.
    Compelled employment, pp. 196, 197.
    Damages.
      Generally, p. 205.
      Interest on damages, pp. 213, 214.
      Liquidated damages, pp. 205 to 212.
      Refusal to hire, p. 201.

FEDERAL AGE DISCRIMINATION IN EMPLOYMENT ACT—Cont'd
Violations—Cont'd
  Remedies—Cont'd
    Damages—Cont'd
      Refusal to refer, pp. 201 to 205.
      Wrongful discharge, pp. 197 to 201.
    Injunctions.
      Permanent injunctive relief, pp. 208 to 211.
      Procedure, p. 171.
    Reinstatement, pp. 196, 197.
Wage-hour administrator.
  Opinions.
    Prohibited practices by employers, pp. 87, 88.
Waiver of rights by plaintiff, pp. 90, 91.

FEDERAL GOVERNMENT EMPLOYMENT.
Protection from discrimination, pp. 214 to 216.

FEES AND COSTS.
Attorneys. pp. 211, 212.

FUNDS.
Appropriations.
  Administration of federal age discrimination in employment act, p. 226.

G

GERONTOLOGY.
Defined, p. 11.
Industrial gerontology.
  Studies of older workers, pp. 18 to 22.
Social gerontology.
  Defined, pp. 32, 33.
  Research, pp. 33 to 36.

H

HUMAN RIGHTS LAW.
State challenges to age discrimination.
  See LEGAL CHALLENGES TO AGE DISCRIMINATION IN
    EMPLOYMENT.

I

INJUNCTIONS.
Procedure, p. 171.
Violations of federal age discrimination in employment act.
  Permanent injunctive relief, pp. 208 to 211.

INTEREST.
Computation on damages, pp. 213, 214.

J

JOB APPLICATIONS.
Lawful practices under federal age discrimination in employment act, pp.
131, 132.

L

LABOR DEPARTMENT.
Wage and hour division.
See WAGE AND HOUR DIVISION.
LAW SUITS.
Civil actions.
Generally.
See CIVIL ACTIONS.
Constitutional and equitable challenges.
See LEGAL CHALLENGES TO AGE DISCRIMINATION IN
EMPLOYMENT.
LEGAL CHALLENGES TO AGE DISCRIMINATION IN EMPLOYMENT.
Constitutional and equitable challenges.
"Right" to obtain and keep employment, pp. 37 to 40.
Course of employment.
Involuntary retirement, etc., pp. 40 to 58.
Federal law.
Prior to 1967, pp. 69 to 71.
State statutes.
Fair employment practices laws.
Employer defined, p. 60.
Enforcement, pp. 61 to 64.
Generally, pp. 66, 67.
Human rights laws, p. 65.
LIMITATIONS.
Enforcement of federal age discrimination in employment act, pp. 163 to
166.

N

NATIONAL INSTITUTION OF AGING.
Created, p. 11.

NOTICES.
    Advice to employees of rights under federal age discrimination in
        employment act.
    Employers required to post, pp. 135, 136.

O

OLDER WORKERS.
    Civilian labor force.
        Percentage employed, pp. 4 to 9.
        Unemployed, pp. 4 to 9.
    Definition.
        Chronological view, p. 8.
    Employment.
        Percentage of civilian labor force, pp. 4 to 9.
    Functional age.
        Safety and convenience of public.
            Lawful practices under federal age discrimination in employment act,
                pp. 100 to 105.
    Studies.
        Functional age, pp. 27 to 31.
        Industrial gerontology, pp. 18 to 22.
        Laboratory research, pp. 31, 32.
        Training and testing, pp. 22 to 27.
    Unemployment.
        Percentage of civilian labor force, pp. 4 to 9.

P

PENSIONS.
    Plans.
        See RETIREMENT.
PROOF.
    Burden of proof.
        Defendant claiming exception to federal age discrimination in employment
            act, pp. 101, 103 to 105.
        General guidelines, pp. 182 to 192.
        Prima facie evidence, pp. 184 to 186.
            Plaintiff required to make case before burden shifts to defendant, p. 189.
        Methods of proof, pp. 192 to 195.
        Prima facie evidence.
        Records kept pursuant to regulations, p. 217.

PROOF—Cont'd

Standard of proof.

Exceptions to federal age discrimination in employment act, pp. 103, 104.

R

RECORDKEEPING.

Employers, pp. 217 to 219.

Exceptions, p. 218.

Employment agencies, pp. 219, 220.

Exceptions, p. 219.

Exceptions.

Generally, p. 222.

Inspection, p. 221.

Past record of employees in job applications.

Lawful practices under federal age discrimination in employment act, pp. 131, 132.

Proof of prima facie cases, p. 217.

Secretary of labor.

Power of secretary to require, p. 216.

Unions, pp. 220, 221.

REMEDIES.

Violations of federal age discrimination in employment act.

See FEDERAL AGE DISCRIMINATION IN EMPLOYMENT ACT.

REPORTS TO CONGRESS.

Secretary of labor.

Report to U. S. Congress, June 30, 1965, pp. 69 to 71.

Required to make, p. 225.

RESEARCH.

Federal age discrimination in employment act. pp. 77, 78.

RETIREMENT.

Involuntary retirement.

Federal statutory and regulatory limitations for safety and convenience of public.

Lawful practice under age discrimination in employment act, p. 99.

Legal challenges to discrimination.

See LEGAL CHALLENGES TO AGE DISCRIMINATION IN EMPLOYMENT.

Prohibited practices under federal age discrimination in employment act, p. 88.

Studies, pp. 239, 240.

Secretary of labor required to undertake, p. 224.

Plans.

Lawful practices under federal age discrimination in employment act, pp. 124 to 129.

S

SECRETARY OF LABOR.
Enforcement of federal age discrimination in employment act.
See ENFORCEMENT.
Investigations pursuant to provisions of federal age discrimination in employment act.
Statistics and commentary, pp. 227 to 237.
Reports to congress, p. 225.
Report of June 30, 1965, pp. 69 to 71.
Study of involuntary retirement.
Secretary required to make, p. 224.

SEPARATION.
Discharge.
See DISCHARGE.

STATE-FEDERAL RELATIONSHIPS.
Enforcement of federal age discrimination in employment act.
See ENFORCEMENT.

STATE STATUTES.
Federal age discrimination in employment act.
Influence of state law upon act, pp. 74, 75.
Generally, pp. 59 to 67.

STATUTES OF LIMITATIONS.
See LIMITATIONS.

STUDIES.
Investigations undertaken by department of labor pursuant to federal age discrimination in employment act and commentary thereon, pp. 227 to 237.
Involuntary retirement, pp. 239, 240.
Secretary of labor required to undertake, p. 224.
Older workers.
See OLDER WORKERS.

T

TERMINATION OF EMPLOYMENT.
See DISCHARGE.

TIME.
Statutes of limitations.
See LIMITATIONS.

U

UNIONS.
Labor organization.
  Federal age discrimination in employment act.
    Definition in act, p. 83.
  Prohibited practices under federal age discrimination in employment act,
    pp. 90, 91.
  Recordkeeping. pp. 220, 221.
    Exceptions.
      Generally, p. 222.
    Inspection, p. 221.
  Refusal to refer.
    Damages awarded to applicants, pp. 201 to 205.
  State law, p. 60.

V

VIOLATIONS.
Federal age discrimination in employment act.
  Enforcement.
    See ENFORCEMENT.
  Remedies.
    See FEDERAL AGE DISCRIMINATION IN EMPLOYMENT ACT.

W

WAGE AND HOUR DIVISION.
Investigations.
  Violations of federal age discrimination in employment act, p. 135.
WAGE-HOUR ADMINISTRATOR.
Opinions.
  Benefit plans.
    Bona fide employee benefits plans, pp. 117-125.
  Retirement, pp. 126, 127.
WAIVERS.
Plaintiff.
  Waiver of rights under federal age discrimination in employment act, pp.
    90, 91.